Wordsworth's reading 1800-1815 lists all of the authors and (where possible) books known to have been read by William Wordsworth during the years which saw the composition of some of his greatest poetry, including *Poems, in Two Volumes*, *The Thirteen-Book Prelude*, *The White Doe of Rylstone* and *The Excursion*. The information is presented in an easy-to-use form, and includes dates of reading and full discussions of evidence. It draws on analyses of Wordsworth's manuscripts contained in current and forthcoming scholarly editions of his works, and incorporates hitherto unpublished research into the poet's intellectual development, including a thorough survey of manuscript materials. Together with Duncan Wu's companion volume, *Wordsworth's Reading 1770-1799*, this is the most complete study of Wordsworth's reading to date, and it will be an essential reference tool for all scholars and students of his work.

WORDSWORTH'S READING 1800–1815

WORDSWORTH'S READING 1800–1815

*

DUNCAN WU
Reader in English Literature
University of Glasgow

Published by the Press Syndicate of the University of Cambridge
The Pitt Building, Trumpington Street, Cambridge CB2 1RP
40 West 20th Street, New York, NY 10011-4211, USA
10 Stamford Road, Oakleigh, Victoria 3166, Australia

© Duncan Wu 1995

The right of Duncan Wu to be identified as author of this work
has been asserted in accordance with the Copyright, Designs
and Patents Act 1988.

First published 1995

Printed in Great Britain by Woolnough Bookbinding Ltd.,
Irthlingborough, Northants.

A catalogue record for this book is available from the British Library

Library of Congress cataloguing in publication data
Wu, Duncan.
Wordsworth's reading, 1800-1815 / Duncan Wu.
p.   cm.
'Continues the story begun by Wordsworth's reading, 1770-1799' - P.ix.
Includes bibliographical references and index.
ISBN 0 521 49674 8 (hardback)
1. Wordsworth, William, 1770-1850 - Books and reading.
2. Wordsworth, William, 1770-1850 - Library - Catalogs.
3. Books and reading - England - History - 19th century.
4. Poets, English - 19th century - Biography.
I. Wu, Duncan. Wordsworth's reading, 1770-1799. II. Title.
PR5892.B6W82 1995
821'.7 - dc20   95-20579 CIP

ISBN 0 521 49674 8   hardback

Contents

Preface	*page* ix
Acknowledgements	xix
List of abbreviations	xxi
Dates of readings	xxviii
A note on texts	xxix
Wordsworth's reading 1800-1815	1
Appendix I	
Wordsworth's reading 1770-1799	
1. Additions	253
2. Points of information	259
Appendix II	
Wordsworth's reading 1800-1815: some queries	260
Appendix III	
The Longman accounts	265
Appendix IV	
Libraries used by Wordsworth	267
Appendix V	
Fugitive texts read by Wordsworth, 1800-1815	269
Appendix VI	
Tale Imitated from Gower: MS text	273
Bibliography	276
Index	285

Preface

This is an annotated list of the books and authors known to have been read by Wordsworth during the years 1800-15. It continues the story begun by *Wordsworth's Reading 1770-1799*, which chronologized his intellectual life up to the point at which he moved into Dove Cottage. Like its predecessor, this volume shadows Mark L. Reed's monumental chronologies; it thus terminates at the same point as his *Chronology of the Middle Years* (1975) - with the first half of the year 1815, when the poet departed London after the long visit in the course of which he had overseen publication of the *White Doe of Rylstone*.

Stylistic and organizational methods conform to those in the earlier volume, as discussed in its Preface; however, there is a distinction in the methodology followed here. The relative paucity of evidence for Wordsworth's reading during the first thirty years of his life led me frequently to depend on internal evidence in his poetry - such as echoes, allusions, and borrowings of various kinds. When he moved into Dove Cottage in late 1799 Wordsworth began a way of life more settled than before, and more conducive to his occupation; the change suited Dorothy's writing habits too, as the *Grasmere Journals* testify. Accordingly, they gathered their books around them - one imagines that the 'Somersetshire goods'[1] unpacked by Dorothy on 25 July 1800 included volumes acquired at Alfoxden - and read, for the first time, at leisure, from the small collection they had each accumulated. In succeeding years they set out to transform that random assortment into a working library, building up a comprehensive array of poetry in particular. This alone would explain the comparative wealth of factual evidence for Wordsworth's reading from 1800 onwards: the number of extant books formerly in his library increases after that date. In addition, a good deal of evidence arises out of his use of books owned by friends; his increasing tendency to discuss literary matters in correspondence; Dorothy's journal entries; and his occasional, documented, book-buying sprees.

As in *Wordsworth's Reading 1770-1799*, I have made it my primary task to present all such evidence to the reader. Where the present volume differs from its predecessor is in placing less emphasis on allusions and echoes than before. Such a multitude have been documented for Wordsworth's mature poetry that I have tended to use them usually only when they confirm circumstantial details, or constitute the earliest discoverable evidence for confirmable readings. There are a prodigious number of echoes of *Paradise Lost* in the poetry from 1800 onwards; to have listed these would have been of little use in gauging when Wordsworth actually read this important poem. Repeated borrowings from the Bible, Shakespeare,[2] Virgil, Horace, Ovid, and other works or authors already known to him are thus not entered unless some compelling reason presents itself[3] - for example, an ascertainable reading of some

---

[1] *Grasmere Journals* 14.

[2] For a wide-ranging discussion of Shakespearean echoes and allusions in Wordsworth see Jonathan Bate, *Shakespeare and the English Romantic Tradition* (Oxford, 1986), chapter 5.

[3] Documentation of Wordsworth's borrowings from these sources has been going on for many years; see, for instance, W. J. B. Owen, 'Some Wordsworthian Borrowings', *N&Q* 193 (1948) 429-30, and J. C. Maxwell, 'Wordsworth and Prospero', *N&Q* 194 (1949) 477. It is worth noting Hazlitt's scepticism as to W's regard for

Preface

specific passage (as in the case of note 283[viii]), or the earliest-known reading of a particular work. All the same, readers will find this book more positivistic, more preoccupied with the circumstances and probabilities of the poet's reading, than was its predecessor.

I have attempted to enforce some distinction between readings undertaken by Dorothy and William. This was not consistently possible in *Wordsworth's Reading 1770-1799* because evidence was often too vague to permit it. However, major sources of information for the years 1800-15 are Dorothy's journals and letters, which are usually quite specific about who read what. My policy has been to include all readings undertaken by Dorothy in her brother's presence; those undertaken in his absence, such as those of *A Midsummer Night's Dream* and *As You Like It* on 22 June 1802, are omitted.

* * *

'We live out of the way of new books; I have not seen a single book since I came here, now 13 months ago' - Wordsworth to Francis Wrangham, February 1801 (*EY* 318)

'I neither read reviews, magazines, nor any periodical publications whatsoever except the Morning [Post]' - Wordsworth to John Thelwall, January 1804 (*EY* 433)

'His Library is in fact little more than a chance collection of odd books' - Dorothy Wordsworth to De Quincey, July 1808 (*MY* i 257)

'I see no new books except by the merest accident' - Wordsworth to Francis Wrangham, spring 1812 (*MY* ii 9)

'Nevertheless (small and paltry as my Collection is) I have not read a fifth part of it' - Wordsworth to Francis Wrangham, 19 February 1819 (*MY* ii 524)

If Wordsworth was neither as ambitious a bibliophile as Francis Wrangham, nor as voracious a reader as Coleridge, it is true, I think, that he sometimes exaggerated the lack of reading matter at his disposal - especially when writing to correspondents who, out of sympathy, were likely to respond to his requests for more. In fact, for someone living in what at that time was still a fairly remote part of the Kingdom,[1] he displayed considerable resourcefulness in his pursuit of books. During his residence first at Dove Cottage, Allan Bank, and Rydal Mount, he sought out a multitude of titles, using friends and relatives (including his brothers Richard

---

these writers: 'That as to poetry, there was something in Shakespear that he [Wordsworth] could not make up his mind to, for he hated those interlocutions between Lucius and Caius: and as to Milton, the only great merit of the Paradise Lost was in the conception or in getting rid of the horns and tail of the Devil, for as to the execution, he thought he could do as well or better himself' (Howe ix 5).

[1] Lamb, as might be expected, was delicate on this matter; copying a number of works for Wordsworth from volumes not readily available in Grasmere, he wrote: 'In your obscure part of the world, which I take to be ultima Thule, I thought these verses out of Books which cannot be accessible, would not be unwelcome' (Marrs ii 105).

Preface

and John, the Beaumonts,[1] De Quincey,[2] Lamb,[3] even, apparently, Mary Monkhouse[4]) as agents. He also made full use of his accounts with such publishers as Daniel Stuart and Thomas Norton Longman to order books from London - such as Withering's *Botany* and Davy's *Researches*. Literary friends like Wrangham, Southey and Scott loaned or gave volumes, and there was, of course, Coleridge, parts of whose extensive collection were with the Wordsworths, wherever they were.[5]

However, Wordsworth's resources during these years did not allow him to purchase a copy of every book he read, and soon after moving to Dove Cottage he was using local libraries. There were book clubs in Grasmere and Kendal, of course, and both he and Dorothy were using these during the 1800s.[6] But one of the most interesting facts to emerge from the current study is that Wordsworth had little hesitation about following Coleridge into other people's private libraries. Coleridge, as John Livingston Lowes and George Whalley have observed,[7] lived up to his self-description as a library cormorant. When enticing Southey to Keswick in April 1801, the chief bait was the libraries: 'As to books, my landlord, who dwells next door, has a very respectable library, which he has put with mine; histories, encyclopaedias, and all the modern gentry. But then I can have, when I choose, free access to the princely library of Sir Guilfred Lawson, which contains the noblest collection of travels and natural history of, perhaps, any private library in England; besides this, there is the Cathedral library of Carlisle, from whence I can have any books sent to me that I wish; in short, I may truly say that I command all the libraries in the county.'[8] Indeed, on 4 April

---

[1] 'We have received the Books from Coleorton', Dorothy told Lady Beaumont on 28 December 1809 (*MY* i 380); what these were, we do not know.

[2] See, for instance, Dorothy's letter to De Quincey of 7 July 1808, listing the works not then in Wordsworth's possession and requesting cheap copies from London (*MY* i 257).

[3] For some of the titles Lamb collected for Wordsworth, see Marrs ii 203-4. It is worth remembering that on 13 October 1804 Lamb wrote to say: 'you may depend upon my sparing no pains to furnish you as complete a library of old Poets & Dramatists as will be prudent to buy' (Marrs ii 147). Wordsworth's stated requirements at that time included Jonson, Beaumont and Fletcher, Massinger, 'Congreve and the rest of King Charles's moralists', Spenser's *View of the Present State of Ireland*, and Marlowe. In addition, Lamb sent 'certain books belonging to Wordsworth' up by the Kendal wagon on 4 November 1802, but it is not known what these were (Marrs ii 84).

[4] 'The Poem came safe in the Box', Sara Hutchinson told Mary on 27 March 1809 (*SHL* 17). I should like to know *which* poem.

[5] The Rydal Mount catalogue of 1829 designates those books belonging to Coleridge; for further discussion see Shaver pp. xx-xxiii.

[6] See Appendix IV.

[7] See especially Whalley's unpublished doctoral thesis, 'Samuel Taylor Coleridge: Library Cormorant' (1950).

[8] Griggs ii 717. The bait worked; Southey made at least two visits to Lawson's library at Brayton - one in December 1803, and another the following year. In December 1803 he told Wynn: 'To-morrow I go for a day or two to Sir Wilfred Lawson's, induced by the fame of his library, of which he is Heberishly liberal; but, unlike Heber, he knows nothing about their contents' (Warter i 249).

Preface

1801 Coleridge borrowed a number of books from Carlisle Cathedral through an old friend, James Losh.[1] On 14 August 1800 he told Poole about Greta Hall:

> In gardens, etc we are uncommonly well off, & our Landlord who resides next door in this twofold House, is already much attached to us - he is a quiet sensible man, with as large a Library as your's - & perhaps rather larger - well stored with Encyclopaedias, Dictionaries, & Histories &c - all modern. - The gentry of the Country, titled & untitled, have all called or are about to call on me - & I shall have free access to the magnificent Library of Sir Gilfred Lawson, a weak but good natured Man -.[2]

Wordsworth too had access to Lawson's collection; indeed, in a letter to Poole as early as 4 January 1799, Coleridge reported that Wordsworth 'thinks that he can procure a house near Sir Gilford Lawson's by the Lakes, & have free access to his immense Library'.[3] He must therefore have seen Lawson's library at some point prior to January 1799, and, if Coleridge was right, the choice of Grasmere as a home was made partly for its relative proximity to Lawson's handsome residence - Brayton Hall, Aspatria. Coleridge's emphasis on 'free access' also draws attention to the importance to both poets of using libraries without subscription fees. Lawson's generosity is confirmed in a letter to Godwin of September 1800, in which Coleridge describes his management of his library as 'liberal in the highest degree'.[4] He seems to have made his first visit there in October 1800, when he saw 'a princely Library, chiefly of natural History'.[5] Two years later he remarked: 'in Voyages, Travels, & Books of Natural History it is no doubt the first in the Island - next to Sir Joseph Banks's'.[6] In addition, the landlord and cotenant of Greta Hall, William Jackson, owned a large collection of books which was available to Coleridge and, presumably, Wordsworth; as Coleridge remarked: 'in *my* Library you will find all the Poets & Philosophers, & many of our best old Writers - below in our Parlor, belonging to my Landlord, but in my possession, are almost all the usual Trash of the Johnsons, Gibbons, Robertsons, &c with the Encyclopaedia Britannica, &c &c.'[7] On 1 November he told Josiah Wedgwood that his landlord 'has collected nearly 500 volumes of our most esteemed modern Writers, such as Gibbon, Hume, Johnson, &c &c.'[8] What may have been available to Wordsworth through the books belonging to Lawson, Jackson, and Coleridge himself during the 1800s can only be conjectured on the basis of these comments, but I believe that those three collections may account for many of the titles and authors listed here, the provenance of which cannot

---

[1] He had used another intermediary, Cottle, when borrowing from the Bristol Library (see *WR* 181, 186).
[2] Griggs i 618.
[3] Griggs i 455.
[4] Griggs i 619.
[5] Griggs i 645.
[6] Griggs ii 869.
[7] Griggs i 619; his italics.
[8] Griggs i 644. The phrase 'most esteemed' is, of course, ironic.

Preface

otherwise be traced. Coleridge also made use of the libraries at Carlton House, St Bees School, and Hawkshead Grammar School.

Coleridge's own books were probably at Wordsworth's disposal from the Alfoxden period onwards, and it is likely that Dove Cottage became the repository for part of Coleridge's collection soon after the Wordsworths moved in. He accumulated a large quantity of volumes at Allan Bank during work on *The Friend*, leaving most of them there when he fell out with Wordsworth in 1810.[1]

Two other nearby libraries deserve mention. John Spedding's growing collection at Mirehouse was probably at Wordsworth's disposal from 1800 onwards. Dorothy visited Mirehouse on 14 August 1800, and we know that, at the very least, her brother and Coleridge borrowed Spedding's copies of Cobbett's *Weekly Political Register*. They probably made use of other volumes too. Southey's move to Greta Hall in 1803 brought another, constantly expanding collection to within easy reach of Grasmere - and Wordsworth was not slow to use it. The greater part of Southey's existing library reached Keswick only in 1808, when Duck Row was established to house twenty-two packages of books.[2]

I hope that this volume and its predecessor will serve to rectify the misconception, to some degree encouraged by the poet, that he not only read little, but had scant regard for book-learning.[3] The truth is that Wordsworth loved certain kinds of books and not others. He took particular pleasure in travel books and poetry, but abstruse German philosophy (three boxes of which, all belonging to Coleridge, were packed off to London in May 1812)[4] held little appeal for him.

What kind of book caught his fancy? During the years covered by this study he composed *The Convention of Cintra*, and, as one might expect, his interest in current affairs flourished during the first two decades of the nineteenth century. The poet who had been 'pretty hot' in revolutionary causes during the 1790s[5] continued to scour the newspapers as Napoleon's fortunes rose and fell. He became an avid reader of newspapers, including the *Morning Post*,

---

[1] See Shaver 313-63.

[2] On 5 May 1808 Southey told Danvers: 'I have had a range of shelves run up along one side of the passage which connects the two houses from the floor to the ceiling. It holds about 1350 volumes, and is denominated Duck Row, though there is only the dark end to which that name can properly be applied, those which are in the light being Drakes. There must be yet a small stand of shelves on the upper landing-place to hold about 200 which are still kicking to windward, and to receive droppers-in' (Warter ii 62).

[3] In this respect this volume and its predecessor are the consequence of Lane Cooper's 'A Glance at Wordsworth's Reading', *MLN* 22 (1907) 83-9, 110-17, one of the earliest articles to have argued against the misconception that Wordsworth was ill-read. All the same, Cooper's argument has taken many years to gain acceptance. As late as 1940 one writer suggested: 'Wordsworth was not a well-read man, and did not desire to be anything of the sort' (Senex, 'Wordsworth and Greek', *N&Q* 178 [1940] 172-3, p. 173). Such arguments depend on the skewed testimony of De Quincey (see Masson ii 287-8). For further discussion see 'The Myth of Wordsworth's Reading but Little', Appendix A of Thomas and Ober's *A Mind For Ever Voyaging*, pp. 183-90.

[4] *MY* ii 13

[5] See *WR* 161.

the *Morning Chronicle*, the *Courier* and the *Times*, and even thought at one point of becoming a journalist (see note 385[ii], below). He was an enthusiastic reader, too, of books about recent political and military history - for instance those by Leckie and Pasley (notes 248 and 311). Soldiering was the profession for which Wordsworth thought himself best suited, and consistent with this fact was his pleasure at Landor's departure for Spain in 1808 to fight with the Spanish army.[1] No doubt his conversations with Coleridge, and involvement with *The Friend*, fuelled these interests.

Certain enthusiasms continued from earlier years: travel books, plays, and novels figure largely in this list. But perhaps his most distinctive trait as a reader was his voracious appetite for poetry. We shall never know exactly how many poets were read by Wordsworth during these years, but the range and variety of those listed here is astonishing. He was as aware of contemporary developments (being, for instance, an early reader of Byron, and a subscriber to Isabella Lickbarrow's *Poetical Effusions* and an early volume of Bernard Barton's)[2] as he was of poetry from classical times onwards. The anthologies edited by Anderson and Chalmers were helpful in this respect, but it is clear that by 1815 he was well-read even among many lesser-known writers excluded by those editors. Who today, in the age of copyright libraries, databases, and the internet, can claim even a nodding acquaintance with the poetry of Richard Edwards, Barnaby Googe, or Laurence Minot? Their work was familiar to Wordsworth. At a period when the works of Medieval writers were hard to come by, he was an admirer of Langland, Malory, and Chaucer. In this light it is no surprise that in due course the anthologists consulted *him*: Dyce sought his counsel while preparing his *Specimens* in later years, and their correspondence provides ample evidence, were any needed, of the poet's bibliographical and scholarly expertise.

During the same period Wordsworth became less keen on periodicals than in earlier years, such that by 1824 he could tell Landor of his regret that the *Imaginary Conversations* had first appeared 'in a Magazine'.[3] This was almost certainly thanks to the adverse criticism directed at his work by the 'depraved Coxcomb'[4] Jeffrey. Wordsworth tried not to be rattled by it, but besides the understandable sense of injustice, he resented the fact that Jeffrey managed to dampen sales of his poetry. He often denied reading Jeffrey, but W. J. B. Owen is probably correct in suggesting that 'he and his family read more of the *Edinburgh Review* than he was sometimes willing to admit'.[5] For instance, Dorothy read Jeffrey's review of Burns in April 1809,[6] the 'foolish' review of Hannah More in August 1809,[7] and that of

---

[1] See Peter Mann, 'Two Unpublished Letters of Robert Southey', *N&Q* NS 22 (1975) 397-9.
[2] See *MY* ii 382.
[3] *LY* i 244. See also his scathing comments on *Blackwood's* in 1819, *MY* ii 522-3.
[4] *MY* ii 197.
[5] W. J. B. Owen, 'Wordsworth and Jeffrey in Collaboration', *RES* 15 (1964) 160-7, p. 163.
[6] *MY* i 326.
[7] *MY* i 365.

Preface

Campbell's *Gertrude*.¹ By July 1810, when Coleridge made an observation on reviewers in his notebook, it was clear that the Wordsworth circle regarded a number of them as 'enemies'.² And by 1814 even Dorothy had tired of Jeffrey's onslaughts (though whether either she or her brother saw Jeffrey's notorious review of *The Excursion* remains debateable).³ Indeed, by 18 February 1815, even Dorothy was expressing astonishment with Sara Hutchinson for spending money 'on those silly Reviews'.⁴ Wordsworth's general dislike of reviewers persisted to the end of his life.⁵

Wordsworth's Library

On 16 June 1811 Dorothy Wordsworth told Catherine Clarkson: 'yesterday we were all employed in bearing the Books out of the Barn, and arranging them':⁶ what were those books? And which titles were stored in the 'large book-case' in the Rydal Mount study in September 1813?⁷ We shall probably never know. True, sometimes we are allowed glimpses (as for instance in the inventory of books sent by Richard Wordsworth of Branthwaite to Dove Cottage in 1805,⁸ or the scan of the Rydal Mount library shelves in the *Essay, Supplementary to the Preface*),⁹ but these are invariably hurried and, alas, all too brief. The full contents of Wordsworth's library at any one time remain virtually impossible to pin down. Admittedly, it *is* possible to say, of some of the books listed here and in *Wordsworth's Reading 1770-1799*, when, and for how long, they came into Wordsworth's possession. It is not, however, possible to draw up a complete catalogue of books in his possession in, say, November 1804. Nor is it safe to assume that because he read a particular title he owned a copy of it. Many of the books listed here were borrowed or read only for a short time. Indeed, the entries in his Commonplace Book must have been copied from books not readily available to him.

From this point of view Chester L. and Alice C. Shaver's *Wordsworth's Library* has been enormously useful. There are several books without which this volume would have been much the poorer: the Shavers' has probably been the most valuable. *Wordsworth's Library* collates all existing loan books, inventories, and auction catalogues of the Rydal Mount library,

---

¹ *MY* i 365.
² *Notebooks* iii 3965. Coleridge refers specifically to 'Mistress Bare and Bald' (Mrs Barbauld), though it is clear from his comments that he has other reviewers in mind.
³ Though see note 228(vi). Wordsworth had heard about its opening sentence by the end of 1814 (*MY* ii 182). There is, intriguingly, a copy of the *Edinburgh Review* for October 1815 (containing Jeffrey's attack on the *White Doe*) at the Wordsworth Library, Grasmere, believed to have belonged to Wordsworth. However, it is worth noting that it bears the ownership inscription of 'Mr Fisher 6 Duke St'.
⁴ *MY* ii 205.
⁵ See *LY* iv 308-9.
⁶ *MY* i 496.
⁷ See *MY* ii 114.
⁸ See my article, 'The Wordsworth Family Library at Cockermouth: Towards a Reconstruction', *The Library* 14 (1992) 127-35.
⁹ See *Prose Works* iii 70-1.

distinguishing titles known to have been Coleridge's from those owned by Wordsworth. I refer to it throughout.

However, it is not a catalogue of Wordsworth's library as it stood at any one moment in time; in fact the books listed by the Shavers were never retained at Rydal Mount simultaneously. All they claim to do is list all the books specifically mentioned in the various catalogues and loan books between 1829 and 1859.[1] There are, as a result, certain anomalous features of *Wordsworth's Library*. For one thing, it omits some titles known to have been in the poet's possession - usually because they go unlisted in any of the extant catalogues.[2] Also, it mentions some books published *after* the poet's death in 1850, because they were given to Mary Wordsworth and subsequently included in the library auction of 1859. And as the earliest of the catalogues dates from no earlier than 1829, caution should be exercised when using *Wordsworth's Library* as a means of confirming readings prior to that year. However, I have taken the view that it is fair to speculate that books listed by the Shavers *may* have come into Wordsworth's ownership earlier than 1829 (providing, of course, that their dates of publication do not make that an impossibility).

There are factors that constrain me from engaging too readily in such speculation. For one thing, Wordsworth's collection was small when he moved into Dove Cottage, and grew only when he began to use Lamb and De Quincey as book buyers from 1804 onwards. Even so, he took many years to acquire standard eighteenth-century texts: the *Tatler* came to Rydal Mount only in 1812, Gibbon's *Decline and Fall* in 1836. As Wordsworth had read both works before he picked up copies of his own, these cases do, I think, prove the general rule that he was a great user of libraries. His usual habit must have been to read books belonging either to a library or to a friend, and only afterwards to buy it, sometimes years later, if he came across a reasonably priced working copy. This explains why, as late as 1808, Dorothy reported to De Quincey that her brother lacked 'Clarendon - Burnet - any of the elder Histories - translations from the Classics chiefly - historical - Plutarch's Lives, - Thucydides, *Tacitus* (I think he said) - (by the bye, he *has* a translation of Herodotus), Lord Bacon's Works - Milton's prose Works - in short, any of the good elder writers'.[3] Not that he hadn't read these authors - in fact, their presence on the list indicates that he probably had: he simply hadn't got round to buying his own copies.

As a buyer of books Wordsworth was eminently practical. Unlike Wrangham, he did not seek them out for their rarity; he bought them to read. Compared with Southey's books, De Quincey recalled, those in Wordsworth's possession were

---

[1] Morley's interesting discussion of Wordsworth's library is also based on the auction catalogue of 1859 (*Robinson* ii 867-74).

[2] Five such titles are listed by James Butler in his review of Shaver, *ELN* 18 (1981) 301-4, and Paul F. Betz owns another six (see Betz 136); there are others, including those listed here as notes 380 and AI12. In addition, some titles are listed in the loan book but not the auction catalogue because they were given away by Mary Wordsworth before her death - and thus before the sale.

[3] *MY* i 257.

Preface

ill bound, or not bound at all - in boards, sometimes in tatters; many were imperfect as to the number of volumes, mutilated as to the number of pages: sometimes, where it seemed worth while, the defects being supplied by manuscript; sometimes not: in short, everything shewed that the books were for use, and not for show; and their limited amount shewed that their possessor must have independent sources of enjoyment to fill up the major part of his time.[1]

The bulk of Wordsworth's volumes were of no particular bibliographical interest. And it is revealing to find their owner telling Scott in November 1806 that he preferred books to be 'of a Pocket size. Any Poetry which I like, I wish for in that size, to which no doubt yours will one day descend'.[2] All the same, the scholarly side to Wordsworth led him to cherish the small number of rare books that came his way: James Patrick Muirhead recorded the pride with which Wordsworth showed him his early edition of *The Seasons*,[3] and the note in his copy of Martin's *Voyage to St Kilda* proves that he appreciated its rarity (see note AI13). However, though erudite in both critical and bibliographical terms, Wordsworth seems to have acquired such rare books as he owned only as exceptions to his usual book-buying habits.[4] Indeed, many of the more valuable items listed by the Shavers were gifts from such admirers as David Laing and Thomas Powell, whose occasional consignments increased Wordsworth's stock of 'first and early editions of Poetry'.[5]

Those who base their speculations about Wordsworth's reading on Shaver's catalogue should be mindful of such factors. The problem with speculating at all is illustrated by William Gilbert's *The Hurricane* (Bristol, 1796). Wordsworth must have known it by 1800, because it is mentioned in a note to *The Brothers*. However, the note professes only an 'imperfect recollection' of Gilbert's poem. So when did Wordsworth read it? The difficulty is compounded by the listing of *The Hurricane* at Shaver 102 - which begs the question of when Wordsworth's copy was acquired. In view of the comparative rarity of Gilbert's volume even in its day, the likeliest scenario is that Wordsworth purchased his copy in Bristol, from its publisher, Joseph Cottle, shortly after publication in 1796. He probably left it either at Alfoxden or London when he went to Germany in 1798, and had it sent on to Grasmere only after *Lyrical Ballads* had gone to press (thus accounting for the imperfect recollection). It was eventually sent to Dove Cottage and remained in Wordsworth's possession for the rest of his life, being listed in the 1829 catalogue as 'Gilbert's Hurricane', and was finally sold at the 1859 auction as lot 516. But those are the only hard facts we have besides the note to *The Brothers*. Wordsworth might just as well have not owned a copy in 1796, and instead bought

---

[1] *Tait's Edinburgh Magazine* 6 (1839) 513.

[2] *MY* i 96.

[3] Muirhead 737. Muirhead was mistaken about *The Seasons*; Wordsworth owned not the first, but the second edition (see note 398[v]).

[4] See his declaration to Wrangham in 1819 that 'on *new* books I have not spent five shillings for the last 5 years' (*MY* ii 524).

[5] *LY* iii 625; see also *LY* iii 756.

Preface

or borrowed one (perhaps from Coleridge) after composing *The Brothers*. We may never know. But in certain cases speculation can shed light on our understanding of the conditions of Wordsworth's reading, and I have regarded it as an essential part of my task to make connections of this kind where they help make sense of the available facts. I have striven to be clear about when I am speculating - and I hope that readers will always be aware that any conjectures involving Shaver cannot claim the status of fact without the support of additional documentation.

The Shavers' volume thus plays a vital part in the present study, even though it is, perhaps surprisingly, the catalogue of a library that never actually existed.

A work of this kind is by its nature incomplete, as new evidence concerning Wordsworth's reading is constantly turning up. Any such information will be gratefully received by the author, in the hope that at some future date it may be possible to provide an even fuller account of Wordsworth's intellectual life.

Acknowledgements

Work on this volume would have taken a good deal longer - and might be less detailed - had it not been for Mark L. Reed's pioneering volume, *Wordsworth: The Chronology of the Middle Years 1800-1815*. This project is a tribute to Professor Reed; having retraced many of the paths first trodden by him some twenty years ago, I was fortunate in finding in him an enthusiastic and helpful correspondent. The information he has provided, and the readiness with which he has attended to my queries, has greatly expedited my progress. I am deeply grateful to him. The other work of scholarship to which this work is indebted is *The Prose Works of William Wordsworth* edited by W. J. B. Owen and Jane Worthington Smyser. The carefully-crafted notes provided by those editors are sometimes the only available evidence for readings by Wordsworth, and I cite them with gratitude to their authors. Professor Owen provided invaluable encouragement during work on *Wordsworth's Reading 1770-1799*, and read early versions prior to publication. I am grateful to him for doing so once more for the present study: his careful and discriminating eye has saved me from many a slip. Bruce Graver is to be credited with one of the most rigorous, and best informed, reviews of *Wordsworth's Reading 1770-1799*, and his comments have been taken into account in preparing its successor. He, too, has provided detailed criticism and corrections to the present work, proving as generous with his learning as he is shrewd in his judgements; without them this volume would be much the poorer.

    I wish also to thank the numerous librarians and curators who have provided help and assistance during my research: Clive Hurst, Bodleian Library, Oxford; Peter and Marian Elkington, Curators, Rydal Mount; Roberta Zonghi, Curator of Rare Books, Boston Public Library; Stephen Z. Nonack, Head of Reference, Library of the Boston Athenæum; Margaret M. Sherry, Rare Books and Special Collections Librarian, Princeton University; Dina Schoonmaker, Special Collections Librarian, Oberlin College Library; Vincent Giroud, Curator of Modern Books and Manuscripts, Beineke Rare Book and Manuscript Library, Yale University; Georgianna Ziegler, Reference Librarian, Folger Shakespeare Library, Washington, DC; Nancy Romero, Head of Rare Books, Special Collections, and Kelly Bridgwater, Circulations Supervisor, University of Illinois Library, Urbana-Champaign; Joel Silver, Curator of Books, and Sue Presnell, Reference Librarian, Lilly Library, University of Indiana; Amanda Saville, Librarian of St John's College, Cambridge; Wendy Fish and Eoin Shalloo, National Art Library, Victoria and Albert Museum; Roberta Davis and Christina Gee, Keats House, Hampstead; and Deborah K. Hedgecock, Guildhall Library, London. I thank the staffs of the Upper Reading Room, Bodleian Library, Oxford; the Carnegie Library, Kendal; the Kendal Record Office; the British Library; the Senate House Library, University of London, and the Colindale Newspaper Library. I am particularly grateful to John Gavin of the Armitt Library, Ambleside, for information relating to book clubs and libraries in the Lake District, and for sending me the typescript of his forthcoming article, 'Westmorland Literary Institutions to 1850'. My primary institutional debt is to the Chairman and Trustees of the Wordsworth Trust, Grasmere, to whom I am grateful for permission to examine and quote

Acknowledgements

from manuscript materials at the Wordsworth Library. The enormous importance of the Trust in its capacities as a research archive and conservation library will be evident from my frequent references to its holdings. In particular I would like to express my gratitude to its Director, Robert S. Woof, who has been generous in imparting advice and information, and its Librarian, Jeff Cowton, who, with his colleagues, has been unfailingly helpful on countless occasions. Present owners of books formerly in Wordsworth's possession, or once read by him, have been no less accommodating: in particular I gratefully acknowledge the kind assistance of Paul F. Betz, John Spedding, and Christopher and Andrea Wordsworth.

Like its predecessor, this volume owes much to the generosity of friends and colleagues who helped along the way, whether by offering encouragement, providing from their own resources the more elusive and fugitive pieces of the jigsaw puzzle, or by chasing on my behalf books once belonging to Wordsworth. For these and other acts of kindness, I thank James A. Butler, David Chandler, Jared Curtis, Damian Walford Davies, David Fairer, Susan Holmes, Ian Jack, Heather Jackson, J. R. de J. Jackson, Stanley Jones, Carol Landon, Sheona Lodge, Roger Lonsdale, Barry McKay, Dorothy A. Porter McMillan, Cecilia Powell, Roger Robinson, Nicholas Roe, Liz Salaman, Barry Symonds, Nicola Trott, Timothy Underhill, John West, D. E. Wickham, and Sylvia Wordsworth. I must give particular acknowledgement to Pat and Rick Tomlinson, who took time out of a hard-earned vacation to pursue a number of Wordsworth's books on my behalf; and to my agent in north-west England, whose generous assistance in numerous matters pertaining to this project has been indispensable. Jonathan Wordsworth suggested this project, and has encouraged it from the first. For their belief in this work I wish also to thank my editors at Cambridge, Kevin Taylor and Josie Dixon.

Their resourcefulness as researchers has led me frequently to the work of two men whose contributions to our knowledge of Wordsworth and Coleridge are incalculable, but whom, alas, I can no longer thank in person: Chester L. Shaver and George Whalley.

My greatest debt is to the British Academy, whose award of a Postdoctoral Fellowship, 1991-4, enabled me to begin work on this book. During that happy period I was fortunate in being a Fellow of St Catherine's College, Oxford. I thank both institutions for generous support. Research continued under different circumstances after I had left Oxford for the wilds of West London: only thanks to the encouragement and support of Caroline Cochrane during that uncertain time was I able to complete it. It is with heartfelt gratitude that I dedicate *Wordsworth's Reading 1800-1815* to her.

Acton, 1995

Abbreviations

Album	*Poems and Extracts Chosen by William Wordsworth for an Album Presented to Lady Mary Lowther, Christmas, 1819* (1905)
Anderson, *British Poets*	*The Works of the British Poets with Prefaces, Biographical and Critical*, ed. Robert Anderson (13 vols., 1795)
Barton	'The Road from Penshurst: Wordsworth, Ben Jonson and Coleridge in 1802', by Anne Barton, *Essays in Criticism* 37 (1987) 209-33
Betz	'Manuscripts, Books, and Related Pictures of the Paul Betz Collection', *British Romantic Art*, by Jonathan Wordsworth, Robert Metzger, and Paul Betz (1990), pp. 38-47
Bicknell	*The Picturesque Scenery of the Lake District*, by Peter Bicknell (1990)
BLS	*A Catalogue of the Books Belonging to the Bristol Library Society*, by Revd. Thomas Johnes (1798)
BNYPL	*Bulletin of the New York Public Library*
Butler *JEGP*	'Wordsworth, Cottle, and the *Lyrical Ballads*: Five Letters, 1797-1800', by James A. Butler, *JEGP* 75 (1976) 139-53
Butler *WC*	'Wordsworth in Philadelphia Area Libraries, 1787-1850', by James A. Butler, *WC* 4 (1973) 41-64
C	Samuel Taylor Coleridge
CC	*Collected Coleridge Series*, Bollingen Series 75
CC *Biographia*	*Biographia Literaria*, ed. James Engell and Walter Jackson Bate (2 vols., 1983)
CC *Essays*	*Essays on his Times*, ed. David Erdman (3 vols., 1978)
CC *Friend*	*The Friend*, ed. Barbara Rooke (2 vols., 1969)
CC *Lectures 1795*	*Lectures 1795 On Politics and Religion*, ed. Lewis Patton and Peter Mann (1971)
CC *Literature*	*Lectures 1808-1819 On Literature*, ed. R. A. Foakes (2 vols., 1987)
CC *Table Talk*	*Table Talk*, ed. Carl Woodring (2 vols., 1990)
CC *Watchman*	*The Watchman*, ed. Lewis Patton (1970)
CLB	*Charles Lamb Bulletin*
Coe	*Wordsworth and the Literature of Travel*, by Charles Norton Coe (1953)
Coe (1952)	'Wordsworth and the Literature of Travel: A Bibliography', by Charles Norton Coe, *N&Q* 197 (1952) 429-33, 457
Coffman	*Coleridge's Library: A Bibliography of Books Owned or Read by Samuel Taylor Coleridge*, by Ralph J. Coffman (1987)

Abbreviations

Cole	*A Bibliographical and Descriptive Tour from Scarborough to the Library of a Philobiblist*, by John Cole (1824)
Comparetti	*The White Doe of Rylstone by William Wordsworth* ed. Alice Pattee Comparetti (1940)
Cornell *Benjamin*	*Benjamin the Waggoner*, ed. Paul F. Betz (1981)
Cornell *Evening Walk*	*An Evening Walk*, ed. James Averill (1984)
Cornell *Home at Grasmere*	*Home at Grasmere*, ed. Beth Darlington (1977)
Cornell *Lyrical Ballads*	*Lyrical Ballads and Other Poems, 1797-1800*, ed. James Butler and Karen Green (1992)
Cornell *Poems 1800-7*	*Poems, in Two Volumes, and Other Poems, 1800-1807*, ed. Jared Curtis (1985)
Cornell *Poems 1807-20*	*Shorter Poems, 1807-1820*, ed. Carl H. Ketcham (1989)
Cornell *Ruined Cottage*	*The Ruined Cottage and The Pedlar*, ed. James Butler (1979)
Cornell *Tuft*	*The Tuft of Primroses, with Other Late Poems for The Recluse*, ed. Joseph F. Kishel (1986)
Cornell *White Doe*	*The White Doe of Rylstone*, ed. Kristine Dugas (1988)
Cornell *13-Book Prelude*	*The Thirteen-Book Prelude*, ed. Mark L. Reed (2 vols., 1991)
Curry	*New Letters of Robert Southey*, ed. Kenneth Curry (2 vols., 1965)
Curtis	*Wordsworth's Experiments with Tradition: The Lyric Poems of 1802*, by Jared R. Curtis (1971)
CW	Christopher Wordsworth, brother of W
DC	Dove Cottage, Grasmere
DC MS	Dove Cottage MS, at the Wordsworth Library, Grasmere
Dendurent	'The Coleridge Collection in Victoria University Library, Toronto', by H. O. Dendurent, *WC* 5 (1974) 225-86
DW	Dorothy Wordsworth
DWJ	*Journals of Dorothy Wordsworth*, ed. Ernest De Selincourt (2 vols., 1951)
EHC	*The Poetical Works of Samuel Taylor Coleridge*, ed. E. H. Coleridge (2 vols., 1912)
ELN	*English Language Notes*
EY	*Letters of William and Dorothy Wordsworth: The Early Years, 1787-1805*, ed. Ernest De Selincourt, rev. Chester L. Shaver (1967)
FN	*The Fenwick Notes of William Wordsworth*, ed. Jared Curtis (1993)
Fullmer	*Sir Humphry Davy's Published Works*, by June Z. Fullmer (1969)

Gordan	'William Wordsworth 1770-1850: An Exhibition', by John D. Gordan, *BNYPL* 54 (1950) 333-48, 384-96
Grasmere Journals	*The Grasmere Journals*, by Dorothy Wordsworth, ed. Pamela Woof (1991)
Griggs	*The Letters of Samuel Taylor Coleridge*, ed. E. L. Griggs (6 vols., 1956-71)
Grosart	*The Prose Works of William Wordsworth*, ed. Revd. Alexander B. Grosart (3 vols., 1876)
Heath	*Wordsworth and Coleridge: A Study of their Literary Relations in 1801-1802*, by William Heath (1970)
HLQ	*Huntington Library Quarterly*
Howe	*The Works of William Hazlitt*, ed. P. P. Howe (21 vols., 1930-4)
Jackson	*Romantic Poetry By Women: A Bibliography 1770-1835*, by J. R. de J. Jackson (1993)
Jacobus	*Tradition and Experiment in Wordsworth's Lyrical Ballads, 1798*, by Mary Jacobus (1976)
Jacobus (1989)	*Romanticism, Writing and Sexual Difference: Essays on* The Prelude, by Mary Jacobus (1989)
Jordan	*De Quincey to Wordsworth: A Biography of a Relationship*, by John E. Jordan (1962)
JW	John Wordsworth, brother of W and DW
JW Sr	John Wordsworth, father of W
Ketcham	*The Letters of John Wordsworth*, ed. Carl H. Ketcham (1969)
Lienemann	*Die Belesenheit von William Wordsworth*, by Kurt Lienemann (1908)
Life of Bell	*The Life of the Revd. Andrew Bell*, ed. Robert and Charles Cuthbert Southey (3 vols., 1844)
Life of Southey	*The Life and Correspondence of the late Robert Southey*, ed. Revd. Charles Cuthbert Southey (6 vols., 1849-50)
Love Letters	*The Love Letters of William and Mary Wordsworth*, ed. Beth Darlington (1981)
Lucas	*The Letters of Charles Lamb and Mary Lamb 1796-1843*, ed. E. V. Lucas (3 vols., 1935)
LY	*The Letters of William and Dorothy Wordsworth: The Later Years*, ed. Ernest De Selincourt, *i: 1821-8*, rev. Alan G. Hill (1978); *ii: 1829-34*, rev. Alan G. Hill (1982); *iii: 1835-9*, rev. Alan G. Hill (1982); *iv: 1840-53*, rev. by Alan G. Hill (1988)
Lyon	*The Excursion: A Study*, by Judson Stanley Lyon (1950)

Abbreviations

Marrs	*The Letters of Charles and Mary Anne Lamb 1796-1817*, ed. Edwin W. Marrs, Jr. (3 vols., 1975-8)
Masson	*The Collected Writings of Thomas De Quincey*, ed. David Masson (14 vols., 1889-90)
Memoirs	*Memoirs of William Wordsworth*, by Christopher Wordsworth (2 vols., 1851)
MH	Mary Hutchinson, from 4 Oct. 1802 Mary Wordsworth, wife of W
MLN	*Modern Language Notes*
Moorman	*William Wordsworth: A Biography*, by Mary Moorman (2 vols., 1957-65)
Moorman *DWJ*	*Journals of Dorothy Wordsworth*, ed. Mary Moorman (2nd edn, 1971)
Moorman *N&Q*	'Wordsworth's Commonplace Book', by Mary Moorman, *N&Q* NS 4 (1957) 400-5
Morley	*Henry Crabb Robinson on Books and Their Writers*, ed. Edith J. Morley (3 vols., 1938)
MP	*Modern Philology*
Muirhead	'A Day with Wordsworth', by James Patrick Muirhead, *Blackwood's Magazine* 221 (1927) 728-43
Musgrove	*Unpublished Letters of Thomas De Quincey and Elizabeth Barrett Browning*, ed. S. Musgrove (1954)
MW	Mary Wordsworth, wife of W
MWL	*The Letters of Mary Wordsworth 1800-1855*, ed. Mary E. Burton (1958)
MY	*The Letters of William and Dorothy Wordsworth: The Middle Years*, ed. Ernest De Selincourt, *i: 1806-11*, rev. Mary Moorman (1969); *ii: 1812-20*, rev. Mary Moorman and Alan G. Hill (1970)
Norton *Prel.*	*The Prelude: 1799, 1805, 1850*, ed. Jonathan Wordsworth, M. H. Abrams, Stephen Gill (1979)
Notebooks	*The Notebooks of Samuel Taylor Coleridge*, ed. Kathleen Coburn (1957-)
N&Q	*Notes and Queries*
OET *Prel.*	*The Prelude*, ed. E. De Selincourt, rev. Helen Darbishire (1959)
Owen, *Preface*	*Wordsworth's Preface to Lyrical Ballads*, ed. W. J. B. Owen (1979)
Owen (1969)	*Wordsworth as Critic*, by W. J. B. Owen (1969)

Abbreviations

Parrish	*The Art of the Lyrical Ballads*, by Stephen Maxfield Parrish (1973)
Patton	*The Amherst Wordsworth Collection*, by Cornelius Howard Patton (1936)
Peacock	*The Critical Opinions of William Wordsworth*, by Markham L. Peacock (1969)
Potts	*Wordsworth's Prelude: A Study of Its Literary Form*, by Abbie Findlay Potts (1953)
Prose Works	*The Prose Works of William Wordsworth*, ed. W. J. B. Owen and Jane Worthington Smyser (3 vols., 1974)
PW	*The Poetical Works of William Wordsworth*, ed. Ernest De Selincourt and Helen Darbishire (5 vols., 1940-9)
Reed i	*Wordsworth: The Chronology of the Early Years, 1770-1799*, by Mark L. Reed (1967)
Reed ii	*Wordsworth: The Chronology of the Middle Years, 1800-1815*, by Mark L. Reed (1975)
Reed *PBSA*	'Wordsworth on Wordsworth and Much Else: New Conversational Memoranda', by Mark L. Reed, *Papers of the Bibliographical Society of America* 81 (1987) 451-8
RES	*Review of English Studies*
Robberds	*A Memoir of the Life and Writings of the Late William Taylor of Norwich*, compiled and ed. J. W. Robberds (2 vols., 1843)
Robinson	*The Correspondence of Henry Crabb Robinson with the Wordsworth Circle*, ed. Edith J. Morley (2 vols., 1927)
Roe	*Wordsworth and Coleridge: The Radical Years*, by Nicholas Roe (1988)
Rogers	*The Table-Talk of Samuel Rogers* (1856)
RW	Richard Wordsworth, brother of W and DW
Sadler	*Diary, Reminiscences and Correspondence of Henry Crabb Robinson*, ed. Thomas Sadler (3 vols., 1869)
Sandford	*Thomas Poole and his Friends*, by Mrs Henry Sandford (2 vols., 1888)
SH	Sara Hutchinson
Shaver	*Wordsworth's Library: A Catalogue*, by Chester L. and Alice C. Shaver (1979)
SHL	*The Letters of Sara Hutchinson*, ed. Kathleen Coburn (1954)
SIB	*Studies in Bibliography*
Southey *SC*	*Sale Catalogues of Libraries of Eminent Persons Vol. 9: Poets and Men of Letters* ed. Roy Park (1974), *Southey*, pp. 83-288

Abbreviations

Stein	*Wordsworth's Art of Allusion*, by Edwin Stein (1988)
Supp.	*The Letters of William and Dorothy Wordsworth VIII: A Supplement of New Letters*, ed. Alan G. Hill (1993)
Thomas and Ober	*A Mind For Ever Voyaging*, by W. K. Thomas and Warren U. Ober (Alberta, 1989)
TWT	*Wordsworth's Hawkshead*, by T. W. Thompson, ed. Robert Woof (1970)
W	William Wordsworth
Warter	*Selections from the Letters of Robert Southey*, ed. John Wood Warter (4 vols., 1856)
WC	*The Wordsworth Circle*
Whalley	'The Bristol Library Borrowings of Southey and Coleridge, 1793-8', by George Whalley, *The Library* 4 (1949) 114-32
Whalley *BC*	'Coleridge Marginalia Lost', by George Whalley, *The Book Collector* 17 (1968) 428-42
Whalley PhD	'Samuel Taylor Coleridge: Library Cormorant', by George Whalley (PhD thesis, 2 vols., 1950)
Whalley (1955)	*Coleridge and Sara Hutchinson and the Asra Poems*, by George Whalley (1955)
Wing	*Short-Title Catalogue of Books printed in England, Scotland, Wales, and British America and of English Books printed in other Countries 1641-1700*, by Donald Wing (3 vols., 1972-88)
Woof PhD	'The Literary Relations of Wordsworth and Coleridge, 1795-1803: Five Studies', by Robert S. Woof (PhD thesis, 1959)
Woof *SIB*	'Wordsworth's Poetry and Stuart's Newspapers: 1797-1803', by Robert Woof, *SIB* 15 (1962) 149-89
Woof (1966)	'A Coleridge-Wordsworth Manuscript and "Sarah Hutchinson's Poets"', by Robert Woof, *SIB* 19 (1966) 226-31
Wordsworth *SC*	*Sale Catalogues of Libraries of Eminent Persons Vol. 9: Poets and Men of Letters* ed. Roy Park (1974), *Wordsworth*, pp. 9-71
Worthington	*Wordsworth's Reading of Roman Prose*, by Jane Worthington (1946)
WR	*Wordsworth's Reading 1770-1799*, by Duncan Wu (1993)
Wrangham *SC*	*Catalogue of the First and Second Portions of the Extensive and Valuable Library of the Venerable Archdeacon Wrangham*, by S. Leigh Sotheby (1843)
Wu *CWAAS*	'The Hawkshead School Library in 1788: A Catalogue', by Duncan Wu, *Transactions of the Cumberland and*

Abbreviations

	Westmorland Antiquarian and Archaeological Society 91 (1991) 173-97
Wu *Library*	'The Wordsworth Family Library at Cockermouth: Towards a Reconstruction', by Duncan Wu, *The Library* 14 (1992) 127-35

Dates of readings

The most problematic part of this list has been assigning dates of reading. For some entries a particular dating is implied by the evidence, but the majority are difficult to place with certainty and datings offered here should be regarded only as a general guide. Nor should they be taken to imply that Wordsworth read a particular book at that moment, straight through. Like most of us, he did not always finish a book he started, nor did he always read it in one sitting. On occasion, he may have picked up a volume with the intention only of reading no more than a page or two. In other cases, readings may have spanned months, even years. Martin's *Description of the Western Islands of Scotland* was certainly in his possession by 1808, and perhaps by his Cambridge years. He was still returning to it when, in 1835, he composed *The Black Stones of Iona*, which instructs the reader to 'See Martin's *Voyage among the Western Isles*' (*PW* iv 43, 408).

How often, and when, did Wordsworth read the books in his possession? We shall probably never know the answer even for one of the titles here listed. The limited task of this study is to document all *known* readings of books in his possession, and to provide estimated dates for those readings: some are specific, some less so, depending on the evidence. An allusion to a work or author is not invariably taken to imply a reading, as Wordsworth had a good memory for poetry and in certain cases was capable of quoting at length without consulting a printed text. Each piece of evidence has been evaluated on its own merits. However, where allusions or borrowings provide Wordsworth's earliest reference to a particular work they are taken to imply a reading by the time at which the allusion was made.

A note on texts

Wherever possible, poetry, manuscript material, and Fenwick Notes by Wordsworth are quoted from the texts and transcriptions provided by the volumes in the Cornell Wordsworth Series. Otherwise, poetry is quoted from *PW*, and Fenwick Notes from *FN*. Quotations from Wordsworth's prose are from *Prose Works*.

Texts transcribed from MS sources, and published here for the first time, have not been altered in respect of orthography, punctuation, or capitalization.

In citations the place of publication may be assumed to be London unless otherwise stated; all italics are mine unless otherwise stated, and material within square brackets is editorial.

In the list, dates within square brackets are those of the first edition; the fact that they are within square brackets indicates that we do not know whether Wordsworth used that edition or not. Dates within round brackets are those of the edition Wordsworth is believed to have read, as in *The Simpliciad* (1808). *English Bards and Scotch Reviewers* [1809], on the other hand, is the title of a work read by Wordsworth, followed by the date of its first publication; whether he read that edition or a later one is unknown.

Wordsworth's reading 1800-1815

1. A., *Dr. Adam Smith, European Magazine* 20 (Aug. 1791) 133-6
Suggested date of reading: by 7 June 1802
References: EY 354-5; *Notebooks* i 775
In his letter to John Wilson of 7 June 1802, W mentioned 'Adam Smith, who, we [are] told, could not endure the Ballad of Clym of the Clough, because the [au]thor had not written like a gentleman' (*EY* 354-5). He had presumably read A.'s *Dr. Adam Smith* in the *European Magazine* for Aug. 1791:

> I pled as well as I could for Allan Ramsay, because I regarded him as the single unaffected Poet whom we have had since Buchanan - *Proximus huic longo sed proximus intervallo*.
> He answered, 'It is the duty of a poet to write like a gentleman. I dislike that homely style which some think fit to call the language of nature and simplicity, and so forth. In Percy's Reliques too, a few tolerable pieces are buried under a heap of rubbish. You have read perhaps Adam Bell Clym of the Cleugh, and William of Cloudeslie?' I answered, Yes. 'Well then,' said he, 'do you think that was worth printing?' He reflected with some harshness on Dr. Goldsmith; and repeated a variety of anecdotes to support his censure. (*European Magazine* 20 [1791] 135)

W may have been referred to A.'s article by C, who mentions this exchange in a notebook entry of Aug. 1800: 'Duty of a Poet to write like a Gentleman. Ad. Smith Europ. Mag. Aug. 1791. 135' (*Notebooks* i 775). The authors of *Lyrical Ballads* would have been as antipathetic to Smith's critical views as they were to *The Wealth of Nations* (see note 359[i]).

2. Adam, Thomas, *Private Thoughts on Religion* (2nd edn, York, 1795)
Suggested date of reading: 1810-30
References: CC *Marginalia* i 9; Shaver 313
This book is now in the British Library. It belonged originally to John James Perceval, 3rd Earl of Egmont, who gave it to Thomas Poole on 15 June 1804. It was in C's possession by June 1807, when he began writing marginalia in it. From 1810-30 it was apparently in W's possession.

3. Addison, Joseph, *The Spectator*
Suggested date of reading: by 10 Nov. 1806
References: MY i 93
On 10 Nov. 1806 W wrote to Beaumont on the subject of winter gardens: 'By the bye, there is a pleasing paper in the Spectator (in the 7th Vol., No 477) upon this subject, the whole is well worth reading, particularly that part which relates to the Winter Garden. He mentions Hollies and Horn-beam as Plants which his Place is full of' (*MY* i 93). This letter was written from Coleorton, and W is so specific in his reference he must have had a copy before him

as he wrote. The reference is, incidentally, accurate: Addison's paper on winter gardens appears in *The Spectator* (8 vols., 1744), vii 21-5 (no. 477 for 6 Sept. 1712). W refers again to this article in a letter of Dec. 1806 to Lady Beaumont (*MY* i 112), and DW mentions it in a letter of 16 Feb. 1807 (*MY* i 138).

The Spectator was prominent in C's thoughts as he prepared *The Friend*. In Feb.-March 1809 he was reading the copy retained by Charles Lloyd at Old Brathay (*MY* i 292), and in Jan. 1810 W and C compared Addison's journal with *The Friend* (Griggs iii 276). C ruminates on it in detail in several letters written at that time (Griggs iii 279, 281). A 1744 edn of *The Spectator* was retained at Rydal Mount (Shaver 4).

4. Aikin, Lucy, 'Lucy Aikins poems'
Suggested date of reading: c. Feb. 1802
References: *Grasmere Journals* 181

The jotted reference to 'Lucy Aikins poems' in DW's journal dates from c. Feb. 1802. Perhaps the Wordsworths had seen her recently published first book - an anthology, *Poetry for Children* (1801) (Jackson 71) - though it is possible that DW refers in fact to Aikin's periodical poetry. I have managed to track down the following periodical poems by her, all published in the *Monthly Magazine* under the initials L.A.: *To the Memory of Miss K.* (5 [Feb. 1798] 123); *On Miss Linwood's admirable Pictures in Needle-work* (5 [March 1798] 287); *Evening* (8 [Oct. 1799] 726); *Sonnet to Fortune, from Metastasio* (8 [Dec. 1799] 890); *On seeing the sun shine in at my window for the first time this year* (9 [May 1800] 364).

W apparently had an unhappy meeting with Lucy Aikin and her family on 14 May 1815 (*Supp.* 72-3). In 1809 Southey described her critiques on poetry in the *Annual Review* as 'absolutely nauseating' (Curry i 506).

5. Alfieri, Vittorio, Count, *The Tragedies of Vittorio Alfieri*, tr. Charles Lloyd (3 vols., 1815)
Suggested date of reading: by 18 Feb. 1815
References: *MY* ii 201; Shaver 6

W's letter to CW of 26 Nov. 1814 mentioned Lloyd's translation as 'printed', with the suggestion that he had seen the proofs, if not a finished copy (*MY* ii 171 and n4). On 18 Feb. 1815 DW reported to SH that 'The publishing of Alfieri has done him [i.e. Lloyd] no good; and I fear that it will not sell' (*MY* ii 201). The mention of Alfieri in W's letter to R. P. Gillies of 14 Feb. 1815 would support the argument that he was at that time reading Lloyd's translation (*MY* ii 197). On 16 March DW encouraged Catherine Clarkson to buy a copy (*MY* ii 214). It was reviewed by Southey in the *Quarterly* for Jan. 1816.

6. Allestree, Richard, *The Ladies Calling* [Oxford, 1673]
Suggested date of reading: by May 1812
References: *Love Letters* 117; Wing A1141-8

On 2 May 1812 MW wrote to her husband from Hindwell: 'I have read the "Ladies calling" one of thy books - which pleased me much - it is such a book as Mrs Luff would say would do *her a deal of good*' (*Love Letters* 117; her italics). W must by that date have acquired a copy of Allestree's volume; it is not listed by Shaver.

7. Amory, Thomas, *The Life of John Buncle* [2 vols., 1756-66]
Suggested date of reading: by 14 Aug. 1811
References: *MY* i 503
On 14 Aug. 1811, DW told Catherine Clarkson that 'I have read nothing since I wrote to you except bits here and there and the Novel of John Bunkle' (*MY* i 503). Her previous extant letter to Clarkson dates from 16 June, so that her reading of Amory's novel must have taken place between then and 14 Aug. *John Buncle* can be presumed to have been in the Wordsworths' possession, and probably known to W, by 14 Aug. 1811. This title was a favourite of Lamb's,[1] who introduced it to C (CC *Marginalia* i 30; Whalley *BC* 1).

8. *An Authentic Narrative of the Loss of the Earl of Abergavenny, East-Indiaman* (1805)
Suggested date of reading: shortly after mid-March 1805
References: *EY* 560-1, 565
There were two pamphlets concerning the sinking of the *Earl of Abergavenny* under JW's captaincy: the second had a preface dated 19 Feb., signed with the initials of William Dalmeida of the East India House. It was from this that Lamb copied details of the inquiry into the sinking in a letter to W of 4 March (Marrs ii 157-60). As a result, DW told Jane Marshall about it and asked her 'to send for it' on 15 and 17 March (*EY* 561); similarly, W asked James Losh to 'procure the pamphlet' in a letter of 16 March (*EY* 565). It is not clear whether the Wordsworths ever saw the pamphlet - they would no doubt have found it painful reading - but it is likely.

9. Anderson, Robert, *The Works of the British Poets. With Prefaces, Biographical and Critical, by Robert Anderson* (13 vols., London and Edinburgh, 1792-5)
Suggested date of reading: end of Jan. 1800 onwards
References: Cornell *Poems 1807-20* 527; Reed ii 202-3n; Shaver 8-9; CC *Marginalia* i 37-87
W used two sets of Anderson: that belonging to JW, now at the Wordsworth Library (Whalley's Copy C),[2] and that belonging to C, now at the Folger Shakespeare Library (Whalley's Copy A).[3] His first regular readings of Anderson at DC date from late Jan. 1800, when JW arrived at DC, bringing Copy C with him. C moved into Greta Hall in July 1800,

---

[1] See his letter to C of 24 June 1797 (Marrs i 112-13). Lamb's copy is now at the Rosenbach Foundation.
[2] See CC *Marginalia* i 37, 76.
[3] See CC *Marginalia* i 39-41.

from which point Copy A would also have been at W's disposal;[1] it contains a number of notes by W associated with his Chaucer translations (CC *Marginalia* i 40). It was in this knowledge that, on leaving DC in Sept., JW took most, but not all, of Copy C with him, leaving W to borrow the absent volumes from Greta Hall. JW sent the rest of his set to DC in Nov. 1802; it contains notes by both C and W. For a detailed account of this see Reed ii 202-3n. W probably had occasional access to Copy A during his residence in Somerset, 1797-8, when C would have kept it on his shelves at Nether Stowey (see *WR* 4-5).

The Latin epigraph on the title-page of both volumes of *Lyrical Ballads* (1800) was drawn from John Selden's foreword to Michael Drayton's *Poly-Olbion* as reprinted in Anderson (see Cornell *Lyrical Ballads* 377).

10. Anderson, Robert, of Carlisle, *Ballads in the Cumberland Dialect* (Carlisle, 1805)
Suggested date of reading: by May 1814
References: *PW* v 441; Shaver 71
It appears that Anderson's *Ballads* was the source for a MS draft for *The Excursion* Book V composed by May 1814 (Reed ii 24, 684); see *PW* v 441. It is likely that W had seen Anderson's volume well before 1814.

11. *Annual Anthology* (Bristol, 1800)
Suggested date of reading: 31 July 1800 and thereafter
References: *Grasmere Journals* 15; Reed ii 76; Shaver 9
DW's journal records that in the afternoon of 31 July 1800 'Coleridge came very hot, he brought the 2nd volume of the Anthology'. It contained, among other things, the first printed text of *This Lime-Tree Bower my Prison*; see *WR* 31. For contents and contributors see Kenneth Curry, 'The Contributors to *The Annual Anthology*', *Papers of the Bibliographical Society of America* 42 (1948) 50-65.

12. *Annual Register*
(i)
Suggested date of reading: by 6 Nov. 1810
References: *MY* i 444 and n1
On 6 Nov. 1810 DW wrote to Robinson: 'Can you procure any Spanish, Portuguese or French papers for Mr Southey? He writes the historical part of the Edinburgh Annual Register and they would be of great use to him' (*MY* i 444). Robinson replied that he hoped to open 'one or two important channels' to Southey (*Robinson* i 63). Southey doubtless gave the Wordsworths copies of the *Register* in which his work appeared, 1809-13.

---

[1] It should be noted that C had left one volume of Copy A in London. Lamb took it to Longman on 6 Aug. 1800, who in turn sent it to Keswick (Marrs i 217).

(ii) *Annual Register* (1761) 19-22
Suggested date of reading: between Sept. 1811 and Nov. 1812
References: *Prose Works* ii 438; *PW* iii 508-22
W's information on Robert Walker, referred to in the *Unpublished Tour* (*Prose Works* ii 299-300), and mentioned at greater length in a note to *The River Duddon* (*PW* iii 508-22), came from the *Annual Register for 1760* (1761), as noted by Owen and Smyser, *Prose Works* ii 438. The materials relating to Walker consist of four letters, prefaced as follows:

> The following Letters being authentic deserve to be inserted, as a remarkable instance of the happy effect of indefatigable and chearful industry. But though they do honour to the very excellent man who is the subject of them, they reflect a heavy disgrace on that part of our national establishment, which makes so wretched and scandalous a provision for great numbers of the most learned and blameless body of ecclesiastics in the world, by which means that industry must be often exerted to procure a scanty livelihood, which ought solely to be employed in their sacred studies, and the work of their ministry.
>
> (p. 19)

The *Unpublished Tour* was composed between Sept. 1811 and Nov. 1812.

13. Anon. (attributed to Chaucer)
(i) *The Floure and the Leafe* (Anderson)
Suggested date of reading: Dec. 1805-Jan. 1806
References: Cornell *Poems 1800-7* 405
W quotes this poem in a note to *Character of the Happy Warrior* (Cornell *Poems 1800-7* 405), composed Dec. 1805-Jan. 1806; he mentions it again in a letter to Lady Beaumont of Dec. 1806 (*MY* i 117). Although, as Curtis points out, 'Modern scholarship disproves attribution of this poem to Chaucer', it was published as his in Urry, the 1782 Bell (see note 38), Anderson, and Chalmers. It is likely that W read it in Anderson, *British Poets* i 532-7. Skeat argues that both this poem and *The Assemble of Ladies* are by the same author - a woman writing in the last quarter of the fifteenth century.[1]

(ii) *The Assemble of Ladies* (Anderson)
Suggested date of reading: by Dec. 1806
References: *MY* i 117-18
W mentions this poem in a letter to Lady Beaumont of Dec. 1806; evidently he had read it before that date. It was published as Chaucer's in Urry, the 1782 Bell (see note 38), and Anderson. In 1810 Chalmers published it under the heading of 'Poems Imputed to Chaucer'. I suspect that W read it in Anderson, *British Poets* i 455-61.

---

[1] For a full account of the arguments concerning the attribution of both works see Eleanor Prescott Hammond, *Chaucer: A Bibliographical Manual* (1933), pp. 423-4, 408-9.

14. *An unfortunate Mother to her infant at her Breast*
Suggested date of reading: probably 1801
References: Reed ii 705; Moorman *N&Q* 402
Reed judges that C copied this poem into the Wordsworth Commonplace Book (DC MS 26, 30r-30v) during early 1804, before 25 March.

15. Arbuthnot, John, *Miscellaneous Works* **(2 vols., 2nd edn, Glasgow, 1751)**
Suggested date of reading: by 27 Sept. 1807
References: *MY* i 166
Advising Walter Scott on his edn of Dryden, W told him that Arbuthnot had commented on *MacFlecknoe* 'in an Essay . . . printed in the Glasgow edition of his works, and entitled "Upon the art of selling Bargains"' (*MY* i 166). The 2nd edn of Arbuthnot's *Miscellaneous Works* was later at Rydal Mount (Shaver 11), and may have been acquired by 27 Sept. 1807.

16. Ariosto
(i) *Orlando Furioso*
Suggested date of reading: ?-c. 19 Nov. 1802
References: Reed ii 201
W translated Ariosto at a rate of nearly 100 lines a day during this time, and covered, apparently, 'two Books' (*LY* iv 8). What little survives of those efforts appears in Cornell *Poems 1800-7* 594-7. It is likely that he was working from the copy of Ariosto's *Opere in versi e in prose, italiane e latine, con dichiarazioni* (4 vols., Venice, 1741), later retained at Rydal Mount, which contained 'Charles Lloyd's Book-plate and Laureate's Autog.' (Wordsworth *SC* 458). Lloyd moved to Ambleside in 1800, and the Wordsworths visited him occasionally from then onwards. They were in the habit of borrowing each other's books (see also note 9), and it is reasonable to suppose that W borrowed Lloyd's handsome edn of Ariosto when he began the translations of 1802. It would have remained in his possession because he probably continued to tinker with his rendering for years after the bulk of work was complete. He appears to have read his translation to De Quincey in London shortly before 25 March 1808 (Jordan 90).

Even if W was not using Lloyd's copy of the *Opere* in 1802, it had almost certainly passed into his possession by 1804: C quotes from vol. 4 in a notebook entry of 15 Sept. 1805, made in Malta (*Notebooks* ii 2670 and n). This indicates that C took at least vol. 4 when he left DC prior to his Mediterranean tour on 14 Jan. 1804. See also *Notebooks* ii 2770.

(ii) *Orlando Furioso,* **tr. John Harington (2nd edn, 1607)**
Suggested date of reading: by May 1813
References: Shaver 11
This volume is now at the Wordsworth Library. It is imperfect in its present state, lacking six leaves, and bears the ownership inscription 'Wm Wordsworth / Rydal Mount' on the flyleaf.

However, the inscription may be misleading: although it may have entered Wordsworth's library shortly after his removal to Rydal Mount in May 1813, my guess is that it came into his possession before that time.

In Oct. 1808 Derwent and Hartley Coleridge began to attend Revd. John Dawes' school in Ambleside, spending most weekends with the Wordsworths at Allan Bank. Hartley, Derwent later remembered, particularly enjoyed his time in the Allan Bank library. This copy of Ariosto contains a number of scribblings by young Hartley on the endpapers, and page 347 has been torn by Hartley and sewn up by Mrs Southey. The various marginalia cannot be firmly dated, but it is evidently that of a schoolboy rather than that of an undergraduate, and on that basis it seems likely that it was entered during Hartley's teens. It was thus almost certainly in W's possession by the time he moved to Rydal Mount in May 1813.

As regards the flyleaf inscription, Wordsworth sometimes entered his name in books years after acquiring them, as he probably did in this case.

17. Aristotle, 'From Aristotle's Synopsis of the virtues and vices'
Suggested date of reading: probably just before 12 March 1805
References: Reed ii 707; *EY* 557-8

> From Aristotle's Synopsis of the virtues and vices
> It is the property of fortitude not to be easily terrified by the dread of things pertaining to death; to possess good confidence in things terrible, & presence of mind in dangers; rather to prefer to be put to death worthily, than to be preserved basely; & to be the cause of victory. Further, it is the property of fortitude to labour and endure, and to make valorous exertion an object of choice. *But* presence of mind, a well-disposed soul, confidence and boldness are the attendants on fortitude: - and besides these industry & patience

This extract from Aristotle was copied into the Wordsworth Commonplace Book (DC MS 26, 45r) by DW probably shortly before it was copied by W into a letter to Lady Beaumont of 12 March 1805. In his letter to Lady Beaumont, W says: 'I will here transcribe a passage which I met with the other day in a review' (*EY* 557). His source has not been traced, though I can at least reveal that it was not John Gillies' translation of Aristotle's *Ethic and Politics*, as Shaver suggests (*EY* 558n1).

18. Armstrong, John, *The Art of Preserving Health* (1744)
Suggested date of reading: c. 1800-2; certainly by 30 May 1812
References: Supp. 97 and n1

Although W's earliest reference to Armstrong's poem occurs in a letter to MW of 30 May 1812, his first reading of it must date from *c.* 1800-2 at the latest, as it appeared in Anderson, *British Poets* vol. 10 (W was reading vol. 10 in 1802; see note 362[i]). He may even have known the poem since childhood. He was particularly keen on Armstrong partly because he regarded him as a borderer (*LY* i 402). A first edn of *The Art of Preserving Health* is listed by the Shavers as present at Rydal Mount (Shaver 12); this was given to him in Dec. 1835 by David Laing (*LY* iii 136). W also owned a copy of Armstrong's *Sketches; or, Essays on Various Subjects. By Launcelot Temple, Esq.* (1758). W included a short extract from *The Art of Preserving Health* in the album he compiled for Lady Mary Lowther in 1819 (*Album* 55); Lyon believes it to be a source for *The Excursion* (Lyon 33).

19. Arnold, Samuel James, *The Devil's Bridge; or, The Piedmontese Alps*
Date of performance: 12 May 1812
References: *Supp.* 67
On 9-13 May 1812, W wrote to MW: 'Miss Lamb looks far better than could be expected and enjoyed herself much at the play; a stupid opera, called "the Devils Bridge," but the Farce, "High Life below Stairs" was very entertaining; it is an excellent Piece' (*Supp.* 67). W accompanied the Lambs to the double-bill of Arnold's *Devil's Bridge* and Townley's *High Life* at the Lyceum Theatre on the Strand on Tuesday 12 May 1812. The double-bill was advertised in the *Morning Chronicle* that day as follows:

> THEATRE ROYAL, LYCEUM
> This Evening will be performed, a grand new Operatic Romance
> in three acts, called The DEVIL'S BRIDGE
> The Principal Characters by Mr. Braham, Mr. Raymond,
> Mr. Lovegrove, and a Young Gentleman; Miss Brereton, Mrs.
> Dickons, Mrs. Bland.
> After which, HIGH LIFE BELOW STAIRS.

The Drury Lane Company had been resident at the Lyceum since 1809, under the direction of Samuel James Arnold. *The Devil's Bridge* was first performed on 6 May 1812.

20. Ashe, Thomas, *Travels, in America, performed in 1806* **(3 vols., 1808)**
Suggested date of reading: probably by early Nov. 1809
References: Reed ii 49; *Prose Works* ii 9, 35-6
In his *Reply to 'Mathetes'*, W refers the reader to Ashe's *Travels*, a volume not listed as present at Rydal Mount in later years, and which was therefore probably borrowed - perhaps from Southey, who did own a copy, and who W saw during the summer of 1809 (Reed ii 433). Coe (1952) 431 notes that Ashe was an influence on *The Excursion*.

21. Bacon, Francis, Lord Verulam
(i) *Of Studies*
Suggested date of reading: by 29 April 1804
References: Cornell *13-Book Prelude* 178

Reed finds an echo of Bacon's *Of Studies* at *Thirteen-Book Prelude* vi 27-8. W had presumably read this work well before 29 April 1804, by which time these lines were composed (Reed ii 13). C had embarked on a serious study of Bacon by Feb. 1801, and probably communicated his enthusiasm to W - which probably led in turn to W's recommendation of Bacon's *Essays* and *Advancement of Learning* to Catherine Clarkson in Dec. 1805 (*EY* 662). Whalley adds: 'There can be little doubt that between 1802 and 1804 Coleridge rediscovered Plato through Bacon and discovered his own Platonism in Bacon' (Whalley PhD ii 152). See also *WR* 8 and Potts 372-9.

(ii) *Works*, ed. David Mallet (4 vols., 1740)
Suggested date of reading: 1808-9; by 3 May 1809
References: *Prose Works* i 372; Jordan 192-5; *MY* i 328
A passage from Bacon's *Advertisement touching the Controversies of the Church of England* provided the motto for W's *Convention of Cintra*; W also refers to the *Meditationes Sacrae* in a passage deleted from the *Convention* (see *Prose Works* i 324-5; 401). The motto as he wished it printed derived from Mallet's edn of 1740 - which he did not possess. As De Quincey observed: 'it has . . . occurred to me as possible (though not very likely) that Mr. Wordsworth quotes from the M.S. extract made by Mr. Coleridge, or even from memory. - My only reason for thinking this . . . is, that Mr. Wordsworth said that the reason why he did not send me the extract was that he did not exactly know where to look for it' (Jordan 195). De Quincey may be correct: W may have been referring to C's notes, or to C's copy of Mallet's *Bacon*, bought from Dyer the Exeter bookseller in 1799 (Griggs i 530 and n3; *Notebooks* i 913n). W had asked De Quincey to send him a copy of Bacon's *Works* on 7 July 1808 (*MY* i 257), but I doubt whether De Quincey had done so - in fact, De Quincey goes out of his way to note their rarity in his letter of 31 May 1809: 'if I were to send out one man to collect *Bacons* - and another to collect *Kangaroos* - I verily believe the Kangaroo man would be the most successful' (Jordan 194). W copies out the correct text of the motto in his letter to Stuart of 3 May 1809, providing a terminal date for his reading of Bacon; I suspect, however, that W consulted C's copy of Mallet's edn on numerous occasions during 1808-9. There was certainly a copy at Allan Bank in Jan. 1809, because C transcribed some of its contents for Basil Montagu (Griggs iii 161).

(iii) *On Revenge*
Suggested date of reading: by 18 May 1812
References: *Supp.* 82 and n2
In his letter to MW of 17-18 May 1812 W alludes to Bacon's *On Revenge*; no doubt it had been known to him since his schooldays.

(iv) *Of Atheism*
Suggested date of reading: by 1815
References: Cornell *White Doe* 77

Bacon's *Of Atheism* provided the epigraph for W's *White Doe of Rylstone* (1815). Dugas reveals that it was 'entered in MW's hand' in the printer's MS (Cornell *White Doe* 77). In the *Essay, Supplementary to the Preface*, W remarks upon Shakespeare:

> But that his Works, whatever might be their reception upon the stage, made but little impression upon the ruling Intellects of the time, may be inferred from the fact that Lord Bacon, in his multifarious writings, nowhere either quotes or alludes to him.
>
> (*Prose Works* iii 68)

From this it may be deduced that a copy of the *Works* was close at hand, if not on the shelves of Rydal Mount. *Essays, Moral, Economical, and Political* (1819), bearing the inscription 'D Wordsworth', is now in the possession of Christopher Wordsworth (see Shaver 290).

22. Bampfylde, John Codrington, *On the Evening* and *Written at a Farm*
Suggested date of reading: May 1808
References: see note

On 1 May 1808 Beaumont wrote to W: 'My dear Friend I have sent two sonnets by John Bamfylde that have not been published, I think you will like their simplicity, I knew him, a more artless unworldly soul never breathed' (Wordsworth Library WLL/Beaumont, G. H./27).[1] He then transcribed two of Bampfylde's sonnets, both of which had in fact been published in *Sixteen Sonnets* (1778), the first as *Sonnet V. On the Evening*, the second as *Sonnet XII. Written at a Farm*. Although he did not apparently own a copy of *Sixteen Sonnets*, Beaumont apparently possessed a MS of Bampfylde's works, which he probably showed W in due course. I am unaware of any readings by W of Bampfylde prior to this; however, it is significant that not only were C and Southey enthusiastic readers of *Sixteen Sonnets* by 1799, but that they had by that year befriended Bampfylde's associate, William Jackson, who allowed Southey to transcribe nineteen of Bampfylde's sonnets and *To the River Teign*.[2] It would be astonishing had W not discussed Bampfylde with Southey and seen his transcription at some point during the ensuing years. Southey included four of Bampfylde's poems in vol. 3 of his *Specimens of the later English Poets* (1807). For Beaumont's transcription see Appendix V.

23. Barbauld, Anna Laetitia
(i) *Hymn to Content*
Suggested date of reading: by Feb. 1808
References: Morley i 62; CC *Literature* i 406-7; *Robinson* i 53

---

[1] Extracts from this letter was first published by Denys Sutton, 'Unpublished Letters from Sir George and Lady Beaumont to the Wordsworths', *N&Q* 175 (1938) 146-9.

[2] For more on this see Griggs i 533; *Life of Southey* ii 26-9; and Roger Lonsdale's introduction to *The Poems of John Bampfylde* (1988).

> But thou, oh Nymph retir'd and coy
> In what brown hamlet dost thou joy
>   To tell thy tender tale;
> The lowliest children of the ground,
> Moss-rose, and violet blossom round,
>   And lily of the vale. (*Hymn to Content* 37-42)

This was, apparently, one of W's least favourite stanzas of poetry - a fact advertised by C in his lecture of 27 Jan. 1812. W appears originally to have made his comments in conversation with C and Lamb during his visit to London in late Feb.-early April 1808. His criticisms appear to have centred on her diction; as Robinson recalled: 'All the remarks, namely on the *brown hamlet*, the "moss rose & violet", &c, were made by Wordsworth to me when in Town' (CC *Literature* i 407; his italics).

In earlier years both W and C had liked her poetry. She was, it should be remembered, an early recipient of a copy of *Lyrical Ballads* (1800), sent with the authors' compliments. In March 1798 C described her as 'that great and excellent woman' (Griggs i 393), an opinion W no doubt shared. Ten years later W is reported to have said that she 'has a bad heart; that her writings are absolutely insignificant, her poems are mere trash and specimens of every fault may be selected from them' (*Robinson* i 53). A crucial factor in this change of opinion must have been the belief that she had written the hostile notice of Lamb's *John Woodvil* in the *Annual Review* (see Griggs ii 1039).

(ii) *Eighteen Hundred and Eleven, a Poem* (1812)
Suggested date of reading: by 24 May 1812
References: Morley i 86

On 24 May 1812 Robinson recorded an encounter between W and Joanna Baillie: 'Miss Baillie was ready to vouch for the excellence of Mrs. Barbauld's *1811*, in which, by the bye, she has six lines of praise and Shakespeare two' (Morley i 86). This does not prove that W read the poem, but he did see Barbauld during this visit to London (see *Supp.* 72, 79), and can be expected at least to have glanced at her latest work. Later in the year, Southey may have referred him to the review by Croker in the *Quarterly* for June 1812, as he did John Murray in Aug. (Curry ii 38).

24. Barker, Mary
(i) *Lines Addressed to a Noble Lord (His Lordship will know why)* in MS
Suggested date of reading: probably Oct. 1814; by 10 Dec. 1814
References: *MY* ii 175-6

As his letter to SH reveals, W contributed to Barker's *Lines*, probably in Oct. 1814, when she visited Rydal Mount (Reed ii 575).

(ii) *Lines Addressed to a Noble Lord (His Lordship will know why)* **(1815)**
Suggested date of reading: early April 1815
References: Reed ii 596-7; Jackson 20
As he contributed to it, W can be expected to have been given a copy of Barker's *Lines* when printing was completed. He gave a copy to Robinson on 9 May (Morley i 167).

25. Barnard, Thomas, *An account of an English Hermit, by a respectable Clergiman* in MS
Suggested date of reading: shortly after 15 Dec. 1809
References: see note
On 15 Dec. 1809 Beaumont sent W a transcription of Barnard's *Account*: 'My dear Friend I send this account for the amusement of your fireside the relator is a character well known in this neighbourhood and the truth unimpeachable.' It ends: 'This account of an English Hermit, was copied from the original copy of Thomas Barnard of Withersfield, who paid him the visit' (Wordsworth Library WLL/Beaumont, G. H./29). This would have reached Grasmere by Christmas; it is at the Wordsworth Library.

26. Barrington, Daines, *Observations on the More Ancient Statutes, from Magna charta to the twenty-first of James I* (3rd edn, 1769)
Suggested date of reading: 1800s
References: Butler *WC* 167; Shaver 18
W's copy of this volume is now at Swarthmore College. It contains a presentation inscription from Anthony Harrison. The most likely time for Harrison to have given it to W is during the 1800s - particularly 30 Aug. 1800, when he stayed at DC overnight (Reed ii 83). For more on Harrison see *Grasmere Journals* 165.

27. Barrow, Isaac, sermon
Suggested date of reading: probably by 5 April 1800
References: Reed ii 704; Moorman *N&Q* 402
The extracts on 'eutrapelia' from Barrow were entered by DW in the Wordsworth Commonplace Book (DC MS 26, 16v-17v) by 5 April 1800. The work from which she took her text was published in Barrow's *Several Sermons Against Evil-Speaking* (1678) as Sermon II on Ephesians 5:4, 'Nor foolish talking, nor jesting, which are not convenient'; the discussion of eutrapelia occurs at pp. 41-2. On 16 Oct. 1803 C told Beaumont that it 'is an old friend & favorite of mine' (Griggs ii 1017); we do not know which edn Beaumont sent C.

28. Barrow, John
(i) *Travels in China* **(1804)**
Suggested date of reading: between July and Oct. 1804

References: Reed ii 707; Moorman *N&Q* 401

Extracts from Barrow's *Travels in China* appear in the Wordsworth Commonplace Book (DC MS 26, 16v-17v). In her letter to Lady Beaumont of 15 Feb. 1807, DW acknowledged receipt of 'Barrow's Travels' (*MY* i 133), and on this basis Reed dates the extracts to after 8 Feb. 1807.

There are, however, problems with this line of argument. Firstly, DW's reference does not indubitably refer to *Travels in China*; in fact, I side with Whalley in thinking it more likely to refer to Barrow's *Travels into the Interior of South Africa* (2 vols., 1801-4) (see next note). Secondly, I question whether extracts would have been copied out from books in W's possession; if *Travels in China* was readily available, why bother copying extracts from it? The surrounding entries in the Commonplace Book appear to date from spring and summer 1805, and that seems a more plausible date for the extracts from *Travels in China*. This is given some weight by the description of Gehol at *Thirteen-Book Prelude* viii 119-43, which draws heavily on Lord Macartney as quoted by Barrow (pp. 127-34 of the 2nd edn; see Cornell *13-Book Prelude* 214).[1] Barrow's *Travels* was published 4 July 1804, and W may have seen or borrowed a copy shortly after - certainly by the time he composed *Prelude* Book VIII in Oct.[2] One possible owner of the copy seen by W is Southey, who reviewed the book in *Annual Review* 3 (1804) 69-83.

It should be noted that, in order to have seen the description of Gehol, W need only have seen it reprinted in a review - as Robert Woof writes: 'one wonders whether the extracts from Barrow's *Travels in China* are from a review or from the volume itself' (Woof PhD 238). In fact Macartney's description of Gehol was mentioned by nearly all the reviewers of the volume, and was quoted extensively by the *Critical Review* 5 (1805) 1-11, 140-7, pp. 141-3. However, it was published in 1805 - too late to have influenced W's *Prelude* lines, composed the previous autumn. I doubt too whether the *Critical Review* was the source for any of the Commonplace Book entries, as not all of them appear in the periodical. There is no evidence that W ever owned *Travels in China*.

(ii) *Travels into the Interior of South Africa* (2 vols., 1801-4)
Suggested date of reading: *c*. 7 Feb. 1807 onwards
References: *MY* i 133

On 15 Feb. 1807 DW wrote to Lady Beaumont to thank her for a consignment of books including 'Barrow's Travels' (*MY* i 133). This is identified by Mary Moorman as *Travels in China*, but Whalley believed that the correct reference was to Barrow's *Travels into the Interior of South Africa* (Whalley PhD i 477). Even if Whalley was incorrect, it is likely that W did see a copy of *Travels into the Interior of South Africa* at this time: on 19 April 1809 SH wrote to Mary Monkhouse from Allan Bank, 'The nicest model of a churn I ever saw was

---

[1] It is worth noting that at p. 134 Macartney compared Gehol with the grounds of Lowther Hall in Westmorland, an observation that would have been of interest to W.

[2] My dating follows that given by Jonathan Wordsworth, Norton *Prel.* 270n1.

in "Barrow's account of the interior of Africa"' (*SHL* 20). This is, apparently, a reference to Barrow's account of Kaffir milk-baskets, *Travels into the Interior of South Africa* i 170. SH's remark is in the past tense, and supports the inference to be drawn from the absence of any title by Barrow in Shaver: that any copy seen by W and his circle was borrowed. In this light DW's remarks to Lady Beaumont in 1807 may be taken to refer not to *Travels in China* but to *Travels in South Africa*. If indeed they do, it would have been sent to the Wordsworths in early Feb. 1807, at Coleorton, and probably left there when they departed. Beaumont may also have owned a copy of Barrow's *Travels in China*. Southey reviewed the title in *Annual Review* 3 (1804) 22-33.

29. Bartram, William, ***Travels through North and South Carolina, East and West Florida, the Cherokee Country, the Extensive Territories of the Muscolgulges or Creek Confederacy, and the Country of the Chactaws*** **(2nd edn, 1794)**
Suggested date of reading: 1800 onwards
References: Ketcham 87; Shaver 19
W had probably acquired his own copy of Bartram by Aug. 1798 (*WR* 9). It went to DC when the Wordsworths moved in, and was an influence on *To Joanna*, composed by 23 Aug. 1800 (Cornell *Lyrical Ballads* 399). At that time it was apparently lent to JW, who took it back to London on 29 Sept. He had finished with it by 10 March 1801, when he wrote to DW to say that he had 'carried Bertrams Travels to Longman - & he promis'd me faithfully that the peoms [*sic*.] should it be sent at the same time' (Ketcham 107) - meaning, I think, that W's copy of Bartram's *Travels* was returned to Grasmere at the same time that Longman sent W a copy of *Lyrical Ballads* (1800), acknowledged on 27 March 1801 (*EY* 321). Reed suggests that Bartram inspired the grove and most of its denizens at *Thirteen-Book Prelude* iii 442-59 (Cornell *13-Book Prelude* 145n).[1] See also Coe 66-79; Coe (1952) 431 notes that Bartram was also an influence on *I wandered lonely as a cloud*, *The Kitten and the Falling Leaves*, and *She was a phantom of delight*.

James Tobin gave his copy of Bartram to C in 1800 (Griggs i 613); it was forwarded to DC by 6 Feb. 1801 (Ketcham 87). C gave it to SH on 10 Dec. 1801 (CC *Marginalia* i lxxxvii, 226); it is now at the Wordsworth Library.

30. Bayley, Peter, ***Poems*** **(1803)**
Suggested date of reading: 9 Oct. 1803
References: *EY* 413
It was on a visit to Southey at Greta Hall, 9 Oct. 1803, when W apparently saw Peter Bayley's *Poems*, with their parodies of the *Lyrical Ballads*, for the first time. Writing to Walter Scott on 16 Oct., he reported that Southey had 'to review a Vol. of Poems by a

---

[1] See also Norton *Prel.* 114n2, Thomas and Ober 75-6, and Lane Cooper, 'Wordsworth Sources. Bowles and Keate', *Athenaeum* 4043 (22 April 1905) 498-500.

somebody Bayley Esqr which contains a long dull Poem in ridicule of the Idiot Boy' (*EY* 413). He probably saw it again, and at greater length, when visiting Keswick again in late Nov., for the criticisms of Bayley's *The Forest Fay* in a letter of 9 Dec. are detailed and specific (*EY* 424-5; see also *EY* 455), and, as David Chandler has argued, fuelled Southey's hostile review of Bayley for the *Annual Review* (see note 365[iii]).[1] Southey's views can be gauged from his comment to Mary Barker of 1804: 'I will break him upon the wheel, and then hook him up alive, *in terrorem*, and make his memory stink in the noses of all readers of English, present and to come. I wish he could know that his book has been sent to me to be reviewed, and that Wordsworth has now got it to claim his own whenever he finds it' (Warter i 254).

31. Beattie, James
(i) ***The Minstrel***
Suggested date of reading: between Sept. 1811 and Nov. 1812
References: *Prose Works* ii 347, 450
W quotes three lines from Beattie's *Minstrel* in his *Unpublished Tour*, composed between Sept. 1811 and Nov. 1812.

(ii) ***The Minstrel***
Suggested date of reading: perhaps *c.* 14 Feb. 1815
References: *MY* ii 196-7
In a letter of 14 Feb. 1815 to R. P. Gillies W said that he preferred

> the *Classical* model of Dr Beattie to the insupportable slovenliness and neglect of syntax and *grammar* by which Hogg's writings are disfigured. It is excusable in him from his education, but Walter Scott knows, and ought to do, better. They neither of them write a language which has any pretension to be called English; and their versification - who can endure it when he comes fresh from the Minstrel? (*MY* ii 196-7; his italics)

W need not have reread *The Minstrel* to make these observations, but they do imply some sort of serious reconsideration of Beattie's achievements, which may have entailed a reading in Feb. 1815.

32. Beaumont, Francis
(i) ***Upon the following Poems of my deare Father, Sir John Beaumont, Baronet, deceased***
Suggested date of reading: between 21 and 29 July 1805
References: see note

---

[1] See '"Twisted in Persecution's Loving Ways": Peter Bayley Reviewed by Southey, Wordsworth and Coleridge', *WC* 24 (1993) 256-61. See also Jordan 39.

On 21 July 1805 Beaumont wrote to tell W that he had found a copy of Sir John Beaumont's poems: 'According to the fashion of the times, before the poems are prefixed complimentary verses among the rest some lines by his son Francis nephew to the Dramatist which are transcribed to send you.'[1] The transcription does not survive, but it is clear from Beaumont's description that the poem was *Upon the following Poems of my deare Father, Sir John Beaumont, Baronet, deceased*, published at the front of John Beaumont's *Bosworth-field* (1629), the volume to which Sir George was referring.

(ii) *To his very loving and assured good friend Mr. Thomas Speght* in MS
Suggested date of reading: by 29 July 1805
References: *EY* 611

In correspondence with Sir George Beaumont, W referred on 1 May 1805 to Francis Beaumont. This led Beaumont to send W a copy of one of Francis' poems, which W praised in his reply of 29 July: 'The verses of your ancestor, Francis Beaumont the younger are very elegant and harmonious, and written with true feeling. Is this the only poem of his extant?' Shaver identifies it as *To his very loving and assured good friend Mr. Thomas Speght* (*EY* 611n1). By this date W was acquainted with Beaumont and Fletcher's dramatic works (see next note).

33. Beaumont, Francis, and John Fletcher, works
Suggested date of reading: by Sept. 1800
References: *Prose Works* i 122

W's reference to Beaumont and Fletcher in the Preface to *Lyrical Ballads* (1800), composed by Sept. 1800, indicates that he was aware of their works by that date.

Their *Fifty Comedies and Tragedies* (1679) was at Rydal Mount (Shaver 316), along with George Colman's edition of the *Dramatick Works* (10 vols., 1778) (Shaver 21). When these were acquired is anyone's guess - certainly W commissioned Lamb to buy on his behalf a copy of their works in Sept. or Oct. 1804, but Lamb pleaded on 13 Oct. that 'I am not plethorically abounding in Cash at this present', and 'Beaumont & Fletcher in folio, the right folio, [are] not now to be met with' (Marrs ii 146). And what was the 'right folio'? The 1679 *Fifty Comedies and Tragedies*, Lamb's own copy of which is now at the British Library (C.45.i.7; see CC *Marginalia* i 365-6) - the same edn as that retained at Rydal Mount: perhaps, after all, Lamb did acquire a copy for W.

C reportedly entered marginalia in Lamb's copy of the *Works* as early as 17 April 1807 (Lucas ii 295); he read *Love's Pilgrimage* in March 1810 at Allan Bank - possibly at Lamb's bidding, as that play was one of his favourites (see *Notebooks* iii 3736; Lucas iii 50).

---

[1] See Wordsworth Library WLL/Beaumont, G. H./10.

34. Beaumont, Sir George Howland, Bart.
(i) *Monthly Review* **46 (Jan. 1805) 99-101**
Suggested date of reading: mid-Feb. 1805 onwards
References: EY 548

On 23 Feb. 1805 W thanked Beaumont for 'your excellent Letter about the young Roscius. . . . it has since amused me much and I thank you heartily for it; the account is throughout interesting and in many respects highly valuable' (*EY* 548). He refers to a review of four recent biographies of William Henry West Betty, dubbed the young Roscius, a famous actor of the day, which apparently Beaumont had written for the *Monthly*. It concludes: 'some of his biographers consider him as a phænomenon almost miraculous, and are inclined to think that Nature broke the mould in which she had formed him, in order that there should never be another like him' (p. 101). See also note 58.

(ii) MS poem on the death of his mother
Suggested date of reading: Nov. 1814
References: see note

In a letter of 20 Nov. 1814, Beaumont transcribed for W a poem written on the recent death of his mother: 'The Death also of my venerable Mother has made a strong impression on my mind & I will venture to send you a thought suggested at the time which however maimed by my bungling Muse - was I will presume to say the genuine offspring of filial affection'.[1] W wrote back expressing approval for Beaumont's poem, which Beaumont in turn acknowledged in his response of 30 Nov. The full text can be found in Appendix V.

35. Beaumont, John, Bart., the elder
(i) *An Epitaph upon my dear Brother Francis Beaumont* **in MS**
Suggested date of reading: see note
References: see note

> On Death thy murderer this revenge I take;
> I slight his terror, and just question make,
> Which of us two the best precedence have,
> Mine to this wretched world, thine to the grave.
> Thou shouldst have follow'd me, but Death, to blame,
> Miscounted years, and measur'd age by fame.
> So clearly hast thou bought thy precious lines,
> Their praise, new swiftly, so thy life declines:
> Thy muse, the hearer's queen, the reader's love,
> All ears, all hearts, but Death's, could please & move. J. Beam^t. Kn^t.

---

[1] Wordsworth Library WLL/Beaumont, G. H./49.

Lamb copied this poem into his copy of Beaumont and Fletcher's *Fifty Comedies and Tragedies* (1679), now at the British Library (C.45.i.7). He had probably acquired the volume by Oct. 1804, as in his view it was the 'right folio' with which to read Beaumont and Fletcher (see note 33, above). He was reading and commenting on them as early as June 1796 (Marrs i 30-4). At any rate, it is likely that, given his interest in Beaumont, W would have read the MS text at some time during the early to mid 1800s.

(ii) poems
Suggested date of reading: by 5 Aug. 1806
References: *MY* i 70

W's reference to 'that illustrious and most extraordinary man Beaumont the Poet and his Brother' in a letter to Sir George Beaumont of 1 May 1805 indicates that he was aware of John and Francis Beaumont by that date (*EY* 588). Subsequent correspondence suggests that W's knowledge of their work was not extensive.

On 21 July Beaumont wrote to tell W:

> I have found a volume of his works, among them are some lines on the early death of his brother - there is also a short poem called the Sheperdess which begins thus
> 'A sheperdess who long had fed her flocks
> 'On stony Charnwoods dry & barren rocks . . .'[1]
> According to the fashion of the times, before the poems are prefixed complimentary verses among the rest some lines by his son Francis nephew to the Dramatist which are transcribed to send you.[2]

The 'volume' Sir George had found was *Bosworth-field* (1629). On 29 July W wrote back, admitting that he had not read any of Sir John's works, although he had heard of *Bosworth-field* (*EY* 611). On 11 Aug. Beaumont wrote back, saying 'I have the p[oem][3] called Bosworth field but have [no][4] time to read it.'[5] In due course Lady Beaumont copied out some of John's verses,[6] for which DW thanked her in a letter of 5 Aug. 1806 (*MY* i 70). Beaumont wrote to W on 10 Aug. 1806, saying: 'I am sure you will be pleased with my ancestor (Sir Johns) poems. the more I read them the more I am pleased, his mind was elevated, pious, & pure. - I wish I could say as much for the Dramatist - much however

---

[1] *The Shepherdesse* appears on pp. 101-4 of the 1629 volume; Beaumont's transcription differs slightly from the printed text: 'A Shepherdesse, who long had kept her flocks / On stony Charnwoods dry and barren rocks'. I have collated Beaumont's transcription with all edns of his ancestor's works, and am sure that, in spite of the variants in his transcriptions, he was using that of 1629.

[2] The transcription does not survive; see Wordsworth Library WLL/Beaumont, G. H./10.

[3] MS torn.

[4] MS torn.

[5] Wordsworth Library WLL/Beaumont, G. H./11.

[6] This copy has not survived.

should be allowed for the customs of the times.'[1] On 21 Aug. W was sufficiently enthusiastic about Lady Beaumont's transcriptions to suggest to Sir George that he edit John's poetry: 'nothing would give me more satisfaction, either in the way of prefixing a Life, carrying the work through the press, or anything else' (*MY* i 77). In late Aug. or early Sept. 1806, Beaumont wrote back, transcribing John Beaumont's *An Act of Hope*.[2] W evidently liked it, because Beaumont wrote back on 11 Sept., saying: 'I am very glad you approve of my ancestor's little poem & am pleased the harmony of his versification struck you, because it confirms my own judgement.'[3] W saw the 1629 volume when he visited Coleorton in Oct. 1806 (Reed ii 337), and refers to it in a note to *Song, at the Feast of Brougham Castle*: 'This line is from The Battle of Bosworth Field by Sir John Beaumont (Brother to the Dramatist), whose poems are written with so much spirit, elegance, and harmony, that it is supposed, as the Book is very scarce, a new edition of it would be acceptable to Scholars and Men of taste, and, accordingly, it is in contemplation to give one' (Cornell *Poems 1800-7* 426). In Nov. 1811 W suggested once more that he edit the works, expressing interest in the search for Beaumont's lost eight-book poem, *The Crown of Thorns*. Beaumont replied:

> we certainly will have a private edition & make further enquiries for the Crown of Thorns - I know Southey promised me to write to his friends on the subject but I never heard the result, if he has exerted himself without success *I* should despair. (his italics)[4]

Southey had indeed expressed an intention to search for *The Crown of Thorns* in a letter to Beaumont of 11 Dec. 1807: 'In February I hope to be in town, and to hunt out the Crown of Thorns. . . . I have no doubt of succeeding in this search.'[5] He was not, apparently, successful.

(ii) *An Act of Hope*
Suggested date of reading: late Aug. or early Sept. 1806
References: see preceding note
An Act of Hope appears on pp. 80-1 of Sir John Beaumont's *Bosworth-field* (1629), which was the source of the transcription sent to W.

(iii) *Bosworth-field: with a taste of the variety of other poems, left by Sir John Beaumont, Baronet, deceased* (1629)
Suggested date of reading: Oct. 1806
References: see preceding note

---

[1] Wordsworth Library WLL/Beaumont, G. H./16.
[2] Wordsworth Library WLL/Beaumont, G. H./17.
[3] Wordsworth Library WLL/Beaumont, G. H./18.
[4] Wordsworth Library WLL/Beaumont, G. H./35
[5] *Memorials of Coleorton*, ed. William Knight (2 vols., 1887), ii 27.

A copy of this volume was in Sir George Beaumont's possession, and W would have seen it when he visited Coleorton in Oct. 1806. In a letter of Nov. 1811, W refers to it as 'Sir John Beaumont's little Volume' (*MY* i 514), a phrase that appropriately describes the 1629 edn.

W's *Song, at the Feast of Brougham Castle* 27 is borrowed from Beaumont's *Bosworth-field*, as he acknowledges in a note (Cornell *Poems 1800-7* 426). The *Song* was composed between 30 Oct. 1806 and early April 1807 - at Coleorton. W included an extract from *Bosworth-field* in the album of verse he compiled for Lady Mary Lowther in 1819 (*Album* 79-80).

36. Beaver, Philip, *African Memoranda: relative to an attempt to establish a British settlement on the island of Bulama, on the western coast of Africa, in the year 1792* **(1805)**
Suggested date of reading: by 26 March 1809
References: Musgrove 9; Southey *SC* 186; *MY* i 297, 486; Reed ii 371 and n1
On 29 May 1811 De Quincey wrote to Mrs Coleridge:

> I had intended to accompany this note with a book which I promised to send over for Mr. Southey's inspection; but, - the carrier's wife being gone to bed, and the book too large to be slipped under the door (which is our practice with letters), - I am obliged to defer sending it until Saturday. This book, by the bye, I have been keeping back with the intention of sending it at the same time with Capt. Beavor's *African Memoranda* - supposing that Wordsworth had not yet done with that book: but, to my great surprise, I now find that it was returned some time since. (Musgrove 9)

The first book De Quincey mentions, Pyrard's *Voyage to the East Indies* [1625], belonged to him;[1] Beaver, however, was Southey's. Southey read it in Oct. 1808, and during succeeding months expressed admiration for it in letters to his numerous correspondents (Warter ii 117; Curry i 486, 498; *Life of Southey* iii 192). He lent his copy to W probably in early 1809, and W's description of Beaver on 26 March 1809 as 'one of the most enlightened men any Country ever produced' (*MY* i 297) can be taken to indicate his reading of it. DW had read it by 12 May 1811 (see *MY* i 486), and Southey's copy was evidently returned at that time.

37. Bell, Andrew
(i) ***The Madras School, or Elements in Tuition, Comprising an Analysis of an Experiment in Education made at the Male Asylum, Madras*** **(1808)**
Suggested date of reading: between 5 June and 2 Oct. 1808
References: *MY* i 246, 269

---

[1] It was still in Southey's possession in 1812, when Southey asked whether he could retain it permanently (Curry ii 33).

On 2 Oct. 1808 W told Wrangham: 'Since I wrote to you I have read Dr Bell's Book upon education which no doubt you must have seen' (*MY* i 269). His previous extant letter to Wrangham dates from 5 June, so he must have read Bell's volume between that date and 2 Oct. Although the editors of *MY* note that W is referring to Bell's *Experiment in Education* (1797), I think it more likely that he meant *The Madras School, or Elements in Tuition, Comprising an Analysis of an Experiment in Education made at the Male Asylum, Madras* (1808).

C began corresponding with Bell in April 1808: 'O dear Dr Bell, you are a great man!' (Griggs iii 88). Coburn writes: 'Coleridge perhaps had already seen his first publication, *An Experiment in Education made at the Male Asylum of Madras* (1797), and certainly he was reading at this time, in preparation for his proposed lecture on education,[1] the proof-sheets (the Dedication is dated 10 April 1808) of Bell's *The Madras School, or Elements of Tuition* . . . (Chelsea 1808)' (*Notebooks* iii 3291f4vn). W knew of Bell, and came to be acquainted with him, through C - in May 1808 (Reed ii 387n29). He would have obtained Bell's most readily available publication, *The Madras School* (1808), at C's recommendation. He may have read Bell's *Experiment in Education* in due course, but only a copy of *The Madras School* was retained at Rydal Mount (Shaver 317).

(ii) *The Madras School, or Elements in Tuition, Comprising an Analysis of an Experiment in Education made at the Male Asylum, Madras* **(1808)**
Suggested date of reading: c. May 1812 onwards
References: Supp. 83 and n4
In his letter to MW of 17-18 May 1812 W writes: 'I will send thee another copy of Bells longer work' (*Supp.* 83). MW was at that time staying with Thomas Hutchinson at Radnor. W refers to *The Madras School* (1808), a copy of which he would have sent to Radnor by mid-June, when he left London. It would presumably have returned to Rydal Mount with MW. By this time, as SH reported in a letter of 27 Oct. 1811, W 'is busy teaching at the School, after Dr Bell's fashion' (*SHL* 28).

(iii) *Elements of Tuition, Part II. The English School* **in MS**
Suggested date of reading: Aug. 1812
References: Reed ii 509
Bell's MS was virtually rewritten by DW during Aug. 1812, and was presumably read by W. It was probably at around this time that W composed *Excursion* Book IX, which discusses Bell's theories (*PW* v 473; Reed ii 681[2]).

(iv) *Elements of Tuition; or the Application of the Madras System of Education to British Schools* **(2 vols., 1814-15)**

---

[1] For an account of C's comments on Bell in his lecture, and indeed a helpful summary of Bell's ideas, see CC *Literature* i 96-100.
[2] Reed places composition between Aug. 1811 and May 1814.

Suggested date of reading: 1814-15
References: *Life of Bell* ii 680; Shaver 22
DW apparently rewrote vol. 2 in Aug. 1812, but few of her alterations were incorporated into the final copy (see preceding note). All the same, Bell sent a copy of vol. 1 to her on publication; as he told Southey: 'My heterogeneous composition does not suit the public taste; and in the fashionable world instruction is not sought for, but amusement. I send the earliest copies to you and Miss Wordsworth' (*Life of Bell* ii 680). DW's copy bore Bell's presentation inscription.

38. Bell, John, *The Poets of Great Britain complete from Chaucer to Churchill* (109 vols., Edinburgh, 1776-1801)
Suggested date of reading: 1801 to 11 May 1841
References: *MY* i 90n1; Shaver 23
A set of Bell's *Poets* was retained at Rydal Mount. It belonged to MH, who was given it by Mrs Langley, the wife of the landowner of Gallow Hill, in 1801. As it was incorporated into W's library by the Rydal Mount years I assume that it probably came to DC with Mary in Oct. 1802. It was sold at Sotheby's for £28 on 13 March 1961; according to the catalogue it contains two inscriptions: 'Mary Hutchinson from the Honble Mrs. Langley. Gallow Hill 1801.', and 'To Dora Quillinan from her loving Mother, Mary Wordsworth May 11th 1841'.

39. *Bessie Bell and Mary Gray*
Suggested date of reading: by 19 Aug. 1814
References: *Supp.* 148
Writing to DW from Perth on 19 Aug. 1814, W remarked that he had 'visited here the burial place of Bessy Bell and Mary Gray, which I shall describe to you when we see you' (*Supp.* 148). The ballad of *Bessie Bell and Mary Gray* was widely circulated and W had probably known it since childhood.

40. Bewick, Thomas, works
Suggested date of reading: by 29 July 1800
References: Cornell *Lyrical Ballads* 388
W's allusion to 'the genius of Bewick' in *The Two Thieves* shows that he was aware of Bewick's work by 29 July 1800, when the poem was complete. Butler and Green suggest that W might have seen Bewick's *Select Fables* (1784), *Quadrupeds* (1790) or *British Birds* (1797). On the basis of meetings dating back to the early 1800s Hazlitt wrote that W 'greatly esteems Bewick's wood-cuts', *Spirit of the Age* (1825), p. 246.

41. Bible
Suggested date of reading: 1800-15
References: see note

W must have read or heard parts of this work constantly throughout the years 1800-15, and numerous allusions to it appear in his poetry. By this time, of course, he would have known much by heart. A full-scale study of W's use of biblical allusions has yet to be written; the most I can do here is to direct the reader to one or two suggestive examples.

Edward Wilson, 'An Echo of St Paul and Words of Consolation in Wordsworth's "Elegiac Stanzas"', *RES* 43 (1992) 75-80, notes an echo of Paul's first Epistle to the Thessalonians in W's *Elegiac Stanzas, Suggested by a Picture of Peele Castle, in a Storm*, composed between 20 May and 27 June 1806. W alludes twice to 1 Corinthians in the first instalment of his *Convention of Cintra*, published in the *Courier* on 27 Dec. 1808 (*Prose Works* i 373, 374). It was written between mid-Nov. and 15 Dec., and W may have read 1 Corinthians at around that time. The other quotations from the Bible in the *Convention of Cintra* suggest that W was referring to it in early 1809; books quoted are Matthew, Ezekiel, and Daniel (*Prose Works* i 393, 402, 403). For more on W and the Bible see Lienemann 205-7.

In Oct. 1805 the Wordsworths were reunited with the family Bible once in their father's possession, and now at the Wordsworth Library (see Wu *Library* JW 18).

42. Bingley, William, *North Wales: including its scenery, antiquities, customs, and some sketch of its natural history* **(2 vols., 1804)**
Suggested date of reading: by 18 Oct. 1811
References: *SHL* 29-30
In her letter of 18 Oct. 1811 (redated by Reed ii 483n26), SH told Mary Monkhouse: 'I have been dipping into Bingley's *Tour of N. Wales.*' She goes on to copy two quotations from vol. 2, pp. 87 and 164 (*SHL* 29-30). As SH was with the Wordsworths at this time it is likely that they too saw Bingley's volume. The fact that it appears in none of the Rydal Mount catalogues would suggest that it was borrowed - perhaps from either Southey or Lloyd, both of whom SH had recently seen.

43. Birch, Thomas, *The Heads and Characters of Illustrious Persons of Great Britain, with Their Portraits Engraven by Mr Houbraken and Mr Vertue. With Their Lives and Characters by Thomas Birch* **(2 vols., 1743, 1751)**
Suggested date of reading: July-Dec. 1805
References: *EY* 610, 629
In a letter to Beaumont of 29 July 1805, W reported that he had purchased a copy of 'Houbraken and Vertue's Heads' a few weeks ago at Penrith, and offered it to Beaumont as a gift (*EY* 610). He must therefore have been in Penrith during the first or second week of July 1805 (not noted by Reed). On 11 Aug. Beaumont replied: 'How much obliged to you I am for procuring the book of Houbraken's prints which I have frequently wished to possess - & I shall value it on all accounts.'[1] By 24 Oct. W was preparing to transmit the large folio

---

[1] Wordsworth Library WLL/Beaumont, G. H./11.

to him (*EY* 629). The safest way to do so was by hand, and he accordingly gave the volume to Joshua Bragg on 21 Dec., 'a Friend of ours' on his way to London (*EY* 665). Bragg left this with RW at Staple Inn, and it was shortly after collected by one of Beaumont's servants (possibly Mr Colly).[1]

44. Blair, Hugh, *Lectures on Rhetoric and Belles Lettres* (2 vols., 1783)
Suggested date of reading: by Sept. 1800
References: *Prose Works* i 113, 173, 175, 176, 177
Blair's influence on the Preface to *Lyrical Ballads* is well documented. In a letter to me, Owen cautions: 'Blair spouts commonplaces of the age, and I am not sure of any direct influence.'

45. Blake, William
(i) *Holy Thursday* (*Innocence*), *Laughing Song*, *The Tyger*, and 'I Love the Jocund Dance'
Suggested date of reading: between mid-March and mid-April 1807, or between mid-May and 10 June 1807
References: Reed ii 707; Moorman *N&Q* 403
These four Blake lyrics appear in the Wordsworth Commonplace Book (DC MS 26, 46v-48v) - copied, Reed suggests, by W and MW at Coleorton between mid-March and 10 June 1807. Even so, it is possible that Robert Woof is correct in thinking that they were copied by Thomas Wilkinson: 'the handwriting of these Blake entries is not distinguishable from that of the entries supposedly in the hand of Wilkinson' (Woof PhD 238). If so, the entries cannot have been made at Coleorton at the time suggested by Reed. Woof also casts doubt over Bateson's suggestion that they were copied *c*. 1804:

> In fact, there seems no good reason that they should not have been entered several years after 1804. . . . That they cannot be earlier than 1804 is most certain, but it seems difficult to find a terminal date for the use of the whole book. . . . There is no positive evidence to prevent the Blake entries belonging, say, to 1812, when we know that Crabb Robinson went out of his way to read Blake to Wordsworth. Most probably the Blake poems were entered earlier, but this remains a conjecture. (Woof PhD 238-9)

Moorman's suggestion that their source was Benjamin Heath Malkin's *A Father's Memoirs of His Child* (1806), which contains all the poems copied by the Wordsworths, as well as *The Divine Image* and *How sweet I roamed*, is generally accepted. That volume was referred to, rather critically, by DW, in 1809 (*MY* i 368) - thus providing a likely terminal date for the entries in the Commonplace Book. On the basis of DW's comments, Betz suggests that Catherine Clarkson lent Malkin's volume to the Wordsworths in 1807, and that she had been lent it by Henry Crabb Robinson; I have chosen to accept Betz's conclusions, including the

---

[1] See *MY* i 55 and n1, 69.

dates he suggests for the entries.[1] As an alternative, he posits that the book may have been in Beaumont's library at Coleorton.

(ii) 'Blake's poems'
Suggested date of reading: 24 May 1812
References: Morley i 85

Robinson recorded on 24 May 1812 that 'I read Wordsworth some of Blake's poems; he was pleased with some of them, and considered Blake as having the elements of poetry a thousand times more than either Byron or Scott' (Morley i 85). One can only guess what poems were read to W - not, presumably, *Jerusalem*, which Robinson regarded as 'a perfectly mad poem' (Morley i 41). Hazlitt had liked *The Chimney Sweeper* when Robinson showed it to him on 10 March 1811 (Morley i 25); in addition, Robinson possessed transcripts of at least the following poems: *To the Muses*, *Night*, *The Little Black Boy*, *A Dream*, *The Sunflower*, *Introduction* (*Experience* and *Innocence*), *Earth's Answer*, *The Garden of Love*, *A Little Boy Lost*, *The Poison Tree*, *The Sick Rose*, *The Human Abstract*, the *Dedication* of the designs for Blair's *Grave*, *America* Plate 10, lines 5-10, and *Europe* Plate 1, lines 12-15.[2]

Owen and Smyser suggest that W's *The Sublime and Beautiful*, composed between Sept. 1811 and Nov. 1812, recalls the *Introduction* to *Songs of Innocence* (see *Prose Works* ii 353, 454).

46. Bloomfield, Robert, *The Farmer's Boy* [1800]
Suggested date of reading: by 17 Sept. 1800
References: Griggs i 623; *Grasmere Journals* 123

'What W. & I have seen of the Farmer's Boy (only a few short extracts) pleased us very much', C told James Tobin on 17 Sept. 1800. Those extracts may have been encountered in a review shortly after publication.[3] It is likely that W read all of Bloomfield's poem not long after. JW had done so by 12 Dec. 1800, when he told MH: 'I have got the farmers boy it is not a poem I like much.' He sent his copy to MH, and it would thus have been available to W (Ketcham 79-80).

C knew it by the time he mentioned it in a letter to Longman of 26 March 1801 (Griggs ii 716), and so, presumably, did W by 28 July 1802, when, on a coach to Peterborough, he and DW noticed that a fellow passenger's little girl had a copy: 'She said it was written by a man without education & was very wonderful' (DW's journal, 28 July 1802). Bloomfield's poem was deservedly popular, and sold 26,000 copies within three years.

---

[1] Paul F. Betz, 'Wordsworth's First Acquaintance with Blake's Poetry', *Blake Newsletter* 3 (1970) 84-9.
[2] See Mark L. Reed, 'Blake, Wordsworth, Lamb, etc.: Further Information from Henry Crabb Robinson', *Blake Newsletter* 3 (1970) 76-84, where W's response to Blake's poems is also given.
[3] Likely candidates include the reviews in the *British Critic* 15 (1800) 601-8, *Critical Review* 29 (1800) 66-77, and *European Magazine* 37 (1800) 368-71, all of which carried substantial extracts from *The Farmer's Boy*.

47. Boccaccio, Giovanni, *Il Decamerone*
Suggested date of reading: 14 April 1807 onwards
References: Reed ii 351
The copy of the *Decameron* charged to W in the Longman accounts on 14 April 1807 for 15*s.* was second-hand, '1 Decameron 4to used calf' (see p. 266), and presumably the one later retained at Rydal Mount (Shaver 29). It is possible that W was in London by 14 April, and that he initiated this transaction himself; if so, he can be presumed to have taken possession of the book immediately.

The Wordsworths appear to have helped C with his Italian in Nov. 1803 (CC *Marginalia* i 542;[1] *Notebooks* i 1649, 1653); this may have involved a reading of Boccaccio at that time.

48. Boileau-Despréaux, Nicolas, *Œuvres* **(3 vols., Paris, 1801)**
Suggested date of reading: Aug. 1802 onwards
References: Reed ii 642; Shaver 30
W purchased this title as part of the *Bibliothèque Portative de Voyageur* (5 vols., Paris, 1801-2) in Calais, Aug. 1802. It is now at the Wordsworth Library. Boileau appears to have been an influence on *Excursion* iv 847-87 (*PW* v 28).

49. Bonaparte, Lucien, *Charlemagne; ou L'Eglise delivrée. Poème épique, en vingt-quatre chants* **(1814)**
Suggested date of reading: by 14 Feb. 1815
References: MY ii 198
'Have you read Lucien B's Epic?' W asked Gillies on 14 Feb. 1815, 'I attempted it, but gave in at the 6th Canto, being pressed for time' (*MY* ii 198). W mentions the poem in his *Essay, Supplementary to the Preface*, composed Jan. 1815 (*Prose Works* iii 78).

50. Bonneval, Claude Alexandre de, Count, *Memoirs of the Bashaw Count Bonneval, from his birth to his death* **(1750)**
Suggested date of reading: by March 1810
References: *Notebooks* iii 3738; CC *Marginalia* i 698-9; Shaver 30
W's copy is now at the Wordsworth Library. It bears inscriptions by W, C, and William Wordsworth Jr. C's reference to 'the character of Count Bonneval' (*Notebooks* iii 3738) reveals that he had by March 1810 encountered it (he was at that time resident at Allan Bank). It also contains a marginal note by C, dating from March-May 1810, commenting further on Bonneval's character (see CC *Marginalia* i 698-9). At any rate, this volume was evidently in W's possession by March 1810, and may have been one of the numerous books sent to him during the preceding year by De Quincey from London.

---

[1] Whalley states that C's reading of Boccaccio took place in Nov. 1802.

51. Book of Common Prayer
Suggested date of reading: see note
References: see note
W no doubt heard and saw the *Book of Common Prayer* on many occasions during the years covered by this volume. Owen suggests it as a source for *Prelude* iv 340-5; see 'Understanding *The Prelude*', *WC* 22 (1991) 100-9.

52. Boswell, James, *The Life of Samuel Johnson* [2 vols., 1791, 1793]
Suggested date of reading: c. 30 Aug. 1800
References: Grasmere Journals 19
'I read a little of Boswells Life of Johnson' (DW's journal, 30 Aug. 1800). DW may have directed W's attention to parts of Boswell, as the *Life* seems to have led to a discussion the following day concerning 'Miss Thrale's hatred' (see *Grasmere Journals* 165). In his diary for 28 Nov. 1799, James Losh described Boswell's *Johnson* as 'a very extraordinary book - if we consider its execution, and the talents of its author, there is not much to praise'.[1] Might Losh have lent his copy to DW? It is possible: intriguingly, he called at DC on 5 Sept. 1800, only days after DW recorded her reading of Boswell (Reed ii 84). It is possible, too, that the volume was borrowed from the collection of William Jackson, C's landlord at Greta Hall, which, according to C, was well supplied with 'all the usual Trash of the Johnsons' (Griggs i 619). That W had read Boswell by spring 1812 is the implication of his reference to Johnson's biographers in a letter to Wrangham of that date (*MY* ii 8).

C quotes Boswell, writing from Allan Bank in Jan. 1810 (Griggs iii 280), and W refers to him in the *Essay, Supplementary to the Preface* (*Prose Works* iii 70).

53. Bourne, Vincent, *Miscellaneous Poems: Consisting of Originals, and Translations* (1772)
Suggested date of reading: from March or April 1806 onwards
References: *EY* 657; *MY* i 4-5
On 25 Dec. 1805, W and DW wrote to RW explaining that their friend, Joshua Bragg, was willing to bring W's copy of Bourne's *Miscellaneous Poems* to Grasmere when he returned from London in Jan. (*EY* 657). W had apparently left this volume in Cambridge with CW. In Jan. 1806 DW wrote again to assure RW that 'if Mr. Bragge can bring the parcel down without inconvenience I am sure he will do it' (*MY* i 4-5). W had received his copy by April 1806, for one of Bourne's poems was to influence *Power of Music*, which W composed probably between 4 April and 10 Nov. 1806. As Lienemann notes, *Power of Music* 'ist beeinflußt von Bournes "Ballad-singer in the Seven-dials"' (Lienemann 68). Curiously, the *Miscellaneous Poems* does not appear to have been at Rydal Mount, though Bourne's *Poetical Works* (2 vols., 1808) was (Shaver 32).

---

[1] Paul Kaufman, 'Wordsworth's "Candid and Enlightened Friend"', *N&Q* 207 (1962) 403-8, p. 408.

Lamb's discovery of Bourne in 1815 would have given W cause to reread him. In a letter to W dated 16 April 1815 Lamb remarks: 'Since I saw you I have had a treat in the reading way which comes not every day. The Latin Poems of V. Bourne which were quite new to me. What a heart that man had, all laid out upon town scenes, a proper counterpoise to *some people's* rural extravaganzas.' He goes on to ask 'Do you remember his epigram on the old woman who taught Newton the A.B.C.' (Marrs iii 140; his italics) - indicating that they had discussed, and probably read, Bourne's poems together. Lamb translated Bourne's *Epitaph on a Dog*, published in *The Indicator* on 3 May 1820, p. 420. Both he and W would have known Cowper's translations from Bourne: *Life and Posthumous Writings* ed. Hayley (Chichester, 1803), ii 345-77.

54. Bowles, William Lisle, *The Two Sailors (The Greenwich Pensioners)* **in MS**
Suggested date of reading: 13 June 1815
References: Reed ii 607 and n36
W was present when this poem was composed; a transcription of it exists, in MW's hand, at the Wordsworth Library.

55. Breton, Nicholas, works
Suggested date of reading: by 17 Sept. 1814
References: *MY* ii 153
In his letter to Robert Anderson of 17 Sept. 1814, W suggests that an enlarged edn of Anderson's *British Poets* should include Breton, the lyric poet. This indicates that he was aware of his works by 17 Sept. 1814.

56. *British Critic*
(i) 33 (March 1809) 298-9, review of *Poems, in Two Volumes* **(1807)**
Suggested date of reading: by 21 May 1807
References: *MY* i 145
On 21 May 1807 W wrote to Lady Beaumont: 'Though I am to see you so soon I cannot but write a word or two, to thank you for the interest you take in my Poems as evinced by your solicitude about their immediate reception' (*MY* i 145). This would suggest that he had by that date seen, or heard about, the two reviews of *Poems, in Two Volumes* that had thus far been published: (i) *The Cabinet* 3 (April 1808) 249-52; (ii) *British Critic* 33 (March 1809) 298-9. Lady Beaumont had cause to fret about W's feelings regarding these reviews. Both are scathingly critical, the *British Critic* taking the view that the *Poems* was 'in good truth well worthy . . . of ridicule; for such flimsy, puerile thoughts, expressed in such feeble and halting verse, we have seldom seen'. Charles Lloyd subscribed to the *British Critic* at Old Brathay, where Southey consulted it in Nov. 1804: 'its praise is milk-and-water, and its censure sour small beer' (Warter i 287).

In his letter to Lady Beaumont, W goes on to remark: 'Leaving these, I was going to say a word to such Readers as Mr. Rogers. Such! - how would he be offended if he knew I considered him only as a representative of a class, and not as unique! "Pity," says Mr. R., "that so many trifling things should be admitted to obstruct the view of those that have merit"' (*MY* i 146-7). Rogers' criticisms were not in print: they were presumably in the first place verbal, and recorded by Lady Beaumont in her previous letter to W. It is highly unlikely, given the cordial acquaintance between Rogers and W by 1807, that the elder poet would have penned either of the hostile reviews of *Poems* that had appeared in print by 21 May.

(ii) 3 (May 1815) 449-67, review of *The Excursion* (1814)
Suggested date of reading: late July 1815
References: *MY* ii 243
On 28 June 1815 DW told Catherine Clarkson: 'I have seen the British Critic which contains a Review by a Friend of the Coleridges' which between ourselves I think a very feeble composition. It was highly praised to me' (*MY* ii 243). The review of *The Excursion* appeared in the *British Critic* for May 1815, and would have been seen by W when he returned to Rydal Mount from London towards the end of July.

57. Brougham, Henry, review of Byron, *Hours of Idleness*, Edinburgh Review 11 (1808) 285-9
Suggested date of reading: between 27 Feb. and 3 April 1808
References: *Rogers* 234-5
Rogers reported W's reaction to Brougham's harsh review of Byron's first volume:

> Wordsworth was spending an evening at Charles Lamb's, when he first saw the said critique, which had just appeared. He read it through, and remarked that 'though Byron's verses were probably poor enough, yet such an attack was abominable, - that a young nobleman, who took to poetry, deserved to be encouraged, not ridiculed.' Perhaps if this had been made known to Byron, he would not have spoken of Wordsworth as he has done. (*Rogers* 234-5)

Robinson was also present on this occasion, and gives a similar account:

> I was sitting with Charles Lamb when Wordsworth came in, with fume in his countenance, and the *Edinburgh Review* in his hand. 'I have no patience with these Reviewers,' he said; 'here is a young man, a lord, and a minor, it appears, who has published a little volume of poems; and these fellows attack him, as if no one may write poetry unless he lives in a garret. The young man will do something, if he goes on.'
>
> (Sadler iii 488)

These remarks do not suggest that W had read *Hours of Idleness* at the time he saw Brougham's review, which appeared in the *Edinburgh* for Jan. 1808 (published *c.* 1 Feb.). W was in London between 27 Feb. and 3 April 1808. The review was initially assumed to have been the work of Jeffrey.

58. Brown, John, *Barbarossa* **[1755]**
Date of performance: by 25 Dec. 1804
References: *EY* 518-19

On 25 Dec. 1804, W wrote to Beaumont commenting on William Betty, 'the young Roscius' who had won acclaim as Selim in *Barbarossa*: 'Neither Selim nor Douglas requires much power, but even to perform them as he does talents and genius I should think must be necessary' (*EY* 519). W had probably not seen Betty in performance, as his rise to fame had occurred only recently, but his phrasing does imply some knowledge of Brown's *Barbarossa*. It is likely that W had known Home's *Douglas* since his schooldays (*WR* 75). DW too refers to *Barbarossa*, apparently with some knowledge of it, in a letter written on the same day (*EY* 520). Brown's play was first performed at Drury Lane in Dec. 1754 and remained popular until the mid-nineteenth century.

In subsequent months Beaumont continued to keep W informed of Betty's career, commenting on his performance in *Douglas* in Feb. 1805, and in *Hamlet* in March 1805.[1] Southey saw him in *Douglas* on 13 Oct. 1805 (*Life of Southey* ii 349), and MW saw him on 3 June 1812 (*Love Letters* 224-5).

59. Brown, Thomas, review of Lamb, *John Woodvil,* **Edinburgh Review 2 (April 1803) 90-6**
Suggested date of reading: by mid-Jan. 1804
References: *EY* 435

In his letter to Thelwall of mid-Jan. 1804, W points out that, 'In their review of Lambs Tragedy at the conclusion is a gross piece of disingenuousness . . .' (*EY* 435). Southey too was dismayed by its unfairness (Curry i 315-16).

W may also have seen the notice of *John Woodvil* in the *Annual Review* which C and Lamb believed to be by Mrs Barbauld (*Notebooks* ii 1848 and n), and which may have fuelled their dislike of her.

60. Browne, Sir Thomas
(i) *Religio Medici* **(6th edn, 1669)**
Suggested date of reading: early June 1804 onwards
References: Marrs ii 138; Shaver 36

---

[1] See letters to W of 5 Feb. and 24 March 1805, WLL/Beaumont, G. H./4 and 9.

A letter from Lamb to DW of 2 June 1804 reveals that on that date he sent a copy of Browne to DC, 'which I desire your brother's acceptance of'. It would have reached Grasmere within days. C appears to have annotated his copy of this edn during April-Sept. 1809 at Allan Bank or Greta Hall (CC *Marginalia* i 743). His copy remained at Allan Bank and entered W's library at Rydal Mount. Shaver does not say so, but it is now at the John Rylands Library (see CC *Marginalia* i 742-59). See also *LY* iv 545.

(ii) *Pseudodoxia Epidemica; or, enquiries into very many received tenents and commonly presumed truths* **(4th edn, 1658)**
Suggested date of reading: see note
References: Shaver 36; Gordan 340
Shaver does not say so, but W's copy is now at the New York Public Library. A note by Charles Lamb on the upper right-hand corner of the front flyleaf records that he bought it for C on 9 March 1804. C has added: 'It was on the 10th; on which day I dined and punched at Lamb's.' C also notes: 'Given by S.T.C. to S. Hutchinson March 1804.' The title-page bears the ownership inscription: 'M. Wordsworth Rydal Mount'. It is not clear from any of this when, if ever, W himself might have read this volume. But if the book was in SH's possession from March 1804 onwards, it is highly likely that he would have read it at around that period.

(iii) *Enquiries into Vulgar and Common Errors* **(1658)**
Suggested date of reading: 1809 or 1810 onwards
References: Shaver 291
Shaver reports that the copy retained at Rydal Mount 'contains a long letter to Sara Hutchinson, relative principally to many curious passages in the work, also several MS. marginal notes and corrections, all in the handwriting of S. T. Coleridge, and autographs of Charles Lamb and Mary Wordsworth'. Its present whereabouts is unknown. From his account, it may be deduced that the volume belonged originally to Lamb, and passed into C's possession, probably at some time during the mid-1800s. Towards the end of the decade, probably during his residence at Allan Bank in 1809, during work on *The Friend*, C left it in W's care; in due course it passed into Rydal Mount (on which see also *LY* iv 545). Whalley does not include it in any of his lists or CC *Marginalia*.

61. Browne, William, *Britannia's Pastorals* **(Anderson)**
Suggested date of reading: probably spring 1802; certainly by 30 Aug. 1803
References: *DWJ* i 298
The first reference to Browne by either DW or her brother comes in her journal of the Scottish tour of 1803, in an entry for 30 Aug.: 'I should have liked to have seen a bevy of Scottish ladies sailing, with music, in a gay barge. William, to whom I have read this, tells me that I have used the very words of Browne of Ottery, Coleridge's fellow-townsman' (*DWJ* i 298). She then quotes the lines from *Britannia's Pastorals* which she has inadvertently

echoed - from Book II Song II - and her text matches, almost exactly, that at Anderson, *British Poets* iv 308, her source. Her remark suggests that W had discussed Browne's poem with C, and had perhaps encountered it through him. If so, the most likely time for any such discussion would have been spring and summer 1802, a suggestion supported by Curtis' observation that the 1802 lyrics recall Browne's diction (Curtis 63). Coburn notes that C claimed to be related to Browne (*Notebooks* ii 2777, iii 3652).

62. Bruce, James, *Travels to Discover the Source of the Nile* (2nd edn, 1804)
Suggested date of reading: see note
References: *MY* i 129

On 24 Jan. 1807 DW wrote to Lady Beaumont asking her to send the Wordsworths, then staying at Coleorton, a copy of Bruce's *Travels*: 'Coleridge says that the *last* Edition of Bruce's Travels is a Book that you ought by all means to have. . . . If you purchase it we should be very glad to have the reading of it' (*MY* i 129; her italics). The Beaumonts seem to have had a good collection of travel books, and this would explain why they 'ought' to have had the most recent edition of Bruce's important volume. Presumably it was sent to Coleorton in due course, and read by the Wordsworths.

Alan Liu says that W 'knew about' Bruce's *Travels* by 1803,[1] and argues for its influence on *The Prelude*, but he does not provide any specific evidence for a reading prior to 1807. Liu's suggestion is not impossible, but it is contingent upon other factors. On 2 Sept. 1805 Southey told Charles Danvers: 'I am at present reading Bruce in order to review the new edition' (Curry i 399). He reviewed the 2nd edn of Bruce's *Travels* in the *Annual Review* 4 (1805) 2-16. W might have seen Southey's copy during 1804, and C's recommendation that the Beaumonts acquire one may be based on a perusal of it. C had known the 1st edn for years, as he had cited Bruce in a note to *Religious Musings* (1796) (EHC i 119n; CC *Watchman* 64). Alternatively, the Wordsworths may have known of the volume through Lamb, who read it in Jan. 1806 (Marrs ii 199).

It is not known whether it was in the consignment of books delivered to Coleorton *c.* 7 Feb. 1807 (*MY* i 133); in later years it was, however, at Rydal Mount (Shaver 36).

63. Bruce, Michael, *Lochleven* (Anderson)
Suggested date of reading: perhaps late 1798; certainly by 8 Dec. 1801
References: Stein 181; *Grasmere Journals* 46

The allusions to Bruce's poem observed by Stein 181 in W's *There was a Boy* and *Strange fits of Passion I have known* suggest that W had read *Lochleven* by late 1798. The first confirmable reading is by DW, recorded in her journal: 'Wm at work with Chaucer. I read Bruce's Lochleven & Life' (DW's journal, 8 Dec. 1801). As Pamela Woof observes, DW read

---

[1] *Wordsworth: The Sense of History* (Stanford, Calif., 1989), p. 1.

these texts in Anderson, *British Poets* vol. 11. Heath notes the influence of *Elegy - Written in Spring* on W during 1802 (Heath 124).

In 1819 W said that a monument should be erected to Bruce on the banks of Lochleven (*MY* ii 535); see also his account of a visit to Lochleven, Aug. 1814 (*Supp*. 150).

64. Brun, Frederika, *Die sieben Hügel*
Suggested date of reading: by 17 Aug. 1800
References: Cornell *Poems 1800-7* 406

As W noted, the story of *The Seven Sisters, or the Solitude of Binnorie* 'is from the German of Frederica Brun'. He must therefore have read Brun's *Die sieben Hügel* before 17 Aug. 1800 when he 'read us the 7 Sisters on a stone' (*Grasmere Journals* 17), and perhaps even before 26 Feb., when his other source for the poem, Robinson's *The Haunted Beach*, appeared in the *Morning Post*.

C apparently acquired a copy of Brun's *Gedichte* while in Germany, and it must have been in that volume that W read *Die sieben Hügel*. Here, too, C read Brun's *Chamouny beym Sonnenaufgange*, which provided the inspiration for his *Hymn before Sunrise, in the Vale of Chamouni* (EHC ii 1131; see also Griggs ii 865n1). Bonjour has shown how C's use of the notes to Brun's poem reveal that he owned the first edn of the *Gedichte* (Zürich, 1795), as they were suppressed in later edns.[1] See also Woof *SIB* 176-7 and Landon, 'Wordsworth, Coleridge, and the *Morning Post*: An Early Version of "The Seven Sisters"', *RES* 11 (1960) 392-402.

65. Brydges, Sir Samuel Egerton, *The Ruminator* (2 vols., 1813)
Suggested date of reading: Nov. 1814 onwards
References: *Supp*. 155; Shaver 39; Healey 2221

W received a parcel from R. P. Gillies containing a presentation copy of this volume between 12 and 23 Nov. 1814. On 23 Nov. he told Gillies: 'I have peeped into the Ruminator, and turned to your first Letter, which is well executed, and seizes the attention very agreeably' (*Supp*. 155). On 22 Dec., he told Gillies: 'I have read the *Ruminator*, and I fear that I do not like it quite as much as you would wish' (*MY* ii 179) - the kind of damning understatement no writer ever wants to hear. W's copy is in the Cornell Wordsworth Collection; it bears the title-page inscription, 'W Wordsworth'.

66. Buchanan, George, poems
Suggested date of reading: by Jan. 1815
References: *Prose Works* iii 78, 100

W ranks Buchanan alongside Burns and Thomson in his *Essay, Supplementary to the Preface*; a more extensive tribute to him appears in W's *Guide* (*Prose Works* ii 191, 398). A copy of

---
[1] *Coleridge's 'Hymn Before Sunrise'* (Lausanne, 1942), pp. 216-20.

Buchanan's *Opera omnia* (Edinburgh, 1714-15) was at Rydal Mount (Shaver 39). The reference to Buchanan in the imitation of Juvenal (*EY* 175 and n4) suggests that W had read him by 1797 - not impossible, as C read him at Cambridge.[1] Might W have been introduced to Buchanan by the co-author of the imitation - Francis Wrangham (cf. James I and Marvell, *WR* 78, 96-7)? If so, that would date his earliest encounter with Buchanan's work to July 1795, when he visited Wrangham in Cobham (Reed i 166). A copy of Buchanan's *Eclog of Crownes* (1605) was in Wrangham's possession by 1824 (Cole 34). Late in life, W remarked: 'I think Buchanan's "Maiae Calendae" equal in sentiment, if not in elegance, to anything in Horace' (Grosart iii 459).

67. Buchanan, John Lanne, *Travels in the Western Hebrides, 1782 to 1790* **(1793)**
Suggested date of reading: probably between mid-March and 10 June 1807
References: Reed ii 707; Shaver 39
W copied a set of extracts from Buchanan into the Wordsworth Commonplace Book (DC MS 26, 46r-46v), probably between mid-March and 10 June 1807, while at Coleorton. This book was at Rydal Mount.

68. Bunyan, John
(i) *Pilgrim's Progress*
Suggested date of reading: by 31 Jan. 1802
References: Grasmere Journals 60
The Wordsworths, like most literate people of the period, can be assumed to have known *Pilgrim's Progress* from childhood. Their earliest reference to it occurs in DW's journal for 31 Jan. 1802, when she suggests that W 'may sit for the picture of John Bunyan any day' (journal, 31 Jan. 1802). They must have known the portrait of Bunyan in editions from the 3rd (1679) onwards. W's earliest mention of Bunyan occurs in a letter of 14 May 1834 (*LY* ii 710). See also Potts 220-43.

(ii) *The Holy War, made by Shaddai upon Diabolus, for the Regaining of the Metropolis of the world. Or, the losing and taking again of the town of Mansoul.* **[1682]**
Suggested date of reading: by 1803
References: Wing B5538
In DW's recollections of the Scottish tour, 1803, her entry for 19 Aug. describes

> a large machine or lever, in appear[ance] like a large forge hammer, as we supposed for raising water out of the mines. . . . At all events the object produced a striking effect in that place where every thing was in unison with it particularly the Building itself which

---

[1] See J. C. C. Mays, 'Coleridge's Borrowings from Jesus College Library, 1791-94', *Transactions of the Cambridge Bibliographical Society* 8 (1981-5) 557-81, p. 574.

was turret-shaped, and with the figures upon it, resembled much one of the fortresses in the wooden cuts of Bunyan's holy Wars. (DC MS 55, 12v)

By 1803 DW and, presumably, her brother, were acquainted with Bunyan's *Holy War*.

69. Bürger, Gottfried August
(i) *Der wilde Jäger*
Suggested date of reading: spring 1800; by 5 April 1800
References: Cornell *Lyrical Ballads* 378
Butler and Green note the influence of Bürger's *Der wilde Jäger* on *Hart-Leap Well*, composed spring 1800, and certainly by 5 April. It is not clear when W first read Bürger's poem, but spring 1800 must be the right terminal date. It is likely that W knew Scott's translation, *The Chase* (1796), reprinted in M. G. Lewis' *Tales of Wonder* (1801) - a title in which W also had an interest (see note 254[i]).

(ii) *Die Entführung*
Suggested date of reading: by Jan. 1815
References: *Prose Works* iii 76
W quotes twelve lines from this work in his *Essay, Supplementary to the Preface*.

70. Burges, James Bland, *Richard Coeur de Lion* (2 vols., 1798)
Suggested date of reading: by 14 Jan. 1801
References: *EY* 683
On 14 Jan. 1801 W wrote to Burges, enclosing a copy of *Lyrical Ballads* (1800) 'as an acknowledgement of the pleasure which I have received from your poem' (*EY* 683). Although it appears that C composed the letter to Burges for W to copy out, it is nevertheless possible that W had read Burges' poem.

71. Burgh, James, *Political Disquisitions; or, an enquiry into public errors, defects, and abuses, etc.* (3 vols., 1774-5)
Suggested date of reading: 22 June 1810 onwards
References: Jordan 211; Shaver 40; Healey 2223
W's copy bears a fly-leaf inscription in De Quincey's hand: 'From Thomas de Quincey to William Wordsworth, Grasmere, Friday, June 22 - 1810'. It is now in the Cornell Wordsworth Collection.

72. Burne, Nicol, *A Delectable New Ballad, Intituled, Leader-Haughs and Yarow* [1690]
Suggested date of reading: probably Sept. 1803
References: *EY* 530 and n2; Wing B5749-50
Sending Scott a copy of *Yarrow Unvisited* on 16 Jan. 1805, W introduced it by saying that it was 'in the same sort of metre as the Leader Haughs' (*EY* 530); W's poem was composed

between 14 Oct. 1803 and 6 March 1804. It is likely that Scott recited Burne's poem to W when they first met, Sept. 1803.[1] W probably sought it out in print, and Woof PhD 263 posits that he referred to the text in Ritson's *Scotish Song* (2 vols., 1794). Curtis notes two verbal borrowings from it in *Yarrow Unvisited* (Cornell *Poems 1800-7* 417).

73. Burnet, Gilbert, *Bishop Burnet's History of his Own Time* **[2 vols., 1724-34]**
Suggested date of reading: by May 1812
References: *Love Letters* 117
'I am going to begin with this single volume of Burnet History', MW wrote to her husband on 2 May 1812, 'I wish you may meet with the other' (*Love Letters* 117). Evidently W had by May 1812 acquired one volume of a two-volume set of the *History*. He did not apparently own it in July 1808, when DW asked De Quincey in London to send a copy of 'Burnet' to Grasmere. At some point W acquired both volumes, as a set was sold in the Rydal Mount auction of 1859 (Wordsworth *SC* 12; Shaver 41). C was reading Burnet in 1795, and it would be surprising if, at around the same time, W was not doing the same (see also CC *Marginalia* i 830).

74. Burnet, Thomas
(i) *Telluris Theoria Sacra* **[2 vols., 1681-9]**
Suggested date of reading: c. 1804-5
References: OET *Prel.* 522; Cornell *13-Book Prelude* i 1172, ii 1008
A draft in MS B of the *Thirteen-Book Prelude*, transcribed first by De Selincourt and reproduced in transcription and facsimile by Reed, indicates that W probably knew Burnet's *Sacred Theory of the Earth* by 1804-5:

> and in turn
> To records listening of primeaval hours
> And the dread labours of the earth - ere Form
> From the conflicting powers of flood & fire
> Escaped, and stood fixed in permanence serene (Cornell *13-Book Prelude* 1008)

For the relevant passages from Burnet, see OET *Prel.* 522. C certainly knew this title by the time he delivered his lectures on revealed religion (CC *Lectures 1795* 102), and may have talked about it to W.

(ii) *Telluris Theoria Sacra* **(2nd edn, 4 vols., 1688-9)**
Suggested date of reading: probably between Dec. 1809 and 1814
References: PW v 420-1

---

[1] Scott also recited it to Lockhart while standing on a spur of the Eildon hills (*PW* iii 446).

W's note to *Excursion* iii 112 appends a lengthy quotation from Burnet's *Sacred Theory* which he claimed to have read 'Since this paragraph was composed' - that is, between Dec. 1809 (the earliest date at which these lines may have been composed according to Reed ii 23) and 1814. The copy read by W was probably that given to C by Charles Danvers in 1795-6, by 1814 retained at Rydal Mount; it is now at Victoria University Library (Shaver 320; Dendurent 465; CC *Marginalia* i 851).

75. Burns, Robert
(i) *Works* (4 vols., Liverpool, 1800)
Suggested date of reading: by 29 Sept. 1800
References: Reed ii 704; Moorman *N&Q* 402

'I well remember the acute sorrow with which, by my own fire-side, I first perused Dr. Currie's Narrative, and some of the letters, particularly of those composed in the latter part of the poet's life', W wrote in the *Letter to a Friend of Robert Burns* (1816) (*Prose Works* iii 118). Currie's life of Burns first appeared in the *Works* (4 vols., Liverpool, 1800), which W had seen by 29 Sept. 1800: by then he had transcribed from it into his Commonplace Book *The Queens' Marie, Go Fetch to Me a Pint o' Wine*, and *O that my Father had ne'er on me smil'd* (DC MS 26, 24v-25r). These fragments all appear among Burns' letters in vol. 2.[1]

A copy of the *Works* (1800) was retained at Rydal Mount (Shaver 42); this was probably in W's possession by 19 Aug. 1814, when MW advised DW to refer to 'Currie's life of Burns and Correspondence' (*Supp*. 151).

(ii) *The Ode to Ruin*
Suggested date of reading: by *c*. 18 Aug. 1803
References: Cornell *Poems 1800-7* 534-5; *PW* iii 439-40

In a note to his *Ejaculation at the Grave of Burns*, composed *c*. 18 Aug. 1803, W directs the reader to 'See in his Poem the Ode to Ruin', providing a terminal date for his reading of that work. De Selincourt quotes the second stanza of Burns' poem, which seems to be in W's mind (*PW* iii 439).

(iii) *Poems* **(Dundee, 1802)**
Suggested date of reading: between 14 Sept. 1803 and 10 Sept. 1807
References: *DWJ* i 383; Reed ii 233 and n40

'At Stirling we bought Burns's Poems in one volume, for two shillings', DW recollected of 14 Sept. 1803. As Reed notes, this was the Dundee edn of 1802, now in the Cornell Wordsworth Collection (Healey 2224). On 15 Sept. the Wordsworths read from it on the way to Edinburgh (*DWJ* i 384). DW gave it to Lady Beaumont on 10 Sept. 1807, as the title-page inscription, in DW's hand, indicates: 'D. Wordsworth, Lady Beaumont, September 10, 1807'.

---

[1] Woof PhD 235 first identified Currie as W's source for these entries.

(iv) *The Vision*
Suggested date of reading: Dec. 1806
References: MY i 119
In his letter to Lady Beaumont of Dec. 1806, written from Coleorton, W quotes the final stanza of *The Vision* (*MY* i 119). It is possible that he quoted it from memory, as it first appeared in the Kilmarnock edn of Burns' poems, of which he was one of the earliest readers (see p. 254); though it is equally possible that the Wordsworths took with them to Coleorton the copy of Burns' *Poems* purchased in Stirling in 1803 (see preceding note). I doubt whether W was quoting from a copy in the Beaumonts' library at Coleorton, or DW would not have needed to give theirs to Lady Beaumont in 1807.

(v) *The Poetical Works of Robert Burns*, ed. Alexander Chalmers (London and Edinburgh, 1813)
Suggested date of reading: 20 or 21 Aug. 1814 onwards
References: Reed ii 566-7; Shaver 42
W's copy is now in the Wordsworth Library. It was purchased in Perth in Aug. 1814, and given to William Wordsworth Jr in 1831. Its inscriptions are faithfully transcribed by Reed.

76. Burton, Robert, *The Anatomy of Melancholy* (Oxford, 1621)
Suggested date of reading: 1810 onwards
References: CC *Marginalia* i 854
Lamb's copy (borrowed by C) was left at Allan Bank in 1810 and passed into Rydal Mount (Shaver 320); its present whereabouts are unknown. However, this was not apparently the copy consulted by C c. May 1809 when he referred to it in a notebook entry (*Notebooks* iii 3502). The explanation may be as follows: the notebook entry was not made at Allan Bank, where Lamb's copy had been left. Wherever C made the entry (probably Keswick, possibly Penrith), he borrowed a copy of an edn later than that of 1628. He returned to Allan Bank on 13 June. It is not known when W acquired his own copy (8th edn, 1676), listed Shaver 43.

77. Butler, Samuel, *Hudibras*
Suggested date of reading: by 4 Jan. 1804
References: *Notebooks* i 1803; Cornell *Benjamin* 56
Sydrophel was the name given by the Wordsworths and their circle to the rock on Helm Crag known as 'the astrologer'. It first appears in a notebook entry by C of 4 Jan. 1804, thus providing the earliest date by which W might be presumed to have been aware of the character of that name in Butler's *Hudibras*. Perhaps he had by then acquired the copy of *Hudibras* containing Grey's annotations (3 vols., 1770), later retained at Rydal Mount (Shaver 44). W alludes, more famously, to 'Th' Astrologer, dread Sydrofel' in *Benjamin the*

Waggoner MS 1, line 159 (Cornell *Benjamin* 56). Lienemann writes: 'An Hudibras II 1 v. 567/8 erinnert "Song at the feast of Brougham castle" v. 10' (Lienemann 45).

78. Buxtorfius, Johannes, *Lexicon Hebraicum et Chaldaicum* (6th edn, 1646)
Suggested date of reading: probably by Feb.-March 1800
References: Shaver 44
This title was retained at Rydal Mount and contained 'Autographs of S. T. Coleridge and W. Wordsworth' (Wordsworth *SC* 344). It must therefore have been acquired before 1810, after which time W and C are not known to have bought books jointly. C was using Buxtorfius as early as Feb.-March 1800, when he mentions it in a notebook entry (*Notebooks* i 676 and n), and in the absence of other evidence it is reasonable to assume that he and W had acquired their copy by that date.

79. Byrom, John, *Epigram on the Feuds Between Handel and Bononcini*
Suggested date of reading: by *c*. early Sept. 1810
References: Jordan 258; *MY* i 458
De Quincey's letter of 27 Aug. 1810 to DW contains the last two lines of Byrom's epigram (Jordan 258), which she in turn copied in her letter to Catherine Clarkson of 30 Dec. 1810 (*MY* i 458). De Quincey's letter probably reached DW in early Sept. Timothy Underhill tells me that there are several places where De Quincey might have read the epigram, besides Byrom's *Miscellaneous Poems* (Manchester, 1773): (i) *The London Journal*, 5 June 1725; (ii) [?William Oldys, compiler], *A Collection of Epigrams* (1727), as Epigram CCCXXI, *The Contest*; (iii) [?William Oldys, compiler], *A Select Collection of Epigrams* (1759), as Epigram CCCXLIX, *The Musical Contest*; and (iv) *Morning Chronicle*, 31 Jan. 1792, where the epigram was revived to apply to the Haydn-Pleyel dispute. A more likely source would have been Chalmers' *Works of the English Poets* (21 vols., 1810), xv 243 (see note 90), where it appears under the title *Epigram on the Feuds between Handel and Bononcini*. However, Underhill adds: 'as a pupil at Manchester Grammar School during the High Mastership of Charles Lawson, the young De Quincey could have *heard* the lines (perhaps often), rather than read them' (letter to me). Underhill cites Dorning Rasbotham's *Verses intended to have been spoken at the breaking up of the Free Grammar School in Manchester for the Christmas holidays in the year 1782* (Manchester, 1782) as indicating that Byrom's poetry was known to pupils of the school. Ward's text of the *Epigram on the Feuds Between Handel and Bononcini* reads:

> Some say, compar'd to Bononcini,
> That Mynheer Handel's but a Ninny;
> Others aver, that he to Handel
> Is scarcely fit to hold a Candle.

Strange all this Difference should be
'Twixt Tweedle-dum and Tweedle-dee!

As W had access to Chalmers, and spent time with De Quincey, it is quite possible that he either read or heard the entire text of the *Epigram* at around this period.

80. Byron, George Gordon, 6th Baron
(i) *English Bards and Scotch Reviewers* [1809]
Suggested date of reading: see note
References: see note

This reading is distinctly doubtful, but as there is a possibility of its having occurred the evidence deserves at least to be summarized. Christopher Wordsworth quotes W as having said: 'I never read the "English Bards" through' (*Memoirs* ii 473-4) - which may be interpreted as meaning that he did read *English Bards* in part. This would not be the implication of the comment recorded by Charles Wordsworth: 'My Uncle had never read English Bards & S. Reviewers' (Reed *PBSA* 458). All the same, Byron's popularity would have made the poem hard to avoid on W's occasional trips to London - and it should not be forgotten that W enjoyed cordial meetings with its author. He was aware of the contents of *English Bards* when he wrote to MW on 9-13 May 1812, mentioning that his letter would be franked by Byron: 'He wrote a satire some time since in which Coleridge and I were abused, but these are little thought of' (*Supp.* 65).

Even if W did not read *English Bards* he certainly heard a good deal about it. It first appeared 9 March 1809, and on the basis of a notebook reference to 'young Prodigies' Coburn suggests that it may have been read by C *c*. April 1809 (*Notebooks* iii 3488 and n). De Quincey may have read the first or second issue of the 1st edn; he must, in any case, have read it in early April and probably March, because in a letter to the Wordsworths of 27 May 1809 he said that he had read it 'some weeks - or perhaps months - ago: but it is so deplorably dull and silly that I never thought of mentioning it before'. He pulled no punches when describing its contents to W; it was, he said, 'a wretched satire partly leveled at Mr. Wordsworth and Mr. Coleridge - called "English Bards and Scotch Reviewers": from the virulence of this book towards Mr. Southey and Mr. Wordsworth, I suspect (and for other reasons) that it is written by Peter Bayley - in revenge for Mr. Southey's having exposed him in the Annual Review' (Jordan 184-5).

(ii) *Childe Harold's Pilgrimage* (1812)
Suggested date of reading: 16 May 1812
References: *Supp.* 80

On 17-18 May 1812 W wrote to MW: 'Yesterday I dined alone with Lady B. - and we read Lord Byrons new poem which is not destitute of merit; though ill-planned, and often unpleasing in the sentiments, and almost always perplexed in the construction' (*Supp.* 80). In time, he became more critical. On 24 May he intimated to Robinson that Byron was 'somewhat cracked': 'Wordsworth allowed him power, but denied his style to be English' (Morley i 85). *Childe Harold* was Byron's first big success; the first edition, published 10 March, sold out within three days. The second, issued 17 April, contained six new poems.

The 'popular passage from Lord Byron on solitude' with which, on 3 June 1812, W compared *Tintern Abbey* (Morley i 93), was presumably from *Childe Harold*.

W came to dislike Byron and his poetry intensely, but in succeeding years he nonetheless read *The Corsair, Childe Harold's Pilgrimage* III and IV, *Lara, Don Juan, Beppo,* and *The Prisoner of Chillon.* Byron's *Works* (4 vols., 1830) was at Rydal Mount (Shaver 44).

(iii) *Lara, A Tale. Jacqueline, A Tale.* (1814)
Suggested date of reading: c. 18 Aug. 1814
References: *Supp.* 149
Writing to DW on 19 Aug. 1814, W describes an incident in a Perth bookshop:

> I stepped yesterday evening into a Bookseller's shop with a sneaking hope that I might hear something about the Excursion, but not a word; on the contrary, inquiry of the Bookseller what a poetical parcel which he was then opening consisted of, he said, that it was a new Poem, called Lara, a most exquisite thing, supposed to be written by Lord Byron, and that all the world were running wild after it. . . . I took the book in my hand, and saw 'Jacqueline' in the same column[1] with Lara; what's this, oh said the bookseller, Jacqueline is a sweet Thing supposed to be by Rogers the author of The Pleasures of Memory. (*Supp.* 149)

Byron's *Lara* was published anonymously with Rogers' *Jacqueline*, by John Murray, shortly after 5 Aug. It went through three edns before the end of the year. W does not say that he purchased a copy in Perth - and given his evident disappointment at not hearing that *The Excursion* was selling in large numbers he might not be expected to. However, a copy of *Lara* and *Jacqueline* (1814) was retained in the Rydal Mount library (Shaver 44), suggesting that this incident on 18 Aug. 1814 culminated in a purchase. An extract from *Lara* appeared in W's local paper, the *Westmorland Advertiser*, for 10 Dec. 1814.

(iv) *The Corsair* [1814]
Suggested date of reading: by 28 May 1815
References: Morley i 167-8
On 28 May 1815 Robinson recorded in his diary that W 'was led to give an opinion of Lord Byron which flattered me by its resemblance to my own. He reproached the author with the contradiction in the character of *The Corsair*, etc.' Byron's poem was published first on 1 Feb. 1814 and had reached a 5th edn by 18 Feb. W had no doubt read it before 28 May 1815, but this is the earliest available indication of a reading.

---

[1] W means only that *Jacqueline* was published continuously after *Lara* in the volume.

81. Calvin, Jean, *Institutio Christianae Religionis* **(Geneva, 1569)**
Suggested date of reading: 1809
References: Shaver 45
This book was retained at Rydal Mount and contained 'Autographs of "S. T. Coleridge" & "W. Wordsworth"' (Wordsworth *SC* 204). In all likelihood it passed into W's possession by 1810, probably some time in 1809, when C was apparently discussing Calvin with W, partly in preparation for his theological articles in *The Friend* (see *Notebooks* iii 3452, 3560; CC *Friend* ii 53, 113, 202). So far as I can find, W never made any sustained study of Calvin.

82. Campbell, Thomas
(i) *The Exile of Erin*
Suggested date of reading: after 28 Jan. 1801
References: Reed ii 704; Moorman *N&Q* 402
Reed judges that the first three stanzas and two concluding stanzas of Campbell's poem were copied and pasted by SH into the Wordsworth Commonplace Book (DC MS 26, 24r-24v) by 29 Sept. 1800. However, this cannot be correct because (i) as Woof PhD 234 notes, the poem was not composed until Nov. 1800, and (ii) it was first published in the *Morning Chronicle* on 28 Jan. 1801, anonymously. A more likely date for the copy is therefore after 28 Jan. 1801. The poem was first attributed to Campbell when published in the 1803 edn of his poems. Woof adds: 'There seems no way of determining whether the poem was copied from the newspaper or from the quarto edition of 1803' (Woof PhD 234). The Wordsworths were reading the *Morning Chronicle* at this period (see note 293), and it may have been their source.

(ii) *The Pleasures of Hope; with Other Poems* **(Edinburgh, 1800)**
Suggested date of reading: 1 Feb. 1802 onwards
References: *Grasmere Journals* 61-2; *EY* 342-3n3; Griggs ii 714
Having lent it to Godwin some time before, C wrote to him on 25 March 1801 to request the return of his copy of Campbell's *Pleasures of Hope* 'which Wordsworth wishes to see'. Godwin did not, apparently, send the volume immediately. First he settled down to read it himself, on 7-8 July 1801 (as his diary records); then he appears to have passed it on to RW, who sent it on to DC, where it arrived on 1 Feb. 1802 in a box containing other books. Sitting by W's bedside, DW 'read in the Pleasures of Hope to him' (DW's journals, 1 Feb. 1802). Whalley reported this copy to be in the library of W. H. P. Coleridge; it bears no annotation besides the pencilled initials 'STC' (Whalley PhD ii 212).

In subsequent years W was no admirer of Campbell's verse; he once told Rogers that *The Pleasures of Hope* 'has been strangely overrated' (*Rogers* 251; see also Morley i 90). Campbell's poem had reached its 4th edn by 1801.

(iii) *Gertrude of Wyoming* **(1809)**
Suggested date of reading: probably by 1 Aug. 1809

References: *MY* i 365

On 1 Aug. 1809 DW asked De Quincey: 'have you seen the *Edinburgh Review* on Cam[p]bell's Poem?' (*MY* i 365). This doesn't prove that W had read *Gertrude of Wyoming* by that date, but it suggests that he had at least heard of it. He must have read it by Jan. 1815, when he compared it unfavourably with *The Excursion* (*MY* ii 187 and n2). Given his past interest in Campbell's work (see preceding notes), it is likely that he saw *Gertrude* soon after publication. C's mention of Campbell in a letter to W of Oct. 1810 suggests that both were by then aware of *Gertrude* (Griggs iii 291).

(iv) *Hohinlinden*
Suggested date of reading: probably by 1 Aug. 1809; certainly by 23 Feb. 1811
References: *MY* i 466

'I think if you look up the Hohen Linden yourself you would not find it difficult to prove to Miss Herriot at least if it is not nonsense that there is very little sense in it, and that the author neither understood nor looked steadily at his subject', wrote DW to Catherine Clarkson on 23 Feb. 1811 (*MY* i 466-7). DW was probably relaying opinions shared by her brother; indeed, as W. J. B. Owen has observed to me, the phrase, 'looked steadily at his subject', is W's (*Prose Works* i 132, line 225). The Wordsworths would have read *Hohinlinden* in *Gertrude of Wyoming* (1809) (see preceding note), although it was first published in 1803, in the 7th edn of *The Pleasures of Hope*.

83. Carleton, George, *The Memoirs of Captain George Carleton* (1743)
Suggested date of reading: by 26 March 1809
References: *MY* i 303

'Carleton's *Memoirs* we have procured, so you need not purchase them for us; but if the Book falls in your way at a reasonable rate, buy it for yourself, for it is a most interesting work', W told De Quincey on 26 March 1809. He refers to the *Memoirs* in *The Convention of Cintra* (*Prose Works* i 257, 383, 403). C read it in April (Griggs iii 200), and promoted it among his friends (see note 200[ii]). It was later retained at Rydal Mount (Shaver 47).

84. Carver, Jonathan
(i) *Travels through the Interior parts of North America, in the years 1766, 1767, and 1768* (1768)
Suggested date of reading: between 27 March and 17 June 1802
References: Cornell *Poems 1800-7* 406

A note to *To H.C., Six Years Old*, composed between 27 March and 17 June 1802, indicates a debt to Carver's *Travels*; the same passage is recalled in W's *Guide* (*Prose Works* ii 185). Perhaps by March 1802 W had acquired the copy later retained at Rydal Mount (Shaver 48). To Carver he also owed his knowledge of 'the melancholy Muccawiss' at *Excursion* iii 947 (*PW* v 423). See also Coe 34-5.

(ii) *Travels through the Interior parts of North America, in the years 1766, 1767, and 1768* **(1768)**
Suggested date of reading: Nov. 1809
References: *Prose Works* ii 185, 396
W alludes to Carver in his *Select Views*, composed early Nov. 1809. The inaccuracy of his reference, as noted by Owen and Smyser, would suggest that he was not consulting his copy at the time.

85. Cave, William, *Apostolici; or, the history of the lives, acts, and martyrdoms of those who were contemporary with, or immediately succeeded the Apostles* **(1716)**
Suggested date of reading: by May 1808
References: Cornell *Tuft* 20-4; Shaver 49
Kishel reveals that the passage dealing with Basil and Gregory in *The Tuft of Primroses* was inspired by a reading of Cave's *Apostolici*, pp. 470-508, a copy of which was retained at Rydal Mount (Shaver 49). According to Kishel, Cave was the source 'for most, if not all' of the details of Basil's life (Cornell *Tuft* 21).[1] Graver adds that Cave and W were fellow alumni of St John's College, Cambridge, the library of which contains a copy of *Apostolici*.

It is worth noting that C's copy of Cave's *Scriptorum ecclesiasticorum historia literaria* (2 vols., Oxford, 1740) was at Rydal Mount (Shaver 322); its present whereabouts is unknown. C must have left it at Allan Bank in 1810, and it remained in W's possession thereafter. Whalley dates C's marginalia to 1801 (CC *Marginalia* ii 11-13)

86. Centlivre, Susanna, 'the Volume'
Suggested date of reading: by 3 April 1808
References: *MY* i 209 and n1
Writing from Grasmere, W told Beaumont on 8 April 1808: 'I left the Volume of Mrs Centlivre at Grosvenor square' (*MY* i 209). Apparently Beaumont had lent him one of her books; he returned it to Beaumont's London residence before departing for DC on 3 April (Reed ii 381). Her *Works* were published in three vols. in 1760-1.

87. Cervantes Saavedra, Miguel de
(i) *Don Quixote*
Suggested date of reading: probably between 23 Sept. and 1 Nov. 1800
References: *Grasmere Journals* 30
DW's journal records: 'We met as we walked to Rydale a Boy from Lloyds, coming for Don Quixote' (1 Nov. 1800). The wording is ambiguous, but the likely interpretation is that Charles Lloyd wished to borrow the Wordsworths' copy of *Don Quixote* (which had been in their father's library at Cockermouth until 1783; see Wu *Library* JW 33). The Lloyds were

---

[1] It was previously believed that W's source was St Basil's *Letters* (see Moorman ii 132-3).

in need of reading matter as they were still in temporary accommodation in Ambleside, separated from their belongings. Cervantes' novel features prominently in the Arab dream of *Thirteen-Book Prelude* Book V.

(ii) *The History of the Valorous and Witty Knight Errant Don Quixote of the Mancha*, tr. Thomas Shelton (4 vols., 1740)
Suggested date of reading: *c.* mid-May 1813 onwards
References: *MY* ii 98; Shaver 50
On *c.* 19 Jan. 1813, W wrote to Basil Montagu, whose son, Algernon, then living with the Wordsworths in the Rectory at Grasmere, was

> in possession of a translation of Don Quixote which professes in the Title Page to be printed Verbatim from the Translation of 1616. I wish you would request him to turn this over to me in exchange for one more recent - which I would procure for him. The Old Trans. would be prized by me and one more recently executed would at Algernon's time of life be full as eligible for him. (*MY* ii 75)

W wrote to Basil Montagu on 30 May to acknowledge receipt of the copy of Shelton's translation, and copy out its title-page (*MY* ii 97-8). As W moved into Rydal Mount on 12 May, this volume was one of his earliest acquisitions there.

88. Cevallos, Don Pedro, *Exposition of the Arts and Machinations which led to the Usurpation of the Crown of Spain*, **tr. J. J. Stockdale (1808)**
Suggested date of reading: between 1 and 5 April 1809
References: *MY* i 316
'I have read Cevallos', DW told De Quincey on 5 April 1809. De Quincey had sent a copy of Cevallos' *Exposition* from London to Grasmere on 29 March; it arrived on 1 April (Jordan 121-2; *MY* i 316).

89. Chalkhill, John, works
Suggested date of reading: by 17 Sept. 1814
References: *MY* ii 153
In his letter to Robert Anderson of 17 Sept. 1814, W suggests that an enlarged edn of Anderson's *British Poets* should include Chalkhill. He would by then have known Chalkhill's 'Oh the gallant fisher's wife' which appeared in Walton's *Complete Angler*. Southey's library contained *Chatterton's Revenge* (1795), among other titles (Southey *SC* 565).

90. Chalmers, Alexander, *The Works of the English Poets from Chaucer to Cowper* **(21 vols., 1810)**
Suggested date of reading: between 1810 and 17 Sept. 1814
References: *MY* ii 152

The fact that C was referring to the *Odes* of Charles Cotton in 1809-10 suggests that he had access to Chalmers' *Works of the English Poets*; if so, W may also have seen the work at that time. In his letter to Robert Anderson of 17 Sept. 1814, W remarks: 'Chalmers' Edition, which would probably never have existed without the Example of yours, is also very incomplete' (*MY* ii 152). The letter is based on a close knowledge of the contents not just of Anderson but also of Chalmers. W did not own Chalmers' *Works of the English Poets*, but he had studied one by 17 Sept. 1814. As Southey was partly responsible for the letter to Anderson, he is a likely source: he reviewed Chalmers in the *Quarterly Review* for Oct. 1814. C annotated another set during the 1820s (CC *Marginalia* ii 14; Whalley *BC* 23). Chalmers reprinted Johnson's *Lives of the Poets*, and himself wrote additional *Lives* for the collection.

91. Chamberlayne, William, works
Suggested date of reading: by 17 Sept. 1814
References: *MY* ii 154
In his letter to Robert Anderson of 17 Sept. 1814, W suggests that an enlarged edn of Anderson's *British Poets* should include 'Chamberlain'. This indicates that he was aware of his works by 17 Sept. 1814. Southey's library contained Chamberlayne's *Pharonnida, a Heroick Poem* (1659) (Southey *SC* 569-70).

92. Chapman, George, works
Suggested date of reading: by 17 Sept. 1814
References: *MY* ii 153
In his letter to Robert Anderson of 17 Sept. 1814, W suggests that an enlarged edn of Anderson's *British Poets* should include Chapman. W acquired a copy of Chapman's *Homer* in April or May 1808 (see note 217[iii], below).

93. Chatterton, Thomas
(i) ***The Excellent Ballade of Charitie*** **(Anderson)**
Suggested date of reading: by 3 May 1802
References: Cornell *Poems 1800-7* 408
As Curtis notes, W's *Resolution and Independence* 'imitates the meter of Thomas Chatterton's (1752-1770) *Excellent Ballade of Charitie*' (Cornell *Poems 1800-7* 408). W had probably read it many years before, as a schoolboy at Hawkshead (*WR* 27), but a rereading in 1802 seems likely in view of the fact that Chatterton's works were readily available to W in Anderson, *British Poets* vol. 11. Anderson places Chatterton next to Michael Bruce, whose work DW was reading on 8 Dec. 1801 (see note 63).

(ii) ***Works***, **ed. Robert Southey and Joseph Cottle (3 vols., 1803)**
Suggested date of reading: 1803 onwards
References: *Prose Works* ii 100

W subscribed to this edn, and would have owned a copy, even though it is not listed by Shaver. He may have referred to Gregory's life of Chatterton, which Southey and Cottle reprinted, as he composed the *Essay, Supplementary to the Preface* (*Prose Works* ii 78, 100).

94. Chaucer, Geoffrey (Anderson)
(i)
Suggested date of reading: 15 Nov., 6 Dec., 24 Dec. 1801
References: *Grasmere Journals* 38

'We sate by the fire and read Chaucer' (DW's journal, 15 Nov. 1801); this may have been a reading of *Troilus and Criseyde*, prior to W's translation (see next note). The Wordsworths spent much of Nov. and Dec. discovering this author; see, however, *WR* 27-8.

Although they probably read Chaucer from Anderson, *British Poets* vol. 1, it should be borne in mind that from autumn 1802 they also had at their disposal the texts in Bell's *Poets of Great Britain*, a copy of which was owned by MH from 1801 (see note 38). And from mid-Feb. 1806 W was to own a third: the copy of Urry's edn purchased on his behalf by Lamb (see note xi, below). There is a possibility that DW refers to a fourth copy of Chaucer in her journal entry of 5 Feb. 1802: 'The Chaucer not only misbound but a leaf or two wanting. I wrote about it to Mary & wrote to Soulby' (*Grasmere Journals* 62). Anthony Soulby had bound books for the Wordsworths in earlier years (*WR* 47). The question is whether DW refers here to a copy of Chaucer's *Works* or to a MS containing W's translations from Chaucer. Graver suggests the latter, adding that DW may even be referring specifically to DC MS 13: 'one of the leaves containing *Prioress* material is missing' (letter to me).

(ii) *Troilus and Criseyde* (Anderson)
Suggested date of reading: c. Dec. 1801
References: Reed ii 132

W translated *Troilus* c. Dec. 1801; see *PW* iv 228-33.

(iii) *The Manciple's Tale* (Anderson)
Suggested date of reading: 2-3 Dec. 1801
References: *Grasmere Journals* 44; Reed ii 132

'Wm rose late. I read the tale of Phœbus & the Crow which he afterwards attempted to translate & did translate a large part of it today' (DW's journal, 2 Dec. 1801). Graver observes to me that Anderson's *British Poets* reprinted Thomas Tyrwhitt's text of *The Canterbury Tales*, with Tyrwhitt's glossary and notes, on which W's translations depended.

(iv) *The Prioress' Tale* (Anderson)
Suggested date of reading: 4-5 Dec. 1801
References: *Grasmere Journals* 45; Reed ii 134

'William translating the Prioress's tale' (DW's journal, 4 Dec. 1801). DW records that he finished the translation on 5 Dec.

(v) *General Prologue* (Anderson)
Suggested date of reading: 22 Dec. 1801
References: Grasmere Journals 52
'I read to them the Tale of Custance & the Syrian Monarch, also some of the Prologues' (DW's journal, 22 Dec. 1801).

(vi) *The Man of Law's Tale* (Anderson)
Suggested date of reading: 22 Dec. 1801
References: Grasmere Journals 52
See preceding note. As late as Oct. 1840 W referred to this work as the 'Tale of Constance' (*LY* iv 130).

(vii) *The Miller's Tale* (Anderson)
Suggested date of reading: 26 Dec. 1801
References: Grasmere Journals 53
'I read aloud - The Miller's Tale' (DW's journal, 26 Dec. 1801).

(viii) (Anderson)
Suggested date of reading: 30 Oct. 1802
References: Grasmere Journals 133
'I went to bed, & after tea S[toddart] read in Chaucer to us' (DW's journal, 30 Oct. 1802).

(ix) *General Prologue*
Suggested date of reading: 11 Jan. 1803
References: Grasmere Journals 137
'Mary read the Prologue to Chaucer's tales to me' (DW's journal, 11 Jan. 1803). The *General Prologue* was by this time a favourite of DW's. She appears to have quoted it from memory on 20 Aug., when at Lead Hills (DC MS 55, 12r; *DWJ* i 211). As MW was reading, it is possible that she was using the text in Bell's *Poets*, which belonged to her.

(x) *The Knight's Tale*
Suggested date of reading: 11 Jan. 1803
References: Grasmere Journals 137
'... read part of The Knights Tale with exquisite delight' (DW's journal, 11 Jan. 1803).
 In an autograph album described by T.W., 'A Lesson for Laureates', *N&Q* 2nd Ser. 2 (1856) 487, W is reported to have written:

> The God of Love, ah benedicité,
> How naughty and how great a Lord is he!
> This is my favourite autograph for ladies.

The entry was signed 'William Wordsworth, Rydal Mount, 26 April 1826'. The quotation is from *The Knight's Tale* 1785-6.

(xi) ***The Works of Geoffrey Chaucer, Compared with Former Eds. and MSS. by J. Urry together with a glossary* [1721]**
Suggested date of reading: mid-Feb. 1806 onwards
References: Marrs ii 204-6
On 1 Feb. 1806, Lamb wrote to W to say that he had purchased copies of Urry's Chaucer, Pope's Shakespeare, Spenser and Milton on his behalf, and sent them up on the Kendal wagon that very day. The copy of Urry's edn of Chaucer cost £1.16s.; W would have received Lamb's consignment by mid-Feb. (Reed ii 314).

95. Chiabrera, Gabriello, *Delle Opere di Gabriello Chiabrera* **(3 vols., Venice, 1782)**
Suggested date of reading: Oct.-Nov. 1809
References: see note
W translated ten epitaphs from Chiabrera's *Opere* (see Cornell *Poems 1807-20* 503-9), probably at around the same time that C first became interested in the Italian poet, between 26 Oct. and 4 Nov. 1809. As their interest was shared, it is reasonable to suppose that W and C used the same Italian text - almost certainly C's lost copy of the *Opere* (1782); see CC *Marginalia* ii 23, and George Whalley, 'Note 315. Coleridge Marginalia Lost', *The Book Collector* 18 (1969) 223.[1] W's translations appear to have provided the immediate inspiration for the *Essays Upon Epitaphs* (CC *Friend* ii 335; *Prose Works* ii 49, 100, 111).

96. children's books
(i)
Suggested date of reading: 1803 onwards
References: see note
In her journal of the Scottish tour, 1803, DW recorded, on 18 Aug.: 'Went to the Church-yard where Burns is buried - a Bookseller accompanied us, of whom I had bought some little books for Johnny' (DC MS 55, 5v). John Wordsworth was born 18 June 1803.

(ii)
Suggested date of reading: mid-1800s onwards
References: *MY* i 45
DW's letter to Lady Beaumont of 24 June 1806 makes clear that Johnny Wordsworth had recently been sent a 'beautiful library' by the Beaumonts (*MY* i 45). Young Dora had received a 'little almanack'.

97. Churchill, Charles
(i) ***Independence*** **(Anderson)**

---

[1] W's distinctive rendering of the name 'Balbi' indicates his use of the incorrect text of 1782; this was first noted by W. J. B. Owen, 'Manuscript Variants of Wordsworth's Poems', *N&Q* 203 (1958) 308-10. See also Cornell *Poems 1807-20* 505.

Suggested date of reading: March-April 1802; certainly by 7 May 1802
References: *PW* i 358
De Selincourt notes 'an unconscious borrowing' in *The Sparrow's Nest*, composed around March-April 1802, and certainly by 7 May, of Churchill's *Independence*. This is supported by the next note, which indicates which the Wordsworths were reading Churchill in Anderson, *British Poets* vol. 10, during the spring and summer of 1802.

(ii) *Rosciad* **(Anderson)**
Suggested date of reading: 19 June 1802
References: *Grasmere Journals* 112
'I read Churchills Rosciad' (DW's journal, 19 June 1802). W was presumably acquainted with Churchill's famous first poem by this time.

98. Churchyard, Thomas, works
Suggested date of reading: by 17 Sept. 1814
References: *MY* ii 153
In his letter to Robert Anderson of 17 Sept. 1814, W suggests that an enlarged edn of Anderson's *British Poets* should include Churchyard. This indicates that he was aware of his works by 17 Sept. 1814. Churchyard's *The Legend of Shore's Wife* had appeared in Percy's *Reliques*.

99. Cibber, Colley, *An Apology for the Life of Mr. Colley Cibber, Comedian, and late patentee of the Theatre-Royal* (2nd edn, 1740)
Suggested date of reading: by 7 Nov. 1805
References: *EY* 642; Shaver 54
In his letter of 7 Nov. 1805, W suggests that Scott, in his edn of Dryden's works, might illustrate some of the prologues of Dryden's plays with quotations from 'Cibber's Apology'. By this date, he must have seen C's copy of that work, later retained at Rydal Mount, and now at the Wordsworth Library (Shaver 54; Coffman C95). Its title-page contains the inked inscription 'S.T.C. to S.H.' A later hand has added: 'who lent this Book to her nephew Wm W J^r. on the last day he saw her 1835'. It contains some marginalia not apparently by C. W had probably seen Cibber's adaptations of Shakespeare performed on stage, as they remained the standard acting versions until 1821.

100. Cicero, Marcus Tullius
(i) *De Divinatione*
Suggested date of reading: between 21 May 1802 and 7 Oct. 1803
References: *Prose Works* ii 101-2; Cornell *Poems 1800-7* 583-4

W knew the story about Simonides finding the corpse of a stranger and burying it, Owen suggests, from either Cicero, *De Divinatione* or Valerius Maximus. The story is recapitulated in the first of the *Essays Upon Epitaphs* (*Prose Works* ii 52; *CC Friend* ii 338).

By this time W's knowledge of Cicero was pretty thorough; he had no doubt memorized large chunks of the works during his Hawkshead years (see *WR* 28-9). Worthington comments helpfully on the possible influence of *De Natura Deorum* on the Stoicism of *The Excursion* (Worthington 52-3); elsewhere, Graver writes on the important influence of Cicero's *De Oratore* on W's portrayal of the Wanderer.[1]

(ii) *In Catilinam*
Suggested date of reading: by 22 Feb. 1810
References: *Prose Works* ii 80, 113
In the third of the *Essays Upon Epitaphs*, W refers to 'Cicero, when holding up Catiline to detestation' (*Prose Works* ii 80). W would have read *In Catilinam* at school.

(iii) *Tusculan Disputations*
Suggested date of reading: by March 1814
References: *PW* v 470
Excursion viii 220ff. was inspired by Cicero's *Tusculan Disputations* (*PW* v 470), which W had presumably known since his Hawkshead schooldays. See also Worthington 27n2.

101. Clanvowe, John, *Of the Cuckowe and the Nightingale* (Anderson)
Suggested date of reading: 7-9 Dec. 1801
References: *Grasmere Journals* 46-7; Reed ii 134-5
W seems to have translated this poem (referred to now as *The Boke of Cupid*) on 7 and 8 Dec. 1801, and made a fair copy on 9 Dec. It appeared in printed editions of Chaucer's complete works from Thynne onwards - until, in the 1890s, Skeat proved it to be by Clanvowe. W's source was almost certainly Anderson, *British Poets* i 498-501, where it appears with Chaucer's works. Reed suggests that the poem inspired the popinjays (parrots) and allegory in *Thirteen-Book Prelude* iii 442-59 (Cornell *13-Book Prelude* 145n).

102. Clarke, James
(i) *A Survey of the Lakes of Cumberland, Westmorland, and Lancashire: together with an Account, Historical, Topographical, and Descriptive, of the Adjacent Country* (2nd edn, 1789)
Suggested date of reading: c. 1804-5
References: OET *Prel.* 552

---

[1] 'The Oratorical Pedlar', *Rhetorical Traditions and British Romantic Literature*, ed. Don Bialostosky and Lawrence Needham (Bloomington, 1995), pp. 94-107.

De Selincourt records that Clarke was probably W's source for the belief that Sidney stayed at Brougham Castle while composing the *Arcadia*.

I must here correct my suggestion at *WR* 29 that W acquired his copy of Clarke in 1789, now preserved at the Wordsworth Library. It is clear from an inscription on the front flyleaf that it was given to him in 1843.

(ii) *A Survey of the Lakes of Cumberland, Westmorland, and Lancashire: together with an Account, Historical, Topographical, and Descriptive, of the Adjacent Country* **(2nd edn, 1789)**
Suggested date of reading: between Sept. 1811 and Nov. 1812
References: *Prose Works* ii 444; Shaver 56
Clarke's *Survey* was a source for W's *Unpublished Tour*, composed between Sept. 1811 and Nov. 1812.

103. Clarkson, Thomas
(i) *Essay on the Impolicy of the African Slave-Trade* **(1788)**
Suggested date of reading: 1800s; probably *c.* 1800
References: Shaver 57
A copy of this title and Clarkson's *Essay on the Slavery and Commerce of the Human Species* (1786) were retained at Rydal Mount. In the absence of other evidence it is reasonable to suppose that the author presented them to W during the 1800s, perhaps as early as Sept. 1800, when the Clarksons first visited DC (Reed ii 85), and probably not later than 1808. According to Wordsworth *SC* 20, the latter volume contained 'autographs of Wordsworth and Coleridge': it must therefore have entered W's possession before their falling-out in 1810.

C borrowed a copy from the Bristol Library Society, 15-25 June 1795 (Whalley no. 61); see also CC *Lectures 1795* 232, 237-9.

(ii) *Essay on the Slavery and Commerce of the Human Species, particularly the African* **(1786)**
Suggested date of reading: 1800s; probably *c.* 1800
References: Shaver 57
See preceding note.

(iii) *A Portraiture of Quakerism, as taken from a view of the moral education, discipline, peculiar customs, religious principles, political and civil oeconomy, and character, of the Society of Friends* **(3 vols., 1806)**
Suggested date of reading: between *c.* 20 June and 23 July 1806 (vols. 2 and 3 only)
References: *MY* i 62
Vols. 2 and 3 of the set, bearing a presentation inscription by the author, arrived at DC *c.* 20 June 1806. W apparently received vol. 1 in London, 29 March-20 May, possibly from the author himself, but left it with Basil Montagu when he left. Not the most reliable of chums,

Montagu apparently mislaid it, because DW was still asking Catherine Clarkson for a copy when she wrote on 5 Feb. and 5 June 1808 (*MY* i 193, 253). The set must eventually have been completed, as Dora Wordsworth's catalogue of the Rydal Mount library lists '3 Vol:' (Shaver 57).

Though he initially had only two volumes, W wasted little time in reading them, and on 23 July 1806 DW reported that 'Wm has read most of Mr. Clarkson's book and has been much pleased, but he complains of the latter volume being exceedingly disfigured by perpetual use of the word *tract*' (*MY* i 62). The Wordsworths evidently knew about this book as it was being composed, and may have seen or heard parts in MS in earlier years; DW refers to it as early as 17 July 1803 (*EY* 397).

(iv) *The History of the Rise, Progress, and Accomplishment of the Abolition of the African Slave-Trade* in MS
Suggested date of reading: between 24 and 29 Aug. 1807
References: *MY* i 160

Thomas Clarkson spent the night of 24 Aug. 1807 at DC. He brought his *History* in MS, and left it with the Wordsworths when he left the next day. On 30 Aug. DW reported to Catherine Clarkson that 'We had read his book, indeed it is so interesting that having once begun there was no leaving off. I never read anything more interesting in my whole life than the narration part. . . . William I believe made a few remarks upon paper, but he had not time for much criticism, and in fact having only one perusal of the work he was too much interested' (*MY* i 160-1). As W had left on 29 Aug. for Eusemere, he must have read the MS between 24 and 29 Aug. C read vol. 1 in proof in early Feb. 1808 (Griggs iii 71): I wonder whether W saw these proofs when he joined C in London later that month.

(v) *The History of the Rise, Progress, and Accomplishment of the Abolition of the African Slave-Trade* (2 vols., 1808)
Suggested date of reading: July or Aug. 1808 onwards
References: see note

The *History* was published on 30 May 1808. W and Southey were given copies; as Southey had received his by 3 Aug., W can be presumed to have received his at about the same time (Curry i 479). W's views on the *History* remained consistent; for a summary see his letter to Robinson of June 1840 (*LY* iv 84-5).

C read the *History* in proof during early Feb. 1808 (Griggs iii 71), and a review by him was published, in mutilated form, in the *Edinburgh Review* for July 1808 (pub. 1 Aug.). He owned two copies: one has now disappeared, the other is at the Beineke Rare Book and Manuscript Library, Yale. The flyleaf of vol. 1 bears the inscription 'Mrs Cookson from S. T. Coleridge', and a copy of W's *Sonnet to Thomas Clarkson* in MW's hand, dated Dec. 1844 (its variants are noted by Curtis, Cornell *Poems 1800-7* 246-7, 506-7). A note on the opposite page (verso of free front endpaper) reads: 'The annexed sonnet by Wordsworth was copied at my request by Mrs Wordsworth. The signature is the poets. E. Cookson'. This suggests that C gave his copy to Mrs Elizabeth Cookson, the Kendal friend of the Wordsworths,[1] probably between July 1808 and Aug. 1810, when the falling-out with W would have curtailed further contact. Prior to 1810 there was some reason for his seeing a good deal of them: besides the fact that they were particular friends of SH, he used their Kendal address as a delivery point for the paper on which he printed *The Friend* (Griggs iii 201, 207, 228n1, 243, 244, 262). Perhaps it was out of gratitude that he gave this copy of the *History* to Mrs Cookson.

It is worth noting Clarkson's comment to Henry Taylor of 31 May 1808: 'The Work came out in London yesterday. There will not be one Copy to be had in the Kingdom in two months Time, and Paper being now 40 per cent advanced, there can never be, while this price lasts, another Edition' (Wordsworth Library/WL MS A/Clarkson, T.). Southey reviewed it, *Annual Review* 7 (1808) 127-48.

(vi) *Memoirs of the Private and Public Life of William Penn* (2 vols., 1813)
Suggested date of reading: early Oct. 1813 onwards
References: *MY* ii 116, 124

DW had not received a copy of Clarkson's *Life of Penn* when she wrote to his wife in Sept. 1813 (*MY* ii 116); it had, however, arrived by 4 Oct.,[2] when she wrote: 'I was resolved not to write until I had read your Husband's Book, of which literally I have not even now read ten pages, from want of time to read anything' (*MY* ii 124). W was apparently rereading it in March 1821 (*LY* i 47-8).

104. Claudianus, Claudius, works
Suggested date of reading: by Sept. 1800
References: *Prose Works* i 122

W's earliest reference to Claudian is to be found in his Preface to *Lyrical Ballads* (1800), composed by Sept. 1800. It is likely that, like Southey and C, he first read Claudian at school (see *WR* 166). A copy of Claudian's poetry was at Rydal Mount (Shaver 58).

105. Cleveland, John, works
Suggested date of reading: by 17 Sept. 1814
References: *MY* ii 154

In his letter to Robert Anderson of 17 Sept. 1814, W suggests that an enlarged edn of Anderson's *British Poets* should include Cleveland. This indicates that he was aware of his works by 17 Sept. 1814.

106. Clifford, Lady Anne, Countess of Pembroke, 'Memoirs', possibly in MS
Suggested date of reading: by April 1807

---

[1] For more on the Cooksons, who should not be confused with W's maternal forebears, see *MY* i 29n1 and *Notebooks* i 2903n.

[2] Southey had read his copy by July 1813 (Curry ii 61).

References: Cornell *Poems 1800-7* 425
W's extensive note to *Song, at the Feast of Brougham Castle*, composed between 30 Oct. 1806 and early April 1807, quotes from Lady Anne Clifford's memoirs; his quotation concerns the killing of the young Earl of Rutland, son of the Duke of York, by John Lord Clifford, at the Battle of Wakefield. Anne Clifford attempted to justify her ancestor: 'for the Earl was no child, as some writers would have him, but able to bear arms, being sixteen or seventeen years of age, as is evident from this' (Cornell *Poems 1800-7* 425). Where could W have seen this statement? Clifford's diaries were first edited and published by Vita Sackville-West in 1923, and more recently by D. J. H. Clifford in 1990. They were quoted from, several times, by Thomas Dunham Whitaker in his *History and Antiquities of the Deanery of Craven* (1805), which W appears to have seen in Sept. 1807, and acquired the following month (see note 423[i]). However, the statement quoted by W does *not* appear in Whitaker.[1] A clue may reside in the fact that Whitaker quotes Clifford's diaries from what he calls the 'Appleby MS.' The Lowther family, who lived at Appleby Castle, were among the subscribers to Whitaker's *History*, and it was at Appleby that they retained the diaries prior to their being given to the Kendal Record Office, where they are now. If so, it is possible that W saw the MSS on a visit there; the only problem with this is that the earliest recorded visit by W to Appleby dates from Aug. 1807 (Reed ii 361).

107. Cobbett, William
(i) *Weekly Political Register*
Suggested date of reading: 20-25 Dec. 1803
References: *Notebooks* i 1752
Although Cobbett's *Weekly Political Register* began publishing in 1802, John Spedding (W's contemporary at Hawkshead Grammar School) started subscribing only with vol. 3 no. 13 (2 April 1803). His collection concludes with vol. 19 no. 52 (29 June 1811), and remains at the Spedding family home, Mirehouse, near Keswick. It was bound some time after 1811, and was thus probably unbound on the occasions when W saw it.

The Wordsworths saw the Speddings regularly from the time they moved into DC, and W would have known when Spedding began taking the *Register*. An early reading of the *Register* is suggested by C's entry, *Notebooks* i 1752, attacking Cobbett - specifically remarks made in the *Register* for 2 April 1803, 23 July 1803 and 17 Dec. 1803. Two factors implicate W in this reading: (i) the notebook entry in question was made 20-25 Dec. 1803, when C was at DC; (ii) the earliest of the *Register* comments to which C responds was published on 2 April 1803 - the earliest owned by Spedding. The likely explanation is that copies of the *Register* were at DC on 20-25 Dec. 1803, either W or C having borrowed them. The proximity of Greta Hall to Mirehouse would have made it a simple matter for C to pick up

---

[1] It ought to appear on p. 224, where Whitaker deals with John Lord Clifford and his 'supposed slaughter of the young earl of Rutland'.

copies of the *Register* before visiting Grasmere.¹ He requested that copies be sent to him in Gibraltar in April 1804 (Griggs ii 1135).

(ii) Weekly Political Register
Suggested date of reading: by early June 1809
References: *Supp*. 18
In early June 1809, W wrote to John Spedding to

> return you your Collection of Cobbets, which have been of great use to me. I have to entreat your pardon for having both soiled them and having otherwise disfigured them which it was impossible for me to prevent; as in order to make use of them I was compelled to have them perpetually before me in a room black with smoke and ashes, and to mark in the margin such passages as I meant to use.² (*Supp*. 18-19)

W would have found Cobbett's *Register* useful as he composed *The Convention of Cintra*, and C consulted it while working on *The Friend* - references in letters of Dec. 1808 show that he was comparing it with his own work (Griggs iii 141-2, 143, 144, 276). As is consistent with W's remarks, a number of Spedding's copies (still at Mirehouse) are indeed stained by soot or candle wax.

Owen and Smyser suggest that W also read *Cobbett's Parliamentary Debates*, subsequently taken over by Hansard, as he composed the *Convention* (*Prose Works* i 398, 410). At any rate, it seems likely that W saw both Cobbett's publications at this period, as is suggested by De Quincey's reference to the *Weekly Political Register* in a letter to DW of 28 March 1809 (Jordan 123 and n3).

C's reference to Cobbett in a notebook entry of May 1810 (*Notebooks* iii 3836 and n) indicates that he was reading the *Register* frequently at that time, if not on a weekly basis. In all likelihood he was still borrowing Spedding's copies.

108. Coleridge, Samuel Taylor
(i) notebooks in MS
Suggested date of reading: 20-23 July 1800
References: *Notebooks* i 761
'Poor fellow at a distance idle? in this haytime when wages are so high? Come near - thin, pale, can scarce speak - or throw out his fishing rod' (*Notebooks* i 761). This brief note records the incident on which W based his poem, the fourth of the *Poems on the Naming of Places*, 'A narrow girdle of rough stones and crags'; significantly, it predates W's poem

---

[1] C knew Spedding by 1803; his wife and DW had visited Mirehouse on 21 Nov. 1800 (*Grasmere Journals* 33).

[2] The smoking chimneys of Allan Bank were a serious problem from the time the Wordsworths moved in; according to Southey, it drove them to despair (Reed ii 399n51). From Aug. to Dec. 1809 builders worked on the house to alleviate the problem - successfully, as it turned out (see *MY* i 387).

(probably written in early Oct.). Given the early draft of the Preface in which W says that C 'has also furnished me with a few of those Poems in the second volume, which are classed under the title of "Poems on the Naming of Places"' (Cornell *Lyrical Ballads* 741), several things may be inferred: (i) that W's poem was originally to have been composed by C - hence the presence of the jotting in his notebook; (ii) that by early Oct. C was unable to write it; (iii) that W read, or at least knew of, C's notebook entry recording the incident. For a more extended discussion of this episode see my 'Wordsworth's Fisher King', *CLB* (forthcoming).

(ii) 'a part of Christabel'
Suggested date of reading: 1 Sept. 1800
References: Grasmere Journals 19
In the early hours of the morning, shortly before they retired at 3.30 am, 'Coleridge read us a part of Christabel' (DW's journal, 31 Aug. 1800). This was the first of a series of readings from a poem that, until 6 Oct., W and C were proposing to publish in *Lyrical Ballads* (1800). I have noted only those readings of *Christabel* specifically mentioned by DW, but others certainly took place at this time.

(iii) *Christabel* Part II in MS
Suggested date of reading: 4-5 Oct., 22 Oct. 1800
References: Grasmere Journals 24; Reed ii 92
'Exceedingly delighted with the 2nd part of Christabel', DW recorded in her journal on 4 Oct. 1800; 'we had increasing pleasure' the following day, when it was read a second time. It had only just been completed. The entire work was read to the Wordsworths after supper on 22 Oct. 1800 at DC (*Grasmere Journals* 29; Reed ii 96).

(iv) *Inscription on a jutting Stone, over a Spring*
Suggested date of reading: probably spring-summer 1802
References: Woof (1966); Whalley (1955) 11; *PW* v 251, 465
This poem went under the above title when first published in the *Morning Post*, 24 Sept. 1802, but was changed to *Inscription for a Fountain on a Heath* when reprinted in *Sibylline Leaves*. It deserves mention here because its opening lines are echoed at *Excursion* vii 616-17, and the borrowing acknowledged in a note. Reed dates composition of the relevant lines of the *Excursion* to between 3 Jan. 1813 and *c.* late May 1814 (Reed ii 24). However, W must have seen the *Inscription* shortly after composition. Whalley (1955) 11 suggested that it was written '(?) Sept 1801', but Woof (1966) has argued persuasively that the earliest MS in which it appears, Sara Hutchinson's Poets, dates from spring-summer 1802.

(v) *Ode to the Rain* in MS
Suggested date of reading: by 25 March 1804
References: Reed ii 706; Woof PhD 237
C's *Ode to the Rain* is entered in the Wordsworth Commonplace Book (DC MS 26, 31r-32v) and dated, by DW, 'Thurday Night October 1st or rather on the Morning of Friday October

2nd 1801'. Reed dates the copy to early 1804, by 25 March. Woof PhD 237 concurs with this general conclusion: 'Coleridge's "Ode to Rain" is presumably entered long after its composition. It is a neat copy of Coleridge's own first draft of the poem, which is also preserved at Dove Cottage library. It is quite uninfluenced by the newspaper version of October 7, 1802.' For a text of C's original MS draft see Woof PhD 568-70.

(vi) *A Letter to Sara Hutchinson* **in MS**
Suggested date of reading: 21 April 1802
References: Grasmere Journals 89
'Coleridge came to us & repeated the verses he wrote to Sara' (DW's journal, 21 April 1802). This was the beginning of the poetic dialogue that continued with *Resolution and Independence*, *Dejection: An Ode*, and W's *Ode*. For the MS text which the Wordsworths would have heard, see *Coleridge's Dejection*, ed. Stephen Maxfield Parrish (Ithaca, NY, 1988).

(vii) *The Language of Birds* **and** *The Day Dream* **in MS**
Suggested date of reading: 6 May 1802 and shortly thereafter
References: Grasmere Journals 97
'When we came in we found a Magazine & Review & a letter from Coleridge with verses to Hartley & Sara H. We read the Review &c.' (DW's journal, 6 May 1802). Pamela Woof suggests that the verses were the ten-line poem, 'Do you ask what the birds say?', published *Morning Post* 16 Oct. 1802, as *The Language of Birds*, and the verses beginning, 'If thou wert here, these tears were tears of light!', published *Morning Post* 19 Oct. 1802, as *The Day Dream, From an Emigrant to his Absent Wife*. Parrish has edited a MS version of *The Day Dream*, closer to what the Wordsworths would have read on 6 May 1802 than to that published four months later; see *Coleridge's Dejection*, ed. Stephen Maxfield Parrish (Ithaca, NY, 1988), pp. 65-9. *The Language of Birds* appears in Sara Hutchinson's Poets, which W would certainly have known; see Whalley (1955) 7-8. Woof (1966) 230 has shown that the poem was not composed in spring 1801, as Whalley suggests, but close to 6 May 1802.

(viii) *In the Manner of Spenser*
Suggested date of reading: by 28 May 1803
References: Marrs ii 114
'I have ordered "Imitation of Spencer" to be restored on Wordsworth's authority', Lamb told C on 28 May 1803 (Marrs ii 114). *In the Manner of Spenser* had first appeared as *Effusion XXIV* in C's *Poems on Various Subjects* (1796); W's copy of that volume was broken up and used for the drafting of *Home at Grasmere*, *Michael*, and *The Prelude* during the early 1800s (see Cornell *Home at Grasmere* 139-40; Cornell *Lyrical Ballads* xxiv-vi). It now constitutes DC MSS 28 and 30. Lamb was editing C's *Poems* (1803) prior to publication; *In the Manner of Spencer* appears at pp. 111-14.

(ix) notebooks in MS
Suggested date of reading: c. 5-8 Jan. 1804
References: *Notebooks* i 1813
W's *The Kitten and the Falling Leaves*, composed between early Oct. 1804 and early 1805, is based on an incident which, as he later recalled, was 'Seen at Town-End, Grasmere' (Cornell *Poems 1800-7* 406). It is also related to a draft in C's notebook which provides the poem's germ (see *Notebooks* i 1813 and n). Coburn dates the draft to 5-8 Jan. 1804, when C was at DC; it is likely that W saw this draft and, months later, developed it into his poem.

(x) *Prospectus of The Friend*
Suggested date of reading: Nov. 1808
References: see note
Barbara Rooke records that the *Prospectus* had gone to press by the first week of Nov. 1808 (CC *Friend* i xxxviii). W must have read it soon after. He had certainly seen it by 26 Nov., when he told Robert Grahame that he should by then have received a copy (*MY* i 275).

(xi) *Christabel* in MS
Suggested date of reading: 29 or 30 April 1809
References: *MY* i 326
During his stay at Allan Bank on 29-30 April, John Wilson heard W read *Christabel* and the *White Doe*, 'with both of which he was much delighted' (*MY* i 326). Neither poem was yet in print.

(xii) *The Friend* in MS and print
Suggested date of reading: June 1809-March 1810
References: see note
On 2 Oct. 1844 W told Sara Coleridge: 'The whole of the Friend was written in that place [Allan Bank] by Sarah Hutchinson from your Father's dictation; it went from her pen to the Printer no transcript being taken' (*LY* iv 612). *The Friend* was published from early June 1809 to mid-March 1810, during which time W probably either saw or heard much of it as it was composed. A copy was retained at Rydal Mount (Shaver 61).

(xiii) notebooks in MS
Suggested date of reading: early Nov. 1809; by 17 Nov.
References: *Prose Works* ii 391
W quotes *Notebooks* i 1812, 'from the memorandum-book of a friend' (*Prose Works* ii 177), in his introduction to *Select Views*, composed in early Nov. 1809, and certainly by 17 Nov. Owen and Smyser reason as follows:

> Coleridge was living with the Wordsworths in November 1809, just when Wordsworth was composing the Introduction to *Select Views* (see *MY* i 372). Having witnessed this particular winter together, it would seem perfectly natural for either one to remind the

other of it, and for Coleridge to turn back to his notebook and offer Wordsworth the record he had made while the memory of it was still fresh. (*Prose Works* ii 391)

(xiv) *Letters on the Spaniards* in *The Courier*, Dec. 1809-Jan. 1810
Suggested date of reading: Dec. 1809-Jan. 1810
References: *MY* i 380
In her letter of 28 Dec. 1809 to Lady Beaumont, DW mentions C's 'series of essays in the Courier, on the Spanish affairs' (*MY* i 380); these were published in the *Courier* for 7, 8, 9, 15, 20, 21, and 22 Dec. 1809, and 20 Jan. 1810. W can be presumed to have read these, not least because they were written at Allan Bank. Writing from there, C mentions them in a letter to Stuart of 30 Sept. 1809 (Griggs iii 227).

(xv) three MSS on Logic
Suggested date of reading: late 1810-May 1811
References: see note
'Coleridge has desired me to open my letter to beg you to bring the Sanskrit MS. and his logical manuscripts', DW wrote De Quincey in late June 1809 (*MY* i 362). These MSS were probably the work referred to by C in a letter to his brother George in a letter of 9 Oct. 1809 as 'the History of Logic from Zeno to the French Pseudo-logicians, Condilliac &c, which are ready for the Press as soon as I can procure the Paper' (Griggs iii 238-9). Quite probably this was a version of the unpublished, and now lost, 'Organum verè Organum', about which C told Godwin in June 1803, and which he claimed would shortly 'go to the Press' (Griggs ii 947). It was part of the work C described to John May as the 'Logosophia' in Sept. 1815 (Griggs iv 589), related to the later *Logic*.[1]

The MSS would have been reunited with C by the time De Quincey moved into DC in late Oct. C was at that time resident at Allan Bank, so that the MSS were accessible to W from then. They remained there in late 1810 when C returned to London. In May 1811, Mrs Coleridge wrote to De Quincey on C's behalf, asking after them; on 29 May he told her: 'I had no other MSS. of his than the three logical ones which you mentioned (and which I had lent to Wordsworth some months before)' (Musgrove 9). They were returned to C probably in May 1811 (Reed ii 474).

(xvi) *To Mr. Justice Fletcher* in *The Courier*, 20 Sept.-10 Dec. 1814
Suggested date of reading: Sept.-Dec. 1814
References: MWL 25
In her letter to DW of 29 Oct. 1814, MW mentions: 'By the bye C. is writing under the guise of an "Irish Protestant" in the Courier - his letters are addressed to Mr. Justice Fletcher - on the subject of the Catholic Question - very clever letters. W says there have been 3, but we

---

[1] See S. T. Coleridge, *Logic*, ed. J. R. de J. Jackson (1981), p. xxxix ff. Musgrove suggests that one of these three MSS may have been the MS.A identified by Alice D. Snyder, *Coleridge on Logic and Learning* (New Haven, 1929), pp. xi-xii.

did not see the first' (*MWL* 25). This indicates that by 29 Oct. the Wordsworths had seen the letters published in the *Courier* on 29 Sept. and 21 Oct. It is likely that they looked out for the remainder; see CC *Essays* ii 373-417.

109. Columbus, Ferdinand, ***The History of the Life and Actions of Admiral Christopher Columbus* [1571] in Awnsham and John Churchill,** *A Collection of Voyages and Travels, with a General Preface giving an Account of the Progress of Navigation* **(4 vols., 1704), vol. 2, pp. 557-686**
Suggested date of reading: by late Feb. 1804
References: OET *Prel.* 626; Norton *Prel.* 496

W draws on Columbus in drafts towards the Five-Book *Prelude* made in MS W, late Feb. or early March 1804.[1] He apparently found the *Life* in A. and J. Churchill's *Collection*, which was apparently known to him from Hawkshead days (see *Prose Works* i 14), and retained at Rydal Mount (Shaver 54).

It is not known when W acquired the Rydal Mount copy, but there was evidently one close at hand during late 1803 and early 1804. Not only was he aware of its contents as he drafted the lines in MS W, but only a few months before C had been meditating on Columbus (*Notebooks* i 1677). Possibly the book was either a gift or loan from Beaumont. Beaumont's earliest gifts to W date from Aug. 1803 (Reed ii 220), and he is known to have had a good collection of travel books. Lady Beaumont told W that she was reading Columbus in March 1821.[2] W refers to Columbus again at *Excursion* vi 234.

110. 'Commentaries on the Scriptures'
Suggested date of reading: see note
References: *MY* ii 9

W's offer to Wrangham of 'bulky old Commentaries on the Scriptures' in early spring 1812 (*MY* ii 9) indicates that he owned some volumes of this sort that interested him little. Moorman and Hill suggest that they may have come from his father's library, but no such title appears in the inventory of books from the Wordsworth library in Cockermouth made up by Richard Wordsworth of Branthwaite (see Wu *Library*).

111. Congreve, William, 'odd volume'
Suggested date of reading: 15 April 1802
References: *Grasmere Journals* 85-6

---

[1] The relevant passage is reproduced in OET *Prel.* 625. My dating of the MS W drafts follows that given by Jonathan Wordsworth, Norton *Prel.* 496. For critical discussion of the passage, see Jacobus (1989) 276-86.
[2] See Denys Sutton, 'Unpublished Letters From Sir George and Lady Beaumont to the Wordsworths', *N&Q* 175 (1938) 146-9, p. 147.

After dinner at an inn on Ullswater, W and DW read 'a volume of Enfield's Speaker, another miscellany, & an odd volume of Congreve's plays' (DW's journal, 15 April 1802). W had been familiar with Congreve at least since his Cambridge years; see *WR* 35-6.

In Sept. or Oct. 1804 W commissioned Lamb to purchase a copy of Congreve on his behalf, and it is quite likely that in due course Lamb did so, as he wrote to W on 13 Oct. that 'Congreve and the rest of King Charles's moralists are cheap & accessible' (Marrs ii 146). Perhaps the copy eventually acquired was that of the *Works* (2 vols., 7th edn, 1774), listed Shaver 64.

112. Constable, Henry, works
Suggested date of reading: by 17 Sept. 1814
References: *MY* ii 153
In his letter to Robert Anderson of 17 Sept. 1814, W suggests that an enlarged edn of Anderson's *British Poets* should include Constable. This indicates that he was aware of his works by 17 Sept. 1814.

113. Cook, James, *An Account of a Voyage round the world*, ed. John Hawkesworth in *An Account of the Voyages Undertaken by the Order of his Present Majesty* (3 vols., 1773)
Suggested date of reading: by 1803
References: see note
In her recollections of the Scottish tour of 1803, DW recorded her responses to Cora Linn and the nearby pleasure-house:

> We came to a pleasure house of which the little Girl had the key - She said it was called the *Fog* house because it was lined with *Fog*, namely moss. On the outside it resembled some of the huts in the prints belonging to Capt. Cook's Voyages, and within was like a haystack scooped out . . . (DC MS 55, 23r; her italics)

DW has in mind Cook's description of a 'town' in Tierra del Fuego, accompanied by Francesco Bartolozzi's engraving of local natives in a crude hut (*Account* ii 54-5).

114. Cooper, Anthony Ashley, 3rd Earl of Shaftesbury, *Characteristicks of Men, Manners, Opinions, Times* [1711]
Suggested date of reading: by Jan. 1815
References: *Prose Works* iii 72, 94; Shaver 65
W refers to Cooper in his *Essay, Supplementary to the Preface*, composed in Jan. 1815. He may, by then, have acquired the copy of *Characteristicks* (3rd edn, 1723), later retained at Rydal Mount (Shaver 65). Stallknecht árgues persuasively for the influence of *The Moralists* on *The Excursion*; see *Strange Seas of Thought* (1958), pp. 134-40.

115. Copy of the Proceedings upon the Inquiry relative to the Armistice and Convention, &c. made and concluded in Portugal, in August 1808, between the Commanders of the British and French Armies; - held at the Royal Hospital at Chelsea, on Monday the 14th of November; and continued by Adjournments until the 27th of December 1808. Ordered by the House of Commons, to be printed, 31st January 1809
Suggested date of reading: between 1 and 26 April 1809
References: Jordan 121

As Owen and Smyser note, a summary of the contents of the *Proceedings* was published in the *Courier* on 3 Jan. 1809, and read by W. Aware of W's interest in the Convention of Cintra, Stuart offered him a copy of the pamphlet in a letter written during Jan. 1809. On 5 Feb. W wrote back to say: 'Many thanks for your kind offers. I should like to see all the Documents you mention, particularly the official Report of the Board' (*MY* i 289). Accordingly, De Quincey sent one to Grasmere on 29 March, where it arrived on 1 April 1809 (Jordan 121). W had read it by 26 April, when he thanked Stuart, adding that had it been in his possession as he composed his *Convention of Cintra*, it 'would have been of use to me, to have made out a stronger case in some instances, particularly upon the subject of plunder' (*MY* i 322).

116. Corbet, Richard, *To Mr. Francis Beaumont (then newly dead)*
Suggested date of reading: by 29 July 1805
References: *EY* 611 and n2

> HE that hath such acuteness, and such wit,
> As would ask ten good heads to husband it;
> He that can write so well that no man dare
> Refuse it for the best, let him beware:
> > BEAUMONT is dead, by whose sole death appears,
> > Wit's a Disease consumes men in few years.

In his letter to Beaumont of 29 July 1805, W recalled 'some pleasing verses (I think by Corbet Bishop of Norwich) on the death of Francis Beaumont the elder', and quoted the concluding couplet of *To Mr. Francis Beaumont (then newly dead)* (*EY* 611). He probably saw this poem in Lamb's copy of Beaumont and Fletcher's *Fifty Comedies and Tragedies* (1679), now at the British Library.

117. Cottle, Joseph, *Alfred* **(Bristol, 1800)**
Suggested date of reading: probably not long after 19 Dec. 1800, and by early 1804
References: Reed ii 106; Cornell *13-Book Prelude* 17n; *WR* 37

Reed notes that Cottle's *Alfred* probably suggested W's consideration of Mithridates as a subject at *Prelude* i 186-9 (see also Reed ii 629-30n2). Although he had not seen Cottle's poem in print as of 19 Dec. 1800 (Butler *JEGP* 153), it is probable that W would have sought it out soon after. The *Prelude* passage it seems to have influenced was composed between April 1801 and early 1804. Given W's contempt for Cottle's famously bad epic, it is unlikely that any reading would have been extensive.

118. Cotton, Charles
(i) *Winter*, stanzas 20-53
Suggested date of reading: early March 1803
References: Marrs ii 98-102
Lamb copied these stanzas out for W in a letter of 5 March 1803, saying: 'You know Cotton, who wrote a 2d part to Walton's Angler. A volume of his miscellaneous poems is scarce. Take what follows from a poem call'd Winter. I omit 20 verses, in which a storm is described, to hasten to the best' (Marrs ii 98). If W did not know the poem by early March 1803, he had memorized it by 3 June 1812, when Robinson recorded in his diary that W quoted 'a fine description of cold from Cotton's *Winter*' (Morley i 93). The text of Cotton's poems in Bell's *Poëts of Great Britain* would have been available to W from 1802 onwards. In addition, Shaver lists the 1725 and 1689 edns of his works (Shaver 67).

(ii) *Cn. Cornelii Galli; vel potius Maximiani Elegia I. Trans.*
Suggested date of reading: early March 1803
References: Marrs ii 102-3
Lamb copied lines 135-54, 185-8, 259-62, and 304-7 into a letter sent to W on 5 March 1803, saying: 'I just excerp here & there, to convince you, if after this you need it, that Cotton was a first rate' (Marrs ii 102). The only available printed text of Cotton's translation of Gallus Cornelius was in Cotton's *Poems on Several Occasions* (1689). There are a number of substantive variants between the two texts, not least Lamb's 'bespeaks' (line 2 of the transcription), which reads ''forespeaks' in the printed text.

(iii) *Winter*
Suggested date of reading: Feb. 1815
References: *Prose Works* iii 37-9, 51
W quotes and discusses Cotton's poem in his Preface to *Poems* (1815). The quotation is fairly long and takes care to omit one 'obscene' line: as W. J. B. Owen suggests to me, W must have had a text before him as he wrote.

119. Courtenay, Rt. Hon. Thomas Peregrine, *Observations on the American Treaty, in Eleven Letters, by Decius* **(1808)**
Suggested date of reading: probably between 1 and 5 April 1809
References: *MY* i 289; Jordan 121
On 5 Feb. 1809, W wrote to Daniel Stuart to request a copy of 'a small pamphlet of Letters published under the name of Decius' (*MY* i 289). This was forwarded to Grasmere by De Quincey on 29 March; it arrived at Allan Bank on 1 April (Jordan 121). W can be presumed

to have read it within short order, probably before 5 April, when DW told De Quincey that 'Decius looks so very dry that I have not heart to attack him' (*MY* i 316). Interestingly, Southey knew Courtenay by 1813 (Curry ii 66).

120. Cowley, Abraham, *The Works of Mr Abraham Cowley* (7th edn, 1681)
Suggested date of reading: by 10 Oct. 1801
References: CC *Marginalia* ii 102-6; *Prose Works* iii 71, 92-3; Shaver 68
W's copy is now at the University of Indiana, Lilly Library. It bears the signature 'Wm Wordsworth' in pencil, overtraced in ink, on the title-page. W bought it second-hand, as the previous owners' signatures appear on the recto of the portrait facing the title-page. It is mentioned in W's all too rare, and brief, glance at his library shelves in the *Essay, Supplementary to the Preface*: 'Turning to my own shelves, I find the folio of Cowley, seventh edition, 1681.' He goes on to recall how, 'twenty-five years ago, the booksellers' stalls in London swarmed with the folios of Cowley' (*Prose Works* iii 71). This does, I think, supply us with a clue as to when W's copy might have been acquired, but in the absence of further evidence we can be confident that he owned it by 10 Oct. 1801. On that date C, then at Grasmere prior to departure for Keswick later in the day, entered several marginal notes and a doodle in the volume (see CC *Marginalia* ii 102-6). Notebook entries dating from 1807-8 are also associated with W's copy of the *Works* (*Notebooks* ii 3196-9, 3203). As for influences on W's poetry, Lienemann 46 writes: 'An einen Vers bei Cowley: And robin redbreasts whom men praise for pious birds erinnert "The redbreast chasing the butterfly" v. 1/2.' This argument supports the case for a reading of Cowley by W in 1801-2, as *The Redbreast and the Butterfly* was composed on 18 April 1802.

My guess is that W acquired his copy of the *Works* in the 1780s or early 1790s, and that he quickly absorbed its contents. In later years he remarked: 'Read all Cowley; he is very valuable to a collector of English sound sense' (*Memoirs* ii 477).

121. Cowper, William
(i) poems
Suggested date of reading: 25 Oct. 1800
References: *Grasmere Journals* 29
'We read Rogers, Miss Seward, Cowper &c.' (DW's journal, 25 Oct. 1800). Possibly the Wordsworths were reading their copy of Cowper's *Poems* (6th edn, 2 vols., 1794-5), later retained at Rydal Mount (Shaver 69).

(ii) *Verses, Supposed to be Written by Alexander Selkirk, During his Solitary Abode in the Island of Juan Fernandez* [1782]
Suggested date of reading: c. Jan.-April 1802
References: *Prose Works* i 163-4

W quotes lines 25-40 of Cowper's poem in his Appendix on Poetic Diction to the Preface to *Lyrical Ballads* (1802).

(iii) *On the Loss of the Royal George* (1803)
Suggested date of reading: early March 1803
References: Marrs ii 103-5
Shortly after its first appearance in Hayley's *Life and Posthumous Writings of Cowper* (1803), Lamb copied this poem out in a letter to W of 5 March. He commented: 'A Song written by Cowper which in stile is much above his usual, and emulates in noble plainnes any old balad I have seen. Hayley has just published it &c. with a Life. - I di[d] not think Cowper up to it' (Marrs ii 103). This must have been the first W heard of Hayley's edn. On 31 March Lamb copied the same poem into C's notebook (*Notebooks* i 1381). When presented with a box made from the remains of the Royal George in 1848, W observed: 'The Poet Cowper would have had a better claim to these Reliques than I feel that I possess' (*Supp.* 257). *On the Loss of the Royal George* was admired also by Southey, who in Nov. 1811 told Montgomery that it was 'unrivalled' (Curry ii 14). The poem can be found at *Life and Posthumous Writings* (3 vols., Chichester, 1803-4), i 126-8.

(iv) *To Mary* (1803)
Suggested date of reading: by 25 March 1804
References: Reed ii 705-6

> I see thee daily weaker grow,
> Thy spirits take a fainter flow:
> 'Twas my distress that brought thee low,
>   My Mary.   Cowper

C's three-line misquotation from Cowper in the Wordsworth Commonplace Book (DC MS 26, 31r) is judged by Reed to date from early 1804, by 25 March. Like *Yardley Oak*, this poem was published first by Hayley in 1803, so that the reason for making a copy was probably the fact that neither C nor W had yet acquired Hayley's edn. The most likely source for the copy of Hayley from which this came was Southey, who reviewed the *Life and Posthumous Writings* in the *Annual Review* 3 (1804) 471-5; Southey had acquired it by March 1803 (*Life of Southey* ii 203-4). The poem can be found at *Life and Posthumous Writings* (3 vols., Chichester, 1803-4), ii 194-6.

(v) *Life and Posthumous Writings of Cowper*, ed. William Hayley, vol. 3 (Chichester, 1804)
Suggested date of reading: probably by 24 Sept. 1804, and frequently thereafter
References: *EY* 577; Reed ii 37-8n31, 707
As is widely acknowledged, *Yardley Oak* inspired *Yew-trees*, composed 24 Sept. 1804 or shortly after. The composition of *Yew-trees* thus provides a terminal date by which W must

have seen *Life and Posthumous Writings* (3 vols., Chichester, 1803-4), iii 409-16, where *Yardley Oak* was first published. This is given further support by Woof PhD 237-8: 'One wonders whether this poem was the one that Wordsworth looked at on the advice of Lady Beaumont in October, 1804' (see *EY* 508).

W does not appear to have owned a copy, but Southey did (see preceding note), as did C, who was given one by Beaumont (see Whalley PhD ii 307). Whichever W was using, this borrowed copy was probably in DW's mind when on 11 April 1805 she told Lady Beaumont: 'I am going to read the Life of Cowper, and the last Volume of letters published since' (*EY* 577).

At some point after 8 Feb. 1807 *Yardley Oak* 1-124 was copied into the Wordsworth Commonplace Book (DC MS 26, 38r-40v) by SH. On that occasion the source may have been either the copy owned by C (which the Wordsworths may have taken to Coleorton, where they then were), or that owned by Beaumont himself, which W could have seen at Coleorton, 30 Oct. 1806-10 June 1807. SH accompanied him and could have made the copy during that time. The fact that it was made at all indicates that, even at this late date, W did not possess *Life and Posthumous Writings* vol. 3. Evidently, however, he pursued it soon after its first publication in 1804, and referred to it (particularly to *Yardley Oak*) on numerous occasions after. C copied *Yardley Oak* 117-19 into his notebook at Allan Bank in March 1810 (*Notebooks* iii 3713).

122. Crabbe, George, *Poems* (1807)
Suggested date of reading: by 29 Sept. 1808
References: *MY* i 268

Writing to Samuel Rogers on 29 Sept. 1808, W commented that 'there was nothing in the last publication so good as the description of the Parish workhouse, Apothecary, etc.' (*MY* i 268). His remaining criticisms indicate that he had read much, if not all, of Crabbe's *Poems* (1807), a copy of which was retained at Rydal Mount (Shaver 70). In 1815, Robinson reported that W 'blamed Crabbe for his unpoetical mode of considering human nature and society' (Sadler i 484).

123. Culpeper, Nicholas, *Culpeper's English Family Physician; or, Medical herbal enlarged . . . and a New Dispensatory, from the MS. of the late Dr. Saunders . . . By Joshua Hamilton* (2 vols., 1792)
Suggested date of reading: early Dec. 1814
References: *MY* ii 175

When William Wordsworth Jr caught a severe cold in early Dec. 1814, his parents called in Dr Scambler from Ambleside. At the same time they consulted their copy of Culpeper; as W told SH on 10 Dec. 1814: 'Mary begs me to say that she does not believe in her own mind notwithstanding Mr Scambler's unqualified assertions, and the exact coincidence of Wm's symptoms with the description of the disease in Dr Hamilton's book, that Wm Ever had the *inflammatory* Croup' (*MY* ii 175). The reference to Dr Hamilton must be to Joshua Hamilton, who revised the 1792 edn of *Culpeper*. Shaver lists an edn of 1652 (Shaver 71).

124. Dampier, William, *A New Voyage round the World* **[1697]**
Suggested date of reading: by late Feb. 1804
References: OET *Prel*. 626; Norton *Prel*. 496
W draws on Dampier in drafts towards the Five-Book *Prelude* made in MS W, late Feb. or early March 1804.[1] He may have been using the copy of Dampier's *Collection of Voyages* (4 vols., 1729) referred to by C in 1807-8 (*Notebooks* ii 3224, 3226), though it is by no means certain. Southey's library contained a copy of the 1697 edn (Southey *SC* 782). Dampier seems to have suggested a central element in the plot of *The Blind Highland Boy*, composed probably March 1804 (Cornell *Poems 1800-7* 420-1); see Coe 36-8.

125. Daniel, Samuel
(i) ***Musophilus***
Suggested date of reading: 24 Nov. 1801
References: Grasmere Journals 41
'Mary read a poem of Daniell upon Learning' (DW's journal, 24 Nov. 1801). Pamela Woof must be correct in suggesting that MH was reading from Anderson, *British Poets* vol. 4 (*Grasmere Journals* 185) - though it is likely also that W's copy of *The Poetical Works of Mr. Samuel Daniel* (2 vols., 1718) had been acquired by this date, and was in regular use (see WR 42-3). The dedicatory sonnet of *Musophilus*, *To the Right Worthy and Judicious Favourer of Virtus, Mr. Fulke Grevill*, is alluded to in W's *Ode* 103.

(ii) ***History of the Civil Wars***
Suggested date of reading: between 21 May and late 1802
References: Cornell *Poems 1800-7* 414
W alludes to Daniel's *Civil Wars* in *It is not to be thought of that the Flood*, written between 21 May and late 1802. Joan Rees, 'Wordsworth and Samuel Daniel', *N&Q* 204 (1959) 26-7, notes that the phrase 'wearied out with contrarieties' (*Thirteen-Book Prelude* x 899), echoes Daniel's *Civil Wars* Book VI, where 'new-defended Faith' brought against 'Faith knowne' will soon 'Weary the Soule with contrarieties' (st. 36, line 6).

(iii) ***Epistle to the Countess of Cumberland***
Suggested date of reading: by July and Oct. 1803
References: Howe vi 309
During his discourses with Hazlitt of July and Oct. 1803, W expressed his love of Daniel's *Epistle to the Countess of Cumberland* (Howe vi 309). On 20 Nov. 1811 he recommended

---

[1] The relevant passage is reproduced OET *Prel*. 626-7. My dating of the MS W drafts follows that given by Jonathan Wordsworth, Norton *Prel*. 496. For critical discussion of the passage, see Jacobus (1989) 276-86.

the *Epistle* to Lady Beaumont (*MY* i 520), and in 1819 he included it in the album of verse compiled for Lady Mary Lowther (*Album* 84-91).

C read from Daniel, including *Hymen's Triumph* and *Musophilus*, during his stay at DC, 20 Dec. 1803-14 Jan. 1804 (see *Notebooks* i 1793-6). Coburn notes that although it would be tempting to suggest that he was reading Daniel from Anderson, 'he was evidently reading Daniel in some other edition' - on the grounds that Anderson does not contain *Hymen's Triumph* (*Notebooks* i 1793). In fact, W's copy of *The Poetical Works of Mr. Samuel Daniel* (2 vols., 1718), does contain the play at i. 85, and, as W owned these volumes by the time of C's reading, it is reasonable to assume that C was using them. It is possible that either or both of the Wordsworths shared in this reading at that time. C was reading Lamb's copy of the 1718 edn (now at the Houghton Library) when staying with the Lambs on 9-10 Feb. 1808 (see CC *Marginalia* ii 116-30).

(iv) *Musophilus*
Suggested date of reading: before 19 April 1808
References: *MY* i 223
On 19 April 1808 MW copied out for C the proposed epigraph to the *White Doe of Rylstone*, which came from Daniel's *Musophilus* (*MY* i 223-4). W knew Daniel's poem well, but was perhaps rereading it at this time.

(v) *The Queenes Arcadia*
Suggested date of reading: between Sept. 1811 and Nov. 1812
References: *Prose Works* ii 342, 449
W quotes Daniel in his *Unpublished Tour*, composed between Sept. 1811 and Nov. 1812.

(vi) *Epistle to the Countess of Cumberland*
Suggested date of reading: spring 1814
References: *The Excursion* (1814), pp. 428-30
In a note to *The Excursion* W acknowledges a quotation from Daniel's *Epistle to the Countess of Cumberland*, and goes on to transcribe four stanzas from the poem 'as they contain an admirable picture of the state of a wise Man's mind in a time of public commotion' (p. 428).

126. Dante Alighieri
(i) *Divina Commedia*
Suggested date of reading: early 1809
References: *Prose Works* i 402
W quotes three lines from the *Inferno* in his *Convention of Cintra*; he may have been referring to C's copy of Placidi's 1732 edn (see next note).

(ii) *Divina Commedia*, ed. G. B. Placidi (Lucca, 1732)
Suggested date of reading: Oct. 1810-1830
References: CC *Marginalia* ii 132
Whalley writes:

> This seems to be the copy sent to London by WW in response to C's request of Feb 1804, the Beaumont gift being the Venice 1774 edition.[1] C left the book behind at Allan Bank in Oct 1810; it is twice marked as C's in Wordsworth LC and was included in WW's list of books to be sent to Highgate in 1829-30. (CC *Marginalia* ii 132)

The Dante was therefore in W's possession between Oct. 1810 and 1829-30. It is now in the possession of N. F. D. Coleridge. W knew his Dante well by 1810, having probably studied the *Divina Commedia* at Cambridge (*WR* 43-4); Dante was evidently a subject of conversation between W and Rogers in subsequent years (see *MY* ii 382). On 3 Sept. 1821 W informed Landor that 'there is, by-the-by, a Latin translation of Dante which you do not seem to know' (*LY* i 79), which Hill identifies as the rendering by Carlo d'Aquino (3 vols., Rome, 1728).

127. Darwin, Erasmus, *The Botanic Garden* Part II, *The Loves of the Plants* (1789)
Suggested date of reading: by Sept. 1800
References: Owen (1969) 17-18; *Prose Works* i 172-3
Owen suggests that W took Darwin's first prose Interlude from *Loves of the Plants* into account as he composed the Preface to *Lyrical Ballads* (1800). In a letter to me, Owen adds that this influence 'is uncertain, but W was, as we know, well into other Darwin works'.

128. Davies, Sneyd, *Against Indolence. An Epistle.*
Suggested date of reading: possibly 15 April 1802; probably by 1815
References: *Grasmere Journals* 85-6; *LY* ii 292; Thomas and Ober 65
On 22 June 1830 W wrote to Dyce about Sir Egerton Brydges' reported obsession with the likes of Sneyd Davies: 'Of some of these Poets whom he would include in a new Corpus I am utterly ignorant; but one of them has produced an exceedingly pleasing poem with a very original air. It begins "There was a time my dear Cornwallis, when". I first met with it in Dr Enfield's[2] Exercises of Elocution or Speaker, I forget which. It is by Davies, and well merits preservation' (*LY* ii 292). W refers to *Against Indolence. An Epistle*, published anonymously in Enfield's *Speaker* from the first edn of 1774 onwards.[3] In fact, its opening lines read:

---

[1] I have not found evidence for the Dante being sent by W to C in Feb. 1804. C's letter to the Wordsworths of 8 Feb. 1804 says: 'Dante & a Dictionary, I shall borrow part from my Brothers, and part from Stuart' (Griggs ii 1059).

[2] The published text reads 'Enfullser's', where the editor of the letters imperfectly deciphered W's script.

[3] When published in George Hardinge's *Biographical Memoirs of the Rev. Sneyd Davies, D.D.* (1816), pp. 70-3, it was entitled *To the Hon. and Rev. F.C.*

In frolick's hour, ere serious thought had birth,
There was a time, my dear CORNWALLIS, when
The Muse would take me on her airy wing
And waft to views romantic . . .[1]

The poem was not published under Davies' name until the edn of Enfield's anthology published in Belfast, 1811. However, it appeared anonymously again in the edn published in Gainsborough, 1814. The attribution to Davies did not appear in the *Speaker* again until 1822. This important detail suggests two possibilities. Either W encountered Davies' poem first in an edn of the *Speaker* which presented it under his name (this would mean that he saw it in either that published in Belfast, 1811, or one derived from the London edn of 1822), or he read it in an edn of the *Speaker* without the attribution but somehow knew it to be Davies'. These factors should be taken into account when dating W's reading. Thomas and Ober believe that W's letter to Dyce refers to a reading recorded in DW's journals, where she mentions that, after dinner at an inn on Ullswater, they read 'a volume of Enfield's Speaker, another miscellany, & an odd volume of Congreve's plays' (DW's journal, 15 April 1802). This does not necessarily follow. The numerous edns of the *Speaker* at this period[2] testify to its popularity, and it cannot be that a voracious reader of poetry such as W encountered it only on 15 April 1802. It is nonetheless likely that his first reading of *Against Indolence* took place at a fairly early date.

129. Davy, Humphry
(i) *Researches chemical and philosophical; chiefly concerning nitrous oxide, or dephlogisticated nitrous air, and its respiration* (1800)
Suggested date of reading: 26 Jan. 1801 onwards
References: Fullmer 1800.2

C's request to Davy in Oct. 1800 to 'tell me how I can get your Essay on the nitrous oxyd' appears to have led, some months later, to W's acquisition of a copy through Longman (Griggs i 632). W's Longman accounts mention '1 Davy's Researches, 8° boards', for which he was debited 9s.6d. on 26 Jan. 1801 (see p. 265). This important volume contains contributions from a number of friends and acquaintances, including John Tobin, Southey, C, and Thomas Beddoes, all of whom described their experiences inhaling nitrous oxide. In fact, C acted as Davy's agent for the publication of this book (Griggs i 556-7), which was issued by W's first publisher, Joseph Johnson, and printed by Joseph Cottle. It is not clear whether the copy acquired by W is that listed by Shaver as having belonged to C (Shaver 324-5); even if it was, W can be assumed to have seen it in early 1801. Davy had been the main proofreader for *Lyrical Ballads* (1800) (*EY* 289).

---

[1] This text is from *The Speaker* (1774).
[2] I have inspected edns of 1774, 1777, 1779, 1781, 1791, 1792, 1794, 1795, 1797, 1798, 1799, 1801, 1805, 1808, 1811, 1814, 1815, 1822. New edns continued to appear into the mid-nineteenth century.

(ii) *A Syllabus of a Course of Lectures on Chemistry Delivered at the Royal Institution of Great Britain* (1802)
Suggested date of reading: c. 1802; by 16 Dec. 1809
References: Fullmer 1802.1

With Thomas Poole, C attended a number of Davy's lectures, delivered at the Royal Institution 21 Jan.-Feb. 1802. C saw much of Davy at this period and was among the few to acquire a signed copy of the *Syllabus*; he may even have seen it in MS. W probably saw the published version soon after. He must have seen C's copy by 16 Dec. 1809, when, at Allan Bank, C gave it to John Monkhouse (see *Notebooks* i 1098 and n; Reed ii 444n61). It is now in the possession of Paul F. Betz.

The *Syllabus* appears to have been retained at Rydal Mount (Shaver 324); either this was the copy given by C to John Monkhouse, or it was another, belonging to W.

130. Day, Thomas, *Sandford and Merton* **[1783-9]**
Suggested date of reading: by 6 March 1804
References: Cornell *13-Book Prelude* 21, 169

Reed suggests that the infant prodigy of *Thirteen-Book Prelude* v 294-349 was modelled on Thomas Day's novel *Sandford and Merton*; see also OET *Prel.* 544 and Norton *Prel.* 164n7. The Infant Prodigy passage was among those entered in MS WW by 6 March 1804.

131. Defoe, Daniel, *The Life and Adventures of Robinson Crusoe, written by himself*
Suggested date of reading: 2 May 1807 onwards
References: Reed ii 353

W's Longman accounts contain a debit for 'Crusoes Life - Sheep', for which he was charged £1.3.0 on 2 May 1807 during a visit to London (see p. 266). This must refer to a vellum-bound copy of Defoe's novel, published as *The Life and Adventures of Robinson Crusoe*; it may have been a birthday present for Johnny Wordsworth, whose fourth birthday fell on 18 June. Perhaps this was the two-volume edn of 1804 later retained at Rydal Mount (Shaver 75), which may have been read to Johnny during his convalescence in spring 1808; the work is mentioned in a letter of 5 June 1808 to Wrangham (*MY* i 249), and De Quincey wrote to Johnny about it on 8 Oct. 1809 (Jordan 254).[1] That it was popular throughout the Wordsworth circle testifies to W's own love of it: in 1811 SH mentioned that Herbert Southey 'can read *Robinson Crusoe* or any Book' (*SHL* 33); in 1804 Southey noted that Hartley Coleridge 'never has read, nor will read, beyond Robinson's departure from the island' (Warter i 312). For W's thoughts on it see *Memoirs* ii 481-2; Grosart iii 468; and Hazlitt's *Spirit of the Age* (1825), p. 246.

---

[1] The 1804 edn carries engravings after Thomas Stothard; two-volume edns had been widely available since 1726.

132. Delille, Jacques, *Discours Preliminaire, Georgiques* [1769]
Suggested date of reading: c. Jan.-April 1802
References: *Prose Works* i 179
W's reference to the 'translator' in the 1802 additions to the Preface to *Lyrical Ballads* is, Owen suggests, to Delille's *Discours Preliminaire* to his translation of the *Georgics*. W 'almost certainly knew' this work; Owen (1969) 12n16.

133. Dennis, John
(i) works
Suggested date of reading: by Sept. 1800
References: see note
Owen has argued that Dennis influenced the Preface to *Lyrical Ballads*, composed Sept. 1800; see, for instance, *Prose Works* i 170-1, 173, 174, 177 and ff. See also Owen (1969) 215-21.

(ii) works
Suggested date of reading: Jan. 1815
References: *MY* ii 188; *Prose Works* iii 82, 104-5
Owen argues that W knew Dennis' works by 1800. W's first mention of Dennis comes in a letter to Catherine Clarkson of Jan. 1815 (*MY* ii 188), the month in which he composed the *Essay, Supplementary to the Preface*, which reworks ideas and phrases used by him. He refers again to Dennis in a letter to Southey of 1815 (*MY* ii 268). See *Prose Works* iii 86, 104-5; and Owen, 'Wordsworth, the Problem of Communication, and John Dennis', *Wordsworth's Mind and Art: Essays*, ed. A. W. Thomson (Edinburgh, 1969), pp. 140-56. W also draws on Dennis in his Preface to *Poems* (1815); see *Prose Works* iii 46-7.

134. Derham, William, works
Suggested date of reading: perhaps by 26 Oct. 1803
References: *Notebooks* i 1616; Shaver 212
C's notebook records 'A most unpleasant Dispute with W. & Hazlitt' on 26 Oct. 1803:

> But *thou*, dearest Wordsworth - and what if Ray, Durham, Paley, have carried the observation of the aptitudes of Things too far, too habitually - into Pedantry? . . . O dearest William! Would Ray, or Durham, have spoken of God as you spoke of Nature?
> (his italics)

Ray, Derham and Paley seem to have represented to W the kind of intellectual who, as he put it in a 1798 draft towards *The Ruined Cottage*, 'Forever dimly pore[s] on things minute' (Cornell *Ruined Cottage* 373). Whalley suggested that C's reading of Ray and Derham was part of 'a tentative scheme for a book on natural history for Hartley's use, like the Greek Grammar he started to write for the children after his return from Malta' (Whalley PhD i 335). None of this proves that W had actually read any of these authors (though he had probably read Paley, on whom he was examined at Cambridge in Jan. 1791; see *WR* 110), but C at least raises the possibility. Coburn suggests that C knew Derham's *Physico-Theological Discourses* (1713) (*Notebooks* i 1147n).

135. Descartes, René, quotations
Suggested date of reading: Feb. 1801
References: Reed ii 113n7
W copied quotations from Descartes into DC MS 31, leaves 71-2, *c*. Feb. 1801. They appear to have been copied from C's own transcriptions and do not imply serious study of Descartes by W (though it should be noted that two books by Descartes were retained at Rydal Mount; see Shaver 76). Significantly, C's first serious study of Descartes also dates from Feb. 1801 (Griggs ii 672, 675, 677-703). Descartes' dream, which provided the basis for the Arab Quixote episode of *Thirteen-Book Prelude* v 71-139, was communicated to W probably by C (Norton *Prel.* 158n4).[1]

136. 'Dictionary'
Suggested date of reading: early 1803
References: *EY* 380; Ketcham 134
On 25 Dec. 1802 DW asked JW to send on a dictionary acquired for the Wordsworths by Mary Lamb (*EY* 380). It would have arrived in Grasmere in Jan. or Feb. 1803.

137. Digby, Kenelm, *Two Treatises, in the one of which, the nature of bodies; in the other, the nature of mans soule; is looked into: in way of discovery of the immortality of reasonable bodies* **(Paris, 1644)**
Suggested date of reading: 1-9 Nov. 1801
References: *Notebooks* i 1002, 1004, 1005; Shaver 77
Notebooks i 1002, 1004 and 1005 reveal that, 1-9 Nov. 1801, C was reading a copy of Digby's *Two Treatises* (1645) borrowed from Carlisle Cathedral Library. W is implicated in this for the following reasons: (i) 6-10 Nov., C was in the company of the Wordsworths, at DC and then at Greta Hall; (ii) a copy of Digby's *Two Treatises* was later retained at Rydal Mount (Shaver 77). Pittman has suggested that W read Digby at Cambridge but I find no evidence for it (*WR* 157). It is more likely that in Nov. 1801 W had not yet acquired his copy of Digby but saw that borrowed by C. On the basis of that reading he would later have sought out the *Two Treatises* for purchase. For an examination of the surviving copy of the volume

---

[1] Jonathan Wordsworth writes that 'the material certainly came *via* Coleridge, and he could well have modified it in the telling, or even (at Grasmere in January 1804) discussed with Wordsworth how it might be changed' (*The Borders of Vision* [1982], p. 194). Jacobus (1989) 120 agrees that 'There is no evidence that Wordsworth himself had first-hand knowledge of Baillet's *Vie de Descartes*.'

borrowed by C and a discussion of its relevance to his work see John Beer, *Coleridge's Poetic Intelligence* (1977), pp. 245-6.

138. Diogenes Laërtius, *Diogenis Laertii de vitis, dogmatis & apophthegmatis clarorum philosophorum, libri X* **(1616)**
Suggested date of reading: by 1810
References: Shaver 78
W's copy is now in the Bodleian Library (Vet. D2 f.23). The first two flyleaves contain a number of notes by a seventeenth-century owner of the book. In addition the first flyleaf carries a faded inscription, still clearly legible, in an eighteenth-century hand: 'E. Libris Gul. Coleridge Ex Aede Christi Ox.' The second flyleaf carries the inscription 'Wm Wordsworth.' This reveals that the book was originally the property of William Coleridge (1758-80), C's brother, who matriculated at Christ Church, Oxford, on 3 June 1774, graduating BA at Wadham in 1779.[1] It must have come into his possession during the years 1774-7, during his time at Christ Church. Presumably it was passed on to C some time after William's death - by Feb. 1801, probably, when C quoted Diogenes in a letter to Josiah Wedgwood (Griggs ii 683).[2] C must have given the volume to W before their falling-out in 1810.

139. D'Israeli, Isaac, *Curiosities of Literature* **(1793)**
Suggested date of reading: by Jan. 1815
References: *Prose Works* iii 76, 98
In his *Essay, Supplementary to the Preface*, W refers the reader to 'D'Israeli's 2d Series of the Curiosities of Literature' (*Prose Works* iii 76).

140. Donne, John, *LXXX Sermons* **(1640)**
Suggested date of reading: 1807 onwards
References: CC *Marginalia* ii 245; Shaver 79
W's copy is now at the Houghton Library; see CC *Marginalia* ii 245. Its marginalia were entered c. Jan. 1809-May 1810 at Allan Bank. W's ownership inscription indicates its purchase at Ashby de la Zouch in 1807; as Reed suggests, it must have been purchased by 10 June, when W left Coleorton. Reading the *Sermons* in April 1830, W commented: 'I prefer this Writer because he is so little likely to be explored by others; and is full of excellent matter, though difficult to manage for a modern audience' (*LY* ii 257).

C read Donne's poetry from Anderson, *British Poets* vol. 4, including *Obsequies on the Lord Harrington*, *The Progress of the Soul*, verse letter *To the Countess of Bedford* and *To*

---

[1] See *Coleridge: The Early Family Letters*, ed. James Engell (1994), p. 34n1. Not to be confused with William Hart Coleridge (1789-1849), afterwards Bishop of Barbados, nephew of C.

[2] Diogenes also provided the source for one of C's notebook entries in Dec. 1805 (*Notebooks* ii 2755 and n).

Mr T.W., during his stay at DC, 20 Dec. 1803-14 Jan. 1804 (see *Notebooks* i 1786-90). It is likely that the Wordsworths shared in that reading.

141. Douglas, Thomas, 5th Earl of Selkirk, *A Letter Addressed to John Cartwright, Esq. on the Subject of Parliamentary Reform* **(1809)**
Suggested date of reading: early June 1809 onwards
References: *MY* i 349; Jordan 190
On 26 May 1809 MW requested De Quincey to send 'Lord Selkirk's letter to Major Cartwright' (*MY* i 349), and on 31 May De Quincey replied: 'I will at any rate use this opportunity to send you the "letter to Major Cartwright"' (Jordan 190). They would have received it within the week. Douglas' *Letter*, written in response to Cartwright's *Reasons for Reformation* (1809), is essentially anti-reform, but does admit to flaws in the system - notably the prevalence of rotten boroughs.

C owned a copy of Cartwright's *The People's Barrier Against Undue Influence and Corruption* (1780) and went out of his way to criticise it in *The Friend* nos. 9 and 10 (12 Oct., 19 Oct. 1809) (CC *Friend* ii 130-40). His comments are recalled in notebook entries of May 1810 (*Notebooks* iii 3836, 3839). Given his interest in Cartwright at this moment, it would have been strange indeed if he did not see W's copy of Douglas' *Letter* - especially as C resided at Allan Bank intermittently from 13 June 1809 onwards.

142. Drayton, Michael
(i) *Poly-Olbion* **(Anderson)**
Suggested date of reading: by *c*. 13 Aug. 1800
References: Reed ii 133n31; Cornell *Lyrical Ballads* 398-9
The Latin epigraph on the title-page of both volumes of *Lyrical Ballads* (1800) was drawn from John Selden's foreword to Michael Drayton's *Poly-Olbion* as published in Anderson, *British Poets* iii 236-8, p. 238 (see Cornell *Lyrical Ballads* 377). It was sent to the printer *c*. 13 Aug. 1800 (*EY* 292-3), thus providing a date by which W can be assumed to have read it.

C described *To Joanna* (composed by the last week of Aug. 1800) as a 'noble imitation of Drayton' (CC *Biographia* ii 104). By Aug. 1803, W was capable of quoting *Poly-Olbion* from memory (see *DWJ* i 201). Graver suggests to me that during his schooldays at Hawkshead W may have been directed to read *Poly-Olbion* by William Taylor. There are marginalia about Drayton's sonnets, in W's hand, in C's copy of Anderson's *British Poets* (now at the Folger Shakespeare Library).

(ii) *Elegy to my dearly loved Friend, Henry Reynolds, Esq. of Poets and Poesy* **(Anderson)**
Suggested date of reading: probably by Dec. 1801
References: see note

On the recto of a fragment of W's Prospectus to *The Recluse* (DC MS 24), there appear the following lines:

> That noble Chaucer, in those former times,
> The first enrich'd our English with his rhimes,
> And was the first of ours that ever brake
> Into the Muses' treasure, and first spake
> In weighty numbers, <u>delving in the mine</u>
> Of perfect knowledge. (W's underlining)

W's source for this draft is almost certainly Anderson, *British Poets* iii 548. Reed suggests that it was 'intended for use in connection with Chaucer translations' made in Dec. 1801 (Reed ii 133-4n31); however, Graver questions this on the grounds that the *Troilus* drafts are not mentioned in DC MS 24. W. J. B. Owen has observed that *To the Daisy* ('With little here to do or see'), composed in part between 16 April and 8 July 1802, and completed by March 1805, contains a borrowing from Drayton's poem.[1] See also Cornell *Home at Grasmere* 265.

(iii) *Moses's Birth and Miracles* (Anderson)
Suggested date of reading: c. Jan.-April 1802
References: *Prose Works* i 165, 189
W quotes this poem in his Appendix on Poetic Diction (1802); his source is probably Anderson, *British Poets* iii 653.

(iv) *Nymphida: The Court of Fairy* (Anderson)
Suggested date of reading: by 8 July 1802
References: Reed ii 161n31
Reed notes that *The Green Linnet*, composed between 16 April and 8 July 1802, employs the same stanza form as *Nymphida*. W would have read it in Anderson, *British Poets* iii 177-9.

(v) *The Muses Elysium* (Anderson)
Suggested date of reading: by 10 Nov. 1806
References: Cornell *Poems 1800-7* 421
Curtis notes an echo of *The Muses Elysium* in W's *By their floating Mill*, composed between 4 April and 10 Nov. 1806; W had probably read Drayton's poem well before then, his most likely source being Anderson, *British Poets* iii 606-33.

(vi) *Poly-Olbion* (Anderson)
Suggested date of reading: between Sept. 1811 and Nov. 1812
References: *Prose Works* ii 344
W refers to 'the old topographer Michael Drayton' in his *Unpublished Tour*, composed between Sept. 1811 and Nov. 1812. As Owen and Smyser point out, 'Borrowdale is

---

[1] 'Some Wordsworthian Borrowings', *N&Q* 193 (1948) 429-30, p. 430.

mentioned three times in Song XXX of *Poly-Olbion*' (*Prose Works* ii 450). W was well-acquainted with this work by 1811-12, but a copy was close at hand, and he might have returned to Drayton's poem at around this time.

143. Dryden, John
(i) *Palamon and Arcite* **(Anderson)**
Suggested date of reading: 9 Dec. 1801
References: *Grasmere Journals* 47

'I read Palamon & Arcite - Mary read Bruce - William writing out his alteration of Chaucers Cuckow & Nightingale' (DW's journal, 9 Dec. 1801). This sentence offers a useful insight into reading habits at DC at this period. DW had been reading Michael Bruce the previous day (see note 63), and had evidently recommended him to MH. W was at this moment working on his translations from Chaucer, and was consulting Dryden as he proceeded; he evidently recommended that DW take a look at Dryden's rendering of *The Knight's Tale*. Pamela Woof notes that DW's reference is 'possibly' to Dryden (as opposed to Chaucer); Graver is more certain: 'It must refer to Dryden. The whole Chaucer enterprise is an attempt to define himself in relation to Dryden, as the late remarks about his methods of translation (in letters of the 1840s) make clear' (letter to me). See also W's comments on Dryden's *Palamon*, *LY* iii 756.

I have usually assumed that during the 1800s W was using the text of Dryden's poems and translations provided by Anderson, *British Poets* vol. 6. However, it should be remembered that Bell's *Poets*, also available to him during these years, contained Dryden's works in vols. 40-2.

(ii) works (Anderson)
Suggested date of reading: by 7 Nov. 1805
References: *EY* 641-3

W had known Dryden's works since his schooldays (see *WR* 49). His letter to Scott of 7 Nov. 1805 gives some attention to Dryden, suggesting that he had recently returned to him. Even if he hadn't, it is worth noting that, besides *Palamon and Arcite* and *Absalom and Achitophel* (which by now he would probably have known by heart), W had by 7 Nov. 1805 read all of Dryden, including the translations from Boccaccio: 'I have read Dryden's Works (all but his plays) with great attention' (*EY* 642). This implies only that he had given more attention to the poems than to the plays, not that the plays were unknown to him.

On 20-23 July 1800 C noted: 'Alexander's Feast - a noble subject still for a bold fellow' (*Notebooks* i 759). As C and his family were at that date at DC, it is possible that the note arose out of talks with W (who had known *Alexander's Feast* since boyhood - see *WR* 49).

(iii) works (Anderson)
Suggested date of reading: by 18 Jan. 1808
References: *MY* i 190-1

W's detailed remarks on Dryden in a letter to Scott of 18 Jan. 1808 may have been inspired by another glance at his work. In particular, the letter contains direct quotations from *To my dear Friend Mr. Congreve* and *Religio Laici* - although W possibly knew those works well enough to recall them without consulting the printed text.

(iv) *Works*, ed. Walter Scott (18 vols., 1808)
Suggested date of reading: by 4 Aug. 1808
References: *MY* i 264
'I had a peep at your edition of Dryden', W told Scott on 4 Aug. 1808. As he had been advising Scott on it since 1805, it is unfortunate that he was disappointed with its notes. Although he does not seem to have acquired his own copy of this work, it appears to have been one of his sources for the third of the *Essays Upon Epitaphs* (*Prose Works* ii 116), in which case he must have seen it during Jan. or Feb. 1810.

(v) *An Ode. To the Pious Memory of the accomplished Young Lady, Mrs. Anne Killigrew, excellent in the two Sister-Arts of Poetry and Painting* (Anderson)
Suggested date of reading: by late Oct. 1814
References: Cornell *Poems 1800-7* 602, 680
W alludes to this poem in *Address to my Infant Daughter*, composed between 9 Sept. and late Oct. 1814.

(vi) *Essay of Dramatic Poesy*
Suggested date of reading: by Jan. 1815
References: *Prose Works* iii 88
W alludes to Dryden's *Essay* in his *Essay, Supplementary to the Preface* (*Prose Works* iii 68, 88).

(vii) *The Indian Emperor*
Suggested date of reading: by Jan. 1815
References: *Prose Works* iii 73, 95
W quotes six lines from the play in his *Essay, Supplementary to the Preface*.

144. Du Bartas, Guillaume de Saluste
(i) *Dubartas his Second Weeke: Babylon. The Second Part of the Second Day of the II. Weeke*, tr. Joshua Sylvester
Suggested date of reading: by 22 Feb. 1810
References: *Prose Works* ii 109
As Owen and Smyser note, W quotes a phrase from Sylvester's *Dubartas* in the second of the *Essays Upon Epitaphs*. They go on to say that W's source was probably Winstanley's *England's Worthies*, a copy of which he probably owned by this time (Shaver 276), and which quotes the relevant line. I include Du Bartas here, however, because there nevertheless remains a chance that W sought out Sylvester's translation: C, after all, was evidently reading

it in 1807 (*Notebooks* ii 3107). And W commends Sylvester in his letter to Anderson of Sept. 1814 (*MY* ii 153). Southey had certainly read *Dubartas* by 2 March 1815 (Curry ii 116), and a copy of *A Summarie upon his famous Poeme*, tr. Thomas Lodge (1637), is listed Southey *SC* 952. It should be noted that his copy of the *Oeuvres* (2 vols., Paris, 1611), listed Southey *SC* 951, was acquired on 23 Dec. 1825, and is now in the Dyce Collection, National Art Library, Victoria and Albert Museum (b.w.879 Fo.3323).

(ii) Works
Suggested date of reading: by Jan. 1815
References: *Prose Works* iii 87
W's 'hasty retrospect of the poetical literature of this Country' in the *Essay, Supplementary to the Preface* begins with the question: 'Who is there that now reads the "Creation" of Dubartas?' (*Prose Works* iii 67). This does not of itself prove that W read either *La Semaine* (Paris, 1584) or *La Seconde Semaine* (Paris, 1584), though in the light of the preceding note it is likely that he read at least some of Sylvester's translation.

145. Dunbar, William, poems
Suggested date of reading: by Jan. 1815
References: *Prose Works* iii 78
The earliest confirmation of a reading occurs when W ranks Dunbar alongside Burns and Thomson in his *Essay, Supplementary to the Preface*. His next encounter with Dunbar did not occur until the summer of 1822, when David Laing, visiting Rydal Mount, seems to have brought a copy of the *Works* with him. As DW told Mary Laing on 17 July 1823: 'when I mentioned the Poet Dunbar to him, every circumstance connected with that day when Mr David Laing dined with us flashed upon his mind. . . . My Brother begs me to say that it is so long since he read Dunbar's Works that it is impossible for him to give any critical opinion of them at present; and he has no opportunity here of referring to the works themselves' (*LY* i 209). Laing lent W a copy of Dunbar in early 1827 (*LY* i 506), and gave him a copy of his own edn of the *Poems* in July 1834 (*LY* ii 723; Shaver 294). In Dec. 1835 W confessed that the state of his eyes was 'a sufficient excuse for not paying the attention to the Poems of Dunbar which I have long anxiously wished to give' (*LY* iii 137).

146. Duppa, Richard
(i) *The Life and Literary Works of Michel Angelo Buonarotti* (1806)
Suggested date of reading: May 1806 onwards
References: Reed ii 324
Reed notes that Duppa's volume was published on 26 May 1806; it contained W's *Translation from the Italian of Michael Angelo I* ('Yes! hope may with my strong desire keep pace'). W saw Duppa on 7 May, and probably on other occasions during that stay in London; he can be presumed to have received a copy of the *Life* before he left *c*. 20 May. Beaumont

had received one by 6 Aug., when he praised W's translations, saying that 'the glorious aspirations of M. Angelo were a perfect cordial to [a] languid soul - what the original can be I know not, but if it exceed the translation it must be sublime indeed'.[1] A copy of the volume was retained at Rydal Mount (Shaver 82). Southey, through whom W met Duppa, also contributed to the volume (*FN* 20-1; Curry i 397).

(ii) *The Life and Literary Works of Michel Angelo Buonarotti* (1806)
Suggested date of reading: between Sept. 1811 and Nov. 1812
References: *Prose Works* ii 291
W quotes Duppa's praise for Lancaster Castle in his *Unpublished Tour*, composed between Sept. 1811 and Nov. 1812. As Owen and Smyser remark, W introduces abbreviations and careless errors in punctuation into Duppa's remarks.

147. D'Urfey, Thomas, works
Suggested date of reading: by 17 Sept. 1814
References: *MY* ii 154
In his letter to Robert Anderson of 17 Sept. 1814, W suggests that an enlarged edn of Anderson's *British Poets* should include 'A selection from Tom D'Urfey'. This indicates that he was aware of his works by 17 Sept. 1814. He may have seen the volume of D'Urfey's works owned by Southey (*Life of Southey* ii 270).

148. Dwight, Timothy, *The Conquest of Canäan; a poem in eleven books* (Hartford, Conn., 1788)
Suggested date of reading: between Sept. 1811 and Nov. 1812
References: *Prose Works* ii 305, 440
W quotes *The Conquest of Canäan* ii 57-62 in his *Unpublished Tour*, composed between Sept. 1811 and Nov. 1812. A copy was retained at Rydal Mount (Shaver 83).

149. Dyer, George
(i) *Poems* (1801)
Suggested date of reading: 1800s
References: CC *Marginalia* ii 353-6
It is likely that W saw C's copy of Dyer's *Poems* (1800) containing the famous cancelled Preface. Perhaps a copy of *Poems* (1800) was among the volumes sent by Lamb to W on 1 Feb. 1806 (see next note). At any rate, C acquired his unique copy shortly before publication, probably in late 1800 or early 1801, and would probably have shown it to W soon afterwards. It is now in the British Library.

---

[1] Wordsworth Library WLL/Beaumont, G. H./15. Beaumont seems to have commended Duppa to W, saying, on 17 Feb. 1805, that 'I am not personally acquainted with Mr Duppa - but his works & his friends speak highly of him' (Wordsworth Library WLL/Beaumont, G. H./5).

(ii) *Poems* (1792)
Suggested date of reading: perhaps mid-Feb. 1806 onwards
References: Marrs ii 205

On 1 Feb. 1806, Lamb wrote to W to say that he had purchased copies of Urry's Chaucer, Pope's Shakespeare, Spenser and Milton on his behalf, and sent them on the Kendal wagon that very day. He went on: 'With the Books come certain Books & Pamphlets of G. Dyer, Presents or rather Decoy-ducks of the Poet to take in his thus-far obliged friends to buy his other works' (Marrs ii 205). It is possible that these included the copy of Dyer's *Poems* (1792) now at the Wordsworth Library. At any rate, W probably acquired his copy of this volume at around this time - as well as his copy of the *Poems* (2 vols., 1802). He would have received Lamb's consignment by mid-Feb. (Reed ii 314).

(iii) *On the Death of Gilbert Wakefield. Meditated in a garden, near a church-yard, at the close of autumn*
Suggested date of reading: by 1809-10
References: PW v 416

> he will live and die
> Forgotten, - at safe distance from 'a world
> Not moving to his mind.' (*Excursion* ii 314-15)

W's alludes in these lines to Dyer's *On the Death of Gilbert Wakefield. Meditated in a garden, near a church-yard, at the close of autumn*, which was first published in Dyer's *Poems* (2 vols., 1802):

> But I have wander'd: let me then recount
> The sum of life, and profit by th' amount:
> A little learning, and a little weakness;
> A little pleasure, and enough of pain:
> A little freedom, with its tale of slavery;
> Passions and reasons struggle; where, tho' oft
> Reason claims empire, passion governs still;
> Believing much, yet doubting not a little;
> Till sickness comes, and with it gloom of thought; -
> When man, quite wearied with a world, perhaps,
> Not moving to his mind, a foolish world,
> Seeks inward stillness, and lies quiet down. (lines 109-20)

The date of composition for the *Excursion* lines is unclear (see Reed ii 23), but 1809-10 is likely. Dyer also composed *Gilberto Wakefield*, a Latin work published in *Poems* (1801), pp. 98-106 (with an English rendering by Thomas Busby), with which *On the Death of Gilbert Wakefield* should not be confused.

150. Dyer, John, *The Fleece*
Suggested date of reading: Nov. 1811
References: *MY* i 521

'If you have not read *The Fleece*, I would strongly recommend it to you', W wrote to Lady Beaumont on 20 Nov. 1811, enclosing with his letter a copy of *To the Poet, Dyer*, which he said was composed 'some time ago' (*MY* i 521). Ketcham, however, suggests that the poem was 'written within the last several weeks' (Cornell *Poems 1807-20* 518); if so, it is likely that W had reread *The Fleece* recently. At a meeting with John Payne Collier some time between 1811 and 1814, W 'was strong in his admiration of Dyer's "Fleece," a poem I had not read';[1] it is also commended in the *Preface* (1815) (*Prose Works* iii 28). W must have known this poem since his schooldays, and as late as 1835 was in the habit of 'muttering' lines from Dyer's poems from memory (*LY* iii 79).

151. Eachard, Laurence, *The History of England, from the first entrance of Julius Caesar and the Romans (to the conclusion of the reign of King James the Second, and the Establishment of King William and Queen Mary)* (2 vols., 3rd edn, 1720)
Suggested date of reading: by 18 Jan. 1808
References: *MY* i 190

John Ogilby, Eachard writes, was

> a *Scotch* Man by Birth, and only a Dancing-Master by Education, who by his own great Labour and Pains made himself famous for a great many things, and gain'd the Favour and Acquaintance of the King, and the chief Men of the Kingdom. The great Poets he translated, the voluminous Books that he publish'd, the Cuts, Maps and Surveys that he made, together with the Projects he contriv'd, all shew him to be a Person of uncommon Reach and wonderful Industry; and it is said, that if he had been carefully educated when young, he might have prov'd the Glory of the *Scotch* Nation. (p. 925; his italics)

On 18 Jan. 1808 W told Walter Scott that 'There is in Echard's History a most laughable account of Ogilby, who, by the bye, was a countryman of yours' (*MY* i 190) - suggesting that the copy at Rydal Mount (Shaver 85) had been acquired by Jan. 1808. This would also indicate that W was by that date acquainted with Ogilby's translations of Virgil.

152. Edgeworth, Maria, *Castle Rackrent* [1800]
Suggested date of reading: 13 Nov. 1805
References: *Prose Works* ii 377

Stranded at Park House by rain on 13 Nov. 1805, W and DW did some reading - W in a 'Book lent him by T. Wilkinson' (unidentified), DW in *Castle Rackrent*. It can be assumed that W had read Edgeworth's novel by this time. Simon Nowell Smith, *Wordsworth to Robert*

---

[1] S. T. Coleridge, *Seven Lectures on Shakespeare and Milton*, ed. John Payne Collier (1856), p. lii.

Graves and Beyond (1983), p. 6, lists a copy of the 3rd edn (1801) presented by C to Thomas Hutchinson on 19 Dec. 1801. If C was giving copies away by 1801, W may well have read it by that date. The Kendal Book Club ordered a copy on 26 July 1803.

On 30 May 1812 W observed that 'I had read but few of [her] works' (*Supp.* 98) - meaning, I would assume, that he had at least read her most famous, even if he didn't like it (see *Supp.* 114). He met Edgeworth herself in Sept. 1829, and commented: 'the authoress is very lively' (*LY* ii 143).

153. *Edinburgh Review***, reviews of Campbell,** *Gertrude of Wyoming* **and More,** *Coelebs in Search of a Wife***,** *Edinburgh Review* **14 (April 1809) 1-19, 145-51**
Suggested date of reading: between 15 and 27 July 1809
References: *MY* i 365
In a letter of 1 Aug. 1809, DW told De Quincey that 'I took the pains when I was at Kendal of going to the Book Club to look at the last Reviews - By the bye, have you seen the *Edinburgh Review* on Cam[p]bell's Poem? . . . The Review of Miss Hannah More's work is equally as foolish, though in a different way' (*MY* i 365). DW was at Kendal from 15 to 27 July 1809, when she would have seen the *Edinburgh* for April 1809 (published *c.* 1 May).

It is doubtful whether W read these reviews as well, though he would probably have heard about them from DW. DW's increasingly reluctant interest in the *Edinburgh* is symptomatic of W's growing sensitivity to the hostile criticism he was receiving from that quarter.

154. Edwards, John
(i) *All Saints' Church, Derby: A Poem* **(1805)**
Suggested date of reading: by 22 Feb. 1810
References: *Prose Works* ii 54-5; CC *Friend* 340-1
W's approving reference to Edwards as 'an ingenuous Poet of the present day' in the first *Essay upon Epitaphs*, published in *The Friend* for 22 Feb. 1810, provides a terminal date by which he had read this work. The *Essay* also quotes twenty-eight lines of Edwards' *All Saints' Church*.

Edwards appears first as a correspondent of C's; two of his letters to C survive in the Wordsworth Library, dated 25 Sept. and 28 Oct. 1809, in which he writes warmly of W's poetry (see *Prose Works* ii 103). He was a subscriber to *The Friend* (CC *Friend* ii 426).

(ii) poems in MS
Suggested date of reading: by 27 March 1811
References: *MY* i 470
On 27 March 1811, W wrote to Edwards: 'Many thanks for your verses which are spirited and your own criticisms upon them correct' (*MY* i 470). The Wordsworths had met Edwards in Derby in early July 1810, and some time after that Edwards had evidently sent W some poems in MS. Edwards had also sent some to C at the time he subscribed to *The Friend*, on

25 Sept. 1809; W might have seen those too. W sent Edwards a copy of *Poems* (1815) (*Supp.* 157).

155. Edwards, Richard, *Amantium iræ amoris redintigratia est*
('In goyng to my naked bedde')
Suggested date of reading: probably between 25 March 1804 and 11 Feb. 1805
References: Reed ii 706
The excerpt from Edwards' poem copied by W in the Wordsworth Commonplace Book (DC MS 26, 37r-37v) is judged by Reed to date from between 25 March 1804 and 11 Feb. 1805. W's source is not definitely known, but it is likely to have been Edwards' anthology, *The Paradyse of Daynty Devises* [1576], where 'In goyng to my naked bedde' is no. 42, pp. 42-3.

156. *Encyclopaedia Britannica* **(18 vols., 3rd edn, Edinburgh, 1797)**
Suggested date of reading: some time after Jan. 1800, and certainly by 31 Jan. 1802
References: *Grasmere Journals* 61; Shaver 88
On 31 Jan. 1802, DW recorded in her journal that William Calvert visited DC: 'he dined with us & carried away the Encyclopaedias'. Pamela Woof suggests that he needed them for his chemistry experiments in his new house, Greta Bank, near Windy Brow (*Grasmere Journals* 199). The Wordsworths' library was as yet sufficiently small for this to make a considerable difference to their shelves: 'After they were gone I spent some time in trying to reconcile myself to the change, & in rummaging out & arranging some other books in their places' (DW's journal, 31 Jan. 1802). It is not clear when the Wordsworths first borrowed these volumes, but it was probably soon after moving into DC - certainly when they were settled in Grasmere, within easy reach of Calvert (who lived near Keswick). W may have borrowed Tom Poole's copies during their residence at Alfoxden (*WR* 174).

157. Enfield, William
(i) *Is Verse Essential to Poetry?*, *Monthly Magazine* **2 (1796) 455**
Suggested date of reading: by Sept. 1800
References: *Prose Works* i 114, 173
Owen writes that W 'almost certainly' knew this article (*Prose Works* i 173). It was among the *Monthlys* sent to W by Losh in 1797 (*WR* 101). See also Owen (1969) 18-20, 113-14.

(ii) *The Speaker; or Miscellaneous Pieces Selected from the Best English Writers* **[1774]**
Suggested date of reading: 15 April 1802
References: *Grasmere Journals* 85-6
After dinner at an inn on Ullswater, W and DW read 'a volume of Enfield's Speaker, another miscellany, & an odd volume of Congreve's plays' (DW's journal, 15 April 1802). Enfield's was a popular standard anthology of the day, and the Wordsworths had almost certainly

encountered it before this date. It was in an edn of this anthology that W first read Sneyd Davies' *Against Indolence. An Epistle.*

As Pamela Woof notes, DW met Enfield briefly in 1788. In 1810 Johnny Wordsworth asked his father to give him a copy of the *Speaker* (*Love Letters* 96). Among the authors in Enfield's selection were Addison, Sterne, Shakespeare, Chesterfield, Pope, Young, Akenside, Dyer, Gray, Mrs Barbauld, and Thomson.

158. Epitaphs
Suggested date of reading: between late April and 17 Dec. 1799
References: Reed ii 708-9

Reed notes that DW copied a number of epitaphs into DC MS 20 between late April and 17 Dec. 1799, namely: epitaph of Josias Franklin and his wife; Benjamin Franklin's epitaph; and an 'Epitaph taken from the Parish Church-Yard of Marsk in the County of York'. Her source has yet to be traced.

159. Euripides, *Iphigenia at Aulis*
Suggested date of reading: c. Oct. 1814
References: Cornell *Poems 1807-20* 146, 529

Euripides is one of W's acknowledged sources for *Laodamìa*, composed Oct. 1814 (see Cornell *Poems 1807-20* 146, 529). He had probably known Euripides' work at least since his Cambridge days.

Doubt has been expressed as to whether W read Euripides in the original. Senex, 'Wordsworth and Greek', *N&Q* 177 (1939) 366-7, goes further:

> Wordsworth refers to the delay of the Greek fleet in Aulis, but I cannot find in his poem any particular debt to the play of Euripedes. . . . It seems to me likely that, if Wordsworth had read in the originals the Greek incidents to which he refers here and there, he would have said so in one of the complacent little notes he added to his poems.
> (p. 366)

Senex, it should be noted, took the view that W read little of anything, and was possessed of scant classical learning. However, if W was capable of 'considerable merit' in an examination on Sophocles at Cambridge in Dec. 1788 (see *WR* 129), he can be presumed to have been competent - and, probably, eager - to read Euripides.

160. Fergusson, Robert, *Poetical Works of Robert Fergusson with the life of the author*, ed. David Irving (Glasgow, 1800)
Suggested date of reading: 21 April 1802
References: *Grasmere Journals* 89; Shaver 93

'Read Ferguson's life & a poem or two' (DW's journal, 21 April 1802). It is not clear when the Wordsworths acquired this volume, but it remained in their library until the Rydal Mount sale of 1859. See also Heath 129-31.

161. Fichte, Johann Gottlieb, *Das System der Sittenlehre* **(Jena and Leipzig, 1798)**
Suggested date of reading: see note
References: Reed ii 461; CC *Marginalia* ii 627-37
C probably acquired this volume during his stay in Germany, 1798-9. He apparently took it with him to Allan Bank, during composition of *The Friend*, and left it there when he went to London in Oct. 1810. In late 1810, De Quincey borrowed it from W (Reed ii 461). He returned it to Allan Bank in May 1811, during which month Mrs Coleridge wrote to him asking after it. 'The *Sittenlehre* of Fichte was at my house', De Quincey wrote back on 29 May, 'and I took care that it should be immediately returned to the Wordsworths' (Musgrove 9). Shortly after that, W probably sent it back to C (see Reed ii 474 and n11). It is now in the British Library (C.126.f.12).

For all this, W may never have read a word of Fichte. All the same, he probably heard a good deal about him from C; on 9 Feb. 1801, for instance, C wrote to DW with 'a literal Translation of page 49 of the celebrated Fichte's Uber den Begriff der Wissenschaftslehre [1794]' (Griggs ii 673).

162. Fielding, Henry
(i) *Amelia*
Suggested date of reading: 7 Nov. 1800
References: *Grasmere Journals* 31; Shaver 93
'A cold rainy morning Wm still unwell. I working & reading Amelia' (DW's journal, 7 Nov. 1800). A set of Fielding's *Works* had been in the family since before 1783 (*WR* 58); whether on this occasion W shared in DW's reading is not clear.

(ii) *Tom Jones*
Suggested date of reading: 25 Nov. 1800
References: *Grasmere Journals* 33; Shaver 93
'I read Tom Jones' (DW's journal, 25 Nov. 1800). See preceding note. It is likely that W was also rereading *Tom Jones* at this period: he seems to recall it in *Michael*,[1] and alludes to it in a letter to C of 22 May 1801 (*EY* 334 and n3).

(iii) *Joseph Andrews*
Suggested date of reading: probably by Feb. 1804
References: Lienemann 73

---

[1] See C. J. Rawson, '"Tom Jones" and "Michael": A Parallel', *N&Q* 212 (1967) 13.

'In "Joseph Andrews" III chapt. V and I chapt. VI begegnet uns ein ähnlicher Gedanke wie in Prel. III 579-84 und Prel. III 115-8' (Lienemann 73). Lienemann is of course referring to the 1850 *Fourteen-Book Prelude*. His evidence is not conclusive, but it is likely that W had read *Joseph Andrews* by Feb. 1804, when the lines to which he refers were composed (Reed ii 12). The set of Fielding's *Works* formerly in his father's library were not sent to DC until 1805 (see *WR* 58-9; Wu *Library* JW31).

163. Finch, Anne, Countess of Winchelsea, works
Suggested date of reading: by 17 Sept. 1814
References: *MY* ii 154
In his letter to Robert Anderson of 17 Sept. 1814, W suggests that an enlarged edn of Anderson's *British Poets* should include 'Lady Winchelsea'. He had known her work since his Cambridge years if not earlier (*WR* 59), and had by 1814 probably acquired the copy of her *Miscellany Poems* (1713) listed Shaver 94. Finch was well-represented in the album W compiled for Lady Mary Lowther in 1819, which included selections from *The Spleen*, *The Petition for an Absolute Retreat*, *Moral Song*, *The Mussulman's Dream*, *A Nocturnal Reverie*, *Enquiry after Peace*, *Fragment*, *Life's Progress* and *Hope* (*Album* 2-32).

164. Flatman, Thomas, *Poems and Songs* (4th edn, 1686)
Suggested date of reading: by Jan. 1815
References: *Prose Works* iii 71
W reveals that this was in his library in 1815 in his *Essay, Supplementary to the Preface*. This is his earliest known mention of Flatman.

165. Fletcher, Phineas or Giles Fletcher, works (Anderson)
Suggested date of reading: 11 Feb. 1802
References: *Grasmere Journals* 66
DW's journal for 11 Feb. 1802 records that 'I had begun with Fletcher, but he was too *dull* for me'. She was reading one of the Fletchers in Anderson, *British Poets* vol. 4, where they precede Jonson whom she and W went on to read together. She can be expected to have communicated her opinion to her brother.

166. *Flodden Field, in Nine Fits* (1664)
Suggested date of reading: between *c*. 8 May and *c*. 27 Sept. 1807
References: *MY* i 165-6
On 27 Sept. 1807 W told Walter Scott: 'I write to say that I have entrusted your Book, the Flodden field, (which either I neglected to give you at Coleorton, or you forgot to take away) to a person named Sarah Ashburner a Native of this Vale who is now servant with Mr Ferrier of Heriot Row Edingborough' (*MY* i 165-6). The work in question must have been *Flodden Field, in Nine Fits* (1664), which Scott presumably lent to W before 8 May 1807, when he

left Coleorton, where the Wordsworths had entertained him for a couple of days (Reed ii 354).

167. Fox, Rt. Hon. Charles James, *To Mrs. Crewe* **(Strawberry Hill, 1775)**
Suggested date of reading: by 15 May 1812
References: *Supp.* 74
In a letter to DW of 15 May 1812, W described dinner the previous day: 'Lady Crew was also of the party, a person to whom Charles Fox 30 or 40 years ago wrote verses which may be found if you think it worth while to seek for them in that miscellany of Poems printed at Carlisle which I gave Mary' (*Supp.* 74). W had therefore seen Fox's *To Mrs. Crewe* (1775) by 15 May 1812; for the 'miscellany' see note 392. W met Fox on 19 May 1806 (Reed ii 323), when Fox is said to have told him: 'I am very glad to see you, Mr. Wordsworth, though I am not of your faction' (*Rogers* 88).

168. Fox, afterwards Vassall, Henry Richard, 3rd Baron Holland, *Some Account of the Life and Writings of L. F. de Vega Carpio* **(1806)**
Suggested date of reading: c. 19 Aug. 1806
References: Reed ii 331-2n38; *Supp.* 6-7
'I felt myself greatly honoured in receiving (through the hands of Mr Longman) the Copy of your Life of Lope de Vega, sent me at your Lordship's request', W wrote to Holland on 19 Aug. 1806 (*Supp.* 6). W's remarks indicate that he had read it, though it had been in his possession for only a day. It was later retained at Rydal Mount (Shaver 97). Southey reviewed Holland's volume in the *Annual Review* 5 (1806) 397-411.

169. Foxe, John, *Acts and Monuments of Matters Most Special and Memorable*
Suggested date of reading: mid-Nov. 1806
References: *MY* i 100-1
Writing to Lady Beaumont from Coleorton, DW revealed: 'I have been reading in Fox's Book of Martyrs - not straight forward; but choice parts, it is a very interesting Book. The account of the Deaths of Ridley and Latimer (especially the latter) is most affecting and impressive' (*MY* i 100-1). If DW was reading this volume, there is a strong likelihood that W was too; she might at least have discussed it with him. The copy she read probably belonged to the Beaumonts. W had known Foxe since boyhood (*WR* 59-60).

170. Fraunce, Abraham, works
Suggested date of reading: by 17 Sept. 1814
References: *MY* ii 153
In his letter to Robert Anderson of 17 Sept. 1814, W suggests that an enlarged edn of Anderson's *British Poets* should include Fraunce. This indicates that he was aware of his works by 17 Sept. 1814.

171. Frend, William
(i) *Evening Amusements; or, the beauty of the heavens displayed* (1803)
Suggested date of reading: see note
References: see note

Shaver notes a copy of this volume bearing C's inscription 'To Hartley Coleridge from his affectionate father, S. T. Coleridge, Feb., 1809' (Shaver 98). W's copy, however, which Shaver does not mention, is now at the Wordsworth Library. The title-page bears the early ownership inscription, 'W Wordsworth'; the flyleaf is inscribed, 'Wm Wordsworth'. When did W acquire it? My guess is that it was given to W by the author at the same time as *Patriotism* (see next note).

(ii) *Patriotism; or the love of our country: an essay, illustrated by examples from ancient and modern history* (1804)
Suggested date of reading: see note
References: Shaver 295

W's copy is now at the Wordsworth Library. The verso of the front cover bears the inscription: 'Mr Wordsworth, the gift of the author'. When might Frend have presented W with this volume (and, possibly, *Evening Amusements*)? Their only known meeting occurred on 27 Feb. 1795 (Reed i 164), but the existence of this book and its presentation inscription indicates that they remained in touch after 1804. My guess is that Frend gave the books to W on a visit to London soon after publication - 1806, 1807, or 1808.

172. Galfridus, Monumetensis, *The British History, translated into English from the Latin of Jeffrey of Monmouth*, tr. Aaron Thompson (1718)
Suggested date of reading: 1814-15
References: Cornell *Poems 1807-20* 163, 531-3; Shaver 99

Geoffrey of Monmouth's *British History* is one of W's acknowledged sources for *Artegal and Elidure*, composed late 1814-Feb. 1815 (Cornell *Poems 1807-20* 163, 531-3). W may have seen it before then: on 16 Nov. 1807 Southey told Wynn that he owned a copy of 'the English "Geoffrey of Monmouth"' (Warter ii 27). A copy was at Rydal Mount by 1829 (Shaver 99).

173. Gay, John
(i) *Fables* (Glasgow, 1752)
Suggested date of reading: 1800s
References: see note

W's copy surfaced in the hands of a dealer during preparation of this book; its fate is unknown at the time of writing. Its title-page bears the inscription: 'Wm Wordsworth W.W.' This is an early inscription, the initials 'W.W.' being characteristic of volumes acquired during the later decades of the eighteenth century, and early 1800s. A reasonable guess would be that this volume came into W's possession during the DC years. This was presumably the copy of 'Gay's Fables:' mentioned in Dora's catalogue of the Rydal Mount library (Shaver 101).

(ii) *The Shepherd's Week in Six Pastorals* **(1714)**
Suggested date of reading: by Jan. 1815
References: *Prose Works* iii 72, 94
W refers to this work in his *Essay, Supplementary to the Preface*, composed in Jan. 1815.

174. *Gazette*
Suggested date of reading: 30 May 1811
References: Musgrove 12
On 31 May 1811, De Quincey wrote to Southey:

> We received the Gazette last night, and were a little disappointed by it: Wordsworth indeed was greatly mortified: however I think that to have *repulsed* Massena reinforced (as we now find that he had been) . . . may be held equal to having *routed* him if he had brought up only his former diminished army. (Musgrove 12; his italics)

Massena was repulsed at Fuentes Onoro, 5 May 1811. I have been unable to identify the 'Gazette' with any certainty. Southey was in the habit of sending his copies on to Grasmere after reading them.

175. 'German Grammar'
Suggested date of reading: 23 Feb. 1802
References: *Grasmere Journals* 71
DW studied her German grammar in connection with her translations from Lessing (see note 253[i]). As W was also participating in these translations, he might also have consulted this volume.

176. Gibbon, Edward, *The History of the Decline and Fall of the Roman Empire* **[6 vols., 1776-88]**
Suggested date of reading: perhaps *c.* 1801; almost certainly before 1804
References: Cornell *14-Book Prelude* 33n
Owen observes that W's consideration of Mithridates as a subject at *Thirteen-Book Prelude* i 186-202 was inspired not only by Percy's translation of Mallet, but by Gibbon (Cornell *14-Book Prelude* 33n; see also Cornell *13-Book Prelude* i 111n and Norton *Prel.* 38n2). W did not at this period possess a copy of his own, but had he wanted to consult one he had only to visit Greta Hall, where he could have seen the copy belonging to C's landlord, William Jackson. W acquired one only when presented with it by Robinson in 1836, which he wrote

to acknowledge in April of that year: 'My little Library had long been disgraced by want of Gibbons decline a deficiency you have kindly supplied' (*LY* iii 201; see also Shaver 102).

177. Gilbert, William
(i) *The Hurricane: A Theosophical and Western Eclogue* **(Bristol, 1796)**
Suggested date of reading: by spring 1800
References: Cornell *Lyrical Ballads* 381
W may have read Gilbert's remarkable poem as early as 1796 (*WR* 63). A note to *The Brothers*, composed between late Dec. 1799 and 5 April 1800, reveals that W's description of the calenture at lines 50-62 'is sketch'd from an imperfect recollection of an admirable one in prose, by Mr. Gilbert, author of the Hurricane' (Cornell *Lyrical Ballads* 144). This does not imply a reading of Gilbert's poem at the time of writing; indeed, W's admission that he has only an 'imperfect recollection' of the poem suggests that he had not seen it for some time. However, a copy of *The Hurricane* was at Rydal Mount (Shaver 102); for speculations concerning this matter see pp. xvi-xvii, above.

(ii) *The Hurricane: A Theosophical and Western Eclogue* **(Bristol, 1796)**
Suggested date of reading: spring 1814
References: *Excursion* (1814), pp. 427-8
W quotes one of Gilbert's notes in one of his notes to *The Excursion*, remarking: 'The Reader, I am sure, will thank me for the above Quotation, which, though from a strange book, is one of the finest passages of modern English Prose' (p. 428). A copy of Gilbert's volume was at Rydal Mount (Shaver 102).

178. Gillies, Robert Pearce
(i) *Egbert; or The Suicide* in MS
Suggested date of reading: between 12 and 23 Nov. 1814
References: *Supp.* 154; Shaver 103
On 23 Nov. 1814 W wrote to Gillies to thank him for a copy of this poem, apparently in MS, which he found 'pleasingly and vigorously written' (*Supp.* 154). He had presumably received it after 12 Nov., the date of his previous letter. *Egbert* was first published in Gillies' *Illustrations of a Poetical Character* (Edinburgh, 1816), a copy of which he sent W prior to publication in April 1816 (*MY* ii 298).

(ii) *Childe Alarique; a poet's reverie, with other poems* **(Edinburgh, 1814)**
Suggested date of reading: Nov. 1814 onwards
References: *Supp.* 155; Shaver 102
W received a parcel containing a presentation copy of this volume between 12 and 23 Nov. 1814. On 23 Nov. he told Gillies: 'Your Poem I have barely looked into, but I promise myself no inconsiderable pleasure in the perusal of this' (*Supp.* 155). In a letter of 22 Dec.

W reveals that he has been reading *Childe Alarique* to MW (*MY* ii 179); he refers to part of the volume in a further letter of 14 Feb. 1815 (*MY* ii 197).

(iii) *Albert* **in MS**
Suggested date of reading: Jan.-Feb. 1815; by 14 Feb. 1815
References: *MY* ii 195
W received a copy of Gillies' *Albert* some time during Jan. 1815 and his detailed criticisms of 14 Feb. indicate that he had by then read it. It was subsequently published in Gillies' *Illustrations of a Poetical Character* (1816).

179. Gilpin, William
(i) *Observations, Relative Chiefly to Picturesque Beauty, Made in the Year 1772, on Several Parts of England; Particularly the Mountains, and Lakes of Cumberland, and Westmoreland* **(2 vols., 1786)**
Suggested date of reading: c. 14 Jan.-13 June 1804
References: see note
Trott and Wu discuss the influence of Gilpin's description of Rubens' 'Daniel in the Lions' Den' on W's cave simile at *Thirteen-Book Prelude* viii 711-27, composed between c. 14 Jan. and 13 June 1804; see 'Three Sources for Wordsworth's *Prelude* Cave', *N&Q* NS 38 (1991) 298-9. W had probably owned a copy of this book since his Cambridge years; see *WR* 64.

(ii) *Observations on the River Wye . . . Relative Chiefly to Picturesque Beauty: Made in the Summer of the Year 1770* **(2nd edn, 1789)**
Suggested date of reading: 1810
References: *Prose Works* ii 414; Shaver 103
Gilpin's *Observations on the River Wye* is alluded to several times in W's *Select Views*, composed 1810. There was a copy at Rydal Mount.

180. Godwin, William
(i) *Essay on Sepulchres* **(1809)**
Suggested date of reading: spring 1811
References: *MY* i 469-70
'Godwin is well', Lamb reported to C in June 1809, 'He has written a very pretty, absurd, book about Sepulchres' (Marrs iii 14).[1] W might have been expected to have read this before writing his *Essays Upon Epitaphs*, but apparently did not; only on 9 March 1811 did he ask Godwin for a copy: 'If you can command a Copy of your book upon Burial, which I have never seen, let it be sent to Lamb's for my use who in the course of this Spring will be able to forward it to me free of expense' (*MY* i 469-70). It is not clear whether Lamb did forward

---

[1] For a concise account of the *Essay*, and further comment by Lamb, see William St Clair, *The Godwins and the Shelleys* (1989), pp. 306-7.

a copy of the *Essay* to Grasmere. No copy is listed by Shaver, and W's reference to it in 1840 suggests that he knew it but vaguely, if at all (*LY* iv 29 and n1).

(ii) *The Lives of Edward and John Philips, Nephews and Pupils of Milton* (1815)
Suggested date of reading: 22 May 1815
References: Marrs iii 161
On 22 May 1815 Mary Lamb wrote to Mrs Morgan and Charlotte Brent:

> Godwin has just pub[li]shed a new book, I wish it may be successful but I am sure it is very dull. Wordsworth has just now looked into it and found these words 'All modern poetry is nothing but the old, genuine poetry, new [vam]ped, and delivered to us at second, or twentieth hand.' In great wrath he took a pencil and wrote in the margin 'That is false, William Godwin. Signed William Wordsworth.' (Marrs iii 161)

The 'new book' was Godwin's *Lives of Edward and John Philips*, which had only recently been published. It would be a fair guess that W did not read the entire book through on that occasion, and made no effort to do so in later years.

181. Goldsmith, Oliver
(i) *Retaliation*
Suggested date of reading: by 20 July 1804
References: EY 491
W must have known this poem very well by the time he quoted it in a letter to Beaumont of 20 July 1804; he may even have been quoting from memory.

(ii) *The Vicar of Wakefield* [1766]
Suggested date of reading: by 4 Nov. 1805
References: EY 635
The earliest reference to Goldsmith's novel by either W or DW comes in a letter to Lady Beaumont of 4 Nov. 1805, though they must both have read it well before that.

(iii) *An History of England in a Series of Letters from a Nobleman to his Son* [2 vols., 1764]
Suggested date of reading: Jan. 1812 onwards
References: Reed ii 490
W's Longman accounts contain a debit for '2 Goldsmiths England per Mr Jameson' for 5s.10d. on 14 Jan. 1812 (see p. 266). Mr Jameson was a bookseller in Edinburgh (see *MY* ii 341, 342). The two copies of Goldsmith's *History of England* were probably gifts for John and Thomas Wordsworth. A copy of this volume had been in JW Sr's library at Cockermouth, and W had probably read it as a boy (Wu *Library* JW19).

182. Googe, Barnaby, works
Suggested date of reading: by 17 Sept. 1814
References: *MY* ii 153
In his letter to Robert Anderson of 17 Sept. 1814, W suggests that an enlarged edn of Anderson's *British Poets* should include Googe, translator of Montemayor. This indicates that he was aware of his works by 17 Sept. 1814.

183. Gower, John, *Tale Imitated from Gower* in MS
Suggested date of reading: c. Sept. 1802
References: Reed ii 642
Prelude MS W contains the fair copy of a verse adaptation of the tale of the travellers and the angel from Gower's *Confessio Amantis* ii 291-364 in DW's hand, entitled 'Tale Imitated from Gower - Friend and Contemporary of Chaucer' (DC MS 38, 10r-12r). It was not apparently copied from a printed source. Like the transcription of Marvell's *Horatian Ode* (see note 273[ii]), which precedes it in the MS, it may have derived from a text belonging to Lamb, consulted during the Wordsworths' visit to London in Sept. 1802. My guess is that the adaptation was by Mary Lamb, as the adaptation has stylistic features in common with other verse by her; this judgement is far from provable, however. Its first line, 'In antient Books I find it written', is distinctly reminiscent of that of W's 'I find it written of Simonides', composed between 21 May 1802 and 7 Oct. 1803 (see Cornell *Poems 1800-7* 583-4). A full text of the MS is provided in Appendix VI.

184. Graham, James, 1st Marquis of Montrose, *I'll never love thee more*
Suggested date of reading: by autumn 1804
References: Norton *Prel.* 292n6
The allusion at *Thirteen-Book Prelude* viii 507, composed probably in autumn 1804, is to Graham's *I'll never love thee more*, which 'Wordsworth probably read in James Watson's *A Choice Collection of Comic and Serious Scots Poems*, 3 Parts (1706-11), Part III, p. 111' (Norton *Prel.* 292n6).

185. Grahame, James
(i) *The Sabbath: A Poem* (Edinburgh, 1804)
Suggested date of reading: 7 Aug. 1805
References: *EY* 617
On 7 Aug. 1805 the Wordsworths told Lady Beaumont that 'We have just read a poem called *the Sabbath* written by a very good man in a truly christian spirit; it contains several sweet passages - beautiful images and tender thoughts - but it wants harmony, the versification indeed being very unpleasing' (*EY* 617). As a copy is not listed by Shaver it may be that they had access to Southey's; he reviewed it for the *Annual Review* 4 (1805) 588-91.

Intriguingly, Grahame owned a number of letters by Burns, and may have discussed them with W.[1]

(ii) *Birds of Scotland* (Edinburgh, 1806)
Suggested date of reading: by Dec. 1806
References: *MY* i 120; Shaver 106
W copied out seven lines of Grahame's poem in a letter to Lady Beaumont of Dec. 1806, written at Coleorton, commending it as 'exquisite'. Grahame probably gave W a copy, *c*. 19 June 1806, when he and his wife and two daughters called at DC (*MY* i 50, 74; Reed ii 327). The lines quoted in the letter to Lady Beaumont were probably copied from the printed volume, in which case W must have had it with him at Coleorton. His copy is now at Harvard University Library.

Grahame's brother, Robert, was the source of the story that inspired *Alice Fell* (see Cornell *Poems 1800-7* 408; *Grasmere Journals* 206-7).

On 18 Nov. 1809 Southey was given a copy of Grahame's *British Georgics* (Edinburgh, 1809) by its publisher, James Ballantyne; W would probably have seen it in due course. It is now in the Dyce Collection, National Art Library, Victoria and Albert Museum (T4to 4177).

186. [Grant, Anne], *Memoirs of an American Lady; with sketches of manners and scenery in America, as they existed previous to the Revolution* (2 vols., 1808)
Suggested date of reading: summer 1813
References: *MY* ii 121
'My whole summer's reading has been a part of two volumes of Mrs Grant's American Lady, which Southey lent to be speedily returned, and a dip or two in Southey's Nelson', DW told Catherine Clarkson on 4 Oct. 1813 (*MY* ii 121-2). It is not clear whether W read Grant's *Memoirs* too, but he may at least have heard about them. He had already heard of Grant through Lady Beaumont (see note AII3). Dorothy A. Porter McMillan points out to me that, against the evidence of the British Library catalogue, Catalina Schuyler (whom Grant refers to as 'Aunt') was the subject, rather than the author, of the *Memoirs*. DW's remarks raise the interesting possibility that Southey was reviewing the *Memoirs*, but no such review is recorded by Curry.[2] Southey evidently admired Grant, as he called on her during his Scottish tour of 1819, and later corresponded with her (Curry ii 266-7).

187. Graves, John, *The History of Cleveland, in the North Riding of the County of York* (Carlisle, 1808)
Suggested date of reading: between 5 June and 2 Oct. 1808

---

[1] See J. W. Egerer, *A Bibliography of Robert Burns* (Edinburgh, 1964).
[2] See 'Southey's Contributions to the *Annual Review*', *Bulletin of Bibliography* 16 (1939) 195-7, and 'Southey's Contributions to *The Quarterly Review*', *WC* 6 (1975) 261-72.

References: *MY* i 270

On 2 Oct. 1808, W wrote to Francis Wrangham, suggesting that he write a 'topographical History of your neighbourhood' along the lines of White's *Selborne* or Whitaker's *History of Craven*:

> I am induced to mention it from belief that you are admirably qualified for such a work; that it would pleasantly employ your leisure hours; and from a regret in seeing works of this kind which might be made so very interesting, utterly marred by falling into the hands of wretched Bunglers, e.g. the *History of Cleveland* which I have just read, by a Clergyman of Yarm of the name of Grave, the most heavy performance I ever encountered, and what an interesting district! (*MY* i 270)

W previous extant letter to Wrangham dates from 5 June; he must therefore have read Graves' *History* between then and 2 Oct. This book was retained at Rydal Mount (Shaver 107).

188. Gray, Thomas
(i) *The Poems of Mr Gray*, ed. William Mason [2 vols., York, 1775]
Suggested date of reading: mid-Nov. 1806
References: *MY* i 101

'I am now reading Gray's life and letters', DW told Lady Beaumont on 15 Nov. 1806. This must be a reference to Mason's edn, which contains a memoir composed of Gray's letters in garbled form. Presumably the copy she was reading belonged to the Beaumonts, as she was writing from Coleorton. There were copies of this edn at Rydal Mount (Shaver 108).

(ii) *Epitaph on Mrs Clark*
Suggested date of reading: by 22 Feb. 1810
References: *Prose Works* ii 86-7

W quotes this work in the third of his *Essays Upon Epitaphs*. His source, Owen and Smyser suggest, was Knox's *Elegant Extracts* (see note 237[iii]).

(iii) *Works . . . to which are added, Memoirs of his Life and Writings*, **ed. William Mason (4th edn, 2 vols., 1807)**
Suggested date of reading: by 22 Feb. 1810
References: *Prose Works* ii 115-16

Owen and Smyser note that W's source for Gray's epitaph on his mother, quoted in the third of the *Essays Upon Epitaphs*, is this edn of the *Works* (*Prose Works* ii 87). W also referred to Gray's *Works* as he composed the *Select Views* in 1810 (*Prose Works* ii 408).

189. Greene, Robert, *Ah, What Is Love?*
Suggested date of reading: probably by 5 April 1800
References: Reed ii 703 and n1; Moorman *N&Q* 402

Reed judges that Greene's poem was entered by JW in the Wordsworth Commonplace Book (DC MS 26, 26v-27r) by 5 April 1800. It is reasonable to suppose that the Commonplace Book contained copies of texts made from works not owned by W.

190. Greville, Fulke, Baron Brooke
(i) *The Life of the Renowned Sir Philip Sidney* **[1652]**
Suggested date of reading: Oct.-Nov. 1806
References: Cornell *Poems 1800-7* 414
The last two lines of *November 1806* ('Another year! - another deadly blow!') are taken from the first part of chapter 8 of Greville's *Life*. W did not at that time own a copy, but it seems likely that the Beaumonts did, and he would have had the run of their library at Coleorton at the time he composed this poem. The impetus to read Greville may have come from C, who was apparently reading and annotating Lamb's copy of the *Works* in Aug.-Sept. 1806 on his return to London from the Mediterranean (see CC *Marginalia* ii 873-4; Whalley *BC* 55).

(ii) *The Life of the Renowned Sir Philip Sidney* **[1652]**
Suggested date of reading: *c*. March 1809 onwards
References: *MY* i 289
Writing to Daniel Stuart on 5 Feb. 1809, who at that time was wont to send books to Grasmere, W said: 'I also wish much to see Lord Brooke's Life of Sir Philip Sidney. It is not an uncommon Book, and perhaps a Bookseller could procure it' (*MY* i 289). It was at around that moment that he alluded to the work in *The Convention of Cintra* (*Prose Works* i 383), suggesting that he at least had access to a copy. Alternatively - and this is just a possibility - he was referring to notes he had made from the copy he may have seen at Coleorton. I doubt whether he ever acquired his own; none is listed by Shaver.

(iii) *The Remains of Sir Fulk Grevill; Lord Brooke;*
being Poems of Monarchy and Religion **(1670)**
Suggested date of reading: *c*. May or June 1809 onwards
References: Jordan 178
On 5 March 1809 De Quincey told DW that he had found '2 works of Ld. Brooke's which I never before heard of etc.' (Jordan 101); these he identified on 25 May as 'his Posthumous Poems: - and his "5 years of King James: or the State of England &c. and the relation of it to other provinces" - a prose work' (Jordan 178). It is likely that he sent these volumes to Allan Bank shortly after writing to DW; at the latest, the Wordsworths would have received them when De Quincey moved into DC on *c*. 20 Oct.

C read Greville's *A Treatie of Human Learning, An Inquisition upon Fame and Honour, A Treatie of Warres*, and *Alaham* in March 1810 at Allan Bank (*Notebooks* iii 3709-19). Coburn and Whalley agree that he may have been referring to Southey's copy of Greville's *Certaine Learned and Elegant Workes* (1633). He had annotated Lamb's copy in 1806 (*Notebooks* iii

3709; CC *Marginalia* ii 874). Given W's interest in Greville it is possible that he shared in the 1810 readings or discussed them with C.

In his letter to Robert Anderson of 17 Sept. 1814, W suggested that an enlarged edn of Anderson's *British Poets* include 'Lord Brooke' (*MY* ii 153).

(iv) *The Five Years of King James; or, the Condition of the State of England, and the Relation it had to other Provinces* (1643)
Suggested date of reading: c. May or June 1809 onwards
References: Jordan 178
See preceding note.

191. Grimm, Friedrich Melchior von, Baron, *Correspondance littéraire, philosophique et critique, addressée à un souverain d'Allemagne* (16 vols., Paris, 1813)
Suggested date of reading: by Jan. 1815
References: *Prose Works* iii 69, 89
W alludes to Grimm's remarks in his *Essay, Supplementary to the Preface*, indicating that he was acquainted with the *Correspondance littéraire* by Jan. 1815. Perhaps his source was Southey, who had owned a copy (Southey *SC* 1244).

192. *Guide to the City of Perth*
Suggested date of reading: 20 or 21 Aug. 1814 onwards
References: Reed ii 566-7; Shaver 110
Reed records that SH's journal of the Scottish tour of 1814 mentions meeting 'a bookseller of whom W had bought a small Ed. of Ossian & the Perth Guide'.

193. Guyon, Jeanne Marie Bouvières de la Motte, *The Life of Lady Guion*, abridged and translated [by J. Gough] (Bristol, 1772)
Suggested date of reading: by 29 Sept. 1800
References: Reed ii 704; Moorman *N&Q* 402
Reed judges that W and DW copied extracts from the *Life* into the Wordsworth Commonplace Book (DC MS 26, 25v-26r) by 29 Sept. 1800. It is reasonable to suppose that the Commonplace Book contained copies of works not owned by W.

Intriguingly, C alludes to the *Life* in notebook entries of June-July 1810 (*Notebooks* iii 3922, 3946). His source is not known, though he was apparently resident at Greta Hall at the time.

194. Hakewill, George, *An Apologie or Declaration of the Power and Providence of God in the Government of the World. Consisting in an Examination and Censure of the Common Errour Touching Natures Perpetuall and Universall Decay, Divided into Six Books* (3rd edn, Oxford, 1635)
Suggested date of reading: by Jan. 1815

References: *Prose Works* iii 68, 88

W alludes to Hakewill in his *Essay, Supplementary to the Preface*, composed in Jan. 1815. Shaver lists C's copy as present at Rydal Mount (Shaver 332); it was probably left at Allan Bank when C departed for London in 1810.

195. Hakluyt, Richard, ***The Principall Navigations, Voyages, and Discoveries of the English Nation*** **[1589]**
Suggested date of reading: by late Feb. 1804
References: OET *Prel.* 625

W draws on Hakluyt in drafts towards the Five-Book *Prelude* made in MS W, late Feb. or early March 1804;[1] his reference to William de Rubruquis's *Itinerarium* at *Thirteen-Book Prelude* vii 86-8 is probably also indebted to Hakluyt, in whose *Principall Navigations* the *Itinerarium* was first published (Cornell *13-Book Prelude* 196). All of which suggests that W had a copy of Hakluyt close at hand as he worked on the *Prelude* in 1804 - though none are listed by the Shavers. The likeliest source is Southey, from whom W was already borrowing books at this date. Southey owned a black letter copy of the *Navigations* by April 1813, and may have acquired it by 1804 (Southey *SC* 1212; Curry ii 56). W mentions Hakluyt in a letter he wrote with Southey to Robert Anderson, 17 Sept. 1814 (*MY* ii 152).

196. Hall, Joseph, Bishop of Exeter and Norwich
(i) Satires (Anderson)
Suggested date of reading: 15 Nov. 1801
References: *Grasmere Journals* 38, 183

DW records that she and W read Hall on 15 Nov. 1801; Pamela Woof notes that they 'were undoubtedly reading Hall's early Satires in Anderson, *British Poets* vol. 2. The first satires are on the art of poetry and there is praise of the "eternal legends" of "Renowned Spenser", whom W read next day from the same volume.' See *British Poets* ii 731-56. W's copy of Hall's *A Recollection of such Treatises as have been heretofore severally published* (Cambridge, 1615) is now at the Folger Shakespeare Library, Washington, DC. It contains his ownership inscription on the half-title of 'Meditations and Vowes'.

By autumn 1802 C was also an admirer of Hall. He had a set of the *Works* at Keswick by Sept. (Griggs ii 870), and in Oct. told Tom Wedgwood that he would 'in a very few weeks go to the Press with a Volume on the Prose writings of Hall, Milton, & Taylor' (Griggs ii 877). It is likely that the Wordsworths' interest fuelled, or even inspired, his; see Coffman H11-12b.

---

[1] The relevant passage is reproduced OET *Prel.* 625; my dating of the MS W drafts follows that given by Jonathan Wordsworth, Norton *Prel.* 496.

(ii) (Anderson)
Suggested date of reading: 23 Feb. 1802
References: *Grasmere Journals* 72
'William now reading in Bishop Hall' (DW's journal, 23 Feb. 1802).

197. Hamilton, William, *The Braes of Yarrow*
Suggested date of reading: probably Sept. 1803
References: Cornell *Poems 1800-7* 199, 417
Hamilton's *Braes of Yarrow* was an important influence on W's *Yarrow Unvisited*, composed between 14 Oct. 1803 and 6 March 1804. An allusion is acknowledged by W in a note (Cornell *Poems 1800-7* 199, 417). He would have known Hamilton's poem from both Percy's *Reliques*, a copy of which he had purchased in Hamburg in 1798 (*WR* 111), and Knox's *Elegant Extracts* (1791) Book V, pp. 404-5.

198. Hargrave, Francis, *A Complete Collection of State-Trials, and Proceedings for High Treason* (4th edn, 11 vols., 1776-81)
Suggested date of reading: by Nov. 1807
References: Jordan 136; Shaver 115
On 1 April 1809 De Quincey wrote to DW: 'I am very glad to tell you that I have succeeded in finding the 11th. vol. of the State Trials (the whole of what is wanting in your copy). This makes the work worth 20 guineas or more' (Jordan 136). This means that W must have acquired his copy of Hargrave by Nov. 1807 when De Quincey was last in Grasmere, and when he would have seen the set minus vol. 11. It is not clear when the replacement volume arrived at Grasmere; it was still, apparently, with De Quincey when he wrote to DW on 25-7 May 1809, and was presumably given to W by the time De Quincey moved into DC on *c.* 20 Oct. 1809. It passed into Rydal Mount where it remained until the sale of 1859.

199. Harrison, Anthony, *Poetical Recreations* (2 vols., 1806)
Suggested date of reading: *c.* 1806
References: Shaver 116, 333
Harrison was an old schoolfriend of W, having been one of the donors to the New Library of Hawkshead Grammar School in 1792 (TWT 369). By 1800 he was a solicitor in Penrith, where the Wordsworths had lived in earlier years. He was one of their earliest friends when they moved into DC, staying there overnight on 30 Aug. 1800 (Reed ii 83).

Two copies of his *Poetical Recreations* were at Rydal Mount (Shaver 116, 333), one of which was C's. They must have been given to W and C at around the time of publication. This is particularly likely as vol. 2 contains a poem called *The Barkhouse-Beck Leap; An Epic Poem, in Twenty Four Stanzas*, stanza 19 of which reads:

> Some tell of nimble bounding Deer,
>   And Stag of Hart-Leap-Well*:
> But of all Leaps, both far and near,
>   The greatest Leap I tell.
>
> * See Mr. Wordsworth's Poem of Hartleap-Well.

Harrison would certainly have shown his old schoolfriend this backhanded tribute; indeed, all of *The Barkhouse-Beck Leap* is intended to parody W's poem. Characteristically, it was what came to mind when, on 31 Dec. 1814, in response to Harrison's reported disdain of *The Excursion*, W said that 'A.H. selected as a topic for his Muse, the Bark-house Beck; so called from its collecting into its bosom all the sweets of Jack Hindson's tan-yard' (*MY* ii 183).

More intriguingly still, vol. 2 of *Poetical Recreations* contains a poem entitled *Charade XV. To Dorothea*, which, with its setting 'By rural GRASMERE's calm Retreat', is addressed to DW.

Harrison saw a good deal of C and W in 1809 as he had by July become a proof-reader for *The Friend* (Griggs iii 218). He also gave W a copy of Barrington's *Observations* (see note 26). He engaged SH in conversation in March 1812 (*SHL* 46), and was visited by Southey in July (Warter ii 284). He was in contact with the Wordsworths in Oct. 1814, when MW wrote to Thomas Monkhouse through him (*MWL* 22).

200. Harte, Walter
(i) works
Suggested date of reading: by 18 Jan. 1808
References: *MY* i 190

In a letter to Walter Scott of 18 Jan. 1808, W mentions 'Harte's Poems Anderson's edition', going on to observe that 'Harte had read Dryden's works with exceeding care but very little profit' (*MY* i 190-1). W read Harte in Anderson, *British Poets* vol. 11.

(ii) *The History of the Life of Gustavus Adolphus, King of Sweden, surnamed the Great* [2 vols., 1759]
Suggested date of reading: by 18 April 1809
References: Griggs iii 200

In a letter to Stuart of 18 April 1809, C writes: 'O God! to read the life of Gustavus Adolphus by Harte (a book, I earnestly recommend to you) or the Memoirs of Col. (or Captn) Tarlton, which contains the best existing account of Lord Peterborough's Campaign in the N. of Spain - & then to think of the very best of our present Soldiers - almost inspires the melancholy idea, that we are predestined to be baffled' (Griggs iii 200). The second of these books, Carleton's *Memoirs*, was at Allan-Bank by March 1809 (see note 83), from where C was writing. In view of that fact it seems likely that Harte's *History* was also at Allan Bank, and that W would have wanted to read it, particularly in view of his interest in Harte's poems (see preceding note). All the same, these volumes were owned by C rather than W: he recommended them again to Stuart (Griggs iii 225-6) and asked Street to return them on 5 Oct. 1811 (Griggs iii 336). By 1815 he had become separated from them; then living in Calne, he asked Gutch to send him another copy, evidently recalling his earlier reading (Griggs iv 596).

201. Hartley, David
(i) *Observations on Man, His Frame, His Duty, and His Expectations* **[1749]**
Suggested date of reading: Sept. 1800
References: *Prose Works* i 169
Owen notes the use of Hartleian terms in W's *Preface* (*Prose Works* i 169); see also Owen (1969) 28-9. In a letter to me, Owen remarks: 'It is hard to think that W didn't read Hartley, especially considering STC's early enthusiasm; and some of the verbal parallels given in *Prose Works* i 169, 171 are quite close. STC's copy of Hartley was among his books in W's library (Shaver 333).' This is now at the British Library; the marginalia it contains were entered, Whalley suggests, between 1798 and 1802 (CC *Marginalia* ii 959).

(ii) *Observations on Man, His Frame, His Duty, and His Expectations* **[1749]**
Suggested date of reading: by 27 Sept. 1808
References: *MY* i 266
W's first explicit reference to Hartley's *Observations*, a book argued to have influenced his poetry from 1798 onwards, dates from a letter of 27 Sept. 1808 (*MY* i 266 and n2). The reference, which is brief, proves little, but W would hardly have mentioned this title were he unacquainted with it.

202. Hawes, Stephen, works
Suggested date of reading: by 17 Sept. 1814
References: *MY* ii 153
In his letter to Robert Anderson of 17 Sept. 1814, W suggests that an enlarged edn of Anderson's *British Poets* should include Hawes. This indicates that he was aware of his works by 17 Sept. 1814. Hawes appeared in Southey's *Select Works of the British Poets* (1831).

203. Hays, Samuel, *A Practical Treatise on Planting and the Management of Woods and Coppices* **(Dublin and London, 1794)**
Suggested date of reading: ?1810s
References: Shaver 296
W's copy is at the Wordsworth Library, donated by Jonathan Wordsworth. The date of its acquisition by W is unclear, but it contains an inscription, in ink, in his hand, 'Wm Wordsworth', that appears to me to date from the 1810s.

204. Hazlitt, William
(i) *An Essay on the Principles of Human Action* **(1805)**
Suggested date of reading: c. mid-Feb. 1806
References: Marrs ii 205; Shaver 334

On 1 Feb. 1806, Lamb wrote to W to say that he had purchased copies of Urry's Chaucer, Pope's Shakespeare, Spenser and Milton on his behalf, and sent them up on the Kendal wagon that very day. Included with these, he went on, 'there comes W. Hazlitt's book about Human Action for Coleridge' (Marrs ii 205). It is fair to suppose that W would have given this volume more than a quick glance before forwarding it to C; he would have been familiar with its contents as Hazlitt brought the MS to Alfoxden in May 1798. This is supported by his annotation to Field's *Memoirs*, where he admits to having 'little or no knowledge of H's writings except his first metaphysical Work'.[1] In due course C's copy of the *Essay* was housed at Rydal Mount (Shaver 334).

(ii) review of *The Excursion*, **Examiner 21, 28 Aug., 2 Oct. 1814, pp. 541-2, 555-8, 636-8**
Suggested date of reading: by 18 Sept. 1814 (parts 1 and 2); between 22 and 29 Oct. 1814 (part 3)
References: see note

Hazlitt's review of *The Excursion* appeared in *The Examiner* in three parts: on 21, 28 Aug. and 2 Oct. 1814. The most detailed account of W's response is given by Hazlitt himself in *A Reply to 'Z'*. Answering the accusation that W was his protector, Hazlitt replies: 'Mr. Wilson tells, as I understand in all companies the following story of Mr. Wordsworth's particular benevolence and regard to me':

> Some time in the latter end of the year 1814 Mr. Wordsworth received an *Examiner* by the post, which annoyed him exceedingly both on account of the expence and the paper. 'Why did they send that rascally paper to him, and make him pay for it?' Mr. Wordsworth is tenacious of his principles and not less so of his purse. 'Oh,' said Wilson, 'let us see what there is in it. I dare say they have not sent it you for nothing. Why here, there's a criticism upon the Excursion in it.' This made the poet (*par excellence*) rage and fret the more. 'What did they know about his poetry? What could they know about it? It was presumption in the highest degree for these cockney writers to pretend to criticise a Lake poet.' 'Well,' says the other, 'at any rate let us read it.' So he began. The article was much in favour of the poet and the poem. As the reading proceeded, 'Ha,' said Mr. Wordsworth, somewhat appeased, 'there's some sense in this fellow too: the Dog writes strong.' Upon which Mr. Wilson was encouraged to proceed still farther with the encomium, and Mr. Wordsworth continued his approbation; 'Upon my word very judicious, very well indeed.' At length, growing vain with his own and the *Examiner's* applause, he suddenly seized the paper into his own hands, and saying 'Let

---

[1] *Barron Field's Memoirs of Wordsworth*, ed. Geoffrey Little (Sydney, 1975), p. 66n110.

me read it, Mr. Wilson,' did so with an audible voice and appropriate gesture to the end, when he exclaimed, 'Very well written indeed, Sir, I did not expect a thing of this kind,' and strutting up and down the room in high good humour kept every now and then wondering who could be the author, 'he had no idea, and should like very much to know to whom he was indebted for such pointed and judicious praise' - when Mr. Wilson interrupted him with saying, 'Oh don't you know; it's Hazlitt, to be sure, there are his initials to it,' threw our poor philosopher into a greater rage than ever, and a fit of outrageous incredulity to think that he should be indebted for the first favourable account that had ever appeared of any work he had ever written to a person on whom he had conferred such great and unmerited obligations. I think this statement will shew that there is very little love lost between me and my benefactor. If farther proofs are called, I have them at hand, and in a sufficient number. (Howe ix 6)

Stanley Jones tells me that Hazlitt's source for this story was probably Alexander Henderson, who spent time with Hazlitt in summer 1818, just before *A Reply to 'Z'* was composed, rather than Charles Lloyd, Howe's preferred candidate (Howe ix 250). Jones goes on to point out one snag with Hazlitt's account of W's reading of his review: only the last of its three parts bore Hazlitt's initials. Jones continues: 'Now it is somewhat odd that Wilson had to point out the initials "W.H." to Wordsworth; and Wordsworth's wondering who the writer could be is only plausible if the article was unsigned. The second part is rather less flattering than the first so we may perhaps legitimately suppose that the number Wilson showed Wordsworth was that of 21 Aug., and that it impelled Wordsworth to buy the second and third instalments' (letter to me). See also Stanley Jones, *Hazlitt: A Life* (1989), pp. 155-60.

This would be consistent with the documentary evidence, such as it is, for W's reading. MW's letter to DW and SH of 29 Sept. 1814 states: 'Hazlitt *did do* that for the Examiner' (*MWL* 15), revealing that she and W had seen the first two parts of Hazlitt's review by that date. But it also suggests that DW and SH had seen Hazlitt's review prior to their departure from Rydal Mount on 18 Sept. In fact, DW admitted as much in her letter to Catherine Clarkson of 11 Nov.: 'I saw two sections of Hazlitt's Review *at Rydale*' (*MY* ii 165). The first two parts of Hazlitt's review must therefore have been at Rydal Mount by 18 Sept.

On 29 Oct. MW told DW (still at Hindwell) that 'The conclusion of Hazlitt's Critique is come to us - a curious piece, but it must benefit the sale of the book' (*MWL* 24). Presumably, the third part of Hazlitt's review had arrived at Rydal Mount between 22 Oct. (the date of MW's previous letter to DW, which makes no mention of it) and 29 Oct. W can be presumed to have read it at some point during those days.

DW's letters to Catherine Clarkson no doubt embody her brother's opinions of the review; see *MY* ii 160, 165. She had not seen the third part by 11 Nov., but would have caught up with it on her return to Rydal Mount in early Dec., if not before. It is worth adding that Robinson thought that Hazlitt's review was 'excellent . . . excepting from this praise some very coarse and cynical remarks on a country life' (Morley i 151).

(iii) review of *Comus*, *Examiner* 11 June 1815, pp. 381-2
Suggested date of reading: between 11 and 15 June 1815
References: Reed ii 606-7; Morley i 169
In the last paragraph of Hazlitt's review of a recent performance of *Comus* in *The Examiner* of 11 June 1815, he commented:

> We have no less respect for the memory of MILTON as a patriot than as a poet. Whether he was a *true* patriot, we shall not inquire: he was at least a *consistent* one. He did not retract his defence of the people of England; he did not say that his sonnets to VANE or CROMWELL were meant ironically; he was not appointed Poet Laureat to a Court which he had reviled and insulted; he accepted neither place nor pension; nor did he write paltry sonnets upon the 'Royal fortitude' of the House of STUART, by which, however, they really lost something.*
>
> * In the last edition of the Works of a modern Poet there is a Sonnet to the King, complimenting him on 'his royal fortitude,' and (somewhat prematurely) on the triumphs resulting from it. The story of the *Female Vagrant*, which very beautifully and affectingly describes the miseries brought on the lower classes by war, in bearing which the said 'royal fortitude' is so nobly exercised, is very properly struck out of the collection.
> (*Examiner*, 11 June 1815, p. 382; his italics)

W read this at some point between 11 and 15 June, when Robinson recorded in his diary:

> We talked about Hazlitt in consequence of a malignant attack on Wordsworth by him in Sunday's *Examiner*. Wordsworth that very day called on Hunt, who, in a manly way, asked whether Wordsworth had seen the paper of the morning, saying, if he had, he should consider his call as a higher honour. He disclaimed the article. The attack by Hazlitt was a note in which, after honouring Milton for being a consistent patriot, he sneered at Wordsworth as the author of 'paltry sonnets upon the royal fortitude,' etc. and insinuated that he had left out the *Female Vagrant*, a poem describing the miseries of war sustained by the poor. (Morley i 169)

The poem to which Hazlitt took exception was *Now that all hearts are glad, all faces bright* (Cornell *Poems 1807-20* 123-4), a celebration of George III's 'regal fortitude' in the face of his worsening insanity. It was first published in W's *Poems* (1815), the 'last edition of the Works of a modern Poet' which the review mentions. Hazlitt's review was published anonymously, but W knew his prose style well enough to have guessed its authorship; in any case, he had by now come to believe that Hazlitt was waging some sort of campaign against him. On 7 April 1817 he told Haydon: 'The miscreant Hazlitt continues, I have heard, his abuse of Southey Coleridge and myself, in the Examiner' (*MY* ii 377).

205. Heath, James, *Flagellum: or the life and death, birth and burial of O. Cromwell the late usurper: faithfully described* (1672)

Suggested date of reading: ?1809 onwards
References: Shaver 118

W's copy is now at St John's College, Cambridge. An ownership inscription on the title-page reads: 'Wm Wordsworth'. It contains numerous pencilled marginalia, and survives in its original boards. No precise dating for W's ownership is possible, but the inscription is consistent with the argument that it dates from the period when both W and C were interested in Cromwell, *c.* 1809.[1]

206. Heath, William, review of *Lyrical Ballads* (1798), *The Anti-Jacobin Review* 5 (April 1800) 334 [434]
Suggested date of reading: *c.* May 1800
References: Reed ii 62

'It has genius, taste, elegance, wit, and imagery of the most beautiful kind', wrote the Revd. William Heath of *Lyrical Ballads* (1798), adding praise even for *The Ancient Mariner* and *The Idiot Boy*. These kind words from an unexpected source appeared in the *Anti-Jacobin Review* for April 1800; it is not clear whether W or C saw it. Butler and Green suggest that this review and that by Francis Wrangham in the *British Critic* (Oct. 1799) may have encouraged Longman to offer £80 for another edition of *Lyrical Ballads* in June 1800 (Cornell *Lyrical Ballads* 23). Emily Lorraine de Montluzin summarizes what is known of Heath's involvement with *The Anti-Jacobin Review* in *The Anti-Jacobins* (1988), pp. 106-7.

207. Herbert, Edward, Baron Herbert of Cherbury, *Epitaph for Himself*
Suggested date of reading: probably between 25 March 1804 and 11 Feb. 1805
References: Reed ii 706

The copy of this work entered by W in the Wordsworth Commonplace Book (DC MS 26) is judged by Reed to date from between 25 March 1804 and 11 Feb. 1805. A number of Herbert's volumes were retained at Rydal Mount (see Shaver 120).

208. Herbert, George
(i) poems
Suggested date of reading: by spring 1802
References: Curtis 66-7

It is likely, as Curtis argues, that Herbert was an influence on W's lyric poems of 1802. See also Stein 225n12.

C was reading Herbert in July-Sept. 1809, March 1810, during his residence at Allan Bank. He was apparently reading his copy of *The Temple* (10th edn, 1674), now in the Berg Collection, New York Public Library; see *Notebooks* iii 3532-3, 3579-80, 3735, CC

---

[1] For comments on Cromwell by W and C, see *Prose Works* i 256, 336; CC *Friend* ii 107; *Notebooks* iii 3976 (dating from Oct. 1810).

Marginalia ii 1032-3. In later years W regarded Walton's life of Herbert as among 'the most pathetic of human compositions' (*Memoirs* ii 482).

(ii) *Sunday* and *Vertue*
Suggested date of reading: by March 1814
References: *PW* v 467; Lienemann 28
W seems to recall either or both of these poems by Herbert at *Excursion* vii 695.

(iii) poems
Suggested date of reading: by 17 Sept. 1814
References: *MY* ii 153
In his letter to Robert Anderson of 17 Sept. 1814, W suggests that an enlarged edn of Anderson's *British Poets* should include 'Herbert'. This indicates that he was aware of his works by 17 Sept. 1814. I presume, with the editors of *MY*, that W refers here to the author of *The Temple* rather than to Lord Herbert of Cherbury, whose poems he had read by 11 Feb. 1805 (see next note). He mentions George Herbert in *The River Duddon* in a sonnet probably composed in 1818 (*PW* iii 253-4, 522-3).

209. Herd, David, *Ancient and Modern Scottish Songs* [Edinburgh, 1769]
Suggested date of reading: after 28 Jan. 1801
References: Reed ii 704; Cornell *Lyrical Ballads* 352; Woof PhD 245-6
The Cruel Mother, one of the ballads in Herd's collection, is widely noted as a source for W's *The Thorn*. All the same, it was presumably entered in W's Commonplace Book (DC MS 26, 25r-25v) *after* the preceding entry, Campbell's *Exile of Erin*, which cannot have been entered prior to 28 Jan. 1801 - that is, nearly three years after the composition of W's poem. The Commonplace Book entry is published *PW* ii 514 and Woof PhD 245-6, and the relevant stanzas of the published ballad reproduced Jacobus 242.

210. Herodotus
(i) *The History of Herodotus*, tr. Isaac Littlebury (3rd edn, 2 vols., 1737)
Suggested date of reading: by 7 July 1808
References: *MY* i 257; Shaver 121
On 7 July 1808 DW wrote to De Quincey, requesting him to purchase a list of books for W. In its midst, she mentions: 'by the bye, he *has* a translation of Herodotus' (*MY* i 257). This was probably the copy of Littlebury's translation, later retained at Rydal Mount. W probably read Herodotus as a schoolboy (*WR* 165).

(ii) *The History of Herodotus*, tr. Isaac Littlebury (3rd edn, 2 vols., 1737)
Suggested date of reading: perhaps between mid-Nov. and mid-Dec. 1808
References: *Prose Works* i 374, 375

It is likely, as Owen and Smyser suggest, that W's knowledge of Leonidas' defence of Thermopylae was drawn from Herodotus. W mentions it in the instalment of his *Convention of Cintra* published in the *Courier* on 13 Jan. 1809; its composition was complete by mid-Dec. 1808.

(iii) *The History of Herodotus*, tr. **Isaac Littlebury (3rd edn, 2 vols., 1737)**
Suggested date of reading: probably by March 1812
References: *PW* v 426; Shaver 121
De Selincourt notes a debt to Herodotus at *Excursion* vi 686-7, composed probably by March 1812 (Reed ii 23).

211. Heron, Robert, *Observations Made in a Journey through the Western Counties of Scotland* **(2 vols., Perth, 1793)**
Suggested date of reading: probably by 5 April 1800
References: Reed ii 704; Moorman *N&Q* 401
Reed judges that a passage on pedlars from Heron was entered in the Wordsworth Commonplace Book (DC MS 26, 5v) by 5 April 1800; for further discussion see Moorman *N&Q* 401. The evidence summarized at *WR* 74 indicates that Heron influenced the Preface to *Lyrical Ballads* (1800), and was a source for *Effusion, in the Pleasure-Ground* (composed between 1814 and 1820); Coe has suggested that it was also a source for *The Solitary Reaper*.[1] Significantly, W's note at *Excursion* (1814), p. 425, says: 'I regret that I have not the book at hand' - and Shaver lists none at Rydal Mount, suggesting that W read a borrowed copy.

212. Herrick, Robert
(i) works
Suggested date of reading: 1802
References: Curtis 65-6, 83-4
Curtis argues for the influence of Herrick's poetry on W's lyric poems of 1802. Herrick was among the writers in a MS collection of poetry compiled by SH in 1826; see Jared Curtis, 'William Wordsworth and English Poetry of the Sixteenth and Seventeenth Centuries', *Cornell Library Journal* 1 (1966) 28-39, esp. pp. 32, 38n18; and David Ginsberg, 'Wordsworth's *Poems, in Two Volumes* (1807) and the Epideictic Tradition', *Rhetorical Traditions and British Romantic Literature* ed. Don Bialostosky and Lawrence Needham (1995), pp. 108-21, p. 119n11.

(ii) works
Suggested date of reading: by 17 Sept. 1814
References: *MY* ii 153

---

[1] See C. N. Coe, 'A Note on Wordsworth's "The Solitary Reaper"', *MLN* 63 (1948) 493, and Coe 32-3.

In his letter to Robert Anderson of 17 Sept. 1814, W suggests that an enlarged edn of Anderson's *British Poets* should include Herrick.

213. Heywood, Thomas
(i) *A Woman Kill'd with Kindness: A Tragedy* [1607]
Suggested date of reading: by 4 Aug. 1808
References: *MY* i 265
Expressing disappointment with Scott's criticism of Heywood in the notes to his edn of Dryden's *Works* (1808), W urged him to read *A Woman Kill'd with Kindness*: 'There is an exquisite strain of Pathos in many parts of that play which Dryden not only was utterly incapable of producing, but of feeling, when produced' (*MY* i 265). It is not clear when W first read Heywood, but it was probably well before he made this comment to Scott.

(ii) poems
Suggested date of reading: late 1813/early 1814 onwards
References: Reed ii 543
'Between 7 Oct and early 1814, Parry sends a collection of books to W including the poems of [Thomas Heywood]' (Reed ii 543). This may have been the copy of 'Divers Dramas, never before published, and a Miscellane of Sundrie Straines in Poetry, &c. by Thomas Heywood' retained at Rydal Mount (Shaver 122; Wordsworth *SC* 625).

214. Hill, John, *A Review of the Works of the Royal Society of London, containing animadversions, etc.* (1751)
Suggested date of reading: by 1809
References: *Notebooks* iii 3610; Shaver 123
W's copy is now at the Huntington Library; see P. M. and E. W. Zall, 'Wordsworth in the Huntington Library: A Preliminary Checklist', *WC* 1 (1970) 141-60, no. 267. C refers in a notebook entry of 1809 probably to W's copy retained at Allan Bank and later at Rydal Mount. This is the earliest by which it can be said to have been in W's possession (though see also *Notebooks* ii 1380).

215. Hoccleve, Thomas, works
Suggested date of reading: by 17 Sept. 1814
References: *MY* ii 153
In his letter to Robert Anderson of 17 Sept. 1814, W suggests that an enlarged edn of Anderson's *British Poets* should include the works of Hoccleve. This indicates that he was aware of Hoccleve's works by 17 Sept. 1814. He may have seen Southey's copy of Hoccleve's *Poems never before printed* (1796).

216. Hogg, James
(i) *The Queen's Wake* (Edinburgh, 1813)
Suggested date of reading: between 29 Aug. and 23 Nov. 1814
References: *Supp.* 155; Shaver 125
'I thank you for the Queen's Wake', W wrote to R. P. Gillies on 23 Nov. 1814, 'since I saw you in Edinburgh I have read it. It does Mr Hogg great credit' (*Supp.* 155). W dined with Gillies in Edinburgh on 29 Aug. when, apparently, Hogg's volume was presented to him. He saw a good deal of Hogg on his visit to Edinburgh during Aug., and Hogg visited Rydal Mount the following month.

(ii) *The Hunting of Badlewe, A Dramatic Tale* (Edinburgh, 1814)
Suggested date of reading: see note
References: *MY* ii 179
Some time during Dec. 1814, R. P. Gillies appears to have sent W a copy of Hogg's latest production. On 22 Dec. W reacted: 'Mr. Hogg's *Badlew* (I suppose it to be his) I could not get through. . . . Mr. H. is too illiterate to write in any measure or style that does not savour of balladism' (*MY* ii 179-80).

217. Homer
(i) *The Iliad and Odyssey*, tr. William Cowper [2 vols., 1791]
Suggested date of reading: see note
References: *MY* i 129
On 24 Jan. 1807 DW wrote to Lady Beaumont asking her to send the Wordsworths, then staying at Coleorton, a copy of Cowper's *Iliad and Odyssey*: 'We do not want it unless you have it, or have a desire to purchase it' (*MY* i 129). It is not known whether this was sent, although a consignment of books was delivered to Coleorton *c*. 7 Feb. (*MY* i 133).

**(ii) *A translation of the twenty-fourth book of the Iliad of Homer*,
tr. Charles Lloyd Sr. (Birmingham, 1807)**
Suggested date of reading: 25 March 1808 onwards
References: Reed ii 387n16
A copy of this book was apparently presented to W by Priscilla Lloyd when he stayed with her and CW between 25 March and 2 April 1808. It was later retained at Rydal Mount (Shaver 127) alongside C's copy, now at Victoria University Library (Dendurent 509).

(iii) *The Whole Works of Homer*, tr. George Chapman (1624)
Suggested date of reading: April or May 1808 onwards
References: CC *Marginalia* ii 1118
C sent 'the Piranesi Folios for William', a New Testament, Chapman's *Homer*, and Huber's *History of Bees* to SH in Penrith, probably, Whalley suggests, in late March or early April

1808.[1] The *Homer* was later retained at Rydal Mount, and presumably came into W's possession during the DC years - at least before W and C fell out in 1810 (Shaver 126). The fact that two copies of Chapman's *Homer* were retained at Rydal Mount suggests that W acquired his own before C's was added to his collection; either way, W probably owned one by April/May 1808.

C's copy was sent to London in late 1834, and is now at Washington University, St Louis, Missouri (CC *Marginalia* i clviii, ii 1117-28). In his letter to Robert Anderson of 17 Sept. 1814, W suggested that an enlarged edn of Anderson's *British Poets* should include Chapman's *Homer* (*MY* ii 154).

(iv) *The Iliad*, tr. Alexander Pope
Suggested date of reading: by March 1812
References: *PW* v 427

W's source at *Excursion* iv 745-50 was, according to De Selincourt, Pope's note on *Iliad* xxiii 175. I am sure that W reread Pope's *Homer* during 1800-15, but specific evidence is hard to come by. Pope's translation may have been one of the first he read while a schoolboy at Hawkshead (*WR* 75); it was included in Anderson, *British Poets* vol. 12.

218. Horatius Flaccus, Quintus
(i) *Ars Poetica*
Suggested date of reading: perhaps between 29 June and 27 Sept. 1800
References: see note

The influence of the *Ars Poetica* on the Preface to *Lyrical Ballads* (1800) is sufficiently well-established to warrant the suggestion that W might have reread it at the time of composition, between 29 June and 27 Sept. 1800. See, for a summary and extrapolation of past scholarship on this topic, Richard W. Clancey, 'Wordsworth, Horace, and the Preface to *Lyrical Ballads*', *CLB* NS 68 (1989) 131-8. W misquotes Horace in a letter of 14 Jan. 1801 (*Supp.* 3 and n1).

Graver reminds me that W alludes frequently to Horace in his poetry of the period 1800-15, especially in *The Prelude* and *The Excursion*. W's comments to Wrangham in spring 1812 on his thwarted desire to return to Greek authors with his children suggests that he may have encouraged them to read Horace at that time (*MY* ii 8).

(ii) *Ars Poetica*
Suggested date of reading: perhaps early 1802
References: *Prose Works* i 177

W would have known the brief passage from the *Ars Poetica* quoted by Owen and Smyser in a note to their text of the 1850 Preface to *Lyrical Ballads*, derived from the 1802 revised version, probably composed early 1802 and certainly by 6 April.

---

[1] Although it should be noted that Griggs prefers a date of 12 Feb. 1808. C enclosed a letter when he sent the volume to SH; see Griggs iii 67-8.

(iii) *Ars Poetica*
Suggested date of reading: c. Feb./March 1809
References: *Prose Works* i 221, 372
Horace provides the epigraph to the title-page of W's *Convention of Cintra*.

(iv) *Epistles*
Suggested date of reading: by Feb. 1815
References: *Prose Works* iii 46
W quoted the *Epistles* in his *Preface* (1815).

219. Housman, John, *A Descriptive Tour and Guide to the Lakes, Caves, Mountains . . . in Cumberland, Westmoreland, Lancashire, and a part of the West Riding of Yorkshire* **(2nd edn, Carlisle, 1802)**
Suggested date of reading: by 13 June 1804
References: see note
Trott and Wu have discussed the apparent influence of Housman's description of the Cave of Yordas on W's cave simile at *Thirteen-Book Prelude* viii 711-27, composed between c. 14 Jan. and 13 June 1804; see 'Three Sources for Wordsworth's *Prelude* Cave', *N&Q* NS 38 (1991) 298-9. A copy of Housman was at Rydal Mount (Shaver 130).

220. Huber, François, *New Observations on the Natural History of Bees,*
tr. Sir John Graham Dalyell (Edinburgh, 1806)
Suggested date of reading: April or May 1808 onwards
References: CC *Marginalia* ii 1118
C sent 'the Piranesi Folios for William', a New Testament, Chapman's *Homer*, and Huber's *History of Bees* to SH in Penrith, probably, Whalley suggests, in late March or early April 1808. Huber's *New Observations* was present at Allan Bank in Oct. 1810 and was later retained at Rydal Mount (Shaver 336). My guess is that it entered W's possession probably in 1808.

221. Humboldt, Friedrich Heinrich Alexander von, Baron, *Researches concerning the Institutions and Monuments of the ancient Inhabitants of America* **tr. Helen Maria Williams (2 vols., 1814)**
Suggested date of reading: c. March 1815
References: *MY* ii 216; Southey *SC* 1463
In March 1815 W asked Southey to send him 'Humbold's (is that his name) books upon South America' (*MY* ii 216). Presumably he received a copy of the *Researches* during March. W refers to Humboldt's *Personal Narrative of Travels to the Equinoctial Regions of the New Continent*, tr. Helen Maria Williams (vol. 1, 1814), in his River Duddon sonnets (*PW* iii 253, 507), and possibly read that work shortly after publication, c. 1814-15.

Southey owned copies of Humboldt's *de Distributione Geographica Plantarum* presented to him by the author (Southey *SC* 1464), and *Political Essay on the Kingdom of New Spain*, tr. John Black (2 vols., 1811).

222. Hunt, James Henry Leigh
(i) *The Feast of the Poets* **(1811), in** *The Reflector*
Suggested date of reading: probably by 23 June 1814
References: see note
On 2 June 1814, Beaumont wrote to W: 'Leigh Hunt no great favorite of mine - after some severe sarcasms in verse has thought proper to do you some justice in a note which follows.' This is a reference to the note which appears in the 2nd edn of the *Feast*, pp. 87-109; on 23 June W replied:

> Mr Lee Hunt whose 'amende honorable' you mention had not read a word of my Poems, at the time he wrote his sarcasms. This I know from an acquaintance of his; so that neither the censure nor the praise of such people is in *itself* of any value. It however affects the immediate sale of works, and authors who are tender of their own reputation would be glad to secure Mr Hunt's commendations. For my own part, my *dignity* absolutely requires an indifference upon this point. (*Supp.* 144-5; his italics)

On the basis of these comments it is evident that W was at least aware of the 1811 version of the *Feast* in *The Reflector*, and had possibly read it; a copy of *The Reflector* (1811) was at Rydal Mount (Shaver 133). The 'acquaintance' was probably Benjamin Robert Haydon. Whether W had by 23 June seen the 1814 *Feast* is debateable, but he would hardly have referred so readily to Hunt's 'sarcasms' had he been unaware of their contents.

(ii) *The Feast of the Poets* **(1814)**
Suggested date of reading: probably by 25-9 Sept. 1814
References: see note
See preceding note. After June 1814 relations between W and Hunt warmed up. On a visit to Lowther W was told by Brougham that 'his writings were valued by Mr Hunt' (*MY* ii 195). In return W sent Hunt a copy of his collected *Poems* on 12 Feb. 1815, and Hunt went to some pains to pacify him when he complained about Hazlitt's comments on political apostasy in *The Examiner* (Reed ii 606). Copies of Hunt's reprinted *Descent of Liberty: A Mask* (1815) were available by Oct.[1] and W was one of the earliest recipients of a copy bearing the author's presentation inscription (Shaver 133; *MY* ii 273). In Dec. Benjamin Robert Haydon, by then W's principal informant on matters Huntian, told him that 'Leigh Hunt's respect for you seems to encrease daily - His Brother it is who has had your bust made.' By spring 1816

---

[1] Edmund Blunden, *Leigh Hunt: A Biography* (1930), p. 94.

W was contributing sonnets to *The Examiner*,[1] and remarked to R. P. Gillies that 'I have great respect for the *Talents* of its Editor' (*MY* ii 299; his italics). It is unlikely that W would have countenanced these contacts had he not seen the revised version of the *Feast*, with its note acknowledging 'the greatness of Mr. Wordsworth's genius' (p. 89). A likely terminal date for a reading of the 1814 *Feast* would be 25-9 Sept. 1814, when W heard Brougham testify to Hunt's admiration of his work. W had almost certainly read it by the time of his visit to London, May-June 1815.

223. Hurdis, James, *The Favorite Village* [Bishopstone, 1800]
Suggested date of reading: by March 1812
References: *PW* v 425
De Selincourt notes an allusion to Hurdis' *Favorite Village* at *Excursion* iv 387, probably composed by March 1812 (Reed ii 23).

224. Hutchinson, Lucy, *Memoirs of the Life of Colonel [John] Hutchinson, Governor of Nottingham Castle and Town* (1806)
Suggested date of reading: between c. 7 Feb. and 15 Feb. 1807
References: *MY* i 133
This volume was part of a consignment sent by the Beaumonts to the Wordsworths in early Feb. 1807, then residing at Coleorton. On 15 Feb. DW told Lady Beaumont that 'my Brother and Sister have read the Life of Colonel Hutchinson, which is a most valuable and interesting Book. - My Brother speaks of it with unqualified approbation. and he intends to read it over again' (*MY* i 133). Later that month W told Walter Scott that it was 'a most delightful Book' (*MY* i 140). C joined in the enthusiasm, and mentions it in his marginalia to Browne's *Pseudodoxia Epidemica* (CC *Marginalia* i 766); Poole, echoing C and W, told Josiah Wedgwood that it 'will do more good than any which has been published for these last 20 years' (Whalley PhD i 220). W may himself have heard about it from Southey, who commended it in the *Annual Review* 5 (1806) 361-78: 'We have seen few histories in which characters are so fairly appreciated, events so candidly related, and causes so naturally developed; it will set her husband's name in the first rank among English patriots, and her own in the first among English writers' (p. 378). On 29 Dec. 1806 Southey asked John May: 'Have you seen the "Memoirs of Colonel Hutchinson?" Very, very rarely has any book so greatly delighted me. It is in unison with almost every feeling and every principle I have at heart' (Warter i 403; see also Warter ii 113). A copy seems also to have been in Wrangham's library (Wrangham *SC* 1307): might he have been urged to acquire it by W? W's copy was later retained at Rydal Mount (Shaver 135); C's is now at the British Library (CC *Marginalia* ii 1191).

---

[1] See *The Examiner*, 18 Feb. 1816, pp. 97-9.

225. Hyde, Edward, 1st Earl of Clarendon, *The History of the Rebellion and Civil Wars in England, begun in the year 1641*
Suggested date of reading: probably by July 1808
References: *MY* i 257; Shaver 135-6
On 7 July 1808 DW wrote to De Quincey in London, listing a number of authors whose works her brother wanted him to acquire on his behalf. This included 'Clarendon', suggesting that W had by that date read the *History*, and wanted his own copy. De Quincey did apparently find one, probably shortly after, and gave it to W. In mid-April 1836 W thanked Robinson for a second copy, reporting that 'two Vols of my Clarendon had fallen into the Opium eaters hands - they were however I believe a present from him so I have not much reason to complain in this case' (*LY* iii 201). Shaver lists only one copy, 6 vols., Oxford, 1705-6 (Shaver 135-6).

226. *Imago primi saeculi societatis Jesu* **(Antwerp, 1640)**
Suggested date of reading: by July-Sept. 1809
References: *Notebooks* iii 3526
C referred to W's copy of this book in a notebook entry dating from July-Sept. 1809 (*Notebooks* iii 3526). He was then resident at Allan Bank. Although Coburn seems to think that this book was in W's possession, Shaver does not mention it.

227. Isola, Agostino, *Pieces Selected from the Italian Poets by Agostino Isola and Translated into English verse by some Gentlemen of the University* **(2nd edn, Cambridge, 1784)**
Suggested date of reading: between Nov. 1802 and Jan. 1803
References: Cornell *Poems 1800-7* xxvii, 590-3
W's copy of this book is now at the Fitzwilliam Library, Cambridge. Between Nov. 1802 and Jan. 1803 he drafted a number of translations from Metastasio into it, suggesting that he took that opportunity to look again at its contents (see *WR* 77).

228. Jeffrey, Francis
(i) review of Southey's *Thalaba* **(1801),** *Edinburgh Review* **1 (Oct. 1802) 63-83**
Suggested date of reading: perhaps Nov. 1802, or shortly thereafter; by mid-Jan. 1804
References: see note
It is not clear exactly when W read Jeffrey's review of *Thalaba* - probably it was soon after publication, towards the end of 1802. His first mention of it comes in a letter of Jan. 1804 to Thelwall, which makes clear that he regarded it as 'an attack upon me' (*EY* 432); however, he did not read it all, and did not own the issue of the *Edinburgh* in which it appeared:

> That review of the Thalaba I never read entirely, having only seen it in a Country Bookseller's shop, who would not permit me to cut open the Leaves, as he only had it

upon trial. Therefore I do not know in what temper it is written; I only remember to have seen that the Fellow was a Blockhead and knew nothing about the Business.

(*EY* 432)

In a letter to Scott of 18 Jan. 1808, W recalled having 'skimmed over, some time ago, what he [Jeffrey] had written in the article on Thalaba, I then set him down in my mind as a poor Creature' (*MY* i 191). For Southey's response to the review see *Life of Southey* ii 196-8.

(ii) review of Wordsworth, *Poems, in Two Volumes* (1807), Edinburgh Review 11 (Oct. 1807) 214-31
Suggested date of reading: 1-2 Dec. 1807
References: *MY* i 185-6

W told Scott in Jan. 1808 that Jeffrey 'has in this last performance shewn himself so utterly contemptible that I should not have adverted to him at all had it not been that I am writing to one personally connected with him' (*MY* i 191-2). The 'last performance' was Jeffrey's mean-spirited review of *Poems, in Two Volumes* published in the *Edinburgh Review* for Oct. 1807. W saw it at Penrith, 1-2 Dec. (*MY* i 185-6); DW read it at about the same time, at Old Brathay. As she told Lady Beaumont on 28 Dec.: 'Luckily [Charles] Lloyd takes it in, therefore I have seen it' (*MY* i 185). Her phrasing, 'Luckily', underlines the fact that her brother would not keep a copy in the house; see also W's letter to Southey, *MY* i 162.

(iii) review of Burns, *Reliques of Robert Burns*, ed. R. H. Cromek (1808), Edinburgh Review 13 (Jan. 1809) 249-76
Suggested date of reading: by 28 April 1809
References: *MY* i 326

In a letter of 1 May 1809, DW recalled having seen 'the last Edinburgh review . . . at Mr. Wilson's. There never was such a compound of despicable falsehood, malevolence, and folly as the concluding part of the Review of Burns's Poems (which was, in fact, all that I thought it worth while to read being the only part in which my Brother's works are alluded to)' (*MY* i 326). The visit to John Wilson at Elleray took place probably 21-8 April (Reed ii 422n24); I doubt whether W saw the offending article, but DW certainly told him about it (see *MY* i 326). Her irritation was well-founded. Jeffrey concludes by recommending 'the simplicity of Burns' to 'the followers and patrons of that new school of poetry':

> Let them think, with what infinite contempt the powerful mind of Burns would have perused the story of Alice Fell and her duffle cloak, - of Andrew Jones and the half-crown, - or of Little Dan without breeches, and his thievish grandfather. Let them contrast their own fantastical personages of hysterical schoolmasters and sententious leechgatherers, with the authentic rustics of Burns's Cotter's Saturday Night, and his inimitable songs; and reflect on the different reception which these personifications have met with from the public. (p. 276)

For C's view of Jeffrey c. April 1809 see *Notebooks* iii 3496.

(iv) review of Walter Scott, *The Lady of the Lake* (1810), *Edinburgh Review* 16 (Aug. 1810) 263-93
Suggested date of reading: some time after Sept. 1810
References: see note
Owen, 'Wordsworth and Jeffrey in Collaboration', *RES* 15 (1964) 160-7, points out that 'De Quincey's report of the popularity of *The Lady of the Lake* and of Jeffrey's influence upon it, which was found entertaining enough to be transcribed by Dorothy,[1] may have sent Wordsworth to the review' (p. 163).

(v) review of John Wilson, *The Isle of Palms, and Other Poems* (1812), *Edinburgh Review* 19 (Feb. 1812) 373-88
Suggested date of reading: between 1 March and 23 May 1812
References: *Supp.* 91
On 23 May 1812 W told MW that 'Mr Wilson is reviewed', referring to Jeffrey's account in the *Edinburgh Review*. This does not prove that he read the review, but he must at least have heard about it.

(vi) review of *The Excursion*, *Edinburgh Review* 24 (Nov. 1814) 1-30
Suggested date of reading: perhaps by 31 Dec. 1814
References: *MY* ii 182
Evidence for W's reading of Jeffrey's most notorious act of literary terrorism is thin, but worth including here, such as it is. On 31 Dec. 1814 W wrote to Catherine Clarkson:

> I smiled at your notion of Coleridge reviewing the Ex. in the Ed. I much doubt whether he has read three pages of the poem,[2] and Jeff. has already printed off a Review; beginning with these elegant and decisive words: 'This will not do'. The sage Critic then proceeding to show cause why. This precious piece is what the Coxcomb's Idolators call a *crushing* Review. Therefore you see as the evil Spirits are rouzed it becomes the good ones to stir, or what is to become of the poor Poet and his Labours? (*MY* ii 182)

I remain unconvinced as to whether, on the basis of this, W can be assumed to have read Jeffrey's review. Even if he had not, however, he would have heard about it from friends and acquaintances. Those who commiserated with him must include Lamb, who on 16 April 1815 apparently had Jeffrey in mind when he wrote of *The Excursion* to W: 'I am glad that you have not sacrificed a verse to those scoundrels' (Marrs iii 139). Another source of information was Lady Beaumont, who wrote to W on 17 Jan. 1815:

---

[1] See Jordan 257-8 and *MY* i 458.
[2] This comment must be coloured by the falling-out with C; C was one of the earliest supporters of *The Ruined Cottage* and *The Pedlar*, which appeared in *The Excursion* in revised form. He must have read *The Excursion* by 3 April 1815, when he told Lady Beaumont what he thought of it (Griggs iv 564-5).

in the quarterly they wish to praise it, but tho well meant know not how to do it with any effect your brother and M[rs] Wordsworth[1] have spent three days with us, and were here when the former[2] was sent to us, which we all thought too bad, to be entitled to notice by any of your friends. (Wordsworth Library WLL/Beaumont, G. H./51)

She displays characteristic perspicacity: the notice in the *Quarterly Review*, by Lamb, had been manipulated by Gifford, the editor, so as to distort its appreciative observations (see note 241[x], below).

In Jan. 1815 W wrote again to Catherine Clarkson:

> As [to the Ed Review] I hold the Author [of it in entire] contempt, and therefore shall not pollute my fingers [with the touch] of it. There is one sentence in the Ex[n]. ending in 'sublime att[ractions] of the grave'[3] which, - if the poem had contained nothing else that [I valued,] would have made it almost a matter of religion with me to [keep out] of the way of the best stuff which so mean a mind as Mr [Jeffrey's] could produce in connection with it. His impertinences, to us[e the] mildest te[rm,] if once they had a place in my memory, would, for a [time] at least, [sti]ck there. You cannot scower a spot of this kind ou[t of] your mind as you may a stain out of your clothes. If the m[ind] were under the power of the will I should read Mr J[y] merely to expose his stupidity to his still more stupid admirers. This not being the case, as I said before, I shall not pollute my fingers with touching his book. (*MY* ii 190-1)

This is the most explicit evidence we have as to W's reading of Jeffrey's review, and it suggests that although W heard about its harshness from others soon after publication, he deliberately avoided it.

229. *Johnie Armstrang* in Walter Scott, *Minstrelsy of the Scottish Border* (3 vols., Kelso, 1802-3)

Suggested date of reading: probably between 17 and 23 Sept. 1803; by 23 Sept. 1803
References: *EY* 412 and n4

On 16 Oct. 1803 W wrote to Walter Scott about the final part of the Scottish tour: 'We did not omit noticing Johnnie Armstrongs Keep, his hanging place we miss'd, to our great regret' (*EY* 412).[4] Armstrong was a historical character, but the Wordsworths could not have been unaware of the Scottish ballad of that name which Scott had lately reprinted in *Minstrelsy of the Scottish Border* i 35-58. He probably read it to them during his time with them, 17-23 Sept.

---

[1] Priscilla, sister of Charles Lloyd.
[2] i.e. Jeffrey's review.
[3] See *Excursion* iv 232-8.
[4] Southey, too, saw 'Johnnie Armstrong's Castle on the Esk' when he passed by in Oct. 1805 (*Life of Southey* ii 351).

There was good reason for W to have looked out for the 'hanging place'. In an extensive headnote to the ballad, Scott describes, with some precision, its location: 'Johnie, with all his retinue, was accordingly hanged upon growing trees, at a place called Carlenrig Chapel, about ten miles above Hawick, on the high road to Langholm. The country people believe that, to manifest the injustice of the execution, the trees withered away' (*Minstrelsy* i 47).

230. Johnson, Samuel
(i) *The Ant*
Suggested date of reading: c. Jan.-April 1802
References: *Prose Works* i 162-3, 189
Johnson's poem is famously described as a 'hubbub of words' in W's Appendix on Poetic Diction to the Preface to *Lyrical Ballads* (1802). Owen notes that 'Wordsworth appears to follow the text of Johnson's *Works*, 1787' (*Prose Works* i 189); possibly this was one of the volumes owned by C's landlord, William Jackson, at Greta Hall.

(ii) *Life of Addison*
Suggested date of reading: by 6 March 1804
References: Cornell *Poems 1800-7* 407
Curtis notes a verbal reminiscence of Johnson's *Life of Addison* in W's *Ode to Duty*, composed largely by 6 March 1804. Although this is, to the best of my knowledge, the earliest specific evidence for a reading by W of the *Lives*, he had presumably encountered the work as a schoolboy (see *LY* iii 492 and *WR* 78).

A copy was either at Allan Bank or close by when C referred to it *c*. April, June-Sept. 1809 (*Notebooks* iii 3480, 3545); perhaps W had by then acquired the copy of *The Lives of the most Eminent English Poets* (4 vols., 1781) later retained at Rydal Mount (Shaver 141). In 1809-10, C referred to the *Odes* of Charles Cotton (see *Notebooks* iii 3653), indicating that he may have been working from Chalmers' *Works of the English Poets* (21 vols., 1810), which contains both Johnson's *Lives* and, in vol. 6, Cotton's works. If that is so, W was probably also using Chalmers by that period.

By this period W was critical of Johnson's prose, and remained so for the rest of his life. On Tuesday 28 March 1809, Joseph Farington recorded in his diary:

> I breakfasted with Sir G. & Lady Beaumont; Wordsworth & Coleridge were a subject of our conversation. - Lady B. was enthusiastic in admiration of Wordsworth. She desired me to read His preface to His poems. Sir George was more moderate. He told me, & warned me of the danger of not approving it, adding, 'That Lady B. was as intolerant in Her opinion as Bishop Bonnor on religious matters.' She afterwards sd. to me, that Coleridge & Wordsworth thought the bad taste in writing which now prevails, is owing to works of two celebrated authors '*Popes translation of Homer, & the Odyssy*' and '*Johnson's lives of the Poets*' These models of art and an inflated style have been imitated to the destroying of all simplicity. The *Old Testament*, they say is the true

model of simplicity of style. They also highly approve the writings of Dr. *Jeremiah Taylor*, who had also the feelings of a Poet, and of Cowley. - Sir George sd. to me 'That Wordsworth & Coleridge by living in a state of seclusion, might engender notions respecting matters of taste that would not be approved by the world.'[1] (his italics)

Robinson noted that when he gave his lectures on Shakespeare and Milton in 1812, C 'excited a hiss once by calling Johnson a *fellow*, for which he happily apologized by observing that it is in the nature of evil to beget evil, and that we are thus apt to fall into the fault we censure' (Sadler i 369; his italics). As late as 1846 W 'said that since Johnson no writer had done so much to vitiate the English language' (Grosart iii 452).

(iii) *Life of Pope*
Suggested date of reading: by 22 Feb. 1810
References: *Prose Works* ii 49, 100, 103-4; CC *Friend* ii 335
W's first *Essay Upon Epitaphs*, published *The Friend* 22 Feb. 1810, quotes Johnson's 'Dissertation on the Epitaphs Written by Pope' appended to the end of the *Life*.

(iv) *The Rambler*
Suggested date of reading: by Jan. 1815
References: *Prose Works* iii 74, 95, 101, 104
W refers to *The Rambler* twice in his *Essay, Supplementary to the Preface*. He must have seen it before Jan. 1815, though I can find no evidence of an earlier reading. C refers to *The Rambler* in a letter to George Coleridge of 9 Oct. 1809 (Griggs iii 239).

231. Jonson, Ben
(i) poems and Life (Anderson)
Suggested date of reading: 11 Feb. 1802
References: Grasmere Journals 66, 203-4
DW read to W from Jonson's poems on 11 Feb. 1802, including *To Penshurst* and *On my First Daughter*. They were reading from Anderson, *British Poets* iv 552-3 and 534, and appear also to have looked at Anderson's Life of Jonson, which includes a paragraph from Thomas Fuller's *History of the Worthies of England* (1662), from which DW quotes.[2] She reread *To Penshurst* on 14 Feb.; as Pamela Woof suggests, it shares thematic similarities with *Home at Grasmere*. See also Curtis 82.

The Wordsworths continued to read Jonson, whose work, Anne Barton has argued, exercised considerable influence on W at this moment. She begins by suggesting that, 'for both William and his sister, Jonson's non-dramatic verse, up to this point in their lives, was effectively unknown' (Barton 210). She goes on to argue for the influence of *To Penshurst* on *Home at*

---

[1] *Diary* ix (January 1808-June 1809), ed. Kathryn Cave (1982), pp. 3425-6.
[2] See *Grasmere Journals* 66; the sentence quoted by DW may be found at Anderson, *British Poets* iv 528.

Grasmere MS B 807-28, that of Jonson's *Discoveries* on the 1800 Preface (see note 355[i]), reveals that *The Sailor's Mother* (composed 11-12 March 1802) has a hitherto unnoticed source in Anderson's Life of Jonson, and suggests that W's *Ode* was inspired by Jonson's *Ode Pindaric, to the immortal Memory and Friendship of the Noble Pair, Sir Lucius Cary, and Sir H. Morison* (Barton 215-16, 220-1, 225, 231).

(ii) (Anderson)
Suggested date of reading: 9 March 1802 onwards
References: *Grasmere Journals* 76, 81, 82
'William was reading in Ben Jonson - he read me a beautiful poem on Love' - perhaps, Pamela Woof speculates, *Drink to me only with thine eyes* or *Epode* (DW's journal, 9 March 1802). Barton argues that it was *Epode* from *The Forest* (Barton 218). Other close encounters with Jonson occurred in subsequent days: 'Wm read Ben Jonson in the morning' (10 March 1802); on 19 March W and C 'disputed about Ben Jonson', and on 23 March W read Jonson after dinner. These readings occurred at the beginning of a highly creative period; see Reed ii 152-5. Not surprisingly, by the time he came to compose the daisy poems of April 1802, W was using the same stanza as Jonson in *Underwoods* (Reed ii 161n31).

W asked Lamb to purchase on his behalf a copy of Jonson's *Works* in Sept. or Oct. 1804; there is no evidence that Lamb managed to do so, complaining that 'Ben Jonson is a Guinea Book', and 'I am not plethorically abounding in Cash at this present' (Marrs ii 146). Lamb's own copy was the 1692 folio, and ideally he would have wanted to acquire an edn of similar pedigree for W. W quoted from Jonson's epigram on his first son in a letter to Catherine Clarkson of 31 Dec. 1814 (*MY* ii 183). See also Curtis 95-6, *LY* i 90.

232. Jordan, Donaldson, and Edwin Judson Pratt, *The Spoiled Child; a farce*
Suggested date of reading: by 23 May 1812
References: *Supp.* 89
W's letter of 23 May 1812 to MW compares Lady Davy with 'Mrs Jordan acting the Spoilt child' (*Supp.* 89): interestingly enough, *The Spoiled Child* was performed at the Theatre Royal, Haymarket, that very night. Might it have been on W's mind because he was to see it?

233. Keate, George, *An Account of the Pelew Islands* [1788]
Suggested date of reading: 1800
References: see note
Lane Cooper, 'Wordsworth Sources. Bowles and Keate', *Athenaeum* 4043 (22 April 1905) 498-500, argues that Keate was W's source for *The Affliction of Margaret* and *The Forsaken*. The dates of composition of these works is given by Curtis as 'between around 1800 and around early January 1807, perhaps especially around 1800, spring 1802, or between late

March 1804 and around early January 1807' (Cornell *Poems 1800-7* 91). 1800 seems as likely a date as any. See also Coe 84-6.

234. Klopstock, Friedrich Gottlieb, *Memoirs of Frederick and Margaret Klopstock*, tr. Elizabeth Smith (Bath, 1808)
Suggested date of reading: by 5 April 1809
References: *MY* i 316
On 5 April 1809 DW told De Quincey: 'also I have read Miss Smith's Translation of Klopstock's and Mrs. K's letters.' This may have been one of the volumes recently sent to Allan Bank by De Quincey. W was aware of Smith's *Fragments, in Prose and Verse* by the time he wrote his *Unpublished Tour* in 1811-12 (see note 361).

235. Klopstock, Margaret, letters
Suggested date of reading: mid-Feb. 1805 onwards
References: *EY* 577
In a letter to Lady Beaumont of 11 April 1805, DW says that she had read a letter by Mrs Klopstock which appeared in the *Monthly Review*, 'in which she describes the progress of her attachment to her husband, and *who* could read that letter without loving her?' (*EY* 577). This is a reference to Margaret Klopstock's letter of 14 March 1758 to Samuel Richardson, in which she describes how she met her husband after reading *The Messiah* and falling in love with its author. It is reprinted at *Monthly Review* 46 (Jan. 1805) 40-1. The reviewer goes on to comment:

> This truly estimable lady expresses, in another letter, the pleasure which she anticipated in presenting a child to the husband whom she so dearly loved: but this blessing was denied her; and a melancholy note from a Mr. Major to Mr. R., concludes this short correspondence, by which he is informed that Mrs. Klopstock died in child-bed, December 1758, in a very dreadful manner. (p. 41)

Given that DW saw this review in a copy of the *Monthly* in W's possession by 23 Feb., it can be presumed that he saw the letter too, probably *c*. 23 Feb.

236. Knight, Richard Payne
(i) *The Landscape: A Didactic Poem in Three Books* (1794)
Suggested date of reading: 27 July 1800
References: *Grasmere Journals* 14
'. . . in the morning I read Mr Knight's Landscape' (DW's journal, 27 July 1800). It is not clear how, when, or if, the Wordsworths acquired this volume; possibly it was among the goods sent from Somerset two days before. W may have seen the copy retained at the Bristol Library during 1797-8 (*BLS* 55).

As Nabholtz has suggested, this poem was probably an influence on W's *Inscription for the House (an Outhouse) on the Island at Grasmere*, composed between 24 Dec. 1799 and 5 April 1800.[1]

(ii) *An Analytical Enquiry into the Principles of Taste* **[1805]**
Suggested date of reading: July 1806
References: MY i 54
'I have just begun to read Mr Knight's Book', DW wrote to Lady Beaumont on 9 July 1806, 'which you were very kind in sending.' W probably read this volume at around this time too. The copy of the *Analytical Enquiry* (3rd edn, 1806) now at the Huntington Library contains marginalia in W's hand. Although it has been suggested by E. A. Shearer and J. I. Lindsay that the marginalia was dictated to W by C, the evidence remains inconclusive.[2] Jackson and Whalley think it unlikely that the Huntington copy is that sent by Lady Beaumont to DC (CC *Marginalia* iii 400), and, in general, the Wordsworths returned books lent to them by the Beaumonts unless it was clear that they were intended as gifts. It is more likely that the copy in the Huntington is C's, and that it was the one later retained at Rydal Mount (Shaver 338). C met Knight several times in March 1804 (Griggs ii 1078-9).

(iii) *An Analytical Enquiry into the Principles of Taste* **(3rd edn, 1806)**
Suggested date of reading: Feb.-April 1808
References: CC *Marginalia* iii 400
See preceding note. W's marginalia are published CC *Marginalia* iii 401-13, and were, as Jackson and Whalley indicate, probably entered during W's stay in London, Feb.-April 1808. Even if the marginalia were dictated by C, as Shearer and Lindsay argue, that would not rule out a reading of the volume by W at this time. Heather Jackson's opinion is that the marginalia is not C's, but W's.

The *Analytical Enquiry* was on C's mind at this moment, providing material for his first Lecture on the Principles of Poetry, delivered 15 Jan. 1808 (CC *Literature* i 31-4).

237. Knox, Vicesimus
(i) *Elegant Extracts*
Suggested date of reading: between 29 June and 27 Sept. 1800
References: *Prose Works* i 154
In his Preface to *Lyrical Ballads* (1800), W quotes a stanza from the ballad he calls 'Babes in the Wood'. Zall has identified Knox as the source for W's distinctive text (*WC* 10 [1979]

---

[1] '... it is at least possible that Knight's poem, with its hard-hitting assault on Repton's gratification of "proud-purse vanity" in design, was the immediate inspiration for Wordsworth's reference to Repton in the Inscription poem. In any case, the sentiments expressed in Wordsworth's verses certainly support the position of Price and Knight in their dispute with Repton', 'Wordsworth's Interest in Landscape Design and an Inscription Poem of 1800', *Papers on Language and Literature* 2 (1966) 265-9, p. 268.
[2] *HLQ* 1 (1937-8) 63-99.

345-7). Indeed, W would have found Knox's text of *Ballad. The Children in the Wood; or, The Norfolk Gentleman's Last Will and Testament* in *Elegant Extracts* (1791) Book V, pp. 378-9.

(ii) *Elegant Epistles* **[1790]**
Suggested date of reading: by 3 Aug. 1808
References: MY i 263
At the end of her letter to Catherine Clarkson of 3 Aug. 1808, DW says: 'Sara says that a fac simile of this letter may be published after my death, among the *Eloquent Epistles*' (*MY* i 263). This jocular remark refers, I think, to Knox's *Elegant Epistles* (there was no publication entitled *Eloquent Epistles*), a children's anthology containing 'familiar and amusing letters, selected for the improvement of young persons, and for general entertainment, from Cicero, Pliny, Sydney . . . and many others'. It is likely that W and DW had known this work for many years. A copy was retained at Rydal Mount (Shaver 147).

(iii) *Elegant Extracts* **(1805)**
Suggested date of reading: by 22 Feb. 1810
References: *Prose Works* ii 114; Shaver 147
Knox's anthology was a source for the third of W's *Essays Upon Epitaphs*, where it is described as 'a bulky Volume of Poetry . . . which must be known to most of my Readers, as it is circulated every where and in fact constitutes at this day the poetical library of our Schools' (*Prose Works* ii 84). As he refers to edns containing a section of epitaphs, Owen and Smyser suggest that W probably had at hand a copy of the 1805 edn - although Books IV and V of the 1791 edn also contain a good selection of epitaphs. He had known this work since at least his Hawkshead years (see *WR* 82-3); two copies were retained at Rydal Mount.

238. Laborde, Alexander Louis Joseph de, Count, *A View of Spain; comprising a descriptive itinerary of each province, and a general statistical account of the country* **(5 vols., 1809)**
Suggested date of reading: 1810
References: Cornell *Poems 1807-20* 509-11; Shaver 148
Laborde's *View of Spain* is acknowledged as a source in W's headnote to *The Oak of Guernica*, composed 1810, and it informed a number of other poems composed at around the same period, as noted Cornell *Poems 1807-20* 509-11. W evidently acquired a copy of this book, possibly through De Quincey, shortly after publication; it was retained at Rydal Mount. There was also a copy in Southey's library (Southey *SC* 1584).

239. Lafontaine, Jean de
(i) *Les amours de Psyché et de Cupidon, avec le Poëme d'Adonis* **(Paris, 1801)**
Suggested date of reading: Aug. 1802 onwards
References: Reed ii 642; Shaver 149

W purchased this title as part of the *Bibliothèque Portative de Voyageur* (5 vols., Paris, 1801-2) in Calais, Aug. 1802. It is now at the Wordsworth Library.

(ii) *Fables choisis, mise en vers; avec un nouveau commentaire par M. Coste* (Paris, 1785)
Suggested date of reading: probably by 9 March 1811
References: *MY* i 468; Shaver 149
W must have owned this title by 9 March 1811 because he quotes from it in a letter of that date to Godwin (*MY* i 468); it was retained at Rydal Mount.

240. Laing, Malcolm, *The History of Scotland from the Union of the Crowns on the accession of James VI. to the throne of England, to the Union of the Kingdoms in the reign of Queen Anne* (2 vols., 1800)
Suggested date of reading: by Jan. 1815
References: *Prose Works* iii 77-8, 99
W refers to Laing's 'Dissertation on the Supposed Authenticity of Ossian's Poems' in his *Essay, Supplementary to the Preface*.

241. Lamb, Charles
(i) *John Woodvil* in MS
Suggested date of reading: Oct. 1800 onwards; by 30 Jan. 1801
References: *Grasmere Journals* 24; *EY* 316
Lamb sent the Wordsworths a MS copy, which they had received by 4 Oct. 1800, when DW 'Read a part of Lambs play'.[1] W had read it by mid Jan. 1801, when he wrote to Lamb expressing his admiration of it. 'Thank you for Liking my Play! !', Lamb responded on 30 Jan. 1801 (Marrs i 268).

On 22 Dec. 1801 DW recorded that 'We talked about Lamb's Tragedy as we went down the White Moss' (*Grasmere Journals* 50). This discussion may have been inspired by the knowledge that it had been revised and was in the press; it was published by G. and J. Robinson early in 1802.

(ii) *John Woodvil; a tragedy* (1802)
Suggested date of reading: probably early 1802 onwards
References: Shaver 150
The Wordsworths probably acquired a printed copy of Lamb's play soon after publication; W's reference to the harsh review of it in the *Edinburgh* in a letter of mid-Jan. 1804 indicates that he had a copy by then. It was later retained at Rydal Mount.

(iii) *The Londoner*, *Morning Post*, 1 Feb. 1802
Suggested date of reading: c. 1 Feb. 1802

---

[1] Robert Lloyd had been sent a copy in Nov. 1798 and Southey in April 1799.

References: *Grasmere Journals* 181
Some time in Feb. 1802 DW jotted down the words 'Lambs Londoner' in her journal (*Grasmere Journals* 181); this is a reference to Lamb's important essay which appeared in the *Morning Post*, 1 Feb. As Pamela Woof remarks, 'D and W must have seen the essay in the newspaper.' See also Lamb's letter to Manning of 15 Feb. 1802 (Marrs ii 54-9).

(iv) ***On Mary Druit who died aged 19*** **in MS**
Suggested date of reading: early March 1803
References: Marrs ii 105
Perhaps aware of W's love of epitaphs, Lamb sent a MS copy of this to W on 5 March 1803.

(v) ***A Farewell to Tobacco*** **in MS**
Suggested date of reading: early Oct. 1805
References: Marrs ii 177-81
Lamb copied out his versified *Farewell* for the Wordsworths in a letter of 28 Sept. 1805, which would have arrived in Grasmere within the week. W must have expressed approval, for, in a letter of 13 March 1806 to Catherine Clarkson, Mary Lamb remarked: 'If you have not had it from Wordsworth shall I send you a poem Charles wrote on tobacco? Wordsworth likes it very much' (Marrs ii 217).

(vi) ***The King and Queen of Hearts*** **(1806)**
Suggested date of reading: mid-Feb. 1806 onwards
References: Marrs ii 204-6
On 1 Feb. 1806 Lamb dispatched a consignment of books to DC, including 'a Paraphrase on the King & Queen of Hearts, of which I being the Author beg Mr. Johnny Wordsworth's acceptance & opinion' (Marrs ii 205). John Wordsworth was then just two and a half years old, and was known to the Lambs through their correspondence with the Wordsworths.

(vii) ***Specimens of English Dramatic Poets*** **(1808)**
Suggested date of reading: c. Sept. 1808 onwards
References: Shaver 151
On 23 Dec. 1806 Mary Lamb told Catherine Clarkson that 'my brother sometimes threatens to pass his hollidays in town hunting over old plays at the Museum to extract passages for a work (a collection of poetry) Mr Wordsworth intends to publish' (Marrs ii 253). This was, as Reed and Marrs observe, the beginning of Lamb's *Specimens* (Reed ii 344n; Marrs ii 254n1), and given W's involvement at the outset it would be odd had Lamb neglected to send him a copy. John M. Turnbull suggests that their proposed partnership in the production of the *Specimens* was intended partly to recoup some of W's funds expended in the book-buying spree of 1804:

> Whether Wordsworth's part in the business hinted at in Mary Lamb's letter amounted to more than mere negotiation with the publishers will probably never now be known; but

discussion of the scheme, if not its very suggestion, would have been a natural outcome of the £8 book-buying debauch vicariously enjoyed by Lamb on his behalf in 1804, which resulted in the acquisition of Lamb's particular favourites amongst his Elizabethans.[1]

As there appears to have been a copy of the 1st edn at Rydal Mount,[2] it may be assumed that Lamb sent one to W c. Sept. 1808, on publication. This is supported by the fact that he is known to have sent W a copy of the 'supplement' to the *Specimens*, which appeared in Hone's *Table Book* (1827) (*LY* ii 194 and n2). W seems to have used the *Specimens* as a source for the funeral dirge for Marcello which he included in his 1819 album for Lady Mary Lowther (*Album* 42; Lamb, *Specimens* [1808], pp. 232-3).

(viii) *A Tale of Rosamund Gray and old blind Margaret* (1798)
Suggested date of reading: by 22 Feb. 1810
References: *Prose Works* i 63, 105; Shaver 151
W refers to Lamb's *Rosamund Gray* in the second of his *Essays Upon Epitaphs*; he must have known it well before 1810, and it is likely that the copy retained at Rydal Mount was acquired shortly after publication.

(ix) *On the Melancholy of Tailors*, *The Champion* 4 Dec. 1814
Suggested date of reading: between 4 and 28 Dec. 1814
References: Marrs iii 124
Lamb's letter of 28 Dec. 1814 indicates that W had by then read Lamb's essay *On the Melancholy of Tailors* in *The Champion* for 4 Dec. See John M. Turnbull, 'Wordsworth's "Flying Tailor"', *TLS* (24 Oct. 1929), p. 846.

(x) review of *The Excursion*, *Quarterly Review* 12 (Oct. 1814) 100-11
Suggested date of reading: see note
References: see note
This entry is to note the existence of a work that W ought to have read, but possibly did not. It is evident from his letter to W of 28 Dec. 1814 (Marrs iii 124-8) that Lamb had not at that date seen the printed, deformed version of his review of *The Excursion* in the *Quarterly*.[3] His letter to W of 7 Jan. 1815 was written as soon as he had seen it (Marrs iii 128-34). Neither W's letter to Catherine Clarkson nor that to Southey, both written in Jan. 1815, prove that W had read it by then - merely that he had heard about Gifford's manipulations (*MY* ii 186-92). DW's letter to Priscilla Wordsworth of 27 Feb. 1815 says that 'We have seen none of the Reviews' of *The Excursion* (*MY* ii 206), and what she goes on to say about Gifford's rewriting of Lamb's article does not indicate a reading even by that date. Lamb's instruction

---

[1] 'Wordsworth's Part in the Production of Lamb's "Specimens"', *N&Q* 154 (1928) 114-15, p. 115.
[2] Although Shaver was not certain; see Shaver 151.
[3] The *Quarterly* for Oct. 1814 was not published until 8 Jan. 1815.

to W on 28 April - 'Dont read that Q. Review' (Marrs iii 149) - suggests that W had not seen it up to then either. W and MW were in London from 6 May to 19 June and saw much of Lamb at that time. Might they, at that time, have seen Lamb's mangled appreciation?

(xi) *On the Genius and Character of Hogarth*, The Reflector 3 (April-Sept. 1811)
Suggested date of reading: by Feb. 1815
References: *Prose Works* iii 46
W quoted from this work in his *Preface* (1815), having probably seen it shortly after publication. Lamb must have known of his interest in it as he mentions it in a letter to W of Sept. 1816 (Marrs iii 226).

242. Lamb, Charles and Mary Anne
(i) *Tales from Shakespear* (2 vols., 1807)
Suggested date of reading: early Feb. 1807 onwards
References: Marrs ii 256-7
'We have book'd off from Swan & Two Necks Lad Lane this day (per Coach) the Tales from Shakespear', Lamb wrote to W on 29 Jan. 1807. Presumably Lamb sent it to Coleorton, in which case it would have reached the Wordsworths by mid-Feb. This title does not turn up in any of the Rydal Mount catalogues; perhaps it was so well-used by the Wordsworth children that it simply did not survive into the Rydal Mount period.

(ii) *The Sea Voyage* in MS
Suggested date of reading: between 27 Feb. and 3 April 1808
References: Marrs iii 13
On 7 June 1809 Lamb told C that 'I shall have to send you in a week or two two volumes of Juvenile Poetry done by Mary & me within the last six months, and That Tale in Prose which Wordsworth so much liked which was published at Xmas with nine other by us - & has reached a Second Edition' (Marrs iii 13). The 'Juvenile Poetry' was Lamb's *Juvenile Poetry* (2 vols., 1809). Lucas identified 'That Tale in Prose' as *Arabella Hardy: The Sea Voyage* (Lucas ii 76), from *Mrs. Leicester's School*. W must have either read or heard it on his visit to London, 27 Feb.-3 April 1808. Mary Lamb had begun *Mrs. Leicester's School* as early as Dec. 1806 (Marrs ii 247); it was first published *c*. Christmas 1808.

(iii) *Mrs. Leicester's School* (2nd edn, 1809)
Suggested date of reading: 5 October 1811 onwards
References: Shaver 151
W's copy is now in the Rare Book Department at Boston Public Library. It contains his initials 'WW' on the recto of the frontispiece; on the front flyleaf DW has written 'Dorothy Wordsworth Grasmere October 5 1811'. This inscription provides a date by which the volume can be assumed to have entered W's possession. For C's marginalia on this work, see CC *Marginalia* iii 484-5. The 2nd edn was published 1 June 1809.

That year also saw the publication of the Lambs' *Poetry for Children, entirely original* (2 vols., 1809): did the Wordsworths ever see the title? They would certainly have been interested, especially as they had been enthusiastic recipients of Mary Lamb's verse in earlier years (see next notes).

243. Lamb, Mary Anne
(i) *Dialogue between a Mother and Child, The Lady Blanch, regardless of her lovers' fears* **in MS**
Suggested date of reading: early June 1804
References: Marrs ii 139-40
Charles Lamb copied these poems for DW in a letter of 2 June 1804. It is likely that W would have seen his sister's correspondence with the Lambs.

(ii) *Why is he wandering o'er the sea?* **in MS**
Suggested date of reading: shortly after 7 May 1805
References: Marrs ii 166
Mary Lamb sent this poem to DW in a letter of 7 May 1805.

(iii) *Virgin and Child, On the Same* **in MS**
Suggested date of reading: shortly after 14 June 1805
References: Marrs ii 170-1
Charles Lamb copied these poems for DW in a letter of 14 June 1805.

244. Lancaster, Joseph, *Improvements in Education; Abridged, Containing a Complete Epitome of the System of Education Invented and Practised by the Author* **(1808)**
Suggested date of reading: by 3 Dec. 1808
References: *MY* i 278
W encountered Bell through C in May 1808 (see note 37[i], above), and it was presumably through C that he knew about Lancaster's rival system of education (the Bell/Lancaster controversy was, after all, the subject of C's lecture of 3 May; see CC *Literature* i 96-7). This is partially confirmed by the brief allusion to Lancaster in W's letter to Wrangham of 3 Dec. 1808 (*MY* i 278). The allusion doesn't of itself prove that W had by that date read the *Improvements*, but 1808 has to be the most likely time at which he might have read it - as he can be presumed to have done, given the presence of a copy at Rydal Mount (Shaver 152).[1]

---

[1] On the basis of the Rydal Mount catalogue entry, 'Lancaster on Education', the Shavers list a copy of the 1803 *Improvements*. However, that could equally well refer to the 1808 abridgement, which W is more likely to have been reading at that time.

245. Landor, Walter Savage
(i) *Gebir* [1798]
Suggested date of reading: see note
References: *LY* i 79

On 3 Sept. 1821, W wrote to Landor, thanking him for the presentation copy of the latter's Latin *Idyllia* (Shaver 152), and adding: 'had your Idylliums been in English I should long ere this have been as well acquainted with them as with your Gebir' (*LY* i 79). This remark does little to establish a precise date for W's first reading of *Gebir*, but he can be assumed to have read it by the time he read *Count Julian* in April or May 1812 (see next note) - and it is likely that he saw *Gebir* well before that. C knew it well enough by 23 Oct. 1810 to echo it in a notebook entry (*Notebooks* iii 3990), and it is reasonable to suppose that W had read it by that date.

A copy of *Gebir* was retained at Rydal Mount bearing 'Autographs of Sir Humphrey Davy and W.W.' (Shaver 152; Wordsworth *SC* 523). If it was presented to W by Davy, the earliest at which it might have come into W's possession is 18 July 1804 when the two men first met (Reed ii 266). Prior to this, W probably heard about Landor and his work from Southey - a strong admirer of *Gebir*, having reviewed it in the *Critical Review* 27 (Sept. 1799) 29-39. Southey met Landor in Bristol, spring 1808, and again at Llanthony, 1811.[1]

For W's shifting relations with Landor see *Prose Works* ii 395-6; *Dora Wordsworth her book*, ed. F. V. Morley (1924), pp. 113-22; and *LY* iii 374-5n2. See also *PW* v 428-9 for Landor's charge that the description of the 'curious child' listening to a sea-shell in *The Excursion* was plagiarised from *Gebir*. If Landor's accusation was correct, that proves at least that W read *Gebir* before 1814.

(ii) *Simonidea* (Bath, 1806)
Suggested date of reading: some time after spring 1808
References: see note

'In your Simoneida, which I saw some years ago at Mr Southey's, I was pleased to find rather an out-of-the-way image, in which the present hour is compared to the shade on the dial', W told Landor on 20 April 1822 (*LY* i 125). Southey's copy is now at the Bodleian Library (Don.f.99), and bears the title-page inscription: 'Robert Southey, from the Author.' It was probably presented to Southey on, or shortly after, his first encounter with Landor in spring 1808, and Southey would have shown it to W not long after.

(iii) *Count Julian* in MS
Suggested date of reading: by 13 May 1812

---

[1] Southey seems to have been the main intermediary between Landor and W - at least, this is the implication of Landor's later reminiscence: 'Southey praised Wordsworth on every occasion and in every letter he wrote to me. Wordsworth never spoke a good word of him but said that all his poetry was not worth 5 shillings' (Thomas Ollive Mabbott, 'Landor on Chatterton and Wordsworth: Marginal Notes', *N&Q* 156 [1929] 168-9, p. 169).

References: Morley i 82

Robinson recorded in his diary for 13 May 1812 that W 'spoke with respect of Landor's power. The tragedy which he is now publishing has very fine touches, he says' (Morley i 82). This implies that W saw Landor's play in MS, a copy of which was in Southey's possession by 12 March 1811 (Warter ii 216); W could have seen it at any time between then and May 1812. It is likely that Southey would have ensured that W saw the published work, a copy of which he had received by 9 Feb. 1812 (Warter ii 252); that copy is listed by Simon Nowell Smith, *Wordsworth to Robert Graves and Beyond* (1983), p. 6-7, with a reproduction of the title-page.

246. Langland, John, *Piers Plowman*
Suggested date of reading: by 17 Sept. 1814
References: *MY* ii 154

In his letter to Robert Anderson of 17 Sept. 1814, W suggests that an enlarged edn of Anderson's *British Poets* should include 'P. Ploughman's Vision and Creed'. This indicates that he was aware of his works by 17 Sept. 1814; most probably he had seen either the 1550 or 1561 edn of the B-text, although T. D. Whitaker had edited the C-text in 1813 (and W was an admirer of Whitaker's other writings; see note 423). Southey had attempted to persuade Longman 'to publish a collection of the scarcer and better old poets, beginning with Pierce Ploughman' in June 1804 (*Life of Southey* ii 293).

247. Law, William, *A Serious Call to a Devout and Holy Life* [1728]
Suggested date of reading: by 5 June 1808
References: *MY* i 249

Although W's earliest mention of this book dates from 1808, it was known to C at least by Dec. 1798 (*Notebooks* i 377f15 and n), and both poets probably read it before then. There was a copy at Rydal Mount (Shaver 154), and it is likely that it had entered W's possession by 5 June 1808.

In 1870 C. M. Ingleby reported that a copy of Law's *Serious Call* (10th edn, 1772) containing C's marginalia also bore W's 'Autograph'; that copy is now lost, but the evidence suggests that it may have belonged to W (see CC *Marginalia* iii 499; Whalley *BC* 67).

248. Leckie, Gould Francis, *An Historical Survey of the Foreign Affairs of Great Britain with a View to explain the Causes and Disasters of the Late and Present Wars* (1808)
Suggested date of reading: 1 April 1809 onwards
References: *MY* i 289; Jordan 121

C first met Gould Francis Leckie, then Honorary Consul of Syracuse, in early Aug. 1804.[1] On 5 Feb. 1809, W wrote to Daniel Stuart requesting a copy of 'Lecky's Pamphlet' (*MY* i

---

[1] At the time, Leckie drew two pictures of Syracuse harbour in C's *Notebooks* (*Notebooks* ii 2180-1).

289); on 28 March 1809, De Quincey wrote to DW to say that he was sending 'Mr. Leckie's books', which arrived in Grasmere on 1 April 1809 (Jordan 121). W and C evidently read it soon after, as C recommended 'Mr. Leckie's valuable and authentic documents respecting the state of Sicily' in *The Friend* for 30 Nov. (CC *Friend* ii 201).

249. Ledyard, John, *A Journal of Captain Cook's Last Voyage to the Pacific Ocean* [Hartford, 1783]
Suggested date of reading: by 10 May 1808
References: *MY* i 231 and n2
DW's reference to Ledyard in her letter to Catherine Clarkson of 10 May 1808 indicates a reading of his *Journal*; perhaps she had seen it on her recent visit to Coleorton, where the Beaumonts had a good collection of travel books.

250. Lee, Harriet, *The German's Tale*
Suggested date of reading: see note
References: Masson iii 205
In his *Recollections*, De Quincey recalled the time, many years before, when he persuaded W to read Lee's *The German's Tale*:

> This most splendid tale I put into the hands of Wordsworth; and, for once, having, I suppose, nothing else to read, he condescended to run through it. I shall not report his opinion, which, in fact, was no opinion; for the whole colossal exhibition of fiendish grandeur in Conrad, the fine delineation of mixed power and weakness in Siegendorf, and the exquisite relief given to the whole by the truly Shaksperian portrait of feminine innocence and nobility in Josephine, he had failed so much as to guess at.
>
> (Masson iii 205)

De Quincey puts no specific date on this incident, and there are few clues in his narrative, but a likely guess would be Nov. 1808-Feb. 1809, when he was resident with the Wordsworths at Allan Bank. Or perhaps some time after Oct. 1809, when he moved into DC. At any rate, it is likely that this reading took place during the late 1800s or early 1810s. *The German's Tale* was one of Sophia and Harriet Lee's *Canterbury Tales* (5 vols., 1797-1805); it appeared in vol. 4 (1801), pp. 3-368.

251. Le Fanu, Alicia, *The Sons of Erin* (1812)
Date of performance: 30 April 1812
References: *Supp.* 52 and n4
W, then in London, saw this play performed on 30 April 1812, possibly with Lamb.

252. Le Sage, Alain Rene, *The Adventures of Gil Blas of Santillane*, tr. Benjamin Heath Malkin (4 vols., 1809)

Suggested date of reading: Aug. 1810
References: *Supp.* 42
On 19 Aug. 1810, DW told W that she was 'reading Malkin's Gil Blas - and it is a beautiful Book as to printing etc but I think the Translation vulgar' (*Supp.* 42). It is not clear whether this book belonged to the Wordsworths, or whether W saw it.

253. Lessing, Gotthold Ephraim
(i) *Fables*
Suggested date of reading: 6 Feb.-12 March 1802
References: *Grasmere Journals* 63, 65, 71-2, 77
DW began translating Lessing's *Fables* on 6 Feb. 1802, read in Lessing on 8 Feb., and translated, with W, probably from Lessing's *Fables*, on 9 Feb. She returned to her German grammar on 23 Feb., probably with a view to preparing for her reading of 'Lessing's Essay' (perhaps the *Laokoon*) on 25 Feb. On 12 March she records that 'I read the remainder of Lessing.' The words 'Fable of the Dogs', apparently jotted *c*. Feb. 1802 in one of DW's journals, may refer to Lessing's *Die Hunde* (see *Grasmere Journals* 181).

(ii) *Laokoon*
Suggested date of reading: 25 Feb. 1802
References: *Grasmere Journals* 72
'I read a good deal of Lessing's Essay' (DW's journal, 25 Feb. 1802). This may have been *Laokoon*, an essay that shares affinities with W's Preface to *Lyrical Ballads*; see Owen, *Preface* 180-1.

254. Lewis, M. G.
(i) *Tales of Wonder* **(2 vols., 1801)**
Suggested date of reading: by *c*. early Oct.-19 Dec. 1800
References: Parrish 187; Ketcham 79
Parrish 187 notes that the stanza and metre of W's ballad version of *Michael* 'are identical to those of Lewis's "The Stranger: A Norman Tale," in *Tales of Terror* (Kelso, 1799) and "Osric the Lion" in *Tales of Wonder* (1800)'. W may have seen both volumes, but *Tales of Wonder* is included here on the grounds that JW had seen it by 12 Dec. 1800, when he described it as 'very poor' (Ketcham 79). If indeed *Tales of Wonder* was W's source, he can be assumed to have seen it by around early Oct.-19 Dec. 1800, the date of composition allotted to the ballad *Michael* by the Cornell editors.

(ii) *The Felon* **in MS**
Suggested date of reading: by early March 1801
References: Ketcham 104

Writing to MH on 9 and 10 March 1801, JW expressed admiration for Lewis' *The Felon* - verses, he added, that 'were sent as Nonparriel[1] to W^m' (Ketcham 104). In a letter to DW of 10 March, he added that 'Mr Lewis's poem is the most funny one I ever read - it is quite a caricature of its kind' (Ketcham 105-6). A copy of *Lyrical Ballads* was sent to Lewis between 12 and 14 Jan. 1801 (Reed ii 108); it may have been in return for this that Lewis sent W the MS. Or perhaps it was contained in the letter received by W on 8 Nov. 1800 (*Grasmere Journals* 31). At any rate, *The Felon* was published in Lewis' *Poems* (1812), pp. 95-7.

255. Lickbarrow, Isabella, *Poetical Effusions* (Kendal, 1814)
Suggested date of reading: c. 23 July 1814 onwards
References: Shaver 157
Lickbarrow lived in Kendal and may have been known to the Wordsworths. W probably saw the numerous poems she published in the *Westmorland Advertiser*. As has been noted,[2] he was a subscriber to *Poetical Effusions*, her first book-length publication, two copies of which appear to have been retained at Rydal Mount; the *Westmorland Advertiser* announced its publication on 23 July 1814. Jonathan Wordsworth and Stephen Hebron note W's influence on her, *Romantic Women Writers* (1994), p. 58.

256. Lloyd, David, *State Worthies* (2nd edn, 1670)
Suggested date of reading: by 10 Oct. 1809
References: Griggs iii 241; *Prose Works* ii 109; Shaver 161
C's enthusiastic recommendation of this title in his letter to Sharp of 10 Oct. 1809 makes it likely that there was a copy at Allan Bank at that time - which W can be expected to have seen even then. C said that it 'should be the Manual of every public man' (Griggs iii 241). Owen and Smyser suggest that W follows Lloyd's phrasing in his praise of Sidney in the second of the *Essays Upon Epitaphs*. A copy of Lloyd was at Rydal Mount.

257. Logan, John, life and poems, including *Ode: written in a visit to the country in autumn* and *Ode to the Cuckoo* (Anderson)
Suggested date of reading: probably by 29 Sept. 1800; 3 June 1802
References: Ketcham 123; *Grasmere Journals* 104
In a letter of 3 May 1801, JW requested DW to ask her brother to recommend a course of reading in Anderson: 'I would be more particularly *pleased* at his pointing out any good poems in Poets such as *Logan* for instance' (Ketcham 123). My guess is that W had read Logan's works by the time he bade farewell to JW for the last time in Sept. 1800, and that he had by then recommended them to him. The earliest confirmation of a reading appears in

---

[1] I assume that JW means by this that the verses are 'unique' in the sense of being a curiosity, or an oddity. 'Nonpareil' can refer also to a size of type, but I take it that the verses in question were in MS.
[2] See Jackson 201-2; C. R. Johnson, *Provincial Poetry 1789-1839* (1992), 535.

DW's journals, 3 June 1802: 'We have been reading the Life & some of the writings of poor Logan since dinner. "And everlasting Longings for the lost." It is an affecting line. There are many affecting lines & passages in his poems.' As Pamela Woof notes, DW quotes Logan's *Ode: written in a visit to the country in autumn*:

> What voice [can] console the incessant sigh,
> And everlasting longings for the lost?

Their source was Anderson, *British Poets* vol. 11. Woof adds that W knew Logan's *Ode to the Cuckoo* (*Grasmere Journals* 234).

258. Lovelace, Richard, works
Suggested date of reading: by 17 Sept. 1814
References: *MY* ii 153
In his letter to Robert Anderson of 17 Sept. 1814, W suggests that an enlarged edn of Anderson's *British Poets* should include Lovelace. This indicates that he was aware of his works by 17 Sept. 1814.

259. Lucanus, Marcus Annaeus, *Pharsalia, A Continuation of Lucan's Historical Poem till the Death of Julius Caesar* tr. Thomas May [1630]
Suggested date of reading: by 17 Sept. 1814
References: *MY* ii 154
In his letter to Robert Anderson of 17 Sept. 1814, W suggests that an enlarged edn of Anderson's *British Poets* should include 'May's Lucan'. This indicates that he was aware of this translation by 17 Sept. 1814. He had probably seen Southey's copy of the 1657-9 edn (Southey *SC* 1830).

260. Lyttelton, George, Baron Lyttelton
(i) *Epitaph to the Memory of Lucy Lyttelton* (Anderson)
Suggested date of reading: by 22 Feb. 1810
References: *Prose Works* ii 110
W quotes this poem from Anderson's *British Poets* vol. 10 in the second of his *Essays Upon Epitaphs* (*Prose Works* ii 74). He had probably known it since his schooldays, but this appears to be his earliest reference to it. It was also available to him in Knox's *Elegant Extracts* (1791) Book V, p. 310.

(ii) *To the Memory of a Lady Lately Deceased: a Monody*
Suggested date of reading: by 22 Feb. 1810
References: *Prose Works* ii 110-11

W knew this poem by 1786, when he borrowed from it in *The Dog: An Idyllium* (see *WR* 91). In the second of his *Essays Upon Epitaphs* it is adduced as evidence that 'Lord Lyttelton dearly loved his wife' (*Prose Works* ii 75).

261. Macklin, Charles, *The True-Born Scotsman*
Suggested date of reading: perhaps between 17 April and 5 May 1807
References: *SHL* 10
In Oct. 1808, SH recommended that Mary Monkhouse see G. F. Cooke as Sir Pertinax MacSycophant in *The True-Born Scotsman*. The most likely time for SH to have seen it is during her time in London with the Wordsworths, 17 April-5 May 1807 (on which date she departed London). She is likely at least to have mentioned the production to W, and it is quite possible that he and MW accompanied her to it. Macklin's play had been a favourite with London audiences since its first performance on 10 July 1764.

262. Macpherson, James 'Ossian', *Fingal* [1762]; *Temora* [1763]
Suggested date of reading: 20 or 21 Aug. 1814 onwards
References: Reed ii 566-7; Shaver 167
Reed records that SH's journal of the Scottish tour of 1814 mentions meeting 'a bookseller of whom W had bought a small Ed. of Ossian & the Perth Guide'. This may have been the two volume edn of Edinburgh, 1812, listed Shaver 167. MW records that SH was reading Ossian at Alloa on 22 Aug. (*Supp.* 151).

263. magazines
(i)
Suggested date of reading: 27 Jan. 1802
References: *Grasmere Journals* 59
'When we returned from Franks William wasted his mind in the Magazines' (DW's journal, 27 Jan. 1802).

(ii)
Suggested date of reading. 6 May 1802 and shortly thereafter
References: *Grasmere Journals* 97
'When we came in we found a Magazine & Review & a letter from Coleridge with verses to Hartley & Sara H. We read the Review &c.' (DW's journal, 6 May 1802).

(iii)
Suggested date of reading: *c*. 5 March 1804
References: *EY* 447
'I was sorry to see from the Papers that your Friend poor Fawcett was dead; not so much that he was dead but to think of the manner in which he had sent himself off before his time', W told Hazlitt on 5 March 1804. This was an event of some significance for W as Fawcett was

the model for the Solitary in *The Excursion* (see *PW* v 374-5); perhaps his death even inspired W to record his story in verse. His phrasing seems to suggest that W saw Fawcett's obituary in a newspaper, but no mention is made of his passing in any daily paper between 24 Feb. (when he died) and 5 March. The *Gentleman's Magazine*, however, does carry a lengthy notice of Fawcett's decease in its number for Feb. 1804, and W might have seen this on or around 5 March. However, W's mention of 'the manner in which he had sent himself off before his time' refers probably to Fawcett's fondness for alcohol, alluded to in the Fenwick Note to *The Excursion* (*PW* v 375). This is not mentioned in the *Gentleman's Magazine*; see *Gentleman's Magazine* 74 (Feb. 1804) 185. I surmise that W had read an obituary mentioning Fawcett's 'intemperance' in another periodical of the day, as yet untraced. In the mid-1790s he had read Fawcett's *Art of War* (*WR* 57-8) and attended his sermons (*PW* v 375); for more on W and Fawcett see Roe 23-7.

(iv)
Suggested date of reading: 3 May 1809
References: *MY* i 327
On 3 May 1809 W wrote to Stuart: 'I have just been reading an old Magazine where I find that Benjamin Flower was fined £100 and imprisoned in Newgate four months . . . for a libel' (*MY* i 327). The magazine remains unidentified. Flower was jailed in 1799.

264. Malcolm, Sir John, *Observations on the Disturbances in the Madras Army in 1809* (1812)
Suggested date of reading: by 24 Aug. 1812
References: Warter ii 290-1; Shaver 168
On 1 Sept. 1812, Southey told the Revd. Herbert Hill:

> General Malcolm's pamphlet was put into my hand by Wordsworth the other day, merely to show me the very able manner in which he had traced the progress of discontent among the officers, - in the true spirit of philosophical history: I have seen nothing more of it. But Malcolm's other book, that upon the political state of India, is here . . . (Warter ii 290-1)

Southey stayed with the Wordsworths in Grasmere between 24 and 27 Aug., the most likely time for him to have seen Malcolm's *Observations*. W had met Malcolm's brother Gilbert, a good friend of CW and cousin of Captain Pasley, in June 1812 (Reed ii 505). Sir John was known to DW, if only by repute, by 11 Sept. 1813 (*MY* ii 110). In 1814 he published a poem, *Persia*, which had evidently been in MS for some time, and may have been known to W. Southey's comments indicate that he owned Malcolm's *Sketch of the Political History of India* (1811) by 24 Aug.; it was probably in that knowledge that W showed Southey the *Observations*.

265. Malkin, Benjamin Heath, *A Father's Memoirs of His Child* **(1806)**
Suggested date of reading: between mid-March and 10 June 1807
References: Reed ii 707; Moorman *N&Q* 403; *MY* i 368
W and MW copied four Blake lyrics from Malkin's volume into the Wordsworth Commonplace Book (DC MS 26, 46v-48r) some time between mid-March and 10 June 1807. They were during that period at Coleorton, so that the book may have belonged to the Beaumonts. DW evidently read the book through, for she commented on 26 Aug. 1809 that Malkin 'is a coxcomb, and indeed it is plain enough from the manner in which that account of his Son is written' (*MY* i 368). Other owners of Malkin's book include Wrangham (Wrangham *SC* 1547) and Robinson (Sadler i 299). See also note 45(i).

266. Mallet, David, *The Excursion* **(1728)**
Suggested date of reading: probably by 1814
References: *LY* iv 788
'There are two Poems, perhaps more, in the English Language bearing the Title of the "Excursion", one by David Mallet, and another by William Wordsworth', so W told Robinson on 22 June 1846 (*LY* iv 788). While this does not prove a reading by W, I find it hard to believe that he chose the title in ignorance of Mallet's work. It was in Anderson, *British Poets* vol. 9, and was thus readily available at DC and later at Rydal Mount. Lyon 32-3 finds some similarities between the two *Excursions*. Coffman M22 erroneously records a copy of the *Works* (1795) containing C's marginalia in the Victoria and Albert Museum. Heather Jackson confirms its non-existence, apparently the result of Coffman's confusion over the status of Coleridge's marginalia in Anderson (CC *Marginalia* i 75).

267. Mallet, Paul-Henri, *Northern Antiquities*, **tr. Thomas Percy (2 vols., 1770)**
Suggested date of reading: perhaps *c.* 1801; almost certainly before 1804
References: Cornell *13-Book Prelude* 17, 111

> Sometimes, more sternly mov'd, I would relate
> How vanquish'd Mithridates northward pass'd,
> And, hidden in the cloud of years, became
> That Odin, Father of a Race by whom
> Perish'd the Roman Empire . . . (*Prelude* i 186-9)

Reed suggests that in these lines 'WW probably recalls especially accounts in Gibbon's *Decline and Fall of the Roman Empire*, chap. X, and Percy's translation of P.-H. Mallet, *Northern Antiquities*, chap. IV, and possibly Joseph Cottle, *Alfred* (London, 1800), I3n, connecting (but not identifying as the same person) Mithridates (?132-63 B.C.), a king of Pontus, with Odin' (Cornell *13-Book Prelude* 111). It is not clear exactly when these lines were composed, but Reed suggests *c.* 1801, with a terminal date of 1804. W probably would not have needed to consult Mallet in order to compose this passage, but it is possible that a copy was at hand as he wrote; see *WR* 93. Southey's copy is now in the possession of Paul F. Betz (Betz 127).

268. Malory, Sir Thomas, *Morte D'Arthur*
Suggested date of reading: by 29 Sept. 1800
References: Reed ii 704; Moorman *N&Q* 403

> And now I daresay (said Sir Boys), that, Sir Lancelot, there thou liest, thou were never matched of none earthly Knight's hands. And thou were the curtiest Knight that ever beare shield. And thou were the truest Friend to thy lover that ever bestrood horse, and thou were the truest lover, of a sinful man, that ever loved woman. And thou were the kindest man that ever strooke with sword. And thou were the goodliest person that ever came among presse of knights. And thou were the meekest man & the gentlest, that ever eate in hall among Ladies. And thou were the sternest Knight to thy mortal foe that ever put speare in the rest. (DC MS 26, 23v)

Moorman was puzzled by this extract from Sir Bors' lament for Arthur in the Wordsworth Commonplace Book, and which Reed judges to have been entered by 29 Sept. 1800. As she explained, 'No modern edition of Malory was then available, but in 1807 Southey was planning to edit one, though he never did so. It is possible that the Wordsworths copied the passage from a volume in his possession.' In fact, Southey did produce a two-volume edn of *Morte D'Arthur* in 1817.[1] He was indeed preparing it a decade before; on 16 Nov. 1807 he told Wynn: 'I am about to edit "Mort d'Arthur": this will be work after my own heart. Can you lend me your brother's copy to correct the press by? You will see the necessity there is for having it printed verbatim and literatim, and that I must have a copy before me for this purpose' (Warter ii 27). This would indicate that even as late as 1807 Southey had no copy of Malory at his disposal, and casts some doubt over the suggestion that the Commonplace Book draft derived from a book owned by him. A more likely source is Francis Wrangham, who owned 'an Unique copy of an edition of the Romance of Arthur, *printed by Wynkyn de Worde*', published in 1529 (Cole 2; see also Wrangham *SC* 75). W could have called in on Wrangham on one of his customary visits to Gallow Hill (not far from Wrangham's residence in Hunmanby), and we know that he attempted to do so in early June 1800 (Reed ii 66). The only problem with this is that we know only that the book was in Wrangham's possession by 1824, when it appeared in Cole's select catalogue of his library (the earliest known to exist). For Arthuriana with Southey connections, see note 357.

269. Malthus, Thomas Robert, *An Essay on the Principle of Population* **(1803)**
Suggested date of reading: by May 1814
References: PW v 473-4

---

[1] *The Byrth, Lyf, and Actes of Kyng Arthur*, with introduction and notes by Robert Southey (2 vols., 1817).

De Selincourt notes that W refers to Malthus at *Excursion* ix 363-4. W's phrase, 'the fear / Of numbers', does not itself prove that he read the *Essay* from cover to cover, but it is probable that by the time he wrote these lines W knew what Malthus had to say. He always characterized Malthus by his concern with overpopulation: in 1828 he mentioned 'Mr Malthus and the population men' (*LY* i 682), and in 1831 remarked: 'It is monstrous to affirm with Mr Malthus, that the World is overpeopled' (*LY* ii 405).

C had read the *Essay* shortly after its first appearance in 1798 (*WR* 94); possibly W saw that copy. He certainly saw the copy of the 1803 edn which C was given by Daniel Stuart and which C annotated in Jan. 1804 at DC, apparently to help Southey with a review (*Notebooks* i 1832 and n).[1] It was retained subsequently at Allan Bank and Rydal Mount (CC *Marginalia* iii 805-9; Shaver 341; Curry i 350-1).

270. Mant, Revd. Richard, *The Simpliciad; a satirico-didactic poem* (1808)

Suggested date of reading: by early Nov. 1809
References: see note

The first inkling W is known to have had about Mant's satirical attack on the 'Lake School' (following on from Jeffrey's review of *Thalaba*) is in a letter from De Quincey on 27 May 1809, in which the latter describes the contents of Byron's *English Bards and Scotch Reviewers*, and goes on to say: 'The other Satire, called The Simpliciad, I have not yet read; because I have had no opportunity of borrowing it' (Jordan 185). De Quincey no doubt wished to assure his mentor that he would not consider *buying* a book in which he was attacked.

There can be little doubt that W saw it soon after. In early Nov. 1809, C wrote to Southey: 'Have you seen the Simpliciad - if not, it shall be sent to you - Such a thing! - O Jesus!' (Griggs iii 261). That letter was written to Southey from Allan Bank where C was staying with the Wordsworths, making it almost certain that W had seen Mant's volume by early Nov. 1809. De Selincourt notes that a number of revisions to W's poems in the 1815 edn were prompted by Mant's jibes (see *PW* ii 491, iii 448; OET *Prel.* 561).

C knew Mant also in a theological context (*Notebooks* iii 4140); W actually dined with him on 8 Sept. 1830, when he was mindful of his authorship of that early satire (*LY* ii 321, 324). By 1848 Mant's volume on *Church Architecture* (1843) was at Rydal Mount (Shaver 169).

271. Marlowe, Christopher, 'plays & poems'

Suggested date of reading: by 13 Oct. 1804
References: Marrs ii 147

Some time in Sept. or Oct. 1804 W asked Lamb to purchase a copy of Marlowe's works on his behalf. On 13 Oct. Lamb responded, 'Marlow's plays & poems are totally vanished; only

---

[1] Might C have urged Josiah Wedgwood to read Malthus at this time? On 7 Nov. 1803 Tom Wedgwood told Poole: 'Joss says you must study Malthus on Population, second edition' (Sandford ii 123).

one edition of Dodsley retains one, & the other two, of his plays' (Marrs ii 147). W was aware of what works by Marlowe were contained in Dodsley's *Select Collection of Old Plays* (1744; 2nd edn, 1780), as Dodsley was the source for the fragment of *Edward II* copied into DC MS 16, probably in 1798 (see *WR* 94-5). The request to obtain the plays and poems would suggest that W had seen more of Marlowe's work since 1798.

272. Martin, Martin, *A Description of the Western Islands of Scotland* **(2nd edn, 1716)**
Suggested date of reading: by late 1808
References: *Notebooks* iii 3409; Shaver 170
In late 1808 SH copied the description of the gawlin from Martin, pp. 71-2, into C's notebook (*Notebooks* iii 3409 and n), probably working from W's copy. This is the earliest known indication of W's ownership of the volume. He also owned Martin's *A Voyage to St Kilda*, which was in his possession at Cambridge; perhaps this book, too, was acquired there.

273. Marvell, Andrew
(i) *On a Drop of Dew*
Suggested date of reading: by March 1802
References: see note
Lucy Newlyn, 'The Little Actor and his Mock Apparel', *WC* 14 (1983) 30-9, argues that Marvell's poem is 'close to the rhythms and language' of W's *To H.C.* (p. 32). This is further discussed by Stein 157-8. The date of composition of W's *To H.C.* is not precisely known. Curtis follows Reed's dating: 'Composed possibly between March 27 and around June 17, 1802, or more probably early 1804, by March 6; fairly certainly between the earliest and latest of these dates' (Cornell *Poems 1800-7* 100). Newlyn observes that C alludes to *To H.C.* in a letter of Oct. 1803, and argues in support of Hodgson's dating of 'between 4 March . . . and April 4, 1802, possibly as late as May 3, 1802' (pp. 38-9). Furthermore, I find that, in a copy of *Poems* (1815), now in the possession of Christopher Wordsworth, W has written, in pencil, next to *To H.C.*, the date '1802-3'. At all events, W evidently began the poem in March 1802, which provides a reliable terminal date for his reading of Marvell's *On a Drop of Dew*. He included a lightly edited version of it in the album of verse he compiled for Lady Mary Lowther (*Album* 66-8). W's acquaintance with Marvell's works probably dates back to late July 1795 (*WR* 96). C's letter to SH of May 1807 contained a transcription of Marvell's *On a Drop of Dew* (Griggs vi 1018): that transcription survives today in the Wordsworth Library.

(ii) *An Horatian Ode upon Cromwell's Return from Ireland*
Suggested date of reading: c. Sept. 1802
References: Reed ii 642n8
Prelude MS W contains a transcription of Marvell's *Horatian Ode* dating from late 1802 (DC MS 38, 2r-9r). Reed suggests that W's source was probably not Thompson's edn of the *Works*

(1776),[1] which W knew by 1814 (see next note), positing instead that Lamb may have owned a MS text of the poem, and that the MS W copy 'may derive from the Ws' contacts with the Ls in London' in Sept. 1802. While I concur with these general conclusions, I must add that the variants between Thompson and MS W are not so striking as to eliminate the possibility that Thompson was W's source. D. E. Wickham points out that Lamb probably owned a copy of Thompson's text by Sept. 1802, referring to Lamb's letter to Godwin of 14 Dec. 1800: 'I remember two honest Lines by Marvel (whose Poems by the way I am just going to possess)' - Lamb then quoting *Upon Appleton House* 427-8 (Marrs i 256).

(iii) works
Suggested date of reading: by 17 Sept. 1814
References: *MY* ii 154
In his letter to Robert Anderson of 17 Sept. 1814, W suggests that an enlarged edn of Anderson's *British Poets* should include Marvell, and he refers specifically to 'the Poems which the Quarto Edition of his Prose Works contains'. This is probably, as the editors of *MY* suggest, a reference to Thompson's edn of the *Works* (1776).

274. Mason, William
(i) *Epitaph on Mrs Mason, in the Cathedral at Bristol*
Suggested date of reading: by 22 Feb. 1810
References: *Prose Works* ii 82, 113
W quotes this work in the third of his *Essays Upon Epitaphs*, probably from Knox's *Elegant Extracts*, two copies of which were retained at Rydal Mount (Shaver 147).

(ii) *Epitaph on Miss Drummond in the Church of Brodsworth, Yorkshire*
Suggested date of reading: by 22 Feb. 1810
References: *Prose Works* ii 85, 115
See preceding note.

(iii) *The English Garden* (1772-81)
Suggested date of reading: by Feb. 1815
References: *Prose Works* iii 28
W commends Mason's poem in his *Preface* (1815); he must have read it many years before.

275. Massinger, Philip
(i) *The Plays of Philip Massinger; with notes by William Gifford* (4 vols., 1805)
Suggested date of reading: Feb. 1806 onwards
References: Shaver 171

---

[1] *An Horatian Ode* appears at Marvell, *Works* ed. Thompson (3 vols., 1776), iii 495-9.

W had requested Lamb to find him a Massinger in 1804, but, according to Lamb, 'Massinger I never saw but at one shop, but it is now gone' (Marrs ii 146). However, on 15 Feb. 1806 Longman charged W for '1 Massingers Works boards', which cost £1.19.0 (see p. 266). It is likely, as Reed suggests, that this was Gifford's edn of 1805, later retained at Rydal Mount. It was almost certainly in this copy that DW and MW read *The Bashful Lover* in April (see next note), and that C read Gifford's introduction and Ferriar's essay on Massinger in Dec. 1808-9 (*Notebooks* iii 3445-6 and nn). It is not to be confused with Gillman's copy of Gifford's edn, which C annotated in 1817 (CC *Marginalia* iii 813). C used it for his lectures of 1811-12 and 1818 (CC *Literature* i 293-4nn26-7, ii 143).

(ii) *The Bashful Lover*
Suggested date of reading: April 1806
References: *MY* i 21
In April 1806, during W's absence in London, DW and MW 'read only one play, the Bashful Lover' (*MY* i 21), probably out of the edn of Massinger's *Plays* with notes by William Gifford purchased in Feb. (see preceding note).

276. May, Thomas, works
Suggested date of reading: by 17 Sept. 1814
References: *MY* ii 153
In his letter to Robert Anderson of 17 Sept. 1814, W suggests that an enlarged edn of Anderson's *British Poets* should include May. This indicates that he was aware of his works by 17 Sept. 1814. Southey owned a copy of May's *The Victorious Reign of Edward III* (1635) (Southey *SC* 1829).

277. Mayne, John, *By Logan's Streams That Run Sae Deep*
Suggested date of reading: between March 1804 and 12 March 1805
References: Reed ii 707
Three stanzas from Mayne's poem were copied by MW into the Wordsworth Commonplace Book (DC MS 26, 44v-45r) between March 1804 and 12 March 1805.

278. Mela, Pomponius, *De Situ Orbis Libri Tres* **[?Basle, 1536]**
Suggested date of reading: possibly by 1800; by 1810
References: Shaver 173
W's copy is now at St John's College, Cambridge, and bears the flyleaf inscription, 'S. T. Coleridge + W. Wordsworth'. There is no title-page. The inscription suggests that it was jointly purchased; if so, this must have occurred by 1810, after which point C and W are not known to have bought books together. One of C's notebook entries dating from 1800 appears to be dependent on Mela, and it is possible that they had by then acquired this volume (*Notebooks* i 694 and n). Mela seems to have been more integral to C's reading than to W's;

Whalley commented: 'If one assumes, as Professor Lowes has suggested, that Coleridge was an inveterate verifier of footnotes and references, we might expect that we can now trace an excursion into the elder cosmographers: perhaps from Hakluyt, Purchas, Leemius, Crantz, Bartram and Bruce he pivoted on Maupertuis's *Figure of the Earth* to explore geographers of more comprehensive vision - Strabo, Pomponius Mela, Diodorus Siculus, Pliny the Elder, George Buchanan, Walter Ralegh, Peter Heylyn, Philip Cluver, du Bartas' (Whalley PhD i 230). Coffman lists three copies which C is thought to have seen (Coffman M79-81).

279. Melmoth, William, *The Great Importance of a Religious Life Consider'd* **[1711]**
Suggested date of reading: by 5 June 1808
References: MY i 249
W's earliest mention of this book dates from 1808. It was by the father of the more celebrated translator of Pliny and friend of Beckford.

280. *Mercantile Gazette*
Suggested date of reading: mid-1800s; by 26 Sept. 1806
References: MY i 81
On 26 Sept. 1806 W thanked Josiah Wade, editor of the *Mercantile Gazette*, 'for the pleasure I and my family have had from the Newspaper which I have punctually received' (*MY* i 81). W seems to have met Wade through C, who knew him by Sept. 1794 (Griggs i 100).

281. Metastasio, Pietro Antonio, sonnets
Suggested date of reading: between Nov. 1802 and early Jan. 1803
References: Woof *SIB* 185-7; Woof PhD 579-83; Reed ii 33; Cornell *Poems 1800-7* 589-93
W translated six of Metastasio's sonnets at this time, five of which were published in the *Morning Post*, 17, 22 Oct., 2, 15 Nov., 12 Dec 1803. Five of these were drafted in W's copy of Agostino Isola, *Pieces Selected from the Italian Poets* (2nd edn, Cambridge, 1784), now at the Fitzwilliam Museum, Cambridge (Shaver 201). The Italian text of 'Laura, farewell my Laura!', the first of the translations to appear in the *Morning Post*, is not in Isola; its source is not known.

282. Michelangelo, sonnets
Suggested date of reading: by 25 Dec. 1804, and from then onwards
References: Reed ii 278n1; Cornell *Poems 1800-7* 410
Reed ii 278n1 provides a detailed account of W's translations from Michelangelo. W was reading Michelangelo's sonnets with a view to translating them from Dec. 1804; his work on them proceeded, on and off, throughout 1805-6, and apparently less intensively in 1807.

283. Milton, John
(i) *Paradise Lost* **Book XI**

Suggested date of reading: 2 Feb. 1802
References: Grasmere Journals 62
'After tea I read aloud the 11th Book of Paradise Lost we were much impressed & also melted into tears' (DW's journal, 2 Feb. 1802). As Pamela Woof observes, the aggression among the animals that came about as a result of the Fall is the subject of W's *The Redbreast and the Butterfly*, composed 18 April 1802 (*Grasmere Journals* 218). See also W's note to *The Redbreast and the Butterfly*, Cornell *Poems 1800-7* 404.

(ii) sonnets
Suggested date of reading: 21 May 1802
References: Grasmere Journals 101; *LY* i 125-6
'Wm wrote two sonnets on Buonaparte after I had read Milton's sonnets to him' (DW's journal, 21 May 1802). In 1822, W recalled, 'my Sister happened to read to me the sonnets of Milton, which I could at that time repeat; but somehow or other I was singularly struck with the style of harmony, and the gravity, and republican austerity of those compositions. In the course of the same afternoon I produced 3 sonnets' (*LY* i 125-6). This was probably the occasion recalled again in W's Fenwick Note to the *Miscellaneous Sonnets*:

> In the cottage of Town-End, one afternoon, in 1801, my Sister read to me the Sonnets of Milton. I had long been well acquainted with them, but I was particularly struck on that occasion with the dignified simplicity and majestic harmony that runs through most of them - in character so totally different from the Italian, and still more so from Shakespeare's fine sonnets. (*FN* 19)

One of these sonnets was *I griev'd for Buonaparte*, published in the *Morning Post*, 16 Sept. 1802. In addition, a note to *Methought I saw the footsteps of a throne* acknowledges the influence of Milton's *Methought I saw my late espouséd saint* (Cornell *Poems 1800-7* 411). For W's opinion of Milton's sonnets, see also *EY* 379.

(iii) *Il Penseroso*
Suggested date of reading: 3 June 1802
References: Grasmere Journals 105
'A very affecting letter came from MH while I was sitting in the window reading Milton's Penseroso to William' (DW's journal, 3 June 1802). Milton's poem was by this time well known to W.

(iv) *Giovane piano e semplicetto amante*
Suggested date of reading: between around Nov. 1802 and early Jan. 1803
References: Cornell *Poems 1800-7* 586, 678
W translated this work as 'A plain Youth, Lady, and a simple Lover', which he published in the *Morning Post* on 5 Oct. 1803 as *Translated from the Italian of Milton. Written During his Travels* (see Woof PhD 578-9; Woof *SIB* 185).

(v) works, including sonnets, *L'Allegro* and *Il Penseroso*
Suggested date of reading: 24 Dec. 1802
References: *Grasmere Journals* 134-5
DW's journal for 24 Dec. 1802 records that she listened to her brother 'reading some of Milton's [sonnets] & the Allegro & Penseroso' - as well as some sonnets of his own.

(vi) Dedication to *The Doctrine and Discipline of Divorce*
Suggested date of reading: by 6 March 1804
References: Cornell *Poems 1800-7* 407
W alludes to this work at *Ode to Duty* 46, composed largely by 6 March 1804.

(vii) 'Miltons Works 4 vol'
Suggested date of reading: mid-Feb. 1806 onwards
References: Marrs ii 204-6
On 1 Feb. 1806, Lamb wrote to W to tell him that he had purchased copies of Urry's Chaucer, Pope's Shakespeare, Spenser and Milton on his behalf, and had sent them up on the Kendal wagon that very day. The copy of Milton's works cost 3*s*.6*d*.; W would have received Lamb's consignment by mid-Feb. (Reed ii 314).

(viii) *Paradise Lost*
Suggested date of reading: between 30 Oct. and 2 Nov. 1806
References: Reed ii 339-40; *MY* i 133
During his stay with the Beaumonts at Coleorton, 30 Oct. to 2 Nov. 1806, W gave several readings from *Paradise Lost* - including Book I and Book VI, lines 767-84. Beaumont wrote to W on 6 Nov. recalling 'that sublime passage in Milton you read the other night (I am not sure of the words) where he describes his, the Messiah's, coming as shining afar off, & this idea was so prevailing that I could almost have imagined I saw movements not to be accounted for, & shapes without a name'.[1] In fact, *PL* vi 767ff was of particular importance to W and C; it is discussed in *Prose Works* iii 34 and CC *Table Talk* i 489-90.

On this occasion, too, W seems to have read all of Book I; as DW recalled in a letter to Lady Beaumont of 15 Feb. 1807: 'I often think of the happy evening when, by your fireside, my Brother read to us the first book of the Paradise lost; and not without many hopes that we may again have the same pleasure together' (*MY* i 133).

(ix) Digression to *The History of Britain, that part especially now call'd England, from the first traditional beginning, continu'd to the Norman Conquest* (1670)
Suggested date of reading: c. early 1809
References: *Prose Works* i 396, 399, 406

---

[1] Wordsworth Library WLL/Beaumont, G. H./18.

W alludes to Milton's *History of Britain* in the *Convention of Cintra*. De Quincey was told to be on the look-out for a copy of Milton's *Prose Works* for W in July 1808, and one may have been sent to Allan Bank by the autumn; one was retained at Rydal Mount (Shaver 176).

(x) *On Shakespear*
Suggested date of reading: by 22 Feb. 1810
References: *Prose Works* ii 61-2, 105; CC *Friend* ii 346
W quotes part of this poem in the first of his *Essays Upon Epitaphs*. About a month later C was reading Milton's prose works, probably at Allan Bank (see *Notebooks* iii 3723).

(xi) *Paradise Lost* Book V
Suggested date of reading: morning, 27 Oct. 1810
References: *MY* i 447
On 12 Nov. 1810, DW told Catherine Clarkson about the morning of 27 Oct. 1810, which the Wordsworths spent at Hackett in Little Langdale:

> The weather was heavenly, when we were there, and the first morning we sate in hot sunshine on a crag, twenty yards from the door, while William read part of the 5th Book of the Paradise Lost to us. He read The Morning Hymn, while a stream of white vapour, which covered the Valley of Brathay, ascended slowly and by degrees melted away. It seemed as if we had never before felt deeply the power of the Poet -'Ye mists and exhalations, etc., etc.!' (*MY* i 447)

The passage read out by W (*PL* v 153-208) was one of the most important to the first-generation Romantics, a key influence on (besides other works) *Home at Grasmere*.

(xii) *Reason of Church Government*
Suggested date of reading: shortly before 28 April 1814
References: *Prose Works* iii 10; *MY* ii 146
In a letter to Poole of 28 April 1814, W quotes Milton's *Reason of Church Government* (*MY* ii 146). The same phrase seems to have inspired a remark made in the Preface to *The Excursion* (*Prose Works* iii 10).

(xiii) *The History of Britain, that part especially now call'd England, from the first traditional beginning, continu'd to the Norman Conquest* (1670)
Suggested date of reading: 1814-15
References: Cornell *Poems 1807-20* 163, 531-3; Shaver 176
Milton's *History* is one of W's acknowledged sources for *Artegal and Elidure*, composed late 1814-Feb. 1815 (Cornell *Poems 1807-20* 163, 531-3). It is likely that W had by that time acquired the copy listed Shaver 176.

(xiv) *Poems Upon Several Occasions, English, Italian, and Latin, with Translations by John Milton. With notes by Thomas Warton* (2nd edn, 1791)

Suggested date of reading: by Jan. 1815
References: *Prose Works* iii 91; Shaver 300
In a note to W's *Essay, Supplementary to the Preface*, Owen and Smyser observe that 'Wordsworth's information is mainly from Thomas Warton's Preface to Milton's *Poems Upon Several Occasions*' (*Prose Works* iii 91). Shaver lists a copy of the 1791 edn as present in Rydal Mount, indicating that Shaver himself saw it in Richard Wordsworth's possession; however, there is no evidence that Richard Wordsworth ever owned such a volume, and I suspect that, on this rare occasion, Shaver was in error. It is more likely that, as Owen and Smyser note, the volume was owned by Margaret Goalby, and that Shaver saw it while it was in her possession; she obtained it from Dorothy Dickson. Its present whereabouts are unknown.

(xv) *Paradise Lost*, ed. Thomas Newton (1763)
Suggested date of reading: by Feb. 1815
References: *Prose Works* iii 46
Shaver has shown that the 1815 Preface was influenced by Newton; see 'Wordsworth's Debt to Thomas Newton', *MLN* 52 (1947) 344. W had owned a copy of this edn since his Cambridge years (see *WR* 99-100).

284. Minot, Laurence, works
Suggested date of reading: by 17 Sept. 1814
References: *MY* ii 153
In his letter to Robert Anderson of 17 Sept. 1814, W suggests that an enlarged edn of Anderson's *British Poets* should include Minot's works. This indicates that he was aware of them by 17 Sept. 1814, probably from their appearance in Ritson's edn of *Poems on interesting events in the reign of Edward III written in the year 1352 by Laurence Minot* (1795).

285. miscellany
Suggested date of reading: 15 April 1802
References: *Grasmere Journals* 85-6
After dinner at an inn on Ullswater, W and DW read 'a volume of Enfield's Speaker, another miscellany, & an odd volume of Congreve's plays' (DW's journal, 15 April 1802). The 'miscellany' would, in fact, have been an anthology, probably of prose articles and extracts from books.

286. Montagu, Lady Mary Wortley, *The Works of the Right Honourable Lady Mary Wortley Montagu, Including her Correspondence, Poems, and Essays*, ed. James Dallaway (5 vols., 1803)
Suggested date of reading: April-May 1805

References: *EY* 577

'In reading Lady Mary W Montagu's letters, whi[ch] we have had lately, I continually felt a *want* - I had not the lea[st] affec[c]tion for her' (DW to Lady Beaumont, 11 April 1805). DW's reading seems to have continued for some weeks; she referred again to Montagu in a letter to Lady Beaumont of 4 May (*EY* 592). W too read Montagu's letters, as his knowledge of her depended largely on them and those of Pope (*LY* ii 237). Shaver does not list this title, so the Wordsworths probably borrowed their copy from some other source - most likely Southey, who commended the volume in the *Annual Review* 2 (1803) 502-7: 'On the whole it may safely be affirmed, that Lady Mary's present letters confirm the pretensions of her sex to peculiar excellence in the epistolary style; and that however highly France may estimate her Sevigné, England may claim a loftier station for her Montagu' (p. 507). He echoed this judgement in a letter to Wynn of 27 Nov. 1804 (see Warter i 289).

287. Montgomery, James
(i) *The Wanderer of Switzerland, and Other Poems* (2nd edn, 1806)
Suggested date of reading: by 1807
References: Cornell *Poems 1800-7* 403; Shaver 179

In a note to *To the Daisy* (pub. 1807) W acknowledged its similarity to Montgomery's *A Field Flower*, which he almost certainly read in *The Wanderer of Switzerland, and Other Poems* (2nd edn, 1806), pp. 151-3. His copy of this volume is now in the possession of Paul F. Betz (Betz 131). It is in a cottonian binding and contains the inscription: 'Wm Wordsworth Grasmere'. It was evidently a subject of discussion among the Wordsworth circle: Southey reviewed it in the *Quarterly Review* 6 (Dec. 1811) 405-19, and C alluded to *A Field Flower* in a notebook entry of June 1810 (*Notebooks* iii 3859). W recalled his first reading of *The Wanderer of Switzerland* in a letter to Montgomery of Nov. 1836 (*LY* iii 326).

(ii) review of *The Excursion*, *Eclectic Review* 3 (Jan. 1815) 13-39
Suggested date of reading: between 27 Feb. and 16 March 1815
References: *MY* ii 203

On 18 Feb. 1815 DW told SH that 'The Eclectic Review was written by Montgomery. He is very religious therefore your conjecture respecting the sincerity of the opening of the Review must have been unfounded' (*MY* ii 203). This remark implies a reading of Montgomery's review, but it should be noted that DW's letter to Priscilla Wordsworth of 27 Feb. does not confirm this: 'The Eclectic, *we are told*, is highly encomiastic' (*MY* ii 206; her italics). If, by this date, the Wordsworths had not seen the review, they did so shortly afterwards. It was apparently sent by John Edwards, for *c*. 20 March W told Edwards that 'Mr Montgomery's praise was highly grateful to me - pray tell him so when you write' (*Supp*. 157). The *terminus ad quem* for W's reading of the review must be 16 March, when DW summarized its contents for Catherine Clarkson (*MY* ii 214).

As Farington recorded in his diary, W discussed the review on 21 May, at dinner with him and the Beaumonts:

> In the course of Conversation *Poetry* was a Topick. Sir George mentioned the high encomiums for Wordsworth's '*Excursion*' in the *Ecclectic* Review. Wordsworth had seen it, and could not but be pleased with the sentiments expressed in it. The *Edinburgh Review* He never reads. He does not wish to have the opinions and *ribaldry* of *Jeffries*, the author of it, floating in His memory, for however much He may despise such matter He would not have it buz in His thoughts, when occupied on any subject when Poetry engages His mind. He added that He does not read the [blank] Review.[1] (his italics)

Edwards presumably sent a copy of Montgomery's review to W between 27 Feb. and 16 March. W had met Montgomery in London in 1812 (*Supp.* 74).

(iii) *The World Before the Flood: A Poem in Ten Cantos* (1813)
Suggested date of reading: c. March 1815
References: *MY* ii 216
Aware that Southey had reviewed *The World Before the Flood* for the *Quarterly* 11 (April 1814) 78-87, W asked him to send his copy to Rydal Mount in March 1815 (*MY* ii 216). This was probably the consequence partly of Montgomery's encomium upon *The Excursion* in the *Eclectic* (see preceding note). W's admiration of Montgomery continued in subsequent years (*LY* iii 326-7).

288. *Monthly Review*
(i) 33 (Oct. 1800) 127-31
Suggested date of reading: c. 12 Dec. 1800
References: Ketcham 79
On 12 Dec. 1800 JW told MH that 'Colridges Walestein is spoken very lightly of in the month[l]y review' (Ketcham 79). I presume that W would soon after have seen the review of *Wallenstein* in the *Monthly*, if he had not already done so.

(ii) (March 1802)
Suggested date of reading: 6, 8 May 1802
References: *Grasmere Journals* 97
'When we came in we found a Magazine & Review & a letter from Coleridge with verses to Hartley & Sara H. We read the Review &c.' (DW's journal, 6 May 1802). Pamela Woof identifies this as a reference to the *Monthly Review* for March 1802, offering a useful account of its contents (*Grasmere Journals* 228). On 8 May DW read 'a poem upon Cowley's wish to retire to the Plantations' in the *Monthly*.

---

[1] *Diary*, ed. Kathryn Cave (vol. 13, New Haven and London), pp. 4625-6.

(iii) 38 (June 1802) 209, review of *Lyrical Ballads* (1800)
Suggested date of reading: c. July 1802
References: Reed ii 184
A review of *Lyrical Ballads* (1800) appeared in the *Monthly* for June 1802. JW had expected to see it in this publication over a year before (Ketcham 122). It was reprinted in the *Literary and Masonic Magazine* 1 (Sept. 1802) 462 (Reed ii 195n69).

(iv) 46 (Jan. 1805)
Suggested date of reading: mid-Feb. 1805 onwards
References: EY 548, 577
Writing to Beaumont on 23 Feb. 1805, W refers to 'your excellent Letter about the young Roscius' - a biography of William Betty, the newly famous London actor in the *Monthly Review* for Jan. 1805 (*EY* 548). And in a letter to Lady Beaumont of 11 April 1805, DW says that she had read a letter by Mrs Klopstock which appeared in the same issue (see note 235).

289. Moore, Edward, *The Gamester* (1753)
Suggested date of reading: by Sept. 1800
References: *Prose Works* i 183
W mentions Moore's prose drama of family life in the Preface to *Lyrical Ballads* (1800). It was a popular repertory piece and he may have seen it performed in London in earlier years.

290. Moore, Sir John, letters, *The Courier*, 24 March 1809
Suggested date of reading: between 24 and 29 March 1809
References: *MY* i 306-7
'I have only seen such of those Letters as appeared in the Courier of Friday last (March 24) they are in number four, and at the end it is said they are to be continued', W wrote to De Quincey on 29 March 1809. The letters justified W's firm opinions about Moore; see *MY* i 306-7.

291. More, Hannah, *Coelebs in Search of a Wife* [2 vols., 1808]
Suggested date of reading: perhaps by 27 Aug. 1813
References: SHL 63
'Cælebs looked mighty brisk and somewhat younger than when I last saw him', SH told John Monkhouse on 27 Aug. 1813, describing a visit to Allan Bank by Daniel Stuart and his new wife. This allusion to Hannah More's popular novel suggests that W knew something of it by that date. He would almost certainly have heard about the notice of *Coelebs* in the *Edinburgh Review* 14 (April 1809) 145-51, which DW saw in July 1809 (*MY* i 365). And at some time between July and Sept. 1809, C copied a quotation from *Coelebs* into his notebook: this is the strongest evidence for a copy of *Coelebs* having been at Allan Bank

(*Notebooks* iii 3541). The copy from which C was working was probably the seventh or eighth edn.

By 1813 W would have heard a good deal about More's book. De Quincey told him on 5 April 1809 that 'Everybody in London is readg. Miss H. More's "*Coelebs in search of a Wife*" - She has got 1000 guineas for it!!!!!!!' (Jordan 141) - though this is the kind of news that would have made W want to avoid it. On 25 May 1809 De Quincey reported that it had gone to 'a 7th. or 8th. edition!' (Jordan 183), and on 18 Oct. that 'A few days ago we heard that a 12th. edition had been called for!!' (Jordan 252). He got round to reading it only in late June or early July, when 'I read about 40 pages in the 1st. vol: such trash I really never did read' (Jordan 241). Lamb read it at around this time too, and on 7 June he told C that 'it is one of the very poorest sort of common novels with the drawback of dull religion in it' (Marrs iii 14).

There is a chance that a copy of *Coelebs* was retained at Rydal Mount. The Rydal Mount loan book mentions 'H. More 1st Vol.', which Shaver suggests may have been More's *Works* (8 vols., 1801), vol. 1 (Shaver 180). However, the entry might also refer to the first vol. of *Coelebs*. That W knew *Coelebs* is supported somewhat by the fact that he enlisted More's support in the face of Jeffrey's hostile review of *The Excursion* (*MY* ii 213).

292. More, Henry, works
Suggested date of reading: by 17 Sept. 1814
References: *MY* ii 153

In his letter to Robert Anderson of 17 Sept. 1814, W suggests that an enlarged edn of Anderson's *British Poets* should include More's poetry. This indicates that he was aware of his works by 17 Sept. 1814. He may have seen Southey's copy of More's *Philosophical Poems* (Cambridge, 1647) (Southey *SC* 1998). Thomas and Ober discuss More's apparent influence on W (Thomas and Ober 91-2).

293. *Morning Chronicle*
Suggested date of reading: 1800 onwards
References: *EY* 523

The Wordsworths were reading the *Morning Chronicle* during the 1800s. It was the source of their copy of Campbell's *Exile of Erin* (see note 82[i]), and that of the recipe for croup medicine, both entered in the Commonplace Book (DC MS 26, 142r). On 27 Dec. 1804 DW exhorted RW to remember to send them 'the Morning Chronicles - we wish for them very much'.

294. *Morning Post*
(i)
Suggested date of reading: 1797-1803
References: Woof PhD 319-583

W's poetry appeared in the *Morning Post* between 1797 and 1803. He is sure to have seen his own contributions in print, and would have been a regular reader of the paper in any case. By far the most thorough and extensive treatment of W and C's dealings with the *Morning Post* is in Woof PhD 319-583.

(ii)
Suggested date of reading: shortly after 7 Dec. 1799
References: see note

C left the Wordsworths on 18 Nov. 1799 and returned to London via Sockburn. He reached London on 27 Nov. and his first regular piece for the *Morning Post*, an analysis of the new French Constitution proposed by Napoleon, appeared on 7 Dec. Can it be doubted that C sent a copy to the Wordsworths? He certainly sent copies of the *Morning Post* to Poole; on 31 Dec. he wrote: 'I hope you receive the papers regularly. They are regularly sent, as I commonly put them in myself' (Griggs i 556). C continued to do this until at least 22 Feb. 1800, when Poole approved of C's resignation as a writer for the *Morning Post*: 'the regular receipt of the *Morning Post*, and what you have written in it, have given me great delight' (Sandford ii 6).

(iii)
Suggested date of reading: 30 May 1800
References: Grasmere Journals 6

'... luckily I caught Mr Ollifs Lad as he was going for letters, he brought me one from Wm & 12 papers' (DW's journal, 30 May 1800). Pamela Woof points out that C had been at DC, 6 April-4 May, and that the *Morning Post* was still being sent there for him (*Grasmere Journals* 152). On 15 July C asked Daniel Stuart, its owner and editor, to redirect copies to him at Greta Hall in Keswick, adding 'The newspapers come very irregularly indeed' (Griggs i 604).[1] Although DW ceased to note the delivery of newspapers after that date, C seems to have sent them on to DC after he had finished with them.

(iv) 29 Sept. 1800
Suggested date of reading: 3 Oct. 1800
References: Grasmere Journals 23

'Amos Cottle's death in the Morning Post' (DW's journal, 3 Oct. 1800). The *Morning Post* for 29 Sept. 1800 reported, under 'DIED': 'Yesterday morning, at his Chambers in Clifford's Inn, Mr Amos Simon Cottle, late of Magdalen College, Cambridge'. This would have been of interest to W, DW, and C, all of whom had known Amos Cottle through his brother Joseph, publisher of *Lyrical Ballads* (1798); see *WR* 179. W had dined with Amos on 12 June 1798 (*EY* 225n4).

---

[1] This request is repeated in a letter of 28 Sept. (Griggs i 626).

(v)
Suggested date of reading: 4 Oct. 1800
References: Grasmere Journals 24
'Coleridge came in while we were at dinner very wet. - We talked till 12 o clock - he had sate up all the night before writing Essays for the newspaper' (DW's journal, 4 Oct. 1800). As Pamela Woof notes, a number of essays and letters on the subject of Farmers and Monopolists appeared in the *Morning Post* at this period (3 Oct.-14 Oct.; CC *Essays* i 243-56), some by C and some by Thomas Poole (*Grasmere Journals* 171). It is reasonable to suppose that the Wordsworths saw these either in MS or in print.

(vi) 1 Feb. 1802
Suggested date of reading: c. 1 Feb. 1802
References: Grasmere Journals 181
See note 241(iii).

(vii) 4 Oct. 1802
Suggested date of reading: c. 4 Oct. 1802
References: see note
The Wordsworths can be expected to have seen the first published version of C's *Dejection: An Ode*, which appeared in the *Morning Post* for 4 Oct. 1802.

(viii) 9 Oct. 1802
Suggested date of reading: c. 9 Oct. 1802
References: Grasmere Journals 249
The *Morning Post*, 9 Oct. 1802, carried a curious report of W's wedding, reprinted *EY* 615n2. DW regarded it as 'the most ridiculous paragraph that ever was penned' (*Grasmere Journals* 249).

(ix)
Suggested date of reading: between 13 Jan. and Oct. 1803
References: EY 381
Evidently the Wordsworths were regular readers of the *Morning Post*. But they would have sought out copies published between 13 Jan. and Oct. 1803 in particular, which contained a number of W's sonnets (for which see Woof *SIB*): 'Perhaps you may see them in the Morning post', DW wrote to JW on 25 Dec. 1802. It is worth noting W's comment to Thelwall of mid-Jan. 1804: 'I neither read reviews, magazines, nor any periodical publications whatsoever except the Morning [Post]' (*EY* 433).

295. Motte, Thomas, 'Travels to the Diamond Mines of Jumbulpoor in Orissa'
Suggested date of reading: probably by 5 April 1800
References: Reed ii 704; Moorman *N&Q* 401

Reed judges that extracts from Motte were entered into the Wordsworth Commonplace Book (DC MS 26, 19r-23r) by 5 April 1800. He adds: 'These extracts, in the autograph of W and DW, have also been pasted in.' Motte's 'Travels' was not a published volume and must have appeared as an article in a newspaper or periodical read by the Wordsworths before 5 April 1800. Reed reads 'Orissa' as 'India'.

296. 'MS., written about the year 1770'
Suggested date of reading: between Sept. 1811 and Nov. 1812
References: *Prose Works* ii 437
In a note to *Dissolution of the Monasteries* 7-8, one of his *Ecclesiastical Sonnets*, W wrote: 'These two lines are adopted from a MS., written about the year 1770, which accidentally fell into my possession. The close of the preceding Sonnet on monastic voluptuousness is taken from the same source, as is the verse, "Where Venus sits", etc., and the line, "Once ye were holy, ye are holy still", in a subsequent Sonnet' (*PW* iii 565-6). W quoted at some length from this MS in his *Unpublished Tour*, composed between Sept. 1811 and Nov. 1812. Like Owen and Smyser, I have managed to discover nothing about either the MS or its author.

297. Murphy, Arthur, *The Grecian Daughter* [1772]
Suggested date of reading: 2 May 1812
References: *Supp.* 56 and n6
On Saturday 2 May 1812, then in London, W told MW that he and Rogers 'are now going to the tragedy' (*Supp.* 56). Hill suggests that this was Murphy's *The Grecian Daughter*, then playing at Covent Garden on a double-bill with 'a grand new melo-dramatic Spectacle, called The SECRET MINE' (*Morning Chronicle*, 2 May 1812).

298. Murray, Lindley, *Introduction to the English Reader* (York, 1801)
Suggested date of reading: 1801
References: Cornell *Lyrical Ballads* 393
In the Fenwick Note to *The Pet-lamb*, W recalled: 'Within a few months after the publication of this poem, I was much surprised and more hurt to find it in a child's School-book which, having been compiled by Lindley Murray, had come into use at Grasmere School where Barbara [Lewthwaite] was a pupil' (Cornell *Lyrical Ballads* 393). W refers to Murray's *Introduction to the English Reader* (York, 1801), an anthology of prose and poetry for children; *The Pet-lamb* appears at pp. 157-60. He had cause to be 'hurt': Murray's text follows that in *Lyrical Ballads* (1800), but omits lines 9-12, 45-9, and, most importantly, 61-8. W must have seen it some time in 1801, shortly after publication.

299. N., S., *Rawleigh Redivivus, or the life and death of Anthony Earl of Shaftesbury By Philanax Misopappas* (1683)
Suggested date of reading: by 18 Jan. 1808

References: *MY* i 191; Shaver 183

Advising Scott on his annotations to his edn of Dryden on 18 Jan. 1808, W remarked: 'I have a life of Shaftsbury entitled I believe Rawleigh Redivivus, should you like to see it?' He had presumably acquired this since his letter to Scott of 7 Nov. 1805, where he suggests that Scott's connection with the Buccleugh family might enable him to learn something about Shaftesbury (Achitophel in Dryden's poem) (*EY* 641-2). *Rawleigh Redivivus* was published anonymously, but the author's dedicatory epistle is signed 'N.S.' W's copy was later housed at Rydal Mount.

300. *New Annual Register*

Suggested date of reading: *c.* 1810

References: see note

The Charles Lamb Society Archive, now at the Guildhall Library, Aldermanbury, London, contains the title-page of the *New Annual Register* for 1810, bearing W's ownership signature. The signature looks roughly contemporary with the volume's date of publication, and one can only assume that it was acquired by W *c.* 1810. The remainder of the volume was not donated to the Charles Lamb Society and may not be extant.[1]

301. newspapers

(i)

Suggested date of reading: 13 Feb. 1802

References: *Grasmere Journals* 68

'Wm took out his old newspapers, & the new ones came in soon after' (DW's journal, 13 Feb. 1802). It is likely that the newspapers in question included back numbers of the *Morning Post*, in which his and Coleridge's poems had been appearing intermittently over the preceding two years; see Woof *SIB*.

(ii)

Suggested date of reading: 28 Feb. 1802

References: *Grasmere Journals* 73

'We got papers in the morning' (DW's journal, 28 Feb. 1802).

(iii)

Suggested date of reading: 3 June 1805

References: *EY* 593

On 3 June 1805 W told Beaumont that 'I have just been reading two newspapers' (*EY* 593).

---

[1] See Deborah K. Hedgecock, *A Handlist to the Charles Lamb Society Collection at Guildhall Library* (supplement to *CLB* NS 89 [1995]), p. 18.

(iv)
Suggested date of reading: 27 Jan. 1806
References: MY i 4
On 27 Jan. 1806 DW told Catherine Clarkson that 'Mary has been reading to us (I stopped writing to hear it) the account of the death of Mr. Pitt' (*MY* i 4). The 'account' must have appeared in a newspaper. Pitt died on 23 Jan.

(v)
Suggested date of reading: early March 1806
References: MY i 40
In June 1806 W wrote to Scott to 'congratulate you on your appointment, in this I sincerely rejoiced; I had heard of it before from Southey and in the Newspapers, but it was pleasant to know it from yourself' (*MY* i 40). Scott's appointment as Clerk of Session had been announced on 8 March; evidently W had read of it in a paper at around that time.

(vi)
Suggested date of reading: 1810
References: MY i 443
W was at this time an avid reader of the *Courier* but there may have been other newspapers that he sought out. On 6 Nov. 1810 DW told Robinson that 'My Brother goes to seek the newspapers whenever it is possible to get a sight of one, and he is almost out of patience that the tidings are delayed so long' (*MY* i 443).

(vii)
Suggested date of reading: summer 1813
References: MY ii 122
On 4 Oct. 1813 DW told Catherine Clarkson that over the summer she had time for 'snatches at the Newspaper' (*MY* ii 122). W's continuing interest in current affairs ensured the regular arrival of a newspaper at Rydal Mount.

(viii)
Suggested date of reading: March 1815
References: MY ii 216, 219
W's specific opinions on Wilberforce's speech, Napoleon and the Corn Laws at this period indicate that he was following political events closely in the newspapers - probably the *Courier*.

302. Newton, John, ***An Authentic Narrative of Some Remarkable and Interesting Particulars in the Life of [the Revd. J. Newton] Communicated in a Series of Letters to the Revd. T. Haweis* [1764]**
Suggested date of reading: 1804
References: Cornell *13-Book Prelude* 181

The subject of *Thirteen-Book Prelude* vi 160-74 is John Newton; the passage from his *Authentic Narrative* on which W based his lines was copied into DC MS 16 in 1798-9 (see *WR* 107; Cornell *Lyrical Ballads* 725-6). In 1804, when he wrote about Newton in *Prelude* Book VI, he would therefore have had his source close at hand; it is possible, too, that there was a copy of Newton's *Authentic Narrative* nearby, and for that reason I have entered it here. Jacobus (1989) 80n23 speculates that W owned a copy of the *Narrative* and that it was acquired on his behalf by James Tobin; none is recorded by Shaver.

303. Nicolson, Joseph, and Richard Burn
(i) *The History and Antiquities of the Counties of Westmorland and Cumberland* (**1777**)
Suggested date of reading: between 30 Oct. 1806 and early April 1807
References: Cornell *Poems 1800-7* 425
W cites Nicolson and Burn as his source for the note to *Song, at the Feast of Brougham Castle*, composed between 30 Oct. 1806 and early April 1807. The copy known to have belonged to him, now at the Wordsworth Library, was in his possession by the time he moved into DC (see *WR* 108). C was evidently reading it at Allan Bank between Sept. 1808 and March 1810 (CC *Marginalia* ii 980).

(ii) *The History and Antiquities of the Counties of Westmorland and Cumberland* (**1777**)
Suggested date of reading: by 22 Feb. 1810
References: *Prose Works* ii 110, 430
One of the epitaphs in the second of W's *Essays Upon Epitaphs* is quoted from Nicolson and Burn. As he owned his own copy of this volume he would have had no trouble referring to it. Nicolson and Burn was also an important source for W's *Select Views*, composed 1810 (*Prose Works* ii 404, 406). As Owen and Smyser note, W 'sometimes skilfully summarizes and sometimes indirectly copies' from the *History* (*Prose Works* ii 430).

304. Norris, John, works
Suggested date of reading: by 17 Sept. 1814
References: *MY* ii 154
In his letter to Robert Anderson of 17 Sept. 1814, W suggests that an enlarged edn of Anderson's *British Poets* should include 'Norris of Bemerton'. He seems never to have acquired his own copy of Norris' poems, but was evidently well acquainted with them. In the *Essay, Supplementary to the Preface*, he observed that the poems went through nine edns (*Prose Works* iii 71).

305. Opie, Amelia, *Adeline Mowbray; or, Mother and Daughter* [**3 vols., 1804**]
Suggested date of reading: by 23 April 1812
References: *MY* ii 7

'Adeline Mowbray made us quite sick before we got to the end of it', DW told W on 23 April 1812. As no copy of this book appears to have been retained at Rydal Mount, it may have been borrowed - though there is a chance that it was known to W. W seems to have met Opie between 6 May and 19 June 1815 (Reed ii 600).

306. Otway, Thomas, *Venice Preserved* [1682]

Suggested date of reading: probably by 4 Aug. 1808; certainly by 7 Aug. 1810
References: *MY* i 265

W might have seen *Venice Preserved* performed as early as the 1790s, when he was a regular playgoer in London, or discussed it with Lamb during the early 1800s, at a time when Lamb was interested in it (see Marrs ii 3, 8); but his earliest reference to Otway, in his letter to Scott of 4 Aug. 1808, indicates only that he knew of his work.

On either 6 or 7 Aug. 1810, he attended a performance of *Venice Preserved* with Beaumont; on 13 Nov., Beaumont wrote to W recalling the occasion:

> I again & again make myself glad with the favourable character we received from the old farmer at the Leasowes of poor Shenstone, & again sympathise with the sorrows of the starved actors at Birmingham when the empty walls of their extensive pit & boxes echoed back the dispairing routs of the poor forsaken Belvidera in the tone of the sad tragedy of Venice preserved - still more sadly performed.[1]

See also Reed ii 457 and 458n24.

307. Ovidius Naso, Publius

(i) *Ovid's Metamorphoses, in fifteen books, with the arguments and notes of John Minellius*, ed. **Nathan Bailey (7th edn, 1787)**
Suggested date of reading: see note
References: see note

This volume, now at the Wordsworth Library, bears a fairly late ownership inscription by W, though the numerous scrawls on its flyleaves would indicate that it was used by the young Coleridges, Wordsworths and Southeys during the DC and Allan Bank years. It was probably in W's library by 1808.

(ii) *Metamorphoses* **i 758-9**
Suggested date of reading: 26 March 1809
References: *MY* i 301

W quotes these lines in a letter to De Quincey. He may have quoted them from memory, but it is possible that he was referring to a printed text.

---

[1] Wordsworth Library WLL/Beaumont, G. H./33.

(iii) *Electa ex Ovidio, et Tibullo, in usum Regiae Scholae Etonensis* **(1787)**
Suggested date of reading: Aug. 1813
References: Patton 260
W's copy is now at Amherst College. It bears the title-page inscription: 'William Wordsworth, purchased at Whitehaven, August 1813'. W and MW were in Whitehaven 31 July-3 Aug. 1813, where they probably stayed with Robert Blakeney (Reed ii 535). Patton suggests that this volume may have been used by W in connection with *Laodamìa*, composed between mid-Oct. and 27-29 Oct. 1814 (Cornell *Poems 1807-20* 142-52).

(iv) *The XV Books of P. Ovidius Naso, entituled Metamorphosis*, tr. **Arthur Golding [1584]**
Suggested date of reading: by 17 Sept. 1814
References: *MY* ii 154
In his letter to Robert Anderson of 17 Sept. 1814, W suggests that an enlarged edn of Anderson's *British Poets* should include 'Goulding's Ovid'. He had known Ovid since his schooldays, and had perhaps by 1814 acquired the copy of Golding (1593) listed Shaver 192. Southey possessed a copy of the rare 1603 black letter edn (Southey *SC* 2126).

308. Palmer, Mrs, 'O hours of peace and comfort, whither fled?'
Suggested date of reading: Dec. 1808
References: see note
On 12 Dec. 1808, Lady Beaumont wrote to W:

> I send you some lines written by Mrs Palmer eldest daughter to Mr Bowles left a widow at an early age with 8 children, in a state of great affluence but so anxious to perform all her duties as to be often overwhelmed with cares, the sentiments are expressive of the purity of her own mind and I think will give you pleasure.[1]

So far as I can discover, Mrs Palmer did not publish her poem. It is lengthy, but the opening lines give some idea of its content:

> O hours of peace and comfort, whither fled?
> The charm is broken, your glad course is run,
> And now ye seem unto my backward gaze
> Like sunbeams darting thro' a sky
> Lovely yet transient, scarce beheld and gone!
> Fain would I call ye back, fain live anew
> This golden time, in which, as in a dream,
> All gracious forms of Nature and of Arts
> And sweet communion twixt friend and friend
> Have sooth'd my spirit, and such peace restor'd

---

[1] Wordsworth Library/Beaumont, G. H./29.

> I had almost forgot the taste of woe.
> Fled is the vision! yet its traces sweet
> By mem'ry nurs'd shall cheer my lonely path
> Lighten each anxious moment, and diffuse
> A mellow lustre over life's decay.

Lady Beaumont probably acquired the manuscript through Bowles, with whom she was acquainted. W was seeing Bowles on his visits to London by 1812 (see, e.g., *Supp.* 65), and may have been introduced to him by the Beaumonts.

309. Park, Mungo, *Travels in the Interior Districts of Africa* [1798]
Suggested date of reading: by late Feb. 1804
References: OET *Prel.* 626; Norton *Prel.* 496
W draws on Park's *Travels* in drafts towards the Five-Book *Prelude* made in MS W, late Feb. or early March 1804,[1] as is consistent with his response to reports of Park's 'disastrous end' in Aug. and Nov. 1806, which indicates some awareness of his career (*MY* i 73, 97). He did not, apparently, try to obtain his own copy of the *Travels* until Jan. 1807, when it had gone out of print (*MY* i 133). There was an 1816 edn of the *Travels* at Rydal Mount (Shaver 194).

310. Parnell, Thomas, *The Hermit*
Suggested date of reading: by May 1810
References: Lienemann 59
So far as I can discover, the earliest Wordsworthian echo of a Parnell poem is that first noted by C. Lawrence Ford:[2] *Excursion* ii 31-2 reads: 'Each with the other pleased, we now pursued / Our journey . . .' This echoes Parnell's *The Hermit* 39-40:

> 'Till each with other pleas'd, and loth to part,
> While in their Age they differ, joyn in Heart . . .

According to Reed, the relevant lines from *The Excursion* were 'probably written between c Dec 1809 and c late May 1810' (Reed ii 23), thus providing a terminal date for W's reading of *The Hermit*. As it appeared in Knox's *Elegant Extracts*, I have little doubt that it was known to W from childhood. Parnell's poetical works were included in Anderson, *British Poets* vol. 7, which was available to W from 1800 onwards.

The Wordsworth Collection at Simon Fraser University contains a copy of Parnell's *Poems on Several Occasions* (1737). The title-page carries a printed ownership inscription, 'J Wordsworth'. Whether or not this volume ever belonged to W is not clear. It does not appear in Shaver.

---

[1] The relevant passage is reproduced at OET *Prel.* 626. My dating of the MS W drafts follows that given by Jonathan Wordsworth, Norton *Prel.* 496. For critical discussion of the passage, see Jacobus (1989) 276-86.
[2] 'Wordsworthiana', *N&Q* 9th Ser. 4 (1899) 321-3, 342-3.

311. Pasley, Sir Charles William, *Essay on the Military Policy and Institutions of the British Empire* (1810)
Suggested date of reading: between 20 and 28 March 1811
References: *MY* i 473

W borrowed a copy of Pasley's *Essay c.* 20 March 1811, and had read it by 28 March, when he wrote its author a lengthy letter of appreciation (*MY* i 473-82). He tells Pasley: 'I had expected it [the book] with great impatience, and desired a Friend to send it down to me immediately on its appearance, which he neglected to do. On this account, I did not see it till a few days ago' (*MY* i 474). Who was the 'Friend'? A clue may be found in a letter from De Quincey to Southey of 17 April 1811: 'Capt. Pasley's book I shall not be able to bring with me,[1] Wordsworth being now at Penrith' (Musgrove 4). Musgrove surmises that this copy was that read by W, and that it had been borrowed from Southey.[2] That would explain W's hope that his friend might 'send it down to me' - a phrasing consistent with its being sent to Grasmere from Keswick.

De Quincey was acquainted with Pasley by 7 July 1809, when he lent him a copy of the second number of *The Friend*, and it was to him that W turned when he sought Pasley's address in 1812 (Jordan 242, 262). De Quincey knew Pasley through C, who had known him since at least 13 Feb. 1805, when they toured the fortifications on the far side of Malta harbour together (*Notebooks* ii 2449). C respected Pasley for his military expertise and remained in touch with him in succeeding years, breakfasting together at Godwin's on 2 May 1807, and corresponding in 1809. W would have heard about Pasley's book through C, who would have been aware of its composition long before publication. There does seem to be some chance that C was the 'Friend' charged with the task of sending a copy to Grasmere when he returned to London in Oct. 1810. C did not do so, however, because the falling-out with W intervened, and interrupted relations between them; W was thus compelled to borrow a copy from some other source - Southey. Pasley gave C a copy of the *Essay* on 10 May 1811 (Griggs iii 330; Coffman P26). In later years, a copy was retained at Rydal Mount (Shaver 196). See also Cornell *Poems 1807-20* 513.

W's admiration for Pasley may have something to do with the fact he regarded soldiery as 'that Profession to which I was most inclined and for which I was perhaps best qualified' (*MY* ii 2 and n2).

312. Pennant, Thomas, *A Tour in Scotland, 1769* [Chester, 1771, 1772]
Suggested date of reading: by 5 April 1800

---

[1] De Quincey went to Keswick on 19 April and returned 26 April.

[2] Southey had certainly read Pasley's volume by 11 Nov. 1810, when he described it to Wynn as 'a very able narrative' (Curry i 543); he was to review it for the *Quarterly*, but his article was rewritten by Croker and disowned by Southey after publication. Southey reprinted his version of it in *Essays Moral and Political* (1832). He was in Grasmere shortly before Christmas 1810 (Reed ii 467; Curry i 547), and might then have lent his copy to W.

References: Reed ii 704; Moorman *N&Q* 401; Woof PhD 240; Cornell *Lyrical Ballads* 382-3 Reed judges that the extracts from Pennant were entered in the Wordsworth Commonplace Book (DC MS 26, 6r-7r) by 5 April 1800:[1] the first tells the story of Helen of Kirkconnell, on which W based *Ellen Irwin*, composed between 6 Oct. 1798 and 23 Feb. 1799. There is a slight complication, in that the same passage from Pennant is quoted by Ritson in a note to 'Where Helen Lies' in his *Scotish Song* (2 vols., 1794), i 145-6 (see Moorman i 429). Woof PhD 240 suggests that, even if W encountered the passage first in Ritson, the copy was made from Pennant: 'The strange factor is the apparent coincidence of Wordsworth's choosing to copy Pennant at the passage that Ritson had quoted; it does seem possible that he remembered the Ritson passage when he read through Pennant. All the other Pennant quotations come from the pages immediately following this source passage' (Woof PhD 240). Whenever he saw the volume, W would have enjoyed the translations from Gaelic of a number of epitaphs, pp. 261-6.

C was apparently consulting Pennant in the mid-1790s (*Notebooks* i 294n). It is possible that C and W were acquainted with the copy of this work at the Bristol Library Society in 1798 (*BLS* 75).

313. Pennington, Montagu, *Memoirs of the Life of Mrs Elizabeth Carter, with a new edition of her Poems* (2 vols., 1807)

Suggested date of reading: 1808
References: *MY* i 189-90

On 3 Jan. 1808 DW wrote to Lady Beaumont: 'I should be very glad of an opportunity of reading Mrs. Carter's life, perhaps it may be sent to Southey to review, and we may see it through him' (*MY* i 189-90). It is not clear whether DW saw Pennington's *Memoirs*, but the Beaumonts frequently lent books to the Wordsworths, and it is possible that they sent this one to Grasmere shortly after DW made her request. Lady Beaumont had been a friend of Mrs Carter (*MY* i 17).

314. Percy, Thomas
(i) *Reliques of Ancient English Poetry* (3 vols., 4th edn, 1794)

Suggested date of reading: 11 Feb. 1806
References: *MY* i 7; Shaver 198

W's quotation from *The More Modern Ballad of Chevy Chase*, as published by Percy, in a letter to Beaumont of 11 Feb. 1806, suggests a reading - though it may be that W knew the

---

[1] I have followed Reed's dating. It is worth noting, however, that Woof PhD 241 finds affinities between *Ellen Irwin* and *The Seven Sisters*, composed 17 Aug. 1800. This might provide some support for the later dating of *Ellen Irwin*, 'possibly any time between October 6, 1798, and July 29, 1800' (Cornell *Lyrical Ballads* 159). If indeed *Ellen Irwin* was composed in July 1800 the Commonplace Book entry from Pennant may also date from that time - and, consequently, have preceded composition of the poem.

poem well enough to quote from it without consulting the text. He had purchased a copy of Percy in Hamburg in 1798 (*WR* 111).

Woof PhD 303 comments:

> With Coleridge it seems that his absorption with Percy's collection tended to fall off after 1798, but with Wordsworth the opposite seems true. Wordsworth seems to have been only generally acquainted with Percy in 1798, but after that his knowledge seems to have increased. . . . In Wordsworth's library in 1827 there were two copies of the *Reliques* and one of them is marked as belonging to Coleridge; Coleridge's copy was one of the many books he left behind at Grasmere in 1810.

(ii) ***Reliques of Ancient English Poetry*** **(3 vols., 4th edn, 1794)**
Suggested date of reading: summer-autumn 1807; by 18 Oct. 1807
References: see note
As W wrote in his notes: 'The Poem of the White Doe of Rylstone is founded on a local tradition, and on the Ballad in Percy's Collection, entitled "The Rising of the North"' (Cornell *White Doe* 150). The *White Doe* was conceived during the summer and autumn of 1807, and its 'plan' determined by 18 Oct. (*MY* i 168). Comparetti 114-15 discusses the influence of some of the ballads in Percy on the *White Doe*.

(iii) ***The Hermit of Warkworth. A Northumberland Ballad. In Three Fits or Cantos*** **[1771]**
Suggested date of reading: by Jan. 1815
References: *Prose Works* iii 75-6, 97-8
W's remarks in his *Essay, Supplementary to the Preface* indicate that he had read Percy's poem by 1815. As it appears in *The Muse's Pocket Companion*, W may have known it from his Hawkshead years (see note 392).

315. Petrarca, Francesco
(i) poems
Suggested date of reading: 9 Dec. 1803
References: *EY* 425-6
Fulminating about Peter Bayley to C on 9 Dec. 1803, W discussed the phrase 'living Sun' as used by Petrarch. It is clear from his comments that he was consulting an Italian edn as he wrote; he even quotes seven lines from Canzone 18A.

(ii) ***De Vita Solitaria***
Suggested date of reading: by early 1809
References: *Prose Works* i 406
W quotes *De Vita Solitaria* in his *Convention of Cintra*. It is likely that he was directed to this work by C, who was reading it on arrival at Allan Bank in Sept. 1808, and who quoted from it in the first number of *The Friend*, 1 June 1809 (CC *Friend* ii 5). They had at their disposal William Sotheby's 'Folio Edition of all Petrarch's Works' (Griggs iii 431), *Opera*

quae extant omnia (4 vols., Basle, 1581), left by C at Keswick prior to his departure for Malta, and present at Allan Bank during work on the *Friend* (for more on this copy see *Notebooks* iii 3360n). A copy of Petrarch's *Dichiarationi* which also contained some of the poems (Venice, 1564) was retained at Rydal Mount (Shaver 200).

316. Philips, Ambrose, *A Collection of Old Ballads* (3 vols., 1723-5)
Suggested date of reading: between 10 July 1807 and *c.* 5 June 1808
References: Reed ii 708; Woof PhD 258-60
DW made copies of extracts or complete texts of six ballads from Philips' *Collection* in the Wordsworth Commonplace Book (DC MS 26, 48v-62r) some time between 10 July 1807 and *c.* 5 June 1808. The ballads were: *Eighth Henry ruling in this land*; *A Princely Song of the Six Queens that were Married to Henry the 8th*; *Fitte of the Ballad of Lady Jane Grey and Lord Guilford Dudley*; *The Lady Arabella and Lord Seymour*; *The Suffolk Miracle*; and *The Lamentable Complaint of Queen Mary for the Unkind Departure of King Philip*. A full and thorough inventory is provided by Woof PhD 258-9, who comments: 'The ballad taste revealed here need not be that of Wordsworth. Dorothy has long been used to reading ballads for her own delight. Even so the ballads extracted do generally form a group, and would be described by the term, "Historical Ballad"; further they would seem to be a part of Wordsworth's growing interest in the historical and traditional. "The White Doe of Rylstone", "The Force of Prayer", "Brougham Castle", "The Horn of Egremont Castle" are poems that bear witness to this awakening interest' (Woof PhD 259-60).

317. Pindar, *Carmina, cum lectionis varietate et adnotationibus,*
***iterum curavit C. G. Heyne* (4 vols., Göttingen, 1798-9)**
Suggested date of reading: 1810 onwards
References: Shaver 201; Coffman P68
Neither Shaver nor Coffman say so, but vol. 3 of W's copy is now at the Lilly Library, University of Indiana. The set belonged originally to C, and was probably purchased in Göttingen in 1799. C referred to it in notebook entries dating from March 1810, probably made at Allan Bank (*Notebooks* iii 3721-2). He left it there when he left for London just before the falling-out with W later that year. All four volumes passed into Rydal Mount, where W entered the flyleaf inscription, 'Wm Wordsworth Rydal Mount'; it remained there until the auction of 1859. The present whereabouts of vols. 1, 2, and 4 are unknown.

C's study of Pindar in Oct. 1806, apparently begun in London and completed in Bury St Edmunds, was dependent on the copy of Schmied's edn (Wittenberg, 1616) now in the Wisbech Museum and Literary Institute (see *Notebooks* ii 2881-2, 2887 and n). This suggests that he left his copy of the *Carmina* with the Wordsworths when he departed for Malta in 1804.

318. Piranesi, Giambattista, 'Folios'
Suggested date of reading: April or May 1808 onwards
References: CC *Marginalia* ii 1118
C sent 'the Piranesi Folios for William', a New Testament, Chapman's *Homer*, and Huber's *History of Bees* to SH in Penrith, probably, Whalley suggests, in late March or early April 1808. W would have received the Piranesi folios shortly after he returned to Grasmere from London on 6 April. The folios remain unidentified and are not mentioned elsewhere. Could it be that they are the copies of the *Antiquities of Rome* which De Quincey later remembered looking over with C in the *Confessions*?[1]

319. Plato, *The Cratylus, Phædo, Parmenides and Timæus of Plato*, tr. Thomas Taylor (1793)
Suggested date of reading: probably by 14 Dec. 1809; by 1817
References: Shaver 202
Taylor's translation of *The Cratylus, Phædo, Parmenides and Timæus of Plato* (1793) was retained at Rydal Mount, and is now at the Wordsworth Library. Although Shaver lists it among W's books, it belonged in fact to C, and contains his marginalia. It must have passed into the library at Allan Bank by the time C departed for London in 1810. It carries an ownership inscription by W, almost certainly dating from the Rydal Mount years, on its titlepage. When in Nov. 1829 DW wrote to C, enclosing a list of his books at Rydal Mount which would shortly be returned to him, she asked whether her brother might retain 'Taylor's Cratylus' (*Supp*. 199). It did indeed remain at Rydal Mount until the sale of 1859 (Wordsworth *SC* 408).

When might the book have come into C's possession? Whalley observes: 'In view of what Lamb tells us of Coleridge's knowledge of the neoplatonists at Christ's Hospital, it is probable that as a Grecian he read some Plato before going to Cambridge' (Whalley PhD ii 428). He goes on to point out that C was reading Plato during the mid-1790s.[2] We do not know whether C owned Taylor's translation as early as 1797-8, the earliest W might have had access to his library, but it is possible. The earliest clue as to their shared interest in Plato is C's jotting from *Phaedrus* at *Notebooks* i 1002, entered probably 1-9 Nov. 1801, a period spent partly at DC and Greta Hall with the Wordsworths.[3] At this period too (the winter of 1801), C read *Parmenides* and *Timaeus* 'with great care' (Griggs ii 866) - suggesting that he was using Taylor's translation. He may have been reading it alongside the copy of Kenelm Digby's *Two Treatises* (1645) which he borrowed from Carlisle Cathedral Library, and which

---

[1] De Quincey met C in 1807, and C must have introduced him to Piranesi's work at around this time. See Thomas De Quincey, *Confessions of an English Opium-Eater and Other Writings*, ed. Grevel Lindop (Oxford, 1985), p. 70.
[2] For more on this and on C's reading of Plato, see Whalley PhD ii 428-30.
[3] C visited DC on 6 Nov. and returned to Greta Hall with them on 9 Nov. The Wordsworths left for DC on 10 Nov. The volume is referred to also at *Notebooks* iii 3901.

is the source for the notebook entry. Coburn suggests that Digby's work was, 'along with Chapman's *Homer* and Bartram's *Travels*, one of the many books Sara Hutchinson and Coleridge enjoyed together' (*Notebooks* i 1002n). As C almost certainly discussed and 'enjoyed' Chapman's *Homer* and Bartram's *Travels* with W, one would expect Digby to have been shared with W too - perhaps even more so than with SH. Furthermore, a copy of Digby's *Two Treatises* (1665) was at Rydal Mount (Shaver 77); Pittman suggested that W read it at Cambridge, but I find no evidence for that (see *WR* 157). Indeed, the fact that C had to borrow a copy in 1801 would suggest that W had not acquired his copy by that time, or C would almost certainly have borrowed his. As a matter of fact, 1-9 Nov. 1801 must be the earliest date at which W might have acquainted himself with Digby's work (see note 137).

W's earliest reading of Plato is not easy to pin down. Although he did study Greek at school, I doubt whether he ever reached the standard required to read Plato in the original. His earliest explicit reference to Plato occurs in the reply to Mathetes, 14 Dec. 1809 (*Prose Works* ii 11), but it is likely that he knew Plato's writings before that - probably through readings and discussions with C. A note to *I heard (alas, 'twas only in a dream)*, composed perhaps in 1817, directs the reader to 'See the Phedo of Plato, by which this Sonnet was suggested' (see Cornell *Poems 1807-20* 225, 543).[1] Critics have noted the presence of Platonic ideas in poetry composed by W from 1798 onwards.[2]

320. Pliny, *Natural History*
Suggested date of reading: c. Oct. 1814
References: Cornell *Poems 1807-20* 146, 529
Pliny is one of W's acknowledged sources for *Laodamìa*, composed Oct. 1814 (see Cornell *Poems 1807-20* 146, 529; Worthington 76; *FN* 113).

321. Plutarch
(i) *The Lives of the Noble Grecians and Romans*, tr. Thomas North [1579]
Suggested date of reading: by 13 June 1804
References: Norton *Prel.* 332n6; Shaver 202
W's copy of North's *Plutarch* (1676)[3] is now at the Beineke Library, Yale; it bears his ownership inscription on the title-page. When it was acquired is unclear, but a reasonable guess would be some time between 1808 and 1810; it is likely that before 1808 W was reading a borrowed copy, as DW listed Plutarch as *not* owned by W in a list sent to De Quincey on 7 July 1808 (*MY* i 257). He had probably known it since childhood, as there was

---

[1] P. Bagchi, 'A Note on Wordsworth's Sonnet, "I heard (alas! 'twas only in a dream)"', *N&Q* 218 (1973) 44, notes: 'he has combined in the poem the ideas of two widely separated passages of the *Phaedo*, one relating to the swan and the other to the "Hollow"'.

[2] See Potts 366-72; Lane Cooper, 'Wordsworth's Knowledge of Plato', *MLN* 33 (1918) 497-9; and Robert Langbaum, 'The Evolution of Soul in Wordsworth's Poetry', *PMLA* 82 (1967) 265-72, among others.

[3] Shaver erroneously dates the edn '1606'.

a copy at Hawkshead Grammar School in 1788 (Wu *CWAAS* 203). See also Norton *Prel.* 410n6 and Worthington 40-2.

The Norton *Prel.* notes that *Thirteen-Book Prelude* ix 415-26 'are drawn from the *Life of Dion* in North's translation (1579) of Plutarch's *Lives* of eminent Greeks and Romans' (Norton *Prel.* 332n6). Reed dates these lines to between late March and 13 June 1804 (Reed ii 13-14).

(ii) *The Lives of the Noble Grecians and Romans*, **tr. Thomas North [1579]**
Suggested date of reading: April 1806
References: *MY* i 21
In April 1806, during W's absence in London, MW and DW told him that they had read 'one or two of Plutarch's lives since we wrote last' (*MY* i 21). Quite possibly this was the same copy of the *Lives* as that used by W during work on the *Prelude* in 1804 (see preceding note).

(iii) *The Lives of the Noble Grecians and Romans*, **tr. Thomas North (1676)**
Suggested date of reading: probably late 1808
References: *Prose Works* i 383
W's mention of Phocion, Epaminondas and Philopœmon in the *Convention of Cintra* suggests that he had either been rereading Plutarch recently, or was at least recalling the *Lives*. I suspect that he acquired his own copy of the *Lives* at around this time (see note [i], above).

(iv) *The Lives of the Noble Grecians and Romans*, **tr. Thomas North (1676)**
Suggested date of reading: probably between 20 and 27 March 1811
References: Cornell *Poems 1807-20* 513-14
W's source for *On a Celebrated Event in Ancient History* and *Upon the Same Event*, probably composed between 20 and 27 March 1811, was Plutarch's life of Titus Quintius Flaminius (see Cornell *Poems 1807-20* 513-14).

(v) *The Lives of the Noble Grecians and Romans*, **tr. Thomas North (1676)**
Suggested date of reading: by May 1814
References: *PW* v 421
W's reference to the 'Spartan monarch' in a MS draft for *Excursion* Book III was apparently suggested by a reading of Plutarch.

322. *Poetae Latini minores . . . curavit J. C. Wernsdorfius*
(6 vols., Altenburgi et Helmstadii, 1780-99)
Suggested date of reading: 1810 onwards
References: Shaver 347
The Rydal Mount library catalogue entry reads: 'A Pocket vol: of the Minor Latin Poets given by Anthony Harrison to S.T.C. taken by Hartley Coleridge. Ja^y 2^d, 1829'. If indeed the volume here referred to was *Poetae Latini minores*, it was probably presented to C by Harrison (on whom see note 199) at some point before or during 1810. Harrison saw C on

and off during 1809-10, as he was proof-reading *The Friend* in Penrith. The volume must have entered W's possession some time before the falling-out with C of 1810.

323. Pope, Alexander
(i) *Messiah* **[1712]**
Suggested date of reading: by early 1802
References: *Prose Works* i 162
W mentions *Messiah* in his Appendix on Poetic Diction to the Preface to *Lyrical Ballads* (1802).

(ii) *Imitation of the 1st Epistle of the 1st Book of Horace*
Suggested date of reading: by Feb. 1804
References: OET *Prel.* 515; Norton *Prel.* 498
De Selincourt notes that the phrase, 'Doth lock my functions up' at *Thirteen-Book Prelude* i 248 comes from Pope's *Imitation*. This must also be the source of the moonlit horse in MS W, whose functions are 'silently sealed up' (Norton *Prel.* 498, line 70). That draft towards the Five-Book *Prelude* dates from Feb. 1804.

(iii) *Epitaph. On Mrs. Corbet, Who dyed of a Cancer in her Breast*
Suggested date of reading: by 22 Feb. 1810
References: *Prose Works* ii 76, 111
W has little good to say about it, but he quotes this work in the second of his *Essays Upon Epitaphs* (*Prose Works* ii 76-7).

(iv) *Epitaph. On the Honble. Simon Harcourt, Only Son of the Lord Chancellor Harcourt*
Suggested date of reading: by 22 Feb. 1810
References: *Prose Works* ii 88, 116
W quotes from this work in the third of his *Essays Upon Epitaphs* (*Prose Works* ii 88). It was anthologized in Knox's *Elegant Extracts*.

(v) *Moral Essays*
Suggested date of reading: by June 1812
References: *Supp.* 135
On 20 June 1812, W wrote to John Hutchinson:

> You remember the lines of Pope
>> Manners with fortunes, humours turn with climes,
>> Tenets with books and principles with times.-

This quotation from Pope's *Moral Essays* i 166-7 is apparently from memory, and thus supports the contention that W was acquainted with this work well before 1812.

324. Porter, Anna Maria, *The Recluse of Norway* (1814)
Suggested date of reading: by 18 Feb. 1815
References: *MY* ii 203
On 18 Feb. 1815 DW told SH that MW 'is deep in the 2nd volume of the "Recluse of Norway" by Miss Porter' (*MY* ii 203). It is not clear whether W read this book, but DW had some good things to say about it, and she might at least have mentioned it to him.

325. Price, Sir Uvedale, 1st bart.
(i) *Essay on the Picturesque* **[1794]**
Suggested date of reading: by 19 Jan. 1806
References: *MY* i 3
On 19 Jan. 1806, DW told Lady Beaumont that

> My Brother has read Mr Price's Book on the picturesque, but we have not had an opportunity of seeing his Essays on Decorations near the House. Coleridge has the former Book, and I shall desire Mrs C. to send it to me. My Brother thinks that Mr Price has been of great service in correcting the false taste of the Layers out of Parks and Pleasure-grounds. (*MY* i 3)

C had acquired his copy by 21 Nov. 1803, on which date he noted that he had 'paged' it, along with an essay by Christian Garve on mountains which he may also have shown or discussed with W (see *Notebooks* i 1676, 1676n, and 1675n). Although a more precise date for W's reading of Price is hard to come by, I would guess that it did not predate DW's letter to Lady Beaumont by much: perhaps Price inspired W's musings on landscape gardening in the letter to Beaumont of 17 and 24 Oct. 1805 (*EY* 622-9). By June 1806 W was corresponding with Price, and they met in Aug. 1810 (Reed ii 457).

Price played a part of pivotal importance in W's career, as he appears to have been responsible for introducing the Beaumonts to *Lyrical Ballads* in Sept. 1801 (Reed ii 122n).

(ii) *Essay on Decorations near the House* **in MS**
Suggested date of reading: after 19 Jan. 1806
References: *MY* i 3
See preceding note. DW's mention in her letter to Lady Beaumont of Price's *Essay on Decorations near the House* indicates that the Wordsworths were aware of it by 19 Jan. 1806. It would be reasonable to suppose that they read it soon after. As the Beaumonts were friendly with Price, they probably owned a copy, and would have shown it to the Wordsworths in due course. They must have seen it in MS, as it was first published in *Sir Uvedale Price on the Picturesque*, ed. Sir Thomas Dick Lauder, Bart. (1842), pp. 297-327.

(iii) *Essay on the Picturesque* **[1794]**
Suggested date of reading: 1809-10
References: see note

Nabholtz, 'Wordsworth's *Guide to the Lakes* and the Picturesque Tradition', *MP* 61 (1964) 288-97, argues for Price's influence on W's *Select Views*, composed 1809-10.

326. Prior, Matthew, *Charity. A Paraphrase on the Thirteenth Chapter of the First Epistle to the Corinthians*
Suggested date of reading: by early 1802
References: *Prose Works* i 162, 189
W mentions Prior's poem in his Appendix on Poetic Diction to the Preface to *Lyrical Ballads* (1802).

327. Purchas, Samuel, *Purchas His Pilgrimage; or, Relations of the World and the Religions Observed in all Ages* (3rd edn, 1617)
Suggested date of reading: by Jan. 1804
References: *Notebooks* i 1840 and n; Marrs ii 138; Shaver 208
It is not known when W first acquired his copy of this work, the present whereabouts of which is not known. As Coburn explains, C read W's copy of *Purchas* at DC, 11-13 Jan. 1804 (*Notebooks* i 1840 and n). The next mention of it appears in a letter from Lamb to DW of 2 June 1804:

> The least we can do, is to see your commissions fulfilled; accordingly I have booked this 2d June 1804 from the Waggon Inn in Cripplegate the watch & books which I got from your brother Richard, together with Purchas's Pilgrimage and Brown's Religio Medici which I desire your brother's acceptance of, with some pens, of which I observed no great frequency when I tarried at Grasmere. (Marrs ii 138)

So far as I know, no one has yet explained exactly what is going on here (Lamb was writing to DW, who he could depend to understand him, even if his punctuation makes matters less than clear to us). The copy of *Purchas* he mentions is that owned by W by Jan. 1804 and read by C at DC. Evidently C borrowed W's copy when he departed for London on 14 Jan. He reached London on 23 Jan. and before leaving to visit Sir George Beaumont at Dunmow on 7 Feb. dined with Lamb on 2 Feb. Probably on that occasion he gave W's copy of *Purchas* to Lamb with instructions to return it to Grasmere on his behalf, perhaps aware that Lamb would be sending W a large parcel in due course.[1] The parcel would have reached Grasmere in the first week of June; W consulted *Purchas* as he composed *Thirteen-Book Prelude* vii 86-8 not long after (Norton *Prel.* 230n4). The volume which 'I desire your brother's acceptance of' was Browne's (see note 60[i]); possibly among the other contents was included 'a Ms Poem' by Richard Sharp (see *EY* 469).

---

[1] The parcel was expected by the Wordsworths in April 1804, and may have been anticipated even earlier than that (see *EY* 469).

Might W's copy of *Purchas* have been that consulted by C immediately prior to composition of *Kubla Khan*? It is not impossible; they were exchanging books by that time. And there is the precedent of Shelvocke, whose *Voyages* W appears to have read before C, and which provided the central incident for *The Ancient Mariner* (see *WR* 126). Should W's copy of *Purchas* ever turn up, it might contain some clue.

Lyon 60 notes that Purchas contributed a number of details to *The Excursion*.

328. Pye, Henry James, *Some Observations on Gardening*
Suggested date of reading: by 17 Oct. 1805
References: *EY* 623-4
W alludes to Pye's essay in a letter to Beaumont of 17 and 24 Oct. 1805. He would have read it in Pye's *Sketches on Various Subjects; Moral, Literary, and Political* (1796), pp. 118-30.

329. Quarles, Francis, works
Suggested date of reading: by 17 Sept. 1814
References: *MY* ii 153
In his letter to Robert Anderson of 17 Sept. 1814, W suggests that an enlarged edn of Anderson's *British Poets* should include Quarles - presumably his *Emblems*. This was such a well-known work that W must have read it before this date. Southey, whose influence is felt throughout the letter to Anderson, may well have encouraged W's interest; he probably introduced C to Quarles, and on 23 Jan. 1803 he wrote approvingly to William Taylor about the emblem of the soul 'that tries to fly, but is chained by the leg to earth' (Robberds i 445). On 19 Feb. 1834 DW recorded that she was 'Reading Quarles'.[1] His *Divine Poems* (1642) and *Enchiridion* (1658) were at Rydal Mount (Shaver 209). Southey owned a copy of the *Emblems* (Southey *SC* 2311).

330. Quintilianus, Marcus Fabius
(i) *Institutio Oratoria*
Suggested date of reading: c. 14 Jan. 1801
References: *EY* 315
W quotes from Quintilian in his letter to Charles James Fox, 14 Jan. 1801 (*EY* 315). The same quotation is given as a motto on a half-title in vol. 1 of *Lyrical Ballads* (1802 and 1805)[2] (see Cornell *Lyrical Ballads* 377-8). It is likely that C by this time owned a set of Quintilian, and that the quotation and epigraph were provided by him.[3] Even so, W may also have read Quintilian, and it is in that context that critics such as Scott Harshberger have read

---

[1] DC MS 188, as quoted Pamela Woof, 'Dorothy Wordsworth, Writer', *WC* 17 (1986) 95-110, p. 95.

[2] Not on the title-page of *Lyrical Ballads* (1800), as erroneously stated in *WR* 114.

[3] C certainly owned it by 1807 or 1808, when he composed this marginal note in Casaubon's edn of Persius: 'I have the whole works of Cicero, Livy, and Quinctilian, with many others' (Whalley PhD i 495).

Michael; see 'The Rhetoric of Improvisation: *Michael* and Quintilian's *Institutio Oratoria*', *WC* 25 (1994) 37-40; see also Worthington 76-7.

(ii) *Institutio Oratoria*
Suggested date of reading: c. Jan.-April 1802
References: *Prose Works* i 176-7

Quintilian was the source of a notion central to the additions made to the Preface to *Lyrical Ballads* c. Jan.-April 1802; see also Owen (1969) 65. Asked about sources for the Preface, Owen tells me that Quintilian and Reynolds are the only ones 'to which I would swear'. He adds that 'Quintilian might have been a school or Cantab text' (letter to me). Shaver lists two seventeenth-century copies, either or both of which may have been acquired by this date (Shaver 209). According to George Kennedy, the passage from Quintilian which provided W's source expressed the only original idea in the *Institutes*.

Graver reminds me that Quintilian is 'crucial for *The Excursion*', and he has argued that Quintilian had an important influence on W's portrayal of the Wanderer.[1]

331. Racine, Jean, *Oeuvres* (3 vols., Paris, 1801)
Suggested date of reading: Aug. 1802 onwards
References: Reed ii 642; Shaver 210

W purchased this title as part of the *Bibliothèque Portative de Voyageur* (5 vols., Paris, 1801-2) in Calais, Aug. 1802. It is now at the Wordsworth Library. He was reading Racine in the early 1790s (see *WR* 114).

332. Raleigh, Sir Walter, *A Vision upon the Fairy Queen*
Suggested date of reading: by late July 1802
References: Cornell *Poems 1800-7* 411

W acknowledged the influence of Raleigh on *Methought I saw the footsteps of a throne*, probably composed between 21 May and late July 1802. He may have found the poem in *The Works of Sir Walter Ralegh, Kt.*, ed. Thomas Birch (2 vols., 1751), ii 392.

333. Randolph, Thomas, works
Suggested date of reading: by 17 Sept. 1814
References: *MY* ii 154

In his letter to Robert Anderson of 17 Sept. 1814, W suggests that an enlarged edn of Anderson's *British Poets* should include Randolph. He had for many years owned a copy of Randolph's *Poems* (1668); see note AI14, below.

---

[1] 'The Oratorical Pedlar', *Rhetorical Traditions and British Romantic Literature*, ed. Don Bialostosky and Lawrence Needham (Bloomington, 1995), pp. 94-107. Much current discussion of Quintilian's influence on W stems from Dockhorn's important 1944 article, 'Wordsworth und die rhetorische Tradition in England', reprinted helpfully in an abbreviated translation by Bialostosky and Needham, pp. 265-80.

334. Ray, John, *Observations, Topographical, Moral, and Physiological; made in a journey through part of the Low-countries, Germany, Italy, and France; with a catalogue of plants not native to England, found spontaneously growing in those parts, and their virtues* **(1673)**
Suggested date of reading: perhaps by 26 Oct. 1803
References: *Notebooks* i 1616; Shaver 212
In *WR* 159 I expressed my reservations at Pittman's suggestion that W read Ray's volume while an undergraduate at Cambridge; the mere fact that it deals with the flora of Cambridge can hardly be said to prove Pittman's case. In fact, the first suggestion that W had read Ray comes in C's notebook entry recording 'A most unpleasant Dispute with W. & Hazlitt' on 26 Oct. 1803: 'But *thou*, dearest Wordsworth - and what if Ray, Durham, Paley, have carried the observation of the aptitudes of Things too far, too habitually - into Pedantry? . . . O dearest William! Would Ray, or Durham, have spoken of God as you spoke of Nature?' (his italics).

Ray, Derham and Paley seem to have represented to W the kind of intellectual who, as he put it in a 1798 draft towards *The Ruined Cottage*, 'Forever dimly pore on things minute' (Cornell *Ruined Cottage* 373). It is still not clear how extensive W's knowledge of Ray was in 1803, but C's notebook entry does suggest that he might by then have acquired the copy of *Observations* later retained at Rydal Mount. Whalley suggested that C's reading of Ray and Derham was part of 'a tentative scheme for a book on natural history for Hartley's use, like the Greek Grammar he started to write for the children after his return from Malta' (Whalley PhD i 335). W's only mention of Ray comes in *Kendal and Windermere Railway* (1845), where he calls him 'one of the first men of his age' (*Prose Works* iii 341). Coburn suggests that C knew Ray's *Wisdom of God* (1714) (*Notebooks* i 1147n).

335. Reynolds, Sir Joshua
(i) *The Works of Sir Joshua Reynolds*, **ed. Edmond Malone (3 vols., 3rd edn, 1801)**
Suggested date of reading: by Sept. 1800
References: *Prose Works* i 175-6, 186
Asked about sources for the Preface to *Lyrical Ballads*, composed by Sept. 1800, Owen tells me that Quintilian and Reynolds are the only ones 'to which I would swear' (letter to me). The Malone edn is cited by Owen at *Prose Works* i 186, and it is likely that a copy was at W's disposal in 1800, nearly four years before he acquired his own copy. Reynolds had been cited in the 1798 Advertisement (see *WR* 116).

(ii) *The Works of Sir Joshua Reynolds*, **ed. Edmond Malone (3 vols., 3rd edn, 1801)**
Suggested date of reading: 17 July 1804 onwards
References: *EY* 490-1; Shaver 214
On 20 July 1804 W wrote to Sir George Beaumont:

> A few days ago I received from Mr Southey your very acceptable present of Sir Joshua Reynolds works, which with the life I have nearly read through. Several of the

discourses I had read before though never regularly together: they have very much added to the high opinion which I before entertained of Sir Joshua Reynolds.

(*EY* 490-1)

W's first comprehensive reading of Reynolds' works can be dated to four or five days in the middle of July 1804. He had, of course, referred to the *Discourses* in the 1798 Advertisement to *Lyrical Ballads* (see *WR* 116). He continued to read Malone's edn in succeeding weeks, and refers to it in a letter to Beaumont of 31 Aug. (*EY* 499-500). It was later retained at Rydal Mount.

(iii) ***The Works of Sir Joshua Reynolds*, ed. Edmond Malone (3 vols., 3rd edn, 1801)**
Suggested date of reading: between Sept. 1811 and Nov. 1812
References: *Prose Works* ii 457
One of W's sources for *The Sublime and the Beautiful* was Malone's edn of Reynolds.

336. Richardson, Samuel, *The Correspondence of Samuel Richardson, a selection from the original manuscripts***, ed. Anna Laetitia Barbauld (6 vols., 1804)**
Suggested date of reading: shortly before 5 Jan. 1805
References: *EY* 525
On 5 Jan. 1805 DW told Lady Beaumont:

> My Brother chanced to meet with Richardson's letters at a Friend's house, and glancing over them, read those written by Mrs Klopstock, he was exceedingly affected by them and said it was impossible to read them without loving the woman. We have been very desirous to see the Book ever since, and hope to be able to borrow it soon, but any new Book in our neighbourhood passes from house to house, and it is difficult to come at it within any reasonable time. (*EY* 525)

This letter is sometimes taken to indicate some involvement by the Wordsworths with the Grasmere Book Club, though Shaver conjectures that the 'Friend' was Charles Lloyd, as a letter by Southey of 1804 confirms that Lloyd owned a copy of this book (*EY* 525n1). Be this as it may, Richardson's *Correspondence* was widely available. There was a copy at the Kendal Book Club, and another was in the hands of Southey by 27 Nov. 1804, when he told Wynn: 'Richardson's correspondence I should think worse than anything of any celebrity that ever was published, if the life prefixed did not happen to be quite as bad. The few letters of Klopstock's Wife must be excepted from this censure: they are very interesting and very affecting; indeed the notice of her death, coming, as it does, after that sweet letter in which she dwells upon her hopes of happiness from that child whose birth destroyed her, came upon me like an electric shock' (Warter i 289). That DW so closely echoes Southey's approval of Mrs Klopstock's letters makes it likely that either she and/or W discussed them with him, and that they even saw his copy. DW was able to compare these letters by Mrs Klopstock, five years later, with Smith's translations in *Memoirs of Frederick and Margaret Klopstock* (1808) (see *MY* i 316 and n3).

337. Ritson, Joseph
(i) *A Select Collection of English Songs* **(3 vols., 1783)**
Suggested date of reading: c. spring 1808 onwards
References: Shaver 216

W's copy is now at the Wordsworth Library. The flyleaf of each volume contains an inscription in ink: 'To William Wordsworth with the best love of D B Skepper'. D. B. Skepper may be identified as Anna Dorothea Benson, whom C and W knew as Mrs Skepper, the housekeeper of Basil Montagu. She married Montagu, becoming his third wife, in late 1808. It may, at first, seem odd that Montagu's housekeeper should have given books to the likes of W, but both he and C had a particular liking for her, not least because she was a former acquaintance of Burns,[1] and evidently told them about him (she was apparently the source of an anecdote in the *Friend*, CC *Friend* i 293n1). W's particular affection for her in 1808 is indicated by the postscript to his letter to Montagu of 18 March: 'Do not forget to give my best Love to Mrs Skepper' (*Supp*. 10). She had been writing to the Wordsworths since at least July 1806 (*MY* i 63 and n1), and by 1807 was in correspondence with Hartley Coleridge (Warter ii 38; Griggs iii 99). The following year she discussed the then-unpublished *White Doe* with C (Griggs iii 110).[2] Granted that, it is no surprise to learn that she presented books to W. In fact, she gave him no less than three of Ritson's volumes: the *Select Collection*, *Ancient Songs*, and *Pieces of Ancient Popular Poetry* (see following notes). Her presentation inscription indicates that they were given to W prior to her marriage to Montagu. The presence in some of them of C's marginalia, dating from around 1809-10, at Allan Bank, supports a likely presentation date of spring 1808. That year seems to mark the high point of her relations with W and C; in Dec. 1808 she told C: 'Our Children are brought up with the highest reverence for Mr. Wordsworth, and I hope that one day they will be nearer to him' (Moorman ii 191). However, W's opinion of Mrs Montagu appears to have changed after his falling-out with C, in which she was seen as instrumental - DW telling W in April 1812 that she despised her (*MY* ii 6). All the same, W met her in that month (*Love Letters* 112).

W's copy of Ritson's *Select Collection* contains C's marginalia in vol. 1. At about the time it was entered (Dec. 1808-Jan. 1809), C mentioned Ritson alongside 'other Dullards' in a notebook entry (see *Notebooks* iii 3437 and n).

---

[1] For more on this intriguing connection, see *The Letters of Robert Burns*, ed. J. DeLancey Ferguson, rev. G. Ross Roy (2 vols., 1985), ii 439; Burns' letter to Anna Dorothea Benson (as Burns knew her) appears at i 186-7. As it was first published in Currie's edn of 1800, it was probably known to C and W.

[2] For more on Mrs Skepper, see Ralph M. Wardle, 'Basil and Anna Montagu: Touchstones for the Romantics', *Keats-Shelley Journal* 34 (1985) 131-71, esp. pp. 158-71.

(ii) *Ancient Songs, from the time of King Henry the Third to the Revolution* **(1790)**
Suggested date of reading: c. spring 1808 onwards
References: Shaver 216
W's copy is now at the Wordsworth Library. It contains an ownership inscription in ink, not in W's hand, but in that of Mrs Skepper: 'W. Wordsworth'. It was probably given to W at the same time as the copy of Ritson's *Select Collection* (see preceding note) - i.e. c. spring 1808. The volume contains marginalia by C made, apparently, during 1808-9.

(iii) *Pieces of Ancient Popular Poetry; from authentic manuscripts and old printed copies* **(1791)**
Suggested date of reading: c. spring 1808 onwards
References: Shaver 216
W's copy is now at the Wordsworth Library. It contains a presentation inscription in ink, by Mrs Skepper: 'W: Wordsworth from his friend D B Skepper'. It was probably given to W at the same time as the other copies of Ritson from Mrs Skepper - i.e. c. spring 1808.

338. Robert le Diable, *Roberte the Deuyll. A Metrical Romance, from an ancient illuminated manuscript,* **tr. I. Herbert (1798)**
Suggested date of reading: probably by 5 April 1800
References: Reed ii 704; Moorman *N&Q* 400
Reed judges that extracts from this grotesque Elizabethan romance were entered in the Wordsworth Commonplace Book (DC MS 26, 5r-5v) by 5 April 1800. It is intriguing that W saw this rare volume, translated and published by I. Herbert. Which of his friends owned it? It was included in Sotheby's sale catalogue of Wrangham's library, 1843 (Wrangham *SC* 2019), and may have been in Wrangham's possession by 1800. Perhaps W called in on him on one of his customary visits to Gallow Hill (not far from Wrangham's residence in Hunmanby); we know that he attempted to do so in early June 1800 (Reed ii 66).

339. Robertson, Joseph, *A Traveller's Guide through Scotland and its Islands* **(3rd edn, Edinburgh, 1806)**
Suggested date of reading: 17 July 1814 onwards
References: Reed ii 556; Butler *WC* 209
W's copy is now the Wordsworth Library. It contains the following inscription, in ink, on the flyleaf, presumably entered by John Marshall:

> J. Marshall
> given to W[m] Wordsworth
> Rydale Mount - July 17th 1814
> Previous to setting out
> with Mary & Sarah on
> their Tour through Scotland

The volume contains pencilled notes on pp. 285-90, evidently related to W's Scottish tour of 1814. A note on the rear endpaper in an unidentified hand says that the volume was 'Taken by W. W. & his sister on their Scottish tour'. DW did not go on the 1814 tour.

340. Robinson, Henry Crabb, review of *The Convention of Cintra*, *London Review* 2 (Nov. 1809) 231-75
Suggested date of reading: shortly after 18 Nov. 1809
References: *MY* i 374
'We have not seen Henry Robinson's review', DW told Catherine Clarkson on 18 Nov. 1809 (*MY* i 374). This was probably a response to Clarkson's enquiry and it is reasonable to suppose that she would have sent a copy to the Wordsworths, especially as Robinson was enthusiastic. Robinson's own account implies that W saw it: 'My review gained me, I believe, very little credit - not with Wordsworth, though eulogistic' (Morley i 13).

341. Robinson, Mary
(i) *The Haunted Beach*
Suggested date of reading: probably *c*. 26 Feb. 1800
References: Reed ii 80n39
The influence of Robinson's poem was acknowledged in C's introductory note to W's *The Seven Sisters* when first published in the *Morning Post*, 14 Oct. 1800 (see Woof *SIB* 176). W must therefore have seen *The Haunted Beach* when it appeared in the *Morning Post*, on 26 Feb.; it was published also in the *Annual Anthology* (1800) at C's insistence (Griggs i 575-6). For further discussion see Landon, 'Wordsworth, Coleridge, and the *Morning Post*: An Early Version of "The Seven Sisters"', *RES* 11 (1960) 392-402.

(ii) *Lyrical Tales* **(1800)**
Suggested date of reading: probably late 1800
References: *EY* 297
In her letter to Jane Marshall of 10 and 12 Sept. 1800, DW laments the fact that 'Mrs. Robinson has claimed the title and is about publishing a volume of *Lyrical Tales*' (*EY* 297). JW, who had purchased one by 12 Dec. 1800, sent his to MH *c*. 31 Jan. 1801 (Ketcham 79-80, 85); it would have been seen by W. W and Robinson were both published by Longman.

342. Rogers, Samuel
(i) *The Pleasures of Memory* **(6th edn, 1794)**
Suggested date of reading: 25 Oct. 1800
References: *Grasmere Journals* 29; Shaver 219
'We read Rogers, Miss Seward, Cowper &c.' (DW's journal, 25 Oct. 1800). As Pamela Woof suggests, it is likely that W and DW were reading the copy of Rogers given to DW by

William Rawson in 1795 (*Grasmere Journals* 176; see also *WR* 118). W and C met Rogers, apparently for the first time, in May or June 1801 (Reed ii 119).

(ii) *An Epistle to a Friend, with other poems* **(1798)**
Suggested date of reading: 1800s
References: see note

W's copy is now in the Dyce Collection, National Art Library, Victoria and Albert Museum (M4to 8300). Its title-page bears two inscriptions. The first, 'Wm Wordsworth', is in W's hand, and dates from the 1800s. Immediately beneath it, Rogers has written, 'From the Author.' Rogers could have given it to W at any time after their first meeting in summer 1801 (Reed ii 119). This volume does not appear in Shaver but was almost certainly retained at Rydal Mount. If, as I suspect, W gave it to Dyce at some point prior to 1829 (when Dora Wordsworth made up the earliest inventory of W's library), that would explain why it does not appear in any of the Rydal Mount catalogues and loan books.

(iii) *Poems* **(1812)**
Suggested date of reading: c. spring 1814; by 5 May 1814
References: *MY* ii 147; Shaver 219

On 5 May 1814 W told Rogers: 'I have to thank you for a Present of your Volume of Poems, received some time since, through the hands of Southey. I have read it with great pleasure' (*MY* ii 147). W and Southey's previous known meeting took place in early June 1813 (Reed ii 532), but it seems unlikely that W would have waited nearly a year before thanking Rogers for the gift of two books (*The Voyage of Columbus* was the other; see next note). Presumably W and Southey met during the spring of 1814.

(iv) *The Voyage of Columbus* **(1810)**
Suggested date of reading: c. spring 1814; by 5 May 1814
References: *MY* ii 147

'The Columbus is what you intended', W told Rogers on 5 May 1814, 'it has many bright and striking passages, and Poems, upon this plan, please better on a second Perusal than the first' (*MY* ii 147). It is not clear when this was sent to W, but it arrived with a copy of Roger's *Poems* (1812) (see preceding note). Curiously, this book is not listed by the Shavers; perhaps it was lent or given away, and not returned.

(v) *Jacqueline, A Tale.* **(1814)**
Suggested date of reading: c. 18 Aug. 1814
References: *Supp.* 149
See note 80(iii), above.

343. Roscoe, William, *The Life and Pontificate of Leo the Tenth* **(4 vols., Liverpool, 1805)**
Suggested date of reading: Nov.-Dec. 1805
References: *EY* 652

On 29 Nov. 1805, DW told Lady Beaumont: 'I am reading Rosco's Leo the tenth - I have only got through the first Chapter which I find exceedingly interesting. The whole Book can scarcely be so interesting to me' (*EY* 652). The Wordsworths were acquainted with Roscoe's political career, for in March 1809 W found Mr Crump 'saturated with Roscoism' (*MY* i 306). In 1812, W met one of Roscoe's sons (*Supp*. 73). Roscoe had known of C as early as Aug. 1796 (Griggs i 230), and met him in Liverpool in July 1800 (Griggs i 607-8).

As it was not, apparently, retained at Rydal Mount, Roscoe's book was probably a loan. The most likely source is Southey, who was reading *Leo the Tenth* on 5 Aug. 1805 (*Life of Southey* ii 341) in preparation for his review of it in the *Annual Review* 4 (1805) 449-67. He visited Grasmere in Sept. (Reed ii 300) and may well have lent it to the Wordsworths then, who he knew were still recovering from the shock of JW's death. If this was so, his copy was returned to Greta Hall by 11 Jan. 1806, when he was reading it a second time: 'I am come to Roscoe', he told Henry Herbert Southey, 'whose book rises much in my estimation upon a second perusal' (Curry i 415).

344. Rousseau, Jean Jacques, *Discourse on Inequality*
Suggested date of reading: perhaps between 19 Dec. 1800 and 9 April 1801
References: Cornell *Lyrical Ballads* 334, 467
Butler and Green note that revisions made to *Michael* between 19 Dec. 1800 and 9 April 1801 'are very close to Rousseau's ninth note to his *Discours sur l'origine de l'inégalité parmi les hommes* (1755)' (Cornell *Lyrical Ballads* 467). W had first read Rousseau's *Discourse* probably as early as 1793 (*WR* 119).

345. Russell, Thomas, *Sonnets and Miscellaneous Poems*, **ed. W. Howley (Oxford, 1789)**
Suggested date of reading: c. Jan.-April 1802
References: *Prose Works* i 163, 189
Russell's *Sonnet X* is quoted in W's Appendix on Poetic Diction to the Preface to *Lyrical Ballads* (1802). W had probably known Russell's work since his Cambridge years (*WR* 120). In 1844, Charles Wordsworth recorded that W 'spoke of the Wykehamist Poets - at the end of the last Century - with great commendation - Russell, Headley, Bowles, & Crowe'; he went on to recall that 'A volume of Russells Poems was published, after his death, by the present ArchBP. of Cant' (Reed *PBSA* 455). This allusion to Howley suggests that W knew the 1789 Oxford edn.

346. Sadler, ---------, of Chippenham, *Wanly Penson; or, The Melancholy Man: A Miscellaneous Novel* **(3 vols., 1792)**
Suggested date of reading: 5 Feb. 1802
References: *Grasmere Journals* 62; Shaver 223
'I read the story of Snell in Wanly Penson' (DW's journal, 5 Feb. 1802). This is the earliest mention of a book that seems to have remained in the Wordsworths' possession until the

Rydal Mount sale of 1859. For further discussion, see Heath 32-3; Walter B. Crawford, 'A Three-Decker Novel in Wordsworth's Library, 1802', *N&Q* NS 11 (1964) 16-17. Southey knew of this book by 1805; perhaps he had seen the Wordsworths' copy (*Life of Southey* ii 346).

347. Schiller, Johann Christoph Friedrich von
(i) ***The Death of Wallenstein*** **in MS, tr. S. T. Coleridge**
Suggested date of reading: between 6 April and 4 May 1800
References: Reed ii 61
On 16 March 1840 W told Robinson that 'C. translated the 2nd part of Wallenstein under my roof at Grasmere from MSS. - about that time I saw the passages of the Astronomical Times and the antient Mythology, which, as treated in Coleridge's professed translation, were infinitely superior' (*LY* iv 50). By 'the 2nd part of Wallenstein' W probably meant *The Death of Wallenstein*, which was published as the second vol. in 1800 alongside C's translation of *The Piccolomini, or the first part of Wallenstein*. Reed suggests that it was on C's first visit to DC that he translated *The Death of Wallenstein*, completing the work by 22 April (see Griggs i 587); it is likely that on that occasion C would have shown the Wordsworths the MS of *The Piccolomini*. A MS copy of *The Death of Wallenstein* remained at DC until 21 Aug. 1800, when DW apparently sent it to Keswick (*Grasmere Journals* 17; Reed ii 81); it was published by Longman in 1800. De Quincey believed W to be unappreciative of Schiller, and *Wallenstein* in particular; see Masson iii 205.

(ii) ***The Piccolomini, or the first part of Wallenstein*** **in MS, tr. S. T. Coleridge**
Suggested date of reading: between 6 April and 4 May 1800
References: Reed ii 61
See preceding note.

(iii) ***The Piccolomini, or the first part of Wallenstein, a drama in five acts***, tr.
S. T. Coleridge; ***The Death of Wallenstein*,** **tr. S. T. Coleridge (2 vols. in 1, 1800)**
Suggested date of reading: c. late July or early Aug. 1800 onwards
References: Shaver 227-8
On 22 Sept. 1800 C told Godwin: 'I was in the Country when Wallenstein was published. Longman sent me down half a dozen' (Griggs i 626). It would appear that these copies had arrived at Keswick by 24 July, when C asked Josiah Wedgwood whether he had seen one (Griggs i 610). If so, it is likely that C gave one to W either when he visited DC on 31 July (Reed ii 76), or when W visited Keswick on 2 Aug. (Reed ii 77). W's copy is now at the Wordsworth Library. It bears a title-page inscription in C's hand:

>For W. Wordsworth
>>from
>>>S. T. Coleridge
>>>>Vale!

It also contains marginalia by C.

In Feb. 1809, C told Stuart that this translation was 'done by me at Longman's particular request, and printed & published contrary to my repeated Warnings & strenuous Advice, and by which I earned about the tenth part of what the same Toil, Time, and Effort would have procured me from the Morning Post' (Griggs iii 179).

348. Scott, John
(i) *A Visit to Paris in 1814; being a review of the moral, political, intellectual, and social condition of the French Capital* (1815)
Suggested date of reading: by 14 May 1815
References: *MY* ii 237; Shaver 229

On 14 May 1815 W wrote to John Scott to thank him for 'the volume which you have presented to me, for which I return you my sincere thanks' (*MY* ii 237). His comments on Scott's book suggest that he had by that date perused it. Scott had sent him a copy of his *Paris Revisited in 1815* (1816) by 22 Feb. 1816, when W told him that it had 'been in constant use since I received it' (*MY* ii 280; Shaver 228-9). A second copy had arrived at Rydal Mount by 11 March (*MY* ii 285).

(ii) review of *The White Doe of Rylstone*, *The Champion* 25 June 1815, pp. 205-6
Suggested date of reading: late July 1815
References: *MY* ii 243

On 28 June 1815 DW told Catherine Clarkson that 'Longman has sent "the Champion" with a long criticism on William's poems' (*MY* ii 243). The review of the *White Doe* was written by John Scott; W would have seen it when he returned to Rydal Mount from London in late July. Scott published two of W's sonnets, *To R. B. Haydon, Esq* and *November 1, 1815* in the *Champion* of 28 Jan. and 4 Feb. 1816. (Cornell *Poems 1807-20* 174).

349. Scott, Sir Walter
(i) *The Lay of the Last Minstrel* in MS
Suggested date of reading: probably between 17 and 20 Sept. 1803; by 20 Sept. 1803
References: *DWJ* i 399

DW recalled that, while in their lodgings at Jedburgh, 20 Sept. 1803, Walter Scott 'sate with us an hour or two, and repeated a part of the Lay of the Last Minstrel' - though it is likely that they had already heard of the poem and possibly seen parts of it in MS between then and 17 Sept. when they met Scott at Lasswade. He repeated more of his poem after guiding the Wordsworths down the Yarrow on 21 Sept. (*DWJ* i 403). W told Rogers about this, because

Rogers later reported: 'During that tour [i.e. of 1803] they met with Scott, who repeated to them a portion of his then unpublished *Lay*; which Wordsworth, as might be expected, did not greatly admire' (*Rogers* 206).

(ii) *Minstrelsy of the Scottish Border* (3 vols., Kelso, Edinburgh, 1802-3)
Suggested date of reading: by 14 Oct. 1803
References: Cornell *Poems 1800-7* 172
W's *October 1803* ('Six thousand Veterans practis'd in War's game') alludes to an anecdote recounted in Scott's *Minstrelsy* (Cornell *Poems 1800-7* 414). As *October 1803* was composed between 14 and 31 Oct. 1803, W must by then have seen Scott's book. Of course, the Wordsworths owned a copy by that point, but they had not yet taken possession of it and had probably not even seen it (see next note). W would have known of the anecdote probably from having seen a copy of the *Minstrelsy* while visiting Scott in Sept. 1803. C's copy of the 2nd edn of the *Minstrelsy* is now in the possession of Paul F. Betz.

(iii) *Minstrelsy of the Scottish Border* (3 vols., Kelso, Edinburgh, 1802-3)
Suggested date of reading: by July or Aug. 1805
References: *EY* 469; Shaver 230
Richard Sharp purchased this set for W in early 1803. According to C's letter to the Wordsworths of 15 Feb. 1804, it was 'left by Lamb at Richard's Rooms a year ago' (Griggs ii 1064) - that is, with Sharp[1] in London. The Wordsworths still had not received it by 29 April 1804 when W told Sharp that 'I have not yet received the parcel' (*EY* 469). It was presumably in W's possession by July or Aug. 1805, when Sharp visited DC (Reed ii 292).

(iv) *The Lay of the Last Minstrel* (1805)
Suggested date of reading: between 16 Jan. and 7 March 1805
References: Shaver 229
Scott's poem was published in Jan. 1805. W knew that a copy was on its way on 16 Jan., when he wrote to Scott to thank him in advance for it. He appears to have read it by 7 March, when he told Scott that 'you have completely attained your object' (*EY* 553).

One thing gives me pause: Feb. 1805 was marked by the grief occasioned by JW's death. I wonder whether W's reading was either close or considered, given his distraction and that of his household at this time. Privately, W and DW were concerned that Scott's poem 'will tarnish the freshness of Christabel and considerably injure the first effect of it' (*EY* 633).

This is a title of which, for a while, W possessed two copies. In June 1806 he wrote to Scott, thanking him for 'your second elegant copy of the Minstrel' (*MY* i 41); this does not necessarily imply another reading of the poem at that time. On 10 Nov. W confessed to Scott: 'I do not deserve your kindness: for the 2nd Copy of the *Minstrel* I gave away' (*MY* i 96). To whom? Possibly C, who read the *Lay* only in Nov. 1807, probably during his journey

---

[1] Griggs erroneously notes that 'Coleridge refers to Richard Wordsworth, the poet's brother'.

from Grasmere to London, on which occasion he claimed to see no resemblance between it and *Christabel* (Griggs iii 39).

(v) review of *The Works of Edmund Spenser*, ed. Henry John Todd (8 vols., 1805), *Edinburgh Review* 7 (Oct. 1805) 214
Suggested date of reading: shortly after 1 Nov. 1805
References: Comparetti 111-13
Comparetti deduces that W must have read Scott's review of Todd's *Spenser*, which influenced *The White Doe of Rylstone*; if so, he must also have seen the copy belonging to Southey (see note 369[xiii]).

(vi) 'your Song'
Suggested date of reading: shortly before 18 Aug. 1806
References: MY i 73
'Thanks for your Song which I duly received', W wrote to Scott on 18 Aug. 1806, 'shall I be wicked enough to say materiam superabat opus?' The song remains unidentified.

(vii) *Ballads and Lyrical Pieces* (Edinburgh, 1806)
Suggested date of reading: c. 7 March 1807 onwards
References: see note
Scott made the mistake of sending a copy of the *Ballads* to W via Montagu in late 1806, on the understanding that Montagu would take it to DC when he visited the Wordsworths at Christmas (*MY* i 122). Unfortunately Montagu did not visit, as he had promised, and W still had not received the book by Feb. 1807, when he was staying at Coleorton; as he explained to Scott: 'the means which I took to have them conveyed safely have been the very cause of my not yet having received them at all' (*MY* i 140). However, W had received a box from Montagu by 7 March, and it may be presumed that it contained his copy of Scott's *Ballads* (*MY* i 141), later retained at Rydal Mount (Shaver 229).

(viii) *Marmion; a tale of Flodden Field* (Edinburgh, 1808)
Suggested date of reading: between 14 May and 4 Aug. 1808
References: MY i 264; Shaver 229; Gordan 342
W had heard about *Marmion* from Southey and Lord Holland by 25 March 1808 (*Supp.* 13), but did not apparently get a chance to read it until a copy was sent to Grasmere. 'Thank you for Marmion which I have read with lively pleasure', he told Scott on 4 Aug. 1808. His previous extant letter to Scott dates from 14 May, when he reported to Scott that his copy had not yet arrived (*MY* i 237). His copy of the first edn is in the Berg Collection, New York Public Library, and was sent by the publisher. It bears the inscription: 'From the author'. MW has written inside it: 'Walter Scott, W. Wordsworth'. W's copy of the second edn is at the Wordsworth Library, and contains an inscription on the inside front cover in Scott's hand:

William Wordsworth
    from his sincere friend
        Walter Scott

The half-title bears an inscription in ink: 'W Wordsworth Rydal Mount'.

W. J. B. Owen, 'Some Wordsworthian Borrowings', *N&Q* 193 (1948) 429-30 finds a borrowing from *Marmion* in W's *View from the Top of Black Comb*, composed between late Aug. and early Sept. 1811 (see also Cornell *Poems 1807-20* 98-100, 518-19).

(ix) *The Lady of the Lake* (Edinburgh, 1810)
Suggested date of reading: 1810
References: Jordan 257-8; *MY* i 458
Evidence is lacking as to W's reading of this work. The merest hint that he did see it is provided by De Quincey's letter to MW of 27 Aug. 1810, which criticizes it as 'the completest magazine of all forms of the Falsetto in feeling and diction that now exists' (Jordan 257). C was a reader of the volume: he read Southey's copy in Sept. 1810, probably at Greta Hall, and his opinion of it was no better than De Quincey's (*Notebooks* iii 3970). Perhaps W also read Southey's copy.

(x) *The Lord of the Isles, A Poem in Six Cantos* (Edinburgh, 1815)
Suggested date of reading: by Jan. 1815
References: *MY* ii 187; Shaver 229
In Jan. 1815 W wrote to Southey: 'I am obliged to Scott for his book, and I love Scott much, and greatly admire his various Tales etc; but it would be superfluous to say to *you* what I must think of the Lord of the Isles as a *Poem*' (*MY* ii 187; his italics). Evidently, Scott had sent W a copy of his latest work, apparently through Southey.

(xi) *Waverley* (3 vols., Edinburgh, 1814)
Suggested date of reading: by 18 Feb. 1815
References: *MY* ii 203
DW discusses *Waverley* in a letter of 18 Feb. 1815, indicating that she had by then read the copy at Rydal Mount; it was published in July 1814. In his letter to Gillies of 25 April, W compares it with *Guy Mannering* (*MY* ii 203, 232); on this evidence alone, De Quincey may be presumed to have been incorrect in believing that W 'has never read one page of Sir Walter Scott's novels' (Masson iii 206).

(xii) *Guy Mannering* (3 vols., Edinburgh, 1815)
Suggested date of reading: by 25 April 1815
References: *MY* ii 232
In his letter to Gillies of 25 April 1815 W says that he has read *Guy Mannering*, and compares it with *Waverley*.

350. Seneca, Lucius Annaeus

(i) *L. Annæi Senecæ Philosophi, et M. Annæi Senecæ Rhetoris quæ extant opera* **(Raphelengii, 1609)**
Suggested date of reading: probably by 1810
References: Healey 2261; Shaver 304
This volume, now in the Cornell Wordsworth Collection, bears W's ownership inscription on a blank leaf, and C's on the title-page. It may have belonged originally to C, been left at Allan Bank in 1810, and not retrieved. It was retained at Rydal Mount (Shaver 304), and was probably in W's possession from at least 1810 onwards.

(ii) works
Suggested date of reading: by spring 1814
References: *The Excursion* (1814), p. 428
As part of the text of *The Excursion* (1814), W prints eight lines from Daniel's *Epistle to the Countess of Cumberland*, noting that 'the two last lines, printed in Italics, are by him translated from Seneca' (p. 428). Worthington comments: 'Wordsworth was the first to identify the translation. That he was able to do so suggests that his knowledge of Seneca was as wide as it was thorough' (Worthington 45). W had known Seneca since at least his Cambridge years, and by 1814 at least two copies of the works would have been available to him - that mentioned in the preceding note, and that discussed note AI16, below.

351. Sennertus, Daniel, *Opera* (4 vols., in 2, Lyons, 1666)
Suggested date of reading: Feb. 1801
References: Reed ii 113n7
Reed reports that W copied quotations from Sennertus into DC MS 31, leaves 71-2, *c*. Feb. 1801. They appear to have been copied from C's transcriptions and should not be taken to imply serious study of Sennertus by W. C had owned a copy of Sennertus' *Opera Omnia* since 1799 (Griggs i 531n2), and it apparently contained his marginalia. Its present location is not known (Whalley *BC* 106; Whalley PhD ii 485).

352. Seward, Anna

(i) poems
Suggested date of reading: 25 Oct. 1800
References: *Grasmere Journals* 29; Shaver 232
'We read Rogers, Miss Seward, Cowper &c.' (DW's journal, 25 Oct. 1800). Pamela Woof suggests that the Wordsworths were reading Seward's most recent volume of sonnets (1799) (*Grasmere Journals* 176). However, the Rydal Mount library contained copies of Seward's *Louisa, Elegy on Captain Cook, Monody on Major André*, and *Poem to the Memory of Lady Miller*. It is not clear when these were acquired, but they may have been in W's hands by 1800.

(ii) *Original Sonnets on Various Subjects; and Odes Paraphrased from Horace* **(1799)**
Suggested date of reading: c. Dec. 1800
References: Whalley (1955) 39n1; Jackson 294
'On the occasion of her first visit to Greta Hall, Coleridge gave Sara [Hutchinson] the corrected proof-sheets of Anna Seward's *Original Sonnets* (1799) with an inscription that shows his attempt to anagram her name in the official form with the final *-h*: "The Editor to Asahara, the Moorish Maid, Dec. 1800 Greta Hall Keswick." These proof-sheets are now in the Dove Cottage Museum, Grasmere' (Whalley [1955] 39n1). It is likely that the Wordsworths would have seen C's gift, either before or after it was presented to SH. It is not listed in Shaver.

353. Shadwell, Thomas, *The Virtuoso* **(1676)**
Suggested date of reading: probably by 27 Sept. 1807
References: *MY* i 166
While advising Scott on his annotations to his forthcoming edn of Dryden's *Works* on 27 Sept. 1807, W told Scott that *MacFlecknoe* 181 alluded to Shadwell's *The Virtuoso*, which he may by that date be assumed to have read. Kinsley reproduces precisely W's information (*Poems of John Dryden* [1958], iv 1920). Shadwell is mentioned in another letter to Scott of 18 Jan. 1808 (*MY* i 190), and in the *Essay, Supplementary to the Preface* (*Prose Works* iii 68, 87). C's copy of the *Dramatick Works* (4 vols., 1720) was retained at Rydal Mount (Shaver 232), and may have been in W's possession by 1807.

354. Shakespeare, William
(i) *Shakespeare's Dramatic Works; with explanatory note. A new edition*, **ed. Percival Stockdale;** *To which is now added a copious index to the remarkable passages and words, by the Revd. Samuel Ayscough* **(3 vols., 1790)**
Suggested date of reading: Oct. 1800 onwards
References: MWL 1
'I was much obliged to you for the trouble you had about my Shakespeare', MH wrote to John Monkhouse on 26 Oct. 1800. She had probably only just received her copy of Stockdale's edn,[1] and would soon have told W about it and probably shown it to him. It would have entered his library upon their marriage and is indeed listed Shaver 232. Coburn notes that C and W favoured Stockdale's edn, and that C annotated two copies - one of which is now in the British Library, the other in Harvard University Library (*Notebooks* ii 3145; Whalley PhD ii 487; Coffman S137).

(ii) *A Lover's Complaint*
Suggested date of reading: bedtime, 5 May 1802

---

[1] SH had requested John Monkhouse to send it in letters of 12 July and 23 Aug. 1800 (*SHL* 4, 6).

References: *Grasmere Journals* 96
'I read The Lover's Complaint to Wm in bed & left him composed' (DW's journal, 5 May 1802). *A Lover's Complaint* is no longer believed unreservedly to be the work of Shakespeare.

(iii) *Henry V*
Suggested date of reading: 8 May 1802
References: *Grasmere Journals* 97
'We sowed the Scarlet Beans in the orchard I read Henry 5th there - William lay on his back on the seat' (DW's journal, 8 May 1802). It is likely that some of the reading was aloud.

(iv)
Suggested date of reading: 15 May 1802
References: *Grasmere Journals* 100
'I read in Shakespeare' (DW's journal, 15 May 1802).

(v) *As You Like It*
Suggested date of reading: 22 June, 1 July 1802
References: *Grasmere Journals* 117
'William read Spenser & I read "As you like it"' (DW's journal, 1 July 1802). This reading completed that begun on 22 June, during W's absence (*Grasmere Journals* 113).

(vi) *A Winter's Tale*
Suggested date of reading: 8 July 1802
References: *Grasmere Journals* 118
'Wm fell asleep I read the Winter's Tale' (DW's journal, 8 July 1802).

(vii) *Hamlet*
Suggested date of reading: evening, 6 March 1804
References: *EY* 451
Writing to C, DW reported on 6 March 1804 that W 'is sitting beside me reading Hamlet' (*EY* 451). Intriguingly, W told Beaumont on 1 May 1805 that 'I never saw Hamlet acted my self' (*EY* 587).

(viii) 'Pope's Shakespeare'
Suggested date of reading: mid-Feb. 1806 onwards
References: Marrs ii 204-6
On 1 Feb. 1806, Lamb wrote to W to tell him that he had purchased copies of Urry's Chaucer, Pope's Shakespeare, Spenser and Milton on his behalf, and had sent them up on the Kendal wagon that very day. The copy of this six-volume edn of Pope's Shakespeare cost £2.2*s*., and was purchased second-hand, its previous owner having inserted 'variae lectiones . . . in a very neat hand from 5 Commentators'; Lamb went on:

The fault of Pope's edition is, that he has comically & coxcombically marked the Beauties: which is vile, as if you were to chalk up the cheek & across the nose of a handsome woman in red chalk to shew where the comeliest parts lay. (Marrs ii 205)

W would have received Lamb's consignment of books by mid-Feb. (Reed ii 314). He refers to Pope's edn of Shakespeare in his *Essay, Supplementary to the Preface* (*Prose Works* iii 68, 89).

(ix) *Othello*
Suggested date of reading: between mid-Nov. and mid-Dec. 1808
References: *Prose Works* i 376
W quotes *Othello* in the *Convention of Cintra*; he may have recalled the phrase quoted, but it is not impossible that he had recently read it.

(x) *Julius Caesar*
Date of performance: 30 April 1812
References: Reed ii 495 and n17
In a note to J. F. Tuffin of 30 April 1812, during his London visit, W mentions that he has just attended a play (*MY* ii 9). Reed notes that the production at Covent Garden that day was *Julius Caesar*.

(xi) *Plays of William Shakespeare*, ed. George Steevens (1793)
Suggested date of reading: by Jan. 1815
References: *Prose Works* iii 69, 90
W refers to Steevens' edn in his *Essay, Supplementary to the Preface*. It was not, apparently, at Rydal Mount, so that he must have seen a copy belonging to someone else.

(xii) *Richard II*
Suggested date of reading: 25 May 1815
References: Morley i 167
On 25 May 1815 Robinson recorded in his diary: 'After dining with the Colliers I accompanied Miss Lamb to the theatre, where we were joined by the Wordsworths. We sat at the front of Drury Lane, and saw *Richard II*.'

355. Sidney, Sir Philip
(i) *Sir Philip Sydney's Defence of Poetry. And observations on poetry and eloquence, from the Discoveries of Ben Jonson*, ed. Joseph Warton (1787)
Suggested date of reading: spring 1802 onwards
References: see note
W's copy is at the Folger Shakespeare Library, Washington, DC. Its title-page bears his ownership inscription, dating from the 1840s. However, he sometimes inscribed his books many years after acquiring them, and the possibility that this volume was in his possession

by 1802 is persuasively argued by Anne Barton, who thinks it influenced the additions W made to the 1800 Preface:

> In that 1787 edition of the *Defence of Poetry* which Wordsworth owned, Warton had reprinted a substantial extract from Jonson's great prose meditation *Discoveries*, lines 587 to 2,815 in Herford and Simpson's numbering, immediately after Sidney's essay. This extract includes the section in which Jonson asks and answers the question, 'What is a Poet?'. In the Owen and Smyser edition of Wordsworth's prose, the major insertion into the Preface of 1802 of material not present in 1800 occurs between lines 295 and 523. Significantly, at line 319 of this new section Wordsworth asks Jonson's question, 'What is a Poet?', repeating Jonson's precise words. (Barton 225)

(ii) *Arcadia*
Suggested date of reading: by 29 April 1804
References: Cornell *13-Book Prelude* 182
In *Prelude* Book VI W suggests that Sidney might have written 'Some snatches . . . Of his Arcadia' within sight of Helvellyn, indicating that he had read Sidney's poem by 29 April 1804, by which time those lines were composed. I suspect that he had read the *Arcadia* as a schoolboy, but find no supporting evidence. A copy of *Arcadia* is listed Shaver 235.

(iii) *Works*
Suggested date of reading: early 1809
References: *Prose Works* i 405
W quotes Sidney's letter to Walsingham, 24 March 1586, in his *Convention of Cintra*; a copy of the *Works* must have been close at hand. It is clear that, during the spring and summer of 1809, and at any rate before 7 June, C entered marginal notes into Lamb's copy of *Arcadia*; he may have discussed Sidney's poem with W at that time (Marrs iii 13).

(iv) *Works*
Suggested date of reading: by 17 Sept. 1814
References: *MY* ii 153
In his letter to Robert Anderson of 17 Sept. 1814, W suggests that an enlarged edn of his *British Poets* should include Sidney, omitted by both Anderson and Chalmers in his *Works of the English Poets* (1810). W knew Sidney's *Astrophil and Stella* at Hawkshead (*WR* 127) and had probably read most if not all of Sidney's works by 1814. Southey had proposed to Longman in Nov. 1804 that he edit Sidney's works (*Life of Southey* ii 306).

356. Sinclair, Sir John, *A Statistical Account of Scotland, drawn up from the Communications of the Ministers of the Different Parishes* (21 vols., Edinburgh, 1791-9)
Suggested date of reading: by 22 Feb. 1810
References: *Prose Works* ii 106

'We learn from the Statistical account of Scotland that, in some districts, a general transfer of Inhabitants has taken place', W writes in the second of his *Essays Upon Epitaphs* (*Prose Works* ii 66-7). He must have seen Sinclair's *Statistical Account* by 22 Feb. 1810, when the *Essays* were complete.

357. ***Sir Ysumbras, Sir Gowther, Sir Amadas***
Suggested date of reading: c. Sept. 1805
References: *EY* 644 and n2
On 3 Oct. 1805 Southey wrote to Wynn:

> Froude, a clergyman of Devonshire, happened, some little time ago, to tell me that a lady in Nottinghamshire had an old MS. volume of poems, which nobody could make out. I expressed a wish to see it, - and, in short, have it now lying on my desk. It contains all sorts of things; and among others three metrical romances, Sir Ysumbras, Sir Gwother, and Sir Amadas. . . . Each is about 800 lines long; the rest of the volume contains many curious things, with much devotional poetry. I shall show it to Walter Scott, and get the owner's permission to take measures for publishing such of its contents as are worthy. (Warter i 340-1)

On 7 Oct. Southey went to Scotland, returning to Keswick on 19 Oct. after three days with Scott at Ashestiel. The next day Southey wrote once more to Wynn to report Scott's opinion:

> He was delighted with the MS., and has commissioned me to offer fifteen guineas for it, for the Advocates' library. Were there any sale for such things, I would willingly add three more volumes to Ritson's;[1] but this must be left to be done by future academies. (Warter i 342-3)

On 7 Nov. 1805 W wrote to Scott: 'I long to know, as I hope I shall from Southey, how you liked the old Manuscript. I thought it looked rather promising' (*EY* 644). Evidently W had seen the manuscript prior to Southey's visit to Ashestiel, probably in Sept. (Reed ii 300). It is now retained at the Advocates Library, MS.19.3.1., from which Christopher Brookhouse edited *Sir Amadas* in 1968 (see *Anglistica* 15 [1968]).[2]

358. Skelton, John
(i) ***The Bowge of Court***
Suggested date of reading: by 6 March 1804
References: Cornell *Poems 1800-7* 410
Line 8 of 'With ships the sea was sprinkled' was, W noted, 'From a passage in Skelton, which I cannot here insert, not having the Book at hand'. The sonnet has been dated as

---

[1] Joseph Ritson, *Ancient English Metrical Romances* (3 vols., 1802).
[2] *Sir Gowther* was edited in 1886, *Sir Ysumbras* in 1901.

composed probably between 21 May 1802 and 6 March 1804 (Reed ii 171); perhaps W had noted or memorized Skelton's lines in earlier years.

(ii) 'pieces which have lately come to light'
Suggested date of reading: between 1810 and 17 Sept. 1814
References: *MY* ii 152
In his letter to Robert Anderson of 17 Sept. 1814, W suggests that an enlarged edn of his *British Poets* should include 'all that are in Chalmers and not in yours, adding to the works of Skelton many pieces which have lately come to light which C. has not included. Mr Heber has most or all of them' (*MY* ii 152). In a letter to Alexander Dyce of 21 July 1832 he repeats: 'in Mr Heber's Library were certain printed poems of Skelton not to be found in any collection of his works' (*LY* ii 544).[1] Although W had dined with Heber during his stay in London in early 1808 (Reed ii 376), he may be relying on information passed on by Southey.[2] Sotheby's *Bibliotheca Heberiana* (1834-7), iv 2356-67, lists a number of unusual Skelton items, mostly sixteenth-century, any or all of which W may have seen. W regarded Skelton as 'a Demon in point of genius' (*LY* i 403) and 'a Brother Cumbrian' (*LY* ii 413-14).

359. Smith, Adam
(i) *Inquiry into the Nature and the Causes of the Wealth of Nations* [1776]
Suggested date of reading: by c. late 1804
References: see note
In *Prelude* Book XII W discusses 'the Books / Of modern Statists', and refers to 'The utter hollowness of what we name / The wealth of Nations' (lines 78-80). This allusion to Smith's famous book suggests that W was probably acquainted by late 1804 with his arguments. He examines them in *Excursion* Book VIII, composed 1813-14.[3] An additional source may be C, who referred to Smith's *Wealth of Nations* in notebook entries of 1800 (*Notebooks* i 661, 735), and advised Poole to 'skim over Adam Smith' in May 1802 (Griggs ii 799). W referred to Smith's literary views in a letter to John Wilson of 7 June 1802 (*EY* 354-5), having seen them reported in the *European Magazine* (see note 1).

(ii) *Theory of Moral Sentiments* [1759]
Suggested date of reading: by Jan. 1815
References: *Prose Works* iii 93

---

[1] This was ample reason for W to lament, after Heber's death in Oct. 1833: 'Mr Heber's wonderful Collection of Books is about to be dispersed' (*LY* ii 665).

[2] It is worth noting that, when Dyce expressed an interest in editing Skelton in 1831, W encouraged him to talk to Southey about it, supporting my suspicion that Southey himself had a good collection of Skelton material, if not as comprehensive as that owned by Heber (*LY* ii 414).

[3] W's treatment of Smith is dealt with by Mary Wedd, 'Industrialization and the Moral Law in Books VIII and IX of *The Excursion*', *CLB* NS 81 (1993) 5-25, esp. pp. 9-10.

W's *Essay, Supplementary to the Preface* (composed Jan. 1815) refers to Smith as 'the worst critic, David Hume not excepted, that Scotland, a soil to which this sort of weed seems natural, has produced' (*Prose Works* iii 71). Owen and Smyser trace the opinions criticized by W to Smith's *Theory of Moral Sentiments*.

360. Smith, Charlotte
(i) *Elegiac Sonnets* (5th edn, 1789)
Suggested date of reading: 24 Dec. 1802
References: *Grasmere Journals* 135; Shaver 237
'. . . beloved William is turning over the leaves of Charlotte Smith's sonnets' (DW's journals, 24 Dec. 1802). This refers, probably, to the 5th edn of her *Elegiac Sonnets*, to which W had subscribed prior to publication in 1789 (see *WR* 128).

(ii) *Ethelinde, or The Recluse of the Lake* (5 vols., 1789)
Suggested date of reading: by Nov. 1812
References: *Prose Works* ii 440
W's reference in his *Unpublished Tour* to Grasmere Abbey, 'having no existence but in the pages of Romance' (*Prose Works* ii 308) suggests that he had read, or at least heard about, Smith's *Ethelinde*. The *Unpublished Tour* was composed between Sept. 1811 and Nov. 1812.

361. Smith, Elizabeth, *Fragments, in Prose and Verse*, ed. Henrietta Maria Bowdler [1808]
Suggested date of reading: between Sept. 1811 and Nov. 1812
References: *Prose Works* ii 445; Jackson 303-7
W refers with approval to Smith's posthumous *Fragments* in his *Unpublished Tour* (*Prose Works* ii 331). He did not know her, but his friend Thomas Wilkinson had done. He is likely also to have seen the copy of Klopstock's memoirs translated by Smith (see note 234). The numerous listings in Jackson suggest that the *Fragments* was a popular work.

362. Smollett, Tobias
(i) life of (Anderson)
Suggested date of reading: 4 Feb. 1802
References: *Grasmere Journals* 62
'I slept in the sitting room read Smollets life' (DW's journal, 4 Feb. 1802). DW's reading of the life of Smollett in Anderson, *British Poets* vol. 10 might have extended to a reading of Smollett's poems, which follow it. W had known Smollett's *Ode to Leven-water* since 1791-2 (see *WR* 128), and DW alludes to it in her recollections of the Scottish tour of 1803, in her entry for 24 Aug. (DC MS 55, 40r; *DWJ* i 245).

(ii) *The Adventures of Ferdinand Count Fathom* [2 vols., 1753]
Suggested date of reading: by 3 Sept. 1803

References: *DWJ* i 334

In the journal of the Scottish tour, 1803, DW writes of one of their landladies: 'She and the house, upon that desolate and extensive Wild, and everything we saw, made us think of one of those places of rendezvous which we read of in novels - Ferdinand Count Fathom, or Gil Blas, where there is one woman to receive the booty, and prepare the supper at night' (*DWJ* i 334). The Wordsworths had probably read Smollett's novels many years before.

363. Sotheby, William
(i) works
Suggested date of reading: by late June 1802
References: Reed ii 183
On 6 Feb. 1827 W told Sotheby:

> I was gratified the other day by meeting in Mr Alaric Watts' Souvenir with a very old acquaintance, a Sonnet of yours, which I had read with no little pleasure more than 30 years ago. 'I knew a gentle Maid'. (*MY* ii 515)

He must have seen Sotheby's sonnet in *Poems* (1790), which was reprinted in 1794. By the time he met its author at DC in late June 1802, he must have known some of his other works. In 1802 Sotheby was best known as a translator from German,[1] and W probably knew his rendering of Wieland's *Oberon* (see *WR* 148). Quite possibly he had also seen his translation of the *Georgics*, published in 1800, or his *Poetical Epistle to Sir George Beaumont* (1801). C was an enthusiast for Sotheby's *Poems* (1790), and in Aug. 1802 told Sotheby he knew *Netley Abbey*, its most famous work, by heart (Griggs ii 855).

I am intrigued to find that a copy of Sotheby's translation of Euripides' *Orestes; a tragedy in five acts* (1802) was at Rydal Mount (Shaver 240): according to the *Morning Chronicle*, it was published on 29 April 1802, so that it might have been a subject of conversation when Sotheby visited Grasmere in June, and a copy would have made a good gift for his host. Sotheby did send one to C, but it went astray and Charles Lamb was detailed to enquire after it in Penrith in late Aug. (Griggs ii 855). Either it, or another, turned up within the month; C's marginalia to *Orestes*, on a foolscap sheet, are dated 1 Oct. 1802, and are now in the Hugh Paul Collection at the University of Kentucky (Coffman S193).

(ii) *Saul, a Poem* (1807)
Suggested date of reading: 17 April 1807
References: Griggs iii 11
On 18 April 1807, C told Sotheby:

> I read yesterday in a large company, where W. Wordsworth was present, about 150 lines of your Saul, respecting your country, Nelson, & the admirable transition to the main

---

[1] Given DW's recent reading, she may well have questioned him about Lessing.

subject, which follows it - and it was delightful to me, to observe that the enthusiasm which had given animation & depth to my own tones, manifested itself with at least equal strength in the faces & voices of all the auditors. (Griggs iii 11)

A copy of *Saul* was later retained at Rydal Mount (Shaver 240), and it is reasonable to suppose that it was acquired soon after its publication. C wrote to Sotheby with a detailed critique in April 1808 (Griggs iii 94).

(iii) 'a tragedy' in MS
Suggested date of reading: 2 May 1812
References: Supp. 56
On 2 May 1812, W wrote to MW:

> This morning I must devote two hours to the reading of a tragedy to be offered for representation, the Author that indefatigable Scribbler in Verse, Sotheby - One act Sir George L. B., and I have sate in judgement on. Thus far it seems well enough contrived for the stage, but the diction is intolerable for poverty and bad taste. (*Supp.* 56)

Sotheby wrote a number of tragedies at this time, including *The Death of Darnley*, *Ivan*, *Zamorin and Zama*, and *The Confession*, all of which were published under the title *Tragedies* in 1814.

364. Southerne, Thomas, *Isabella; or, the Fatal Marriage*
Date of performance: 18 May 1815
References: Marrs iii 158
Lamb's letter to W of 16 May 1815 appears to suggest that W saw Eliza O'Neill in the part of Isabella on 18 May 1815 (Reed ii 603 and 602n24). Even if he did not on that date, W may have sought out Miss O'Neill in this role at some other time, as she had become famous for it after her debut on 4 Nov. 1814. C was among her early admirers, writing a fan letter to her on 7 Dec. 1814 (Griggs vi 1028); she played Donna Teresa in C's *Remorse* on 28 Jan. 1813.

365. Southey, Robert
(i) *Letters written during a Short Residence in Spain and Portugal* [Bristol, 1797]
Suggested date of reading: 10, 14 Oct. 1800
References: Grasmere Journals 25, 27
'After dinner Wm went to bed - I read Southey's letters'; 'Wm lay down after dinner - I read Southeys Spain' (DW's journal, 10, 14 Oct. 1800). On this evidence, W seems always to have been asleep whenever DW read Southey's anonymous volume, but there is no reason to doubt that he read it at about this time. It was published by Cottle. C owned a copy, and the Wordsworths may have been reading his (Coffman S208); only vol. 1 of the 1808 edn was retained at Rydal Mount (Shaver 242).

(ii) *Thalaba the Destroyer* (1801)
Suggested date of reading: by 5 May 1802
References: Grasmere Journals 96
Having read Southey's poem, the Wordsworths sent it to Gallow Hill on 5 May 1802, where C was staying with the Hutchinsons.

(iii) review of Peter Bayley, *Poems* (1803), *Annual Review* 2 (1803) 546-52
Suggested date of reading: 1803-4
References: see note
As a contributor to Southey's review of Bayley, W can be expected to have seen it in MS and in print (see note 30).

(iv) *Madoc* in MS
Suggested date of reading: May or Nov.-Dec. 1804
References: see note
'Southey's Madoc is printed and will be published very soon', DW told Catherine Clarkson on 9 Dec. 1804 (*EY* 515). This suggests that W may have seen or heard all or part of the poem prior to its publication in April 1805. On his way to discuss publication with Longman, Southey stopped overnight at DC on 8 May 1804; he and his family visited DC in mid-Nov. Either occasion would have provided opportunities for W to preview Southey's latest epic. It is worth noting that James Losh reported in his diary for 4 Sept. 1800 that *Madoc* 'is ready for publication . . . Southey showed me about two years ago two books of this poem which I admired but thought deficient in dignity of sentiment and style'.[1] There is no reason, however, to think that W saw *Madoc* in MS before 1804.

(v) *Madoc* (1805)
Suggested date of reading: 15 April 1805 onwards; by 3 June 1805
References: *EY* 595; Shaver 243
On 15 April 1805 DW told Lady Beaumont that 'Southey's Madoc is published - he is sitting in the next room with my Brother' (*EY* 582). Southey must have given W a copy then, for on 1 May W reported to Sir George that 'We have had Southey's Madoc in the house more than a fortnight and have done no more than admire the elegant title-page and printing of the Book' (*EY* 588). This had been put to rights by 3 June, when W told Sir George that he was 'highly pleased with it'; however, for W's serious reservations concerning the poem see the rest of that letter (*EY* 595). W's copy is now at the Wordsworth Library; it contains an inscription, in Southey's hand: 'William Wordsworth from The Author'.

(vi) *Joan of Arc* (3rd edn, 2 vols., 1806)
Suggested date of reading: early 1806 onwards
References: Shaver 242

---

[1] Paul Kaufman, 'Wordsworth's "Candid and Enlightened Friend"', *N&Q* 207 (1962) 403-8, p. 405.

W's copy is now at the Wordsworth Library. It contains his ownership inscription on the title-page, and was probably acquired soon after publication in early 1806.

(vii) *Chronicle of the Cid* (1808)
Suggested date of reading: late 1808; certainly by 3 May 1812
References: *MY* ii 15; Shaver 304

'I am reading the Cid', DW told W and MW on 3 May 1812 (*MY* ii 15). W's copy is now at the Wordsworth Library. It bears the title-page inscription, in ink: 'Wm Wordsworth'. This is a late inscription, in W's hand. Copies were printed by Oct. 1808, and Southey was sending them to his friends during following months. It is reasonable to suppose that W acquired his at that time, particularly as the two men are known to have met on 19 Oct. to discuss the Convention of Cintra. C had read the *Chronicle* by 7 Dec. 1808, when he pronounced: 'I have read few Books with such deep Interest, as the Chronicle of the Cid' (Griggs iii 136). He was to have reviewed it in the *Courier* some time *c*. March 1809. As he was then living at Allan Bank with the Wordsworths, it would be remarkable had W not also seen it.

In addition to the copy bearing W's ownership inscription, another copy of this volume was apparently in his possession. It is now at the Wordsworth Library, and bears several inscriptions. The earliest appears on the second title-page, and is in ink, in Southey's hand: 'S. T. Coleridge, from Robert Southey'. I would presume that it dates from 1808. The second inscription appears on the first title-page, and is in a late hand, in ink: 'Wm Wordsworth'. A third inscription, on the inside front cover, reads: 'Presented to D^r. Davy by Wm Wordsworth Rydal Mount 12th April 1859'. These inscriptions would indicate that this copy belonged originally to C, having been given to him on publication by its author. It probably remained in W's possession after the falling-out with C in 1810, and moved with the Wordsworths to Rydal Mount. On 12 April 1859, it passed out of the family, being given by William Wordsworth Jr to Dr John Davy, brother of Humphry Davy (see *LY* iii 89n1).

(viii) *Thalaba the Destroyer* (2nd edn, 2 vols., 1809)
Suggested date of reading: spring/summer 1809 onwards
References: Shaver 244

W's copy is now at the Wordsworth Library. The half-title page carries an inscription in ink, in Southey's hand: 'William Wordsworth from the Author'. It was published in April 1809, and it is reasonable to suppose that W received his copy in the spring or summer of that year.

(ix) *History of Brazil* (vol. 1 only, 1810)
Suggested date of reading: Oct. 1810
References: Griggs iii 296

In early Oct. 1810 C wrote to W: 'I send the Brazil which has entertained & instructed me. The Kehama is expected' (Griggs iii 296). Southey had given him a copy of the first volume of this work, and he in turn sent it to W. This copy is now in the British Library (C.61.k.1), and its title-page bears the inscription, in Southey's hand: 'S. T. Coleridge from the Author'.

It contains some Coleridge marginalia. It would have arrived at Allan Bank by mid-Oct. and in later years was retained at Rydal Mount (Shaver 242). DW read it in May 1812 (see *MY* ii 15). See also *Notebooks* iii 3979.

(x) *The Curse of Kehama* (1810)
Suggested date of reading: between early Oct. and 30 Dec. 1810
References: *MY* i 458; Coffman S201; Shaver 241
W's copy is now at the Wordsworth Library, and contains an inscription in Southey's hand: 'William Wordsworth from the Author'. On 30 Dec. 1810 DW told Catherine Clarkson that 'I have not yet read Southey's curse of Kehama; but I believe, from William's account, that it has great merit' (*MY* i 458), thus providing a terminal date for W's first reading of this work. In early Oct. C evidently meant to send his copy to W - but did he manage to do so before their falling-out later that month? I suspect not: the inscription in W's copy seems to imply that he never received C's copy, and instead was presented with another by its author.

C had opinions on *Kehama* in July 1810 when it was still in proof (*Notebooks* iii 3952); W would also have heard about it prior to publication.

(xi) *The Life of Nelson* (2 vols., 1813)
Suggested date of reading: summer 1813
References: *MY* ii 121
'My whole summer's reading has been a part of two volumes of Mrs Grant's American Lady, which Southey lent to be speedily returned, and a dip or two in Southey's Nelson', DW told Catherine Clarkson on 4 Oct. 1813 (*MY* ii 121-2). Southey can be presumed to have given, rather than loaned his *Life of Nelson* to the Wordsworths, as a copy was retained at Rydal Mount (Shaver 242).

(xii) *Carmen Triumphale, for the Commencement of the Year 1814* (1814)
Suggested date of reading: *c.* Jan. 1814 onwards
References: Shaver 241
Shaver does not say so, but W's copy is now at the Wordsworth Library. The half-title bears an inscription, in ink, in Southey's hand: 'Wm Wordsworth from the Author'. It was published in Jan. 1814 and was probably given to W shortly after. The *Westmorland Advertiser*, of which W was a regular reader, published Southey's poem in its entirety on 15 Jan. 1814.

(xiii) *The Retrospect*
Suggested date of reading: before May 1814
References: *Excursion* (1814), p. 430
One of W's notes to *The Excursion* acknowledges a borrowing from Southey's *The Retrospect*, which W must have known for many years. It first appeared in the volume of *Poems* (Bath, 1795) published jointly with Robert Lovell. See also *LY* iv 535.

(xiv) *Roderick, the Last of the Goths* in proof
Suggested date of reading: early Oct. 1814 onwards
References: MWL 21
Writing to DW on 22 Oct. 1814 MW remarked: 'Southey's new Poem has been in the house in sheets ever since he was here and I have never had time to look at it yet' (*MWL* 21). Southey stayed for a week at Rydal Mount at the beginning of Oct. 1814 (Reed ii 575).

Roderick had been in preparation since Feb. 1810, and the Wordsworths would have heard about it for years prior to its publication. Ketcham suggests that it was the inspiration for W's *A few bold Patriots, Reliques of the Fight* (Cornell *Poems 1807-20* 498), composed between June 1808 and June 1813.

(xv) *Ode to His Royal Highness the Prince Regent, His Imperial Majesty the Emperor of Russia, and His Majesty the King of Prussia* (1814)
Suggested date of reading: 1814 onwards
References: Shaver 304
W's copy is now at the Wordsworth Library. It bears an inscription, in Southey's hand, in ink, on the half-title: 'Wm Wordsworth from the Author'. Presumably it was presented to W shortly after publication in 1814.

(xvi) *Roderick, the Last of the Goths* (1814)
Suggested date of reading: c. Jan. 1815
References: *MY* ii 187; Shaver 243
'Did I thank you for Roderic, I hope so, it was very acceptable', W wrote to Southey in Jan. 1815 (*MY* ii 187). W had seen the poem in proof; evidently Southey had sent the finished work to him by Jan. 1815. It was in print by 12 Dec. 1814 (Warter ii 383). W's copy is now at the Wordsworth Library, and contains an inscription in Southey's hand: 'William Wordsworth from the Author'. DW had read it by 8 April 1815; for her reaction, see *MY* ii 228.

366. Southey, Robert, and Samuel Taylor Coleridge, *Omniana; or, horae otiosiores* (2 vols., 1812)
Suggested date of reading: by Feb. 1815
References: *Prose Works* iii 49; Shaver 243
W's copy is now at Yale University. He quotes from it in his Preface to *Poems* (1815).

367. Southwell, Robert, works
Suggested date of reading: by 17 Sept. 1814
References: *MY* ii 153
In his letter to Robert Anderson of 17 Sept. 1814, W suggests that an enlarged edn of Anderson's *British Poets* should include Southwell. This indicates that he was aware of his works by 17 Sept. 1814.

368. Sparrman, Anders, *A Voyage to the Cape of Good Hope towards the Antarctic polar circle, and Round the World* **(1785)**
Suggested date of reading: probably by 5 April 1800
References: Reed ii 704; Moorman *N&Q* 402
Reed judges that extracts from Sparrman were entered in the Wordsworth Commonplace Book (DC MS 26, 7r-16r) by 5 April 1800. It is reasonable to suppose that the Commonplace Book contained copies of texts made from works not owned by Wordsworth.

369. Spenser, Edmund
(i) *Muiopotmos: or, the fate of the butterfly*
Suggested date of reading: March-April 1800
References: PW v 476
De Selincourt points out the influence of Spenser's *Muiopotmos* on his text of *Home at Grasmere*; in fact, the similarity is even more striking if one compares the lines from Spenser with *Home at Grasmere* MS B 24-43 (Cornell *Home at Grasmere* 38-40). If Jonathan Wordsworth's dating is correct, this means that W had read *Muiopotmos* by March-April 1800.[1]

(ii) works (Anderson)
Suggested date of reading: 16 Nov., 18 Nov., 24 Nov., and perhaps Dec. 1801
References: *Grasmere Journals* 38-9, 41
A sustained spell of reading from Spenser began on 16 Nov. 1801 (*Grasmere Journals* 38); the Wordsworths were reading his work in Anderson, *British Poets* vol. 2, the same volume from which they read Hall on 15 Nov. MH was reading *Faerie Queene* Canto I on 6 Dec. (*Grasmere Journals* 45), and W continued to read intermittently in Spenser throughout Nov.-Dec. 1801, and March-April 1802.

(iii) *Muiopotmos: or, the fate of the butterfly* **(Anderson)**
Suggested date of reading: by 13 and 14 March 1802
References: Cornell *Poems 1800-7* 408
Curtis notes a borrowing from Spenser's *Muiopotmos* in W's *Beggars*, composed 13 and 14 March 1802. W and DW were immersed in Spenser at this period. Another recollection of the same stanza is to be found at *Thirteen-Book Prelude* x 838 (Cornell *13-Book Prelude* 289 and n; Norton *Prel.* 404n9; OET *Prel.* 606). W would have read Spenser's poem at Anderson, *British Poets* ii 572-7.

(iv) (Anderson)
Suggested date of reading: 16 March 1802
References: *Grasmere Journals* 79

---

[1] See *William Wordsworth: The Borders of Vision* (1982), p. 390.

'After dinner I read him to sleep - I read Spenser while he leaned upon my shoulder' (DW's journal, 16 March 1802).

(v) *Prothalamion: or, a spousal verse* (Anderson)
Suggested date of reading: 25 April 1802
References: *Grasmere Journals* 91
'Read the Prothalamium of Spenser - walked backwards & forwards' (DW's journal, 25 April 1802). DW's source was Anderson, *British Poets* ii 514-16.

(vi) *Colin Clout's Come Home Again* (Anderson)
Suggested date of reading: May/June 1802
References: *PW* iii 424; Cornell *Poems 1800-7* 411
De Selincourt and Curtis note several echoes of Spenser's poem in W's *The world is too much with us*, composed between 21 May 1802 and 6 March 1804. This sonnet was almost certainly composed in May, possibly June, 1802, and one may conjecture that W was reading *Colin Clout* at that time.

The poem is alluded to by C in a letter of 21 Oct. 1801, and one would expect W to have read it by then (Griggs ii 768-9).

(vii) *Prosopopoia: or, Mother Hubberd's Tale* (Anderson)
Suggested date of reading: 4 June 1802
References: *Grasmere Journals* 105
'I read Mother Hubbard's tale before I went to bed' (DW's journals, 4 June 1802). Pamela Woof identifies this reference to Spenser's *Prosopopoia: or Mother Hubberd's Tale*, which DW would have read in Anderson, *British Poets* ii 501-13 (*Grasmere Journals* 235). The poem is called *Mother Hubberd's Tale* on Anderson's running heads.

(viii) *Faerie Queene* Canto I (Anderson)
Suggested date of reading: 16 June 1802
References: *Grasmere Journals* 110
'I read the first Canto of the fairy Queen to William. William went to bed immediately' (DW's journal, 16 June 1802). Reed suggests that this reading influenced lines written for the *Ode* on 17 June (Reed ii 181n55).

(ix) (Anderson)
Suggested date of reading: 1 July 1802
References: *Grasmere Journals* 117
'William read Spenser & I read "As you like it"' (DW's journal, 1 July 1802).

(x) *View of the Present State of Ireland*
Suggested date of reading: by Nov. 1802
References: *EY* 378-9

In Nov. 1802 W advised JW to buy an edition of Spenser containing his *View of the Present State of Ireland*; as Shaver observes, the first such edition was that of 1679. Although this is W's first mention of this work, he had presumably read it before Nov. 1802. All the same, he had apparently not acquired his own copy even by 13 Oct. 1804, when Lamb wrote to him, apparently responding to a request for one: 'The works on Ireland I will enquire after, but I fear, Spenser's is not to be had apart from his poems; I never saw it' (Marrs ii 147). Lamb finally ran down a copy of 'a Folio which luckily contains besides all the Poems, The View of the State of Ireland, which is difficult to meet with' (Marrs ii 204). This was sent to Grasmere on 1 Feb. 1806, and would have been at DC within the week.

(xi) *Virgil's Gnat* (Anderson)
Suggested date of reading: between 21 May 1802 and 6 March 1804
References: Cornell *Poems 1800-7* 547
The quotation in W's *Pelion and Ossa flourish side by side* 4-5 comes from *Virgil's Gnat*. W read it at Anderson, *British Poets* ii 437-43.

(xii) *The Shepherd's Calendar* (Anderson)
Suggested date of reading: by 1804
References: OET *Prel.* 578
De Selincourt notes that *Thirteen-Book Prelude* viii 191-203 is based on *The Shepherd's Calendar*, and quotes the relevant passages.

(xiii) *The Works of Edmund Spenser*, ed. Henry John Todd (8 vols., 1805)
Suggested date of reading: shortly before 7 Nov. 1805
References: *EY* 641
'Like you, I had been sadly disappointed with Todd's Spencer', W told Scott on 7 Nov. 1805. He must have seen this new edn some time between mid-Aug., when he seems last to have seen Scott (Reed ii 298), and 7 Nov. He did not, apparently, acquire his own copy. Whose did he see? In Sept. 1805 Southey told C. W. Williams Wynn: 'Todds Spenser is on my reviewing shelf. You know I had proposed to edit Spenser myself - what a different book should I have made!' (Curry i 401). Southey reviewed Todd's edn in the *Annual Review* 4 (1805) 544-55, and W probably saw his copy during Sept. or Oct. 1805; it was an important source for the *White Doe* (see Comparetti 110-13).

(xiv) *Works*
Suggested date of reading: mid-Feb. 1806 onwards
References: Marrs ii 204-6
W does not seem to have owned a copy of Spenser's *Works* (besides Anderson) prior to being sent one by Lamb on 1 Feb. 1806. It must have been either a copy of the 1679 folio or a subsequent edn; it contained *View of the Present State of Ireland*, and was purchased second-hand for 14*s*. W would have received it by mid-Feb. (Reed ii 314).

(xv) *Muiopotmos: or, the fate of the butterfly*
Suggested date of reading: between Sept. 1811 and Nov. 1812
References: *Prose Works* ii 291
W quotes *Muiopotmos* 209-16 in his *Unpublished Tour*, composed between Sept. 1811 and Nov. 1812 - lines that influenced other works, as Owen and Smyser note (*Prose Works* ii 436).

(xvi) *The Works of Mr Edmund Spenser. In Six Volumes. Publish'd by Mr Hughes* (6 vols., 1715)
Suggested date of reading: by Jan. 1815
References: *Prose Works* iii 71, 93
W quotes from Hughes' dedication of Spenser's *Works* to Lord Somers in his *Essay, Supplementary to the Preface*.

(xvii) *Faerie Queene*
Suggested date of reading: 18 Feb. 1815
References: *MY* ii 204; Comparetti 108-9
'It is 11 oclock William has been reading the Fairy Queen', DW told SH on 18 Feb. 1815 (*MY* ii 204). This reading may have been undertaken in preparation for the dedicatory poem to the *White Doe* (see next note).

(xviii) *Faerie Queene*
Suggested date of reading: shortly before 20 April 1815
References: Cornell *White Doe* 78-80; Comparetti 108-9
So numerous are the references to Spenser's poem in the dedicatory poem to the *White Doe* that is likely that W reread it shortly before 20 April 1815, when it was composed.

370. Staël-Holstein, Anne Louise Germaine de, Baroness, *A Treatise on Ancient and Modern Literature . . . from the French of the Baroness Stael de Holstein* **(2 vols., 1803)**
Suggested date of reading: by Jan. 1815
References: *Prose Works* iii 78, 99-100
W's reference to Madame de Staël in his *Essay, Supplementary to the Preface* indicates that he had seen her *Treatise* by Jan. 1815. He owned a copy of her *Corinne* (Shaver 245), but not of the *Treatise*. The most likely source seems to be Southey, who came to know de Staël when she visited England in late 1813; it was at that time that he acquired his signed copy of *De l'Allemagne* (3 vols., 1813) (Warter ii 340; Southey *SC* 2731).

371. Stanhope, Philip Dormer, 4th Earl of Chesterfield, *Advice to a Lady in Autumn*
Suggested date of reading: by Feb. 1815
References: *Prose Works* iii 37, 51

W quotes from Chesterfield's poem in his Preface to *Poems* (1815). He seems not to have owned copies of his books, but may have consulted those in Southey's library (Southey *SC* 649, 650). In 1846 W 'said that since Johnson no writer had done so much to vitiate the English language. He considers Lord Chesterfield the last good English writer before Johnson' (Grosart iii 452).

372. Steele, Sir Richard, and Joseph Addison, *The Tatler. By Isaac Bickerstaff* (4 vols., 1710-11)
Suggested date of reading: 7 June 1812 onwards
References: *Supp.* 122; Shaver 246
On 7-8 June 1812 W wrote to MW from London: 'I purchased on Saturday the Tatler, unbound a neat Copy for 4.6 This is surely very reasonable, and we do not possess the Book' (*Supp.* 122). He must have read *The Tatler* before this, having probably seen the copies retained by Charles Lloyd at Old Brathay (*MY* i 292).

373. Stephen, James, *The Crisis of the Sugar Colonies; or, An Inquiry into the Objects and Probable Effects of the French Expedition to the West Indies; and Their Connection with the Colonial Interests of the British Empire* (1802)
Suggested date of reading: by 19 Aug. 1803
References: *DWJ* i 204; Shaver 247
'Coleridge gave our host a pamphlet, "the Crisis of the Sugar Colonies", he was well acquainted with Burns's Poems', DW recorded in her journal of the Scottish tour of 1803 (DC MS 55, 9v). The turnpike man to whom the copy of Stephen was given had shown kindness to C and the Wordsworths on 19 Aug. as they journeyed through Scotland. Why C was carrying it is in itself an interesting question; it might have only incidental relevance to W's reading were it not for the fact that another copy was retained at Rydal Mount (Shaver 247). It can be assumed to have come into W's possession by 19 Aug. 1803. C no doubt felt free to give his away because he knew that W's would be available to him. Southey too had read it by July 1806 (Curry i 426); in later years W met its author (*LY* ii 379 and n1).

374. Sterne, Laurence, *The Life and Opinions of Tristram Shandy, Gentleman* [1760]
Suggested date of reading: c. Jan. 1806
References: *PW* ii 498-9
De Selincourt suggests that W had a passage from *Tristram Shandy* 'at the back of his mind' as he composed *Benjamin the Waggoner* in Jan. 1806. Perhaps he had recently reread Sterne's novel.

375. Stoddart, John
(i) *Remarks on local manners and scenery in Scotland* (2 vols., Edinburgh and London, 1801)

Suggested date of reading: probably mid- to late 1801
References: Cornell *13-Book Prelude* 17n8
W was a friend of the author, who visited DC in Oct. and Nov. 1800 (Reed ii 96-7, 97-8), and probably saw the *Remarks* shortly after publication (July 1801 in Edinburgh and 3 Sept. in London) - certainly by Sept. or Oct. 1801. As Stoddart is known to have presented a copy to C,[1] it would be strange had he not also presented one to W. Lamb seems to have reviewed it in *The Albion*, 9 July 1801 (see Winifred Courtney, *Young Charles Lamb 1775-1802* [1982], p. 318).

According to Reed, the *Remarks* 'certainly suggested' *Prelude* i 214-20, which nominate William Wallace as a fit subject for heroic verse; DW included a quotation from Stoddart in an early version of her 1803 Scottish journal (*MY* i 11 and n2).

(ii) review of *Lyrical Ballads* (1800), *British Critic* 17 (Feb. 1801) 125-31
Suggested date of reading: c. 5 March 1801
References: Reed ii 114n9
Reed suggests that Stoddart's review arrived at DC c. 5 March 1801 and was sent on to C at Keswick. JW, meeting regularly with Stoddart in London, had seen it by 26 Feb., when he told MH that it was 'too indiscriminately flattering' (Ketcham 95).

376. Stolberg, Friedrich Leopold, Graf zu, *On a Cataract*, tr. S. T. Coleridge
Suggested date of reading: between 1799 and 1801
References: see note
C purchased his copy of *Gedichte der Brüder Christian und Friedrich Leopold Grafen zu Stolberg*, ed. Heinrich Christian Boie (Leipzig, 1779) (*Notebooks* i 340), on 22 Sept. 1798 - which provides the *terminus a quo* for a dating of his rendering of Stolberg's *On a Cataract* (dated '?1799' by EHC). The *terminus ad quem* is less easily determinable, though a reasonable guess would be c. 1801, when he was preoccupied with Stolberg's Platonism, and sending translations from his works to Southey (*Notebooks* i 928; Griggs ii 769). That W saw *On a Cataract* shortly after composition is implied by his defence of C from the charge of plagiarism in March 1840: 'As to the passage from Stolberg, it was begun, as I know, as a translation, and amplified. Coleridge took incredible pains with the execution, and has greatly excelled the original; but why he did not in this case also speak the plain truth I am quite at a loss to conceive' (*LY* iv 50). It is likely that W also saw C's other renderings of Stolberg: *Tell's Birth-Place*, *The British Stripling's War-Song*, and *Hymn to the Earth*.

377. Sylvester, Joshua
(i) *O Holy Peace*
Suggested date of reading: 2 Oct. 1801 onwards

---

[1] Present location not known; see Whalley PhD ii 517.

References: Reed ii 705-6

> O holy peace by thee are only found
> The passing joys that every where abound
>
> Sylvester

C's two-line extract from Sylvester in the Wordsworth Commonplace Book (DC MS 26, 31r) is judged by Reed to date from early 1804, by 25 March. W would have known Sylvester's work by then; see *WR* 2.

(ii) works
Suggested date of reading: by 17 Sept. 1814
References: *MY* ii 153
In his letter to Robert Anderson of 17 Sept. 1814, W suggests that an enlarged edn of Anderson's *British Poets* should include Sylvester.

378. Symmons, Dr Charles, *Life of Milton* in Milton, *The Prose Works of John Milton; with a life of the author, interspersed with translations and critical remarks*, by C. Symmons (7 vols., 1806)
Suggested date of reading: between 4 Nov. 1807 and 17 April 1808
References: *MY* i 175, 213; Reed i 371n2
W had not seen Symmons' *Life* on 4 Nov. 1807, but reported to Wrangham that he had done so on 17 April 1808: 'on some future occasion I will tell you what I think of it' (*MY* i 213). The absence of Symmons from any of the Rydal Mount catalogues suggests to me that Wrangham lent his copy to W. At any rate, it was the inspiration for a *Sonnet on Milton* in April 1808 (Cornell *Poems 1807-20* 46, 497).

379. Sympson, Joseph, *Science Revived; or The Vision of Alfred: A Poem in Eight Books* (1802)
Suggested date of reading: 25 April 1802 onwards
References: *Grasmere Journals* 91; Shaver 251
'Mr S sent us some quills by Molly Ashburner & his Brother's book' (DW's journal, 25 April 1802). It is likely that W had known Sympson for some time as both were alumni of Hawkshead Grammar School. In later years W recalled that Sympson 'was a native of Cumberland, and was educated in the vale of Grasmere, and at Hawkshead school. His poems are little known, but they contain passages of splendid description; and the versification of his "Vision of Alfred" is harmonious and animated. . . . He was a man of ardent feeling, and his faculties of mind, particularly his memory, were extraordinary' (*Memoirs* i 177n1). W borrowed from Sympson in the Duddon sonnets. Shaver appears to suggest that W's copy is now in the Boston Athenæum; this is not in fact the case, for the copy in that Library has been there since at least 1810, when it appeared in the first printed catalogue.

380. Tasso, Torquato, *Godfrey of Bulloigne; or, the recoverie of Jerusalem,* **tr. Edward Fairfax [1600]**
Suggested date of reading: by 17 Sept. 1814
References: *MY* ii 154
In his letter to Robert Anderson of 17 Sept. 1814, W suggests that an enlarged edn of Anderson's *British Poets* should include 'Fairfax's Tasso'. W had first read Tasso at Cambridge (*WR* 134) and it is likely that he had first encountered Fairfax's translation then. He may by 1814 have acquired the copies (3rd edn, 1687; 4th edn, 1749) listed Shaver 305, 253. W seems also to have owned a copy of the 1600 first edn of Fairfax's translation: it is not listed by Shaver, but is listed by Quaritch, who describes it as follows: 'the title soiled and mounted, and the three preliminary leaves wanting, with the autograph of WORDSWORTH'.[1]

381. Taylor, Jeremy
(i) works
Suggested date of reading: by 28 March 1809
References: see note
On 28 March 1809, Farington recorded in his diary that Lady Beaumont had told him that W and C 'highly approve the writings of Dr. *Jeremiah Taylor,* who had also the feelings of a Poet, and of Cowley.' It may be assumed that W had by that date read some work or works of Taylor.

(ii) *A Dissuasive from Popery to the People of Ireland* **(3rd edn, 1664)**
Suggested date of reading: by 13 May 1812
References: Morley i 83
On 13 May 1812 Robinson recorded in his diary: 'William Wordsworth was more afraid of the liberal than the methodistic party on the bench of bishops, and read a beautiful passage from Jeremy Taylor on the progress of religious dissensions from his *Dissuasive against Popery*' (Morley i 83). This suggests that W had acquired his copy of the *Dissuasive* by 13 May 1812. He had probably known it for some time, as it was a favourite of C's.[2] His copy was at Rydal Mount, along with C's (Shaver 254, 355); it is now in the British Library (3936.b.36). It bears W's ownership inscription on the title-page, 'W. Wordsworth', underneath which he has written 'Wm Wordsworth'. There are no other markings in the book.

(iii) *Holy Living* **and** *Holy Dying* **(23rd edn, 1719)**
Suggested date of reading: by May 1814
References: *PW* v 459; Shaver 254

---

[1] *A General Catalogue of Books* (7 vols., 1887-92), iv 2272.
[2] C quoted part of it in *The Friend* (*CC Friend* i 283-7).

W misquotes Taylor's *Holy Dying* at *Excursion* vi 532-3; it is further discussed by Stein 158. By the time he composed these lines W may have acquired the copies of *Holy Living* and *Holy Dying* listed by the Shavers. He refers to 'Bishop Taylor's Works' in his Preface to *Poems* (1815) (*Prose Works* iii 37).

382. Taylor, William, of Norwich
(i) *Bluebeard*, **in** *The Iris*
Suggested date of reading: by 9 March 1811
References: *MY* i 469
On 9 March 1811 W told Godwin: 'Wm. Taylor of Norwich took the trouble of versifying Blue Beard some years ago' (*MY* i 469). David Chandler tells me that

> W would have seen Taylor's translation in *The Iris*, a Norwich weekly newspaper that Taylor edited and wrote extensively for between 1803 and 1804. He probably saw *The Iris* through Southey, Taylor's friend, who received free copies. Southey had a high opinion of the paper and helped Taylor obtain subscriptions; it is therefore possible that he showed it to W as a potential subscriber. *Bluebeard* first appeared in the issue of 17 March 1804. Just three weeks later a revised edn appeared in the same paper, 'Conformably to the wish of several correspondents'.[1] The poem was later republished in the *Monthly Magazine* 38 (1814). It does not appear to have been a translation but rather a versification of a traditional folk tale. Taylor's *Cinderilla, or the Little Glass Slippers* had appeared in *The Iris* for 21 Jan. 1804 and his friend Frank Sayers had published comparable versifications of folk tales in his *Nugae Poeticae* (Norwich, 1803).

(ii) *English Synonyms Discriminated* **(1813)**
Suggested date of reading: by Feb. 1815
References: *Prose Works* iii 29-30, 41-2
W quotes and comments from this volume in his *Preface* (1815), composed by Feb. 1815.

383. Temple, Laura Sophia, *Poems* **(1805)**
Suggested date of reading: by 28 Sept. 1806
References: *MY* i 81; Jackson 346-7
'The Verses you pointed out from Laura Sophia Temple did her considerable credit', W wrote to Josiah Wade on 28 Sept. 1806. It is not clear where W saw these verses; it is likely that they were reprinted from her *Poems* (1805) in a periodical or newspaper, perhaps Wade's own *Mercantile Gazette*, which the Wordsworths were regularly sent (see note 280).

---

[1] On 27 March 1804, Taylor wrote to Southey, 'Why did you not tell me what you thought of Bluebeard in the "Iris"? a little detailed abuse would have helped me to mend the second edition' (Robberds i 491). Having received the 'second edition', Southey wrote back with some surprise on 8 April, 'I had no suspicion that you designed to reprint it in the "Iris"' (Robberds i 493).

384. *The Cabinet* 3 (April 1808) 249-52, review of *Poems, in Two Volumes* (1807)
Suggested date of reading: by 21 May 1807
References: *MY* i 145

On 21 May 1807 W wrote to Lady Beaumont: 'Though I am to see you so soon I cannot but write a word or two, to thank you for the interest you take in my Poems as evinced by your solicitude about their immediate reception' (*MY* i 145). This would suggest that he had by that date seen either or both of the two reviews of *Poems, in Two Volumes* that had thus far been published: (i) *The Cabinet* 3 (April 1808) 249-52; (ii) *British Critic* 33 (March 1809) 298-9. Lady Beaumont had cause to fret about W's feelings regarding these reviews. Both are scathingly critical, *The Cabinet* taking the view that in *Poems* W's 'fancy frequently degenerates into conceit, his feeling into puerile affectation, his sublimity into bombast, and his originality of expression into harshness and obscurity'.

In his letter to Lady Beaumont, W goes on to remark: 'Leaving these, I was going to say a word to such Readers as Mr. Rogers. Such! - how would he be offended if he knew I considered him only as a representative of a class, and not as unique! "Pity," says Mr. R., "that so many trifling things should be admitted to obstruct the view of those that have merit"' (*MY* i 146-7). Rogers' criticisms were not in print: they were presumably in the first place verbal, and reported by Lady Beaumont in her previous letter to W. It is highly unlikely, given the cordial acquaintance between Rogers and W by 1807, that the elder poet would have penned either of the hostile reviews of *Poems* in print by 21 May. Even so, it is intriguing that the word 'trifling', which Rogers uses, appears also in the review in *The Cabinet*: perhaps the reviewer had also heard his criticisms.

385. *The Courier*
(i)
Suggested date of reading: 1804-18
References: see note

C contributed to the *Courier* from 1804 to 1818. W can be presumed to have seen some of his articles published prior to 1808.

(ii)
Suggested date of reading: 1808-9
References: see note

The *Courier* was W's main source for information relating to the Convention of Cintra, news of which was reported on 16 Sept. 1808; Owen and Smyser note a number of allusions to the *Courier*'s reports in W's pamphlet (*Prose Works* i 372-415).

W read the *Courier* regularly during these years, and seems on occasion to have been sent copies by its editor; on 4 June 1809, he told Stuart: 'Many thanks for the Newspaper' (*MY* i 354). W felt particularly compelled by current affairs at this period, as much as he had during his early youth. In May 1809 he even decided 'to write upon publick affairs in the *Courier*, or some other newspaper, for the sake of getting money' (*MY* i 325).

It should be noted that W probably did not see the *Courier* on a daily basis at any point at this time: in a letter to Stuart of 9 Oct. 1809, C mentions the 'circuitous post', and reports that he saw the *Courier* 'only very irregularly' (Griggs iii 231).

(iii) 12 May 1808
Suggested date of reading: c. 12 May 1808
References: *Prose Works* i 401
W's mention in the *Convention of Cintra* of the sword of Francis I suggests that he may have seen the *Courier* of this date.

(iv) 1 July 1808
Suggested date of reading: c. 1 July 1808
References: *Prose Works* i 378
W's account of the address from the Council of Leon in the *Convention of Cintra* is taken from the *Courier* of 1 July 1808.

(v) 4 July 1808
Suggested date of reading: c. 4 July 1808
References: *Prose Works* i 375, 378
W's reference to 'that inestimable paper entitled "PRECAUTIONS"' in his *Convention of Cintra* (*Prose Works* i 231) indicates, as Owen and Smyser note, that he had seen the *Courier* for 4 July 1808. This part of the *Convention* was composed between mid-Nov. and mid-Dec. 1808.

(vi) 8 July 1808
Suggested date of reading: c. 8 July 1808
References: *Prose Works* i 376, 378, 395
In his *Convention of Cintra* W apparently quoted the declaration of war by the Spanish Junta from the text given in the *Courier* of 8 July 1808.

(vii) 12 July 1808
Suggested date of reading: c. 12 July 1808
References: *Prose Works* i 378, 395
W's *Convention of Cintra* quotes the address of the Junta of Seville from the *Courier* of 12 July 1808.

(viii) 16 July 1808
Suggested date of reading: c. 16 July 1808
References: *Prose Works* i 377
W's *Convention of Cintra* quotes Morla's address to the citizens of Cadiz from the *Courier* of 16 July 1808.

(ix) 9 Aug. 1808
Suggested date of reading: c. 9 Aug. 1808
References: *Prose Works* i 375
W's paraphrase of Joachim Blake's letter in his *Convention of Cintra* suggests that he saw the text published in the *Courier* for 9 Aug. 1808.

(x) 11 Aug. 1808
Suggested date of reading: c. 11 Aug. 1808
References: *Prose Works* i 376, 384
In his *Convention of Cintra*, W refers the reader to the manifesto of the Court of Portugal, as reproduced in the *Courier* for 11 Aug. 1808.

(xi) 3 Sept. 1808
Suggested date of reading: c. 3 Sept. 1808
References: *Prose Works* i 378
W summarizes and quotes Wellesley's dispatches in his *Convention of Cintra* from the text given in the *Courier* for 3 Sept. 1808. As Owen and Smyser suggest, his information about the 'official communication' may have been taken from the *Courier* for 5 Sept.

(xii) 12 Sept. 1808
Suggested date of reading: c. 12 Sept. 1808
References: *Prose Works* i 385, 388
W's account of Morla's letters in his *Convention of Cintra* draws on the report in the *Courier* of this date.

(xiii) 15 Sept. 1808
Suggested date of reading: c. 15 Sept. 1808
References: *Prose Works* i 377
W's *Convention of Cintra* quotes the manifesto of the Junta of Seville from the *Courier* of 15 Sept. 1808.

(xiv) 16 Sept. 1808
Suggested date of reading: c. 16 Sept. 1808
References: *Prose Works* i 380, 381, 384
It is likely that W saw the *Courier*'s account of the firing of the Park and Tower guns, an event mentioned in his *Convention of Cintra*. His account of the Russian fleet was probably also taken from the *Courier* of this date.

(xv) 17 Sept. 1808
Suggested date of reading: c. 17 Sept. 1808
References: *Prose Works* i 381, 385
W's analysis of the expediency of expelling the French from Portugal in his *Convention of Cintra* is similar to that given in the *Courier* for this date.

(xvi) 22 Sept. 1808
Suggested date of reading: c. 22 Sept. 1808
References: *Prose Works* i 379, 386
Owen and Smyser compare a passage in W's *Convention of Cintra* with editorial comments in the *Courier* for 22 and 27 Sept.

(xvii) 26 Sept. 1808
Suggested date of reading: c. 26 Sept. 1808
References: *Prose Works* i 387, 388
In the *Convention of Cintra*, W refers to the protest against the treaty by the Portuguese, presumably because he had read the *Courier* of this date.

(xviii) 27 Sept. 1808
Suggested date of reading: c. 27 Sept. 1808
References: *Prose Works* i 379
See note for 22 Sept. 1808.

(xix) 1 Oct. 1808
Suggested date of reading: c. 1 Oct. 1808
References: *Prose Works* i 377
W's allusion in his *Convention of Cintra* to Massaredo's address to the Biscayans indicates an acquaintance with the text in the *Courier* of 1 Oct. 1808.

(xx) 10 Oct. 1808
Suggested date of reading: c. 10 Oct. 1808
References: *Prose Works* i 376, 377
In his *Convention of Cintra*, W quotes from Junot's bulletins as reprinted in the *Courier* for 10 Oct. 1808 - his source also for the death toll of 13,000 at the sacking of Beia.

(xxi) 12 Nov. 1808
Suggested date of reading: shortly after 12 Nov. 1808
References: *MY* i 299; *Prose Works* i 409-10
Instructing De Quincey in March 1809 as to the text of *The Convention of Cintra*, W said that he would like to quote directly from 'the blasphemous address to Buonaparte made by some Italian deputies, which you remember we read at Grasmere some time ago, and his answer. . . . If, without much trouble, you could find it in the file of *Couriers* at the office, I should exceedingly like such parts as you might approve of, both of address and answer, to be inserted in the Appendix' (*MY* i 299-300). As Reed notes, this shows that W and De Quincey read the *Courier* for 12 Nov. 1808 (Reed ii 403).

(xxii) 15 Nov. 1808
Suggested date of reading: c. 15 Nov. 1808
References: *Prose Works* i 392, 407

W's phrasing in the *Convention of Cintra* appears to echo the *Courier* of this date.

(xxiii) 18 Nov. 1808
Suggested date of reading: c. 18 Nov. 1808
References: *Prose Works* i 379, 382, 389
W's reference to Wellesley's testimony to the Board of Inquiry in his *Convention of Cintra* is probably dependent on the account given in the *Courier* for 18 Nov. 1808.

(xxiv) 21 Nov. 1808
Suggested date of reading: c. 21 Nov. 1808
References: *Prose Works* i 385-6, 387, 395
In the *Convention of Cintra*, W reports the opinions of the Portuguese apparently from the account given in the *Courier* of this date.

(xxv) 22 Nov. 1808
Suggested date of reading: c. 22 Nov. 1808
References: *Prose Works* i 382, 384-5, 387, 399-400
W reports Wellesley's and Dalrymple's testimonies to the Board of Inquiry in his *Convention of Cintra* probably from the account given in this number of the *Courier*.

(xxvi) 25 Nov. 1808
Suggested date of reading: c. 25 Nov. 1808
References: *Prose Works* i 383-4
The *Convention of Cintra* indicates that W may have been aware, from the report in the *Courier* of this date, of Ferguson's testimony to the Board of Inquiry.

(xxvii) 13 Dec. 1808
Suggested date of reading: c. 13 Dec. 1808
References: *Prose Works* i 382
W was aware of Burrard's testimony to the Board of Inquiry in his *Convention of Cintra* probably from the *Courier* of this date.

(xxviii) 15 Dec. 1808
Suggested date of reading: c. 15 Dec. 1808
References: *Prose Works* i 381, 384, 399
W reports Wellesley's examination of Colonel Torrens in his *Convention of Cintra* apparently from the account given in the *Courier* of this date.

(xxix) 27 Dec. 1808, 13 Jan. 1809
Suggested date of reading: Dec. 1808-Jan. 1809
References: see note
Instalments of W's *Convention of Cintra* appeared in the *Courier* on these dates.

(xxx) 3 Jan. 1809
Suggested date of reading: c. 3 Jan. 1809
References: *Prose Works* i 407
As Owen and Smyser note, a summary of the contents of the *Copy of the Proceedings upon the Inquiry relative to the Armistice and Convention, &c. made and concluded in Portugal, in August 1808, between the Commanders of the British and French Armies; - held at the Royal Hospital at Chelsea, on Monday the 14th of November; and continued by Adjournments until the 27th of December 1808. Ordered by the House of Commons, to be printed, 31st January 1809* was published in the *Courier* on 3 Jan. 1809, and read by W. It provided a good deal of the information mentioned in the Appendix to W's *Convention of Cintra*.

(xxxi) 7 Jan. 1809
Suggested date of reading: c. 7 Jan. 1809
References: *Prose Works* i 393, 402
W recounts the story of the boy of Saragossa in the *Convention of Cintra*, probably because he read about it in the *Courier* of this date.

(xxxii) 21 Jan. 1809
Suggested date of reading: c. 21 Jan. 1809
References: *Prose Works* i 391-2
W's *Convention of Cintra* refers to the King's disapproval of the Convention, presumably because he had read about it in the *Courier* of this date.

(xxxiii) 24 March 1809
Suggested date of reading: between 24 and 29 March 1809
References: *MY* i 306-7; *Prose Works* i 410
'I have only seen such of those Letters as appeared in the Courier of Friday last (March 24) they are in number four, and at the end it is said they are to be continued', W wrote to De Quincey on 29 March 1809. The letters justified W's firm opinions about Moore; see *MY* i 306-7.

(xxxiv) 13 April 1809
Suggested date of reading: 18 April 1809
References: *SHL* 19
Writing to Mary Monkhouse from Allan Bank on 19 April 1809, SH remarked that she had seen a churn 'advertized in the Courier yesterday'. She refers to the advertisement on the front page of the *Courier* for 13 April:

> CHURNS. - An important discovery for Farmers. - J. WOODS, of Ormskirk, Lancashire, recommends to their attention his patent Machine for reducing labour in Churning: it is worked by a lever, with weight and a girt, will perform more work with it than two women can execute in the same time without it. - All orders will be immediately

executed, and the Machine sent on receipt of the money, or a respectable reference for payment. He has a considerable number now ready, and the money price is 2l. 2s. 6d.

The advertisement had already appeared in the *Courier* for 5 April, but perhaps SH had not seen that.

(xxxv) May 1809
Suggested date of reading: c. 14 May 1809 onwards
References: Jordan 154
'A long letter - wondrously dull!', De Quincey wrote on his letter to DW of 10 May 1809, 'therefore do not honor it by reading it before the 3 Couriers; or you will be disappointed' (Jordan 154). The three numbers of the *Courier* sent at this time to W would have reached Grasmere by *c*. 14 May.

(xxxvi)
Suggested date of reading: Dec. 1809
References: *MY* i 380
In her letter of 28 Dec. 1809 to Lady Beaumont, DW mentions C's 'series of essays in the Courier, on the Spanish affairs' (*MY* i 380).[1] W can be presumed to have read these, not least because they were written at Allan Bank.

(xxxvii) 7 March to 5 Dec. 1811
Suggested date of reading: March-Dec. 1811
References: *MY* i 494
On 16 June 1811 DW told Catherine Clarkson:

> I am sorry to say (I would not say it but to you) that poor Coleridge's late writings in the Courier have in general evidenced the same sad weakness of moral constitution to which you alluded in your last letter, as tainting his intercourse with his private Friends and his casual acquaintances also. They are as much the work of a party-spirit, as if he were writing for a place - servile adulations of the Wellesleys. I speak of the general character of his paragraphs and short essays. (*MY* i 494)

The Wordsworths were evidently following C's contributions in the *Courier* from 7 March to 5 Dec. 1811 (CC *Essays* ii 109ff). As regards the Duke of Wellington, C wrote of 'the greatness of his Lordship's talents' on 28 May (CC *Essays* ii 173), though this was by no means his only praise for him at this time.

(xxxviii) 16 Nov. 1811
Suggested date of reading: by 20 Nov. 1811
References: *MY* i 494

---

[1] See CC *Essays* ii 37-100.

'Do you see *The Courier* newspaper at Dunmow?' W wrote to Lady Beaumont on 20 Nov. 1811,

> I ask on account of a little poem upon the comet, which I have read in it to-day. Though with several defects, and some feeble and constrained expressions, it has great merit, and is far superior to the run not merely of newspaper but of modern poetry in general. I half suspect it to be Coleridge's, for though it is, in parts, inferior to him, I know of no other writer of the day who can do so well. It consists of five stanzas, in the measure of the *Fairy Queen*. It is to be found in last Saturday's paper, November 16th. If you don't see *The Courier*, we will transcribe it for you. (*MY* i 521)

W refers to *The Comet, 1811*, which indeed appears in the *Courier* for 16 Nov. 1811; it is reproduced on pp. 270-1, below.

At this period De Quincey shared newspapers with the Wordsworths, as is evident from SH's letter to Mary Monkhouse of 3 Dec. 1811: 'Quincey reads the newspapers standing, or rather stooping with Catherine on his back' (*SHL* 37).

(xxxix) 18 Aug. 1814
Suggested date of reading: 21 Aug. 1814
References: Supp. 151; *MY* ii 198-9

MW wrote to DW from Alloa on 23 Aug. 1814: 'I should have told you before that on our return from our walk on Sunday night in Perth, W. put into my hands Wednesday's *Courier* announcing Mr Wordsworth's Poem with the Dedication - We hailed it with great pleasure' (*Supp.* 151). The *Courier* in question must have been that for 18 Aug., which reproduces the dedicatory poem to Lord Lonsdale from *The Excursion*.

Also during this period the Wordsworths were reading C's letters to Mr Justice Fletcher, which appeared in the *Courier* Sept.-Dec.; see note 108(xvi), above.

(xl) 17 Dec. 1814
Suggested date of reading: shortly after 17 Dec. 1814
References: see note

The *Courier* of this date published an extract from *The Excursion*, ii 546-92, under the title, *The Country Funeral*. As a regular reader of the *Courier*, W can be expected to have seen it.

(xli) 12 Jan. 1815
Suggested date of reading: soon after 12 Jan. 1815
References: MY ii 198-9

'I thank you for the notice of the Excursion in *The Courier*', W told Stuart in a letter which the editors of *MY* conjecturally date Jan. or Feb. 1815, 'It will serve the Book, though I owe the Editor a bit of a grudge for having *appeared* to join in, at least to countenance, the vulgar clamour against me; but I forgive him' (*MY* ii 198-9; his italics). In fact it is possible to date the letter more specifically, as W is evidently referring to the review in the *Courier* for Thursday 12 Jan. 1815. He usually saw copies of the *Courier* within days of publication, and may be expected to have written to Stuart soon after reading the review. A more likely date for the letter would be soon after 12 Jan. 1815, and probably not later than 1 Feb.

W's response to the review was justified, as its praise seems to be somewhat barbed. It begins by observing that the lyrical ballads are

> strangely compounded . . . [but] abound in traits of genuine feeling, and afford glimpses of a genius which must delight and astonish, if beheld in its full splendor. We could be content with this nearer view, even if compelled to tolerate those peculiarities which to the eyes of many obscure his excellencies, and in the opinion of some, amount to an intolerable nuisance. For these reasons we were both surprised and gratified on opening the present Volume, to find that this poet, who has been reproached for communing with leech gatherers and beggars, and for moralizing over a spade or a washing-tub, has chosen a subject fit for the grasp of his mighty mind - a theme so elevated as to tempt only the most daring muse that ever soared.

By this time W had probably also seen the notices of *The Excursion* in the *Courier* for 21 Oct. and 17 Dec. 1814 (Reed ii 588).

(xlii)
Suggested date of reading: 1815
References: *MY* ii 229
On 11 April 1815 DW told Catherine Clarkson: 'We had given over taking a Newspaper (except the Courier which came from Keswick) but we could not exist without one sent directly to us' (*MY* ii 229). W's remark to Southey on a Friday evening in March 1815, that 'We shall here have no more news till Sunday evening, it seems long to wait at such a moment' (*MY* ii 216),[1] gives some indication of his interest in current affairs at this period.

386. *The Cruel Mother*
Suggested date of reading: after 28 Jan. 1801
References: Reed ii 704; Cornell *Lyrical Ballads* 352; Woof PhD 245-6
See note 209.

387. *The Cumberland Pacquet, and Ware's Whitehaven Advertiser*, 15 June, 22 June 1802
Suggested date of reading: c. 15, 22 June 1802
References: *EY* 369

---

[1] One reason for his interest at this moment was Napoleon's escape from Elba and return to Paris, March 1815.

The day after the death of the 'bad' Earl of Lonsdale on 24 May 1802, JW informed his brother, RW, that 'Lord Lonsdale is no more improve this Information if you can to your and your Family's advantage' (*EY* 358n2). News spread quickly through the family, and the Wordsworths' claims on the late Earl were the subject of DW and W's letter to RW of 10 June (*EY* 358-61). On 24 June W told RW: 'An advertisement has appeared twice in the Cumberland Pacquet requesting all persons who have any claims on the late Earl of Londsdale to send them in immediately' (*EY* 369). The first appearance of this advertisement was in the *Pacquet* for 15 June:

> The EARL of LONSDALE
> ALL Persons, who have any DEMANDS upon the late EARL of LONSDALE are desired immediately to send an account of the same, to JOHN RICHARDSON, Esq. at LOWTHER HALL, Westmorland.

This issue of the *Pacquet* also contains a report of the Earl's funeral, along with details of his Will and Codicils, including the request that his debts be discharged. The advertisement appeared a second time in the *Pacquet* for 22 June; the Wordsworths can be assumed to have seen both. It was published again on 24 and 29 June, and 6, 13, 20, and 27 July.

388. *The Evening Mail*
Suggested date of reading: c. 3 June 1809 onwards
References: Jordan 189-90
On the back of his letter to the Wordsworths of 25-27 May 1809, De Quincey added: 'I send 2 Nos. of the Evening Mail - 1 containing *one* of the private letters on Ld. Cochrane's affair: - the other the Decree about Saragossa' (Jordan 189-90; his italics). As his letter of 31 May reveals, the parcel did not begin its journey until Tuesday 30 May, and so would have arrived at Allan Bank probably on 3 June.

389. *The Examiner*, 19 March 1809
Suggested date of reading: c. 25 March 1809 onwards
References: Jordan 120
De Quincey told DW on 25 March 1809 that on 20 March he had sent the previous Sunday's *Examiner*. He had doubts about whether it would arrive, and W's replies give no indication either. If they did, W would probably have received them by c. 25 March.

390. *The Globe*
Suggested date of reading: early April 1809
References: Jordan 139; *MY* i 320
On 5 April 1809 De Quincey wrote to DW to say that

I sent (or rather, ordered to be sent) a *Times* of Monday morning last: - did you receive it? - I called the office of the *Times*; and they were all sold; so that I was obliged to leave an order with a newsman to get one and send it off for me. - I sent it on account of the speeches at the Common Hall; and that you might have the pleasure of knowing, as soon as possible, the humiliation and punishment of this infamous tool of the ministry - the ld. Mayor . . . (Jordan 139)

In fact, De Quincey had sent a copy of the *Globe* to the Wordsworths - not the *Times*, and he was corrected by DW (*MY* i 320). The *Globe* was a London evening paper, unobtainable to those elsewhere.

391. Thelwall, John
(i) *Poems Chiefly Written in Retirement* (Hereford, 1801)
Suggested date of reading: by 16 April 1802, probably also 20-25 April 1802
References: EY 349
In a letter of 16 April 1802, W told C, then at Greta Hall: 'I have sent Thels Book, tell me something about it' (*EY* 349). This is a reference to Thelwall's *Poems* (1801), which contains a poem featuring the Wordsworths and C - *Lines written at Bridgewater, in Somersetshire, on the 27th of July, 1797; during a long excursion, in quest of a peaceful retreat*. As C arrived at DC only a few days later, on 20 April, it is likely that he would have brought Thelwall's *Poems* with him, and discussed its contents with W over the following days. This copy may have passed into W's possession, but, if so, it is not listed by Shaver. On 26 April 1805 Thelwall presented a copy of the *Poems* (2nd edn, Hereford, 1805), to Mrs Coleridge, which was retained at Rydal Mount (Shaver 357); it is now at the British Library (11641.cc.28), and bears the following inscription on the verso of the title-page:

> To Sara Coleridge
> a memorial of friendship & esteem for her & her Samuel - from the Author, made happy by her visit at Preston, & the information imparted of the health & prosperity of him the object of conjugal affection to the receiver, & of ardent friendship to the giver of this trifle[1]
> 26 April 1805
> Preston

Perhaps this was the copy W had in mind when, writing to Thelwall's second wife in Nov. 1838, he remarked: 'I possess a small printed volume of his, containing specimens of an Epic Poem and several miscellaneous Pieces, in some of which he laments the death of a Daughter in strains that shew how grievously he suffered by that event, - Mr Coleridge and I were of

---

[1] C was at this time in Malta; in a letter to his wife of 12 Dec. 1804 he had reported improved health (Griggs ii 1157).

opinion that the modulations of his blank verse were superior to those of most writers in that metre' (*LY* iii 641). It is reasonable to suppose that these views were arrived at during C's visit to DC, 20-25 April 1802. The poems on the death of Thelwall's daughter are collected under the title *Paternal Tears*. W praised it again in a letter to Haydon of 20 Jan. 1817, when he observed that 'Thelwall's were the agonies of an unbeliever, and he expressed them vigorously in several copies of harmonious blank verse' (*MY* ii 361).

(ii) *A Letter to Francis Jeffray, Esq., on Certain Calumnies and Misrepresentations in the Edinburgh Review* **(Edinburgh, 1804)**
Suggested date of reading: shortly after 7 Jan. 1804
References: EY 431-2
For a full explanation of the pamphlet skirmish between Thelwall and Jeffrey in early 1804, see *EY* 431n. In mid-Jan. W told Thelwall that 'I received your Pamphlet some time ago' (*EY* 432), presumably meaning at around the time of its publication on 7 Jan. And on 25 Jan. C told Southey that 'Thelwall has had a grand Rumpus with the Ed. Reviewers, written a pamphlet, of which a 1000 copies have already sold & is said to have laid them prostrate & flat' (Griggs ii 1039).

(iii) *The Peripatetic* **(1793)**
Suggested date of reading: before 1815
References: WR 135-6
The evidence for this entry is set forth at *WR* 135-6. It deserves repetition here if, as seems likely, *The Peripatetic* was a central influence on *The Excursion*; see Lyon 35-7. C's copy was retained at Rydal Mount (Shaver 356).

392. *The Muse's Pocket Companion: A Collection of Poems* **(Carlisle, 1785)**
Suggested date of reading: by 15 May 1812, but probably much earlier
References: Supp. 74; Shaver 183
In a letter to DW of 15 May 1812, W described dinner the previous day: 'Lady Crew was also of the party, a person to whom Charles Fox 30 or 40 years ago wrote verses which may be found if you think it worth while to seek for them in that miscellany of Poems printed at Carlisle which I gave Mary' (*Supp.* 74). Landon identifies the 'miscellany' as *The Muse's Pocket Companion* [London, 1782]. An enlarged edn was published in Carlisle in 1785, containing a number of poems known to W during his Hawkshead years: Beattie's *The Minstrel*, Langhorne's *Owen of Carron*, Tickell's *Lucy and Colin*, Mallet's *William and Margaret* and *Edwin and Emma*, Goldsmith's *The Traveller* and *The Deserted Village*, Gray's *Elegy*, as well as Fox's *Verses on Mrs. Crewe* and many other works. All of which suggests to me that W may have acquired his copy of this volume while a schoolboy, possibly from its publisher, J. Milliken, who was based in Carlisle. Further edns, apparently pirated, were published in Dublin in 1787 and 1800.

393. The Philanthropist; or Repository for Hints and Suggestions Calculated to Promote the Happiness and Comfort of Men
Suggested date of reading: by 31 Dec. 1814
References: *MY* ii 181, 230 and n2

On New Year's Eve 1814 W asked Catherine Clarkson to see whether she could get the Quaker periodical, *The Philanthropist*, to give *The Excursion* a favourable review: 'give it what help you can in the Philanthropist or any well circulated Periodical publication to which you may have easy access. I mentioned the Philanthropist because it circulates a good deal among Quakers, who are wealthy and fond of *instructive* Books' (*MY* ii 181). C, too, had sought Quaker support during production of *The Friend* for similar reasons.[1] And on 11 April 1815, DW wrote to Catherine Clarkson: 'Your Receipt for a Criticism in the Philanthropist is excellent and we pray you earnestly to do the work yourself; for there is no-body here who *can* do it' (*MY* ii 230; her italics). W and DW must by 31 Dec. 1814 have seen a copy of the Quaker periodical, edited by William Allen, which ran from 1811 to 1819, and which contains, in vol. 5 (1815), a review of *The Excursion*, pp. 342-63. Southey also seems to have had access to *The Philanthropist* (*Life of Bell* ii 655).

394. The Statesman
(i) 9 March 1809
Suggested date of reading: *c.* 11 March 1809 onwards
References: Jordan 108

On 11 March 1809 De Quincey wrote to DW: 'On Thursday night I sent you down an Eveng. paper (The Statesman) - which I hope you received: - I sent it not on acct. of the Debates - but of Saragossa' (Jordan 108). De Quincey was writing on the following Saturday, so that it is possible that the Wordsworths received the copy of the *Statesman* describing the siege of Saragossa either on 11 March or thereabouts. The information contained in the *Statesman* (edited at this time by John Hunt) helped inspire W's *Hail Zaragoza! If with unwet eye* and *1810*, composed within days.

(ii) 20 March 1809
Suggested date of reading: *c.* 25 March 1809 onwards
References: Jordan 120

De Quincey sent a copy of the *Statesman* for 20 March 1809 to Allan Bank on that date (Jordan 120). He had doubts about whether it reached the Wordsworths, and no indication is offered in W's extant replies as to whether it arrived. Had it done so, W would have received it probably by *c.* 25 March.

---

[1] See Deirdre Coleman, *Coleridge and The Friend (1809-10)* (Oxford, 1988), chapter 5.

395. *The Times*

(i) 29 June 1808
Suggested date of reading: c. early July 1808
References: *Prose Works* i 376
As Owen and Smyser point out, W quotes the *Times* report of the Proclamation of the Council General of the Principality of Asturias almost verbatim in the *Convention of Cintra*.

(ii) 30 June 1808
Suggested date of reading: c. early July 1808
References: *Prose Works* i 377, 378
The *Times* of 30 June 1808 was apparently a source for the *Convention of Cintra*. As Owen and Smyser point out, it was also the basis for the opening lines of W's *Indignation of a High-Minded Spaniard 1810* (see Cornell *Poems 1807-20* 72).

(iii) 4 Aug. 1808
Suggested date of reading: c. early Aug. 1808
References: *Prose Works* i 378
W quotes this edn of the *Times* almost verbatim in the *Convention of Cintra*.

(iv) 30 Aug. 1808
Suggested date of reading: c. early Sept. 1808
References: *Prose Works* i 377
The *Times* of 30 Aug. 1808 provided an important quotation for use in W's *Convention of Cintra*.

(v) 3 Sept. 1808
Suggested date of reading: c. early Sept. 1808
References: *Prose Works* i 378-9
W probably quotes the wording of the British proclamation to the Portuguese from the report in the *Times* of 3 Sept. 1808.

(vi) 21 Sept. 1808
Suggested date of reading: c. 21 Sept. 1808
References: *Prose Works* i 386
Owen and Smyser suggest that W's *Convention of Cintra* may have been influenced by the *Times* for 21 Sept. 1808.

(vii) 14 Oct. 1808
Suggested date of reading: c. 14 Oct. 1808
References: *Prose Works* i 391
Owen and Smyser suggest that W's *Convention of Cintra* may have been influenced by the *Times* for 14 Oct. 1808.

Wordsworth's reading 1800-1815

(viii) 20 Oct. 1808
Suggested date of reading: c. 20 Oct. 1808
References: *Prose Works* i 390
Owen and Smyser suggest that W's *Convention of Cintra* may have been influenced by the *Times* for 20 Oct. 1808.

(ix) 25 March 1809
Suggested date of reading: c. 25 March 1809
References: *Prose Works* i 413
Did W ever see Sir John Moore's letters in the *Times* for 25 March 1809? By 29 March he had read those published in the *Courier* on 24 March, after Mr Crump mentioned them to him; in turn, he suggested to De Quincey that he compose an appendix for the *Convention of Cintra* in which he could 'give a review of these Letters' (*MY* i 306). By 7 April W had still not seen all of Moore's letters, and told De Quincey that he was 'very sorry that, not having the whole of this correspondence, I cannot write the note on Moore's representation myself' (*MY* i 318). However, by the time he wrote to De Quincey on 24 May, W had seen 'his last Letter' (*MY* i 342).

(x) 13 April 1809
Suggested date of reading: c. 17 April 1809
References: Jordan 141-2
On 15 April 1809 De Quincey wrote to W to tell him that he 'procured from a waiter of a coffee-house the *Times* of Thursday morning. . . . I sent it off last night' (Jordan 141-2). This probably arrived at Allan Bank c. 17 April.

(xi) 30 May 1809
Suggested date of reading: c. 5 June 1809 onwards
References: Jordan 201-2
In his letter to the Wordsworths of 31 May 1809, De Quincey writes: 'I had almost forgotten to mention that I send you a copy of the *Times* of yesterday on account of the German's paper about Schill' (Jordan 201-2). If the letter and newspaper travelled up on Thursday, they can be expected to have arrived in Grasmere probably by the following Monday, 5 June. After this date W may also have had access to Southey's copies. From Oct. 1809 onwards Southey was sent *The Times* to help him research his accounts of Spanish affairs for the Edinburgh *Annual Register* (Curry i 518; see also *Letters from the Lake Poets to Daniel Stuart*, ed. Mary Stuart [1889], pp. 411-12).

396. *The Vision of the Brothers* in MS
Suggested date of reading: by 4 Jan. 1810
References: *MY* i 384

This poem, along with some 'stanzas', was sent to W by John Miller; its unidentified author was 'a young man' of Miller's acquaintance. W gave a generous account of it, concluding that 'both the Poems do their author great credit' (*MY* i 384). No more is known of these works.

397. Thiébault, Dieudonné, *Original Anecdotes of Frederick II, King of Prussia, and of his family, his court, his ministers, his academies, and his literary friends* (**2 vols., 1805**)
Suggested date of reading: c. 7 Feb. 1807 onwards
References: *MY* i 133-4
This volume was part of a consignment sent by the Beaumonts to the Wordsworths in early Feb. 1807, then residing at Coleorton. On 15 Feb. 1807 DW told Lady Beaumont:

> I have not quite finished the anecdotes of Frederick which I find exceedingly amusing; and instructive also, as giving a lively portrait of the hard-heartedness and selfishness, and servility of the Courtiers of a tyrant, and of the unsatisfactoriness of such a life.
>
> (*MY* i 133-4)

Perhaps the Wordsworths left this volume behind for the Beaumonts, as it seems not to have been at Rydal Mount. Southey reviewed it in the *Annual Review* 4 (1805) 488-95.

398. Thomson, James
(i) *The Castle of Indolence*
Suggested date of reading: c. 9 May 1802
References: Grasmere Journals 98
DW records that work on *Stanzas Written in My Pocket-Copy of Thomson's 'Castle of Indolence'* began 9 May and continued through to 11 May. It is likely that W reread Thomson's poem at around this time. MH had been reading Thomson, perhaps from the same volume, on 15 Nov. 1801 (*Grasmere Journals* 38).

W quotes from *The Castle of Indolence* in a letter to Beaumont of 28 Aug. 1811 (*MY* i 507 and n2).

(ii) *The Castle of Indolence*
Suggested date of reading: 1804
References: Norton *Prel.* 196n1
Norton *Prel.* 196n1 notes an allusion to *The Castle of Indolence* at *Thirteen-Book Prelude* vi 202; the same editors also note a recollection of Thomson's poem at *Thirteen-Book Prelude* iii 543-9 (Norton *Prel.* 118n3). It is likely that W was consulting his copy during work on the *Prelude* in 1804.

(iii) *Hymn on Solitude*
Suggested date of reading: Dec. 1806
References: *MY* i 113

Writing from Coleorton, W quotes eight lines of Thomson's *Hymn* in his letter to Lady Beaumont of Dec. 1806. Presumably Beaumont's library contained a copy of Thomson's *Works* from which he was copying.

(iv) *Winter*
Suggested date of reading: Nov. 1809
References: *Prose Works* ii 398
The source for W's reference to Laplanders in his *Select Views*, composed early Nov. 1809, is a note to Thomson's *Winter*.

(v) *The Seasons* (2nd edn, 1730)
Suggested date of reading: *c*. 1809-11
References: see note
'I have perused the second edition of his Seasons', W says in the *Essay, Supplementary to the Preface*. A copy of the 2nd edn was at Rydal Mount (Shaver 257); according to the auction catalogue it bore the inscription: 'James Ellwood to William Wordsworth' (Wordsworth *SC* 671). Ellwood was the Penrith solicitor consulted by W in 1809-10 (*Supp*. 16; *MY* i 435). As he died in 1811, the copy of the *Seasons* must have been given to W at around this time. In later years W attempted to help Ellwood's widow, Jane, find employment (see *MY* ii 406, 410; *LY* i 20).

(vi) *The Castle of Indolence*
Suggested date of reading: 28 Aug. 1811
References: *MY* i 507
W quotes six lines of Thomson's poem in a letter to Beaumont of 28 Aug. 1811. It is likely that he was quoting from memory, but it is not impossible that a printed text was close at hand, particularly in view of the quotation in the *Unpublished Tour* (see next note).

(vii) *The Castle of Indolence*
Suggested date of reading: between Sept. 1811 and Nov. 1812
References: *Prose Works* ii 296
W quotes *The Castle of Indolence* in his *Unpublished Tour*, composed between Sept. 1811 and Nov. 1812.

(viii) *The Works of James Thomson* (3 vols., 1768)
Suggested date of reading: by Jan. 1815
References: *Prose Works* iii 72-3, 94; Shaver 257
W quotes from Patrick Murdoch's life of Thomson, which appeared in this edn of the *Works*, in his *Essay, Supplementary to the Preface*. A copy of this title was present at Rydal Mount (Shaver 257).

399. Thurlow, Edward Hovell, 2nd Baron, 'a volume of Poems'
Suggested date of reading: by 17 May 1812
References: *Supp.* 83 and n3

W wrote to MW on 17-18 May 1812, reporting one of C's less creditable acts: 'for example Lord Thurlow a young Man lately sent him a volume of Poems which he has published, superbly Bound. The Poems have great merit far beyond any thing usually published. Coleridge never looked into the Book nor took any notice of this mark of attention, of course the Young Lord must be bitterly wounded in mind' (*Supp.* 83). The implication would appear to be that W had read Thurlow's volume while C hadn't. It is not clear which of Thurlow's productions W is referring to; it might be either *Hermilda in Palestine with other poems* (1812) or *Verses Prefixed to the Defence of Poesy* (1812). Lamb may have been another recipient of Thurlow's publications; in 1815 he told W: 'I was lately fatiguing myself with going thro' a volume of fine words by *Ld. Thurlow*, excellent words . . . but what an aching vacuum of matter' (Marrs iii 140; his italics).[1]

400. Tickell, Thomas, *To a Lady Before Marriage* (Anderson)
Suggested date of reading: between Sept. 1811 and Nov. 1812
References: *Prose Works* ii 340-1, 448-9

W quotes Tickell's verses in his *Unpublished Tour*, composed between Sept. 1811 and Nov. 1812. He was probably using the text in Anderson, *British Poets* viii 438-9.

C noted in April 1800: 'Tickell, Auth. of Kensington Garden, born two miles from Cockermouth' (*Notebooks* i 725). Anderson says that Tickell was 'born at Bridekirk, near Carlisle, in 1686' (*British Poets* viii 403); as this entry was made during C's stay at DC, it is possible - indeed likely - that this information was discussed with W. If so, it might be inferred that W, as well as C, had by then read *Kensington-Garden*, probably from Anderson, *British Poets* viii 434-8.

401. Tobin, John, *The Honey Moon: A Comedy in Five Acts* (1805)
Suggested date of reading: c. 1805 onwards
References: Butler *WC* 170; Shaver 306

According to Butler, W's copy is inscribed by the author's brother, James Webbe Tobin - perforce, as it was published posthumously, shortly after the playwright's death on 31 Jan. 1805. John Tobin's theatrical career was blighted by failure, for he submitted no less than thirteen plays to the managers of various theatres before acceptance of *The Honey Moon*. He died seven weeks before it was performed, and did not live to witness its considerable

---

[1] Incidentally, Byron described Thurlow's *Poems on Several Occasions* (1813) as 'damn'd nonsense' (see *On Lord Thurlow's Poems*, *Lord Byron: The Complete Poetical Works*, ed. Jerome J. McGann [7 vols., Oxford, 1980-93], iii 88, 426).

success.¹ In Malta, C did not hear about Tobin's death until 18 April; he wrote a letter of consolation to James Webbe Tobin the following day (Griggs ii 1130-1). It seems likely that W was given the published copy of *The Honey Moon* shortly after publication in 1805.

402. Townley, James, *High Life Below Stairs*
Date of performance: 12 May 1812
References: *Supp.* 67
On 9-13 May 1812, W wrote to MW: 'Miss Lamb looks far better than could be expected and enjoyed herself much at the play; a stupid opera, called "the Devils Bridge," but the Farce, "High Life below Stairs" was very entertaining; it is an excellent Piece' (*Supp.* 67). W had accompanied the Lambs to the double-bill of Arnold's *Devil's Bridge* and Townley's *High Life* at the Lyceum Theatre on the Strand on Tuesday 12 May 1812. *High Life* had been a favourite with audiences since its first performance at Drury Lane in 1759. For more information see note 19.

403. Turberville, George
(i) works, including poems on Russia
Suggested date of reading: probably by late Feb. 1804
References: *MY* ii 152
In his letter to Robert Anderson of 17 Sept. 1814, W suggests that an enlarged edn of Anderson's *British Poets* should include the works of Turberville, including 'what Chalmers has omitted, His letters from Russia which are in Hackluyt' (*MY* ii 152). This confirms that he was aware of the works by Turberville included by Chalmers in his *Works of the English Poets* (1810), and of the verse-letters from Russia in Hakluyt's *Principall Navigations* (a copy of which he had seen by late Feb. 1804; see note 195, above). Hakluyt presents the latter under the heading 'Certaine letters in verse, written by Master George Turbervile out of Moscovia, which went as Secretarie thither with Master Tho. Randolph, her Majesties Ambassadour to the Emperour 1568, to certeine friends of his in London, describing the maners of the Countrey and people'. They are: *To his especiall friend Master Edward Dancie*, *To Spencer*, and *To Parker*.

(ii) works included in Chalmers' *Works of the English Poets* **(1810)**
Suggested date of reading: between 1810 and 17 Sept. 1814
References: *MY* ii 152
See preceding note.

---

¹ It quickly became a staple of the professional and amateur repertoire; John Hamilton Reynolds performed in it in Nov. 1810 (see Joanna Richardson, *Letters from Lambeth* [1981], p. 61).

404. Turner, William, *A Compleat History of the most Remarkable Providences, both of Judgment and Mercy, which have hapned in this present age* **(1697)**
Suggested date of reading: early Dec. 1807 onwards
References: Shaver 261

W's copy is now at Simon Fraser University. One of the front flyleaves contains an inscription by W stating that he bought it at Barnard Castle in 1807 - probably in Dec., on his way to or from Stockton (see Reed ii 369). I am grateful to Mark L. Reed and Jared Curtis for help with this note.

405. Tytler, Henry William
(i) *Extract of a Letter on Literary Subjects, Particularly Poetry, to Eaglesfield Smith, Esq., from Dr. H. W. Tytler*, Scots Magazine **65** (Aug. **1803**) 530-3
Suggested date of reading: by 17 Sept. 1803
References: *EY* 413 and n1

In a letter to Scott of 16 Oct. 1803, W mentions a review soon to be written by Southey: 'By the Bye, he occasionally reviews and he has at present, among other things, a Poem to review of that very Tytler who made the illiberal attack upon him and Coleridge in the Edinburgh Magazine which I showed you at Liswaide, so no mercy for poor Tytler' (*EY* 413). W had evidently read Tytler's *Extract of a Letter*, which appeared in the *Scots Magazine* (formerly the *Edinburgh Magazine*) for Aug. 1803. W and DW arrived at Lasswade on 17 Sept., which provides a terminal date for their reading of Tytler's article. Presumably they had purchased a copy of the *Scots Magazine* some time during the previous day, which they spent in Edinburgh, and where copies would have been easy to come by. Tytler's 'attack' is mild by comparison with what was to come; it consists primarily of the following allusion to one of Southey's best-known poems:

> Southey's Joan of Arc (one of the wonderful productions of imagination, according to the common taste), I have looked into, and always turned from it with disgust; which, I scarcely think, any one, speaking impartially, will say that they have done from even the worst of *my own* writings. (p. 531; his italics)

At the conclusion of the *Letter* Tytler quotes Pope, *Essay on Criticism* 195-200, and comments: 'When Southey, Coleridge, or any other modern *Imaginationist* has equalled these six lines, I may perhaps incline to give up my long continued admiration, and imitation of Pope, and the ancients' (p. 533; his italics). This issue of the *Scots Magazine* also contains a report of the trial of John Hatfield, the forger and bigamist who married Mary of Buttermere, from Carlisle, 15 Aug., informing readers of the guilty verdict and death sentence, pp. 577-8: I suspect this was why the Wordsworths bought it. DW had encouraged C to visit Hatfield in prison on 16 Aug. (*Notebooks* i 1432).

(ii) *The Voyage Home from the Cape of Good Hope, with other poems relating to the Cape, and notes* **(1803)**
Suggested date of reading: 9 Oct. 1803
References: *EY* 413 and n1
See preceding note. Tytler's *Voyage* was the poem which Southey had been asked to review, probably by the *Monthly*, which gave it short shrift in its May 1804 issue (vol.4, pp. 46-8). W would have had the chance to take a look at it when he saw Southey on 9 Oct. (Reed ii 238-9).

406. Valerius Maximus, Caius, *Facta et Dicta Memorabilia*
Suggested date of reading: between 21 May 1802 and 7 Oct. 1803
References: *Prose Works* ii 101-2; Cornell *Poems 1800-7* 583-4
W knew the story about Simonides finding the corpse of a stranger and burying it, Owen suggests, from either Cicero, *de Divinatione* or Valerius Maximus. Two copies of the latter were retained at Rydal Mount (Shaver 262-3). The story is recapitulated in the first of the *Essays Upon Epitaphs* (*Prose Works* ii 52; CC *Friend* ii 338).

407. Vaughan, Sir Charles Richard, *Narrative of the Siege of Zaragoza* **(2nd edn, 1809)**
Suggested date of reading: by 26 March 1809
References: see note
Owen and Smyser demonstrate that W read the 2nd edn of Vaughan's pamphlet (*Prose Works* i 405). He was apparently sent one by De Quincey, who did not have time to read it himself (Jordan 122). W must have read it by 26 March 1809, when he instructed De Quincey to send Vaughan a copy of *The Convention of Cintra* (*MY* i 302-3).

408. Vieyra Transtagano, Anthony, *A New Portuguese Grammar in Four Parts* **(2nd edn, 1777)**
Suggested date of reading: ?1800s
References: Shaver 264
W's copy is now at the Wordsworth Library. It bears his ownership inscription on its title-page, dating, I think, from the 1800s. Southey was given a copy by James Grahame in 1808 (Curry i 469), and W probably acquired his at about the same time.

409. Vincent, Augustine, *A discoverie of errours in the first edition of the catalogue of nobility, published by R. Brooke . . . At the end whereof, is annexed a review of a later edition, by him stolne into the world 1621* **(1622)**
Suggested date of reading: between 30 Oct. 1806 and early April 1807
References: Cornell *Poems 1800-7* 425

W cites page 622 of Vincent's volume as a source for the note to *Song, at the Feast of Brougham Castle*, composed between 30 Oct. 1806 and early April 1807. It seems not to have belonged to him but may have been in Beaumont's library at Coleorton.

410. V.[incent], T.[homas], *God's Terrible Voice in the City* (1667)
Suggested date of reading: by 18 Jan. 1808
References: *MY* i 190; Shaver 264; Wing V440

On 18 Jan. 1808 W wrote to Scott about the notes for his forthcoming edn of Dryden's works: 'I think the character of the Annus Mirabilis as a Poem might be illustrated by some extracts from a long sermon entitled God's terrible voice in the City, in which the fire of London is minutely described; Dryden's is a sorry Poem, and the Sermonist though with a world of absurdity has upon the whole greatly the advantage of him' (*MY* i 190). W had evidently acquired a copy of Vincent's sermon by 18 Jan. 1808; it was later retained at Rydal Mount. Vincent's powerful description of the Great Fire of 1666 appears in section VI of his tract, pp. 46-59.

411. Virgilius Maro, Publius
(i) *Georgics*
Suggested date of reading: 1800
References: see note

Graver has pointed out that *Michael* and other poems among *Lyrical Ballads* (1800) allude to the *Georgics*; see 'Wordsworth's Georgic Pastoral: *Otium* and *Labor* in "Michael"', *European Romantic Review* 1 (1991) 119-34. It is hard to be certain, but there is a reasonable chance that W returned to Virgil during the spring and summer of 1800.

As Graver points out, allusions to Virgil are plentiful throughout *The Prelude*, *The Excursion*, *Home at Grasmere*, and many of the works associated with *The Recluse*:

> These range from precise translations of key phrases ('labor improbus' becomes, via Milton, 'irksome toil') to imitation (the Wanderer's prophecy about the glories of universal, state-sponsored education is directly dependent on Jupiter's prophecy in *Aeneid* Book I). Even the portrait of Margaret, who let the leaves of her books lie where they dropped, alludes to the Cumaean Sybil in Book III. (letter to me)

As stated in the Preface, it is no part of my job to note every allusion here, though allusions form the basis for entries when they indicate that a reading may have taken place. W knew his Virgil well by this period and did not always need to refer to a printed text.

(ii) *Works*, tr. John Ogilby
Suggested date of reading: by 18 Jan. 1808
References: *MY* i 190

On 18 Jan. 1808 W told Scott: 'There is in Echard's History a most laughable account of Ogilby, who, by the bye, was a countryman of yours' (*MY* i 190). I don't believe that W would have taken any notice of Echard's account of Ogilby had he not known Ogilby's translation of Virgil - the work for which he was best known. As I found no hard evidence for a Hawkshead reading I did not include it in *WR*; all the same, a copy of Ogilby's rendering (1679) was present in the Hawkshead Grammar School library and might well have been used by W during his time there (Wu *CWAAS* 279).

W owned a copy of *The Works of Publius Virgilius Maro*, tr. John Ogilby (1650), now at the Wordsworth Library (Shaver 307). There is no ownership inscription inside this volume and no indication of when it was acquired, although it does contain marginalia by Dora. It also carries a note by Gordon Graham Wordsworth: 'This translation of Virgil was found tied up in a bundle with the M.S.S. of the translations by W.W.' This would suggest that it was in W's possession by July 1823 when work on his *Aeneid* translations began.

(iii) *Georgics* **and** *Aeneid*
Suggested date of reading: perhaps late 1808
References: *Prose Works* i 386, 401
W quotes the *Georgics* and the *Aeneid* in the *Convention of Cintra*; he was capable of doing so without reference to a printed text but it seems not impossible that he did look at one all the same.

(iv) *Georgics* **ii 126-33**
Suggested date of reading: 26 March 1809
References: *MY* i 301-2
W quotes these lines in a letter to De Quincey of 26 March 1809. He may have quoted from memory, but it is possible that he was referring to a printed text.

(v) *The Thirteene Bookes of Æneidos. The first twelve being the worke of the divine poet Virgil Maro, and the thirteenth, the supplement of Maphæus Vegius*, **tr. Thomas Phaer [1596]**
Suggested date of reading: by 17 Sept. 1814
References: *MY* ii 154
In his letter to Robert Anderson of 17 Sept. 1814, W suggests that an enlarged edn of Anderson's *British Poets* should include 'Phaer's Virgil'. This indicates that he was aware of Phaer's translation by 17 Sept. 1814.

(vi) *The First Foure Books of Virgil his Aeneid translated into English Heroicall Verse*, **tr. Richard Stanyhurst [Leyden, 1582]**
Suggested date of reading: by 17 Sept. 1814
References: *MY* ii 154

In his letter to Robert Anderson of 17 Sept. 1814, W suggests that an enlarged edn of Anderson's *British Poets* should include 'as a curiosity the few books of Stanyhurst's Virgil' (*MY* ii 154).

(vii) *Aeneid* Books I, VI
Suggested date of reading: c. Oct. 1814
References: Cornell *Poems 1807-20* 529-30
Aeneid Books I and VI are acknowledged sources for *Laodamìa*, composed Oct. 1814 (see Cornell *Poems 1807-20* 529-30).

412. Volney, Constantin François de Chasseboeuf, comte de, *Travels through Syria and Egypt, in the years 1783, 1784, and 1785* [2 vols., 1787]
Suggested date of reading: between early 1796 and late 1800
References: see note
An early W MS containing drafts towards *Home at Grasmere*, *Benjamin the Waggoner* and *Michael*, DC MS 28, also contains the following note:

> When the Semoum or Samiel begins to blow the sky at other times so clear becomes dark and heavy, the Sun loses his splendour and becomes of a violet colour. The air is not cloudy but grey and thick, an[d] is filled with an extremely subtile dust which penetrates everywhere. The camels in the desert surprized by this wind bury their noses in the sand and keep them there till the squall is over. - Respiration is short and difficult, the skin parched and dry and the body consumed by an internal heat. No thing can restore perspiration (DC MS 28, 23r)

I have collated the draft with Volney's *Travels* (2nd edn, 2 vols., 1788), and find that it consists of three brief extracts from Volney, chapter 4, 'Of the Winds and their Phænomena'. All are from vol. 1: the first two sentences are from p. 61; the second sentence from pp. 62-3; the last two sentences from p. 61. Reed comments: 'A date more exact than between early 1796 and perhaps c late 1800 seems unjustified' (Reed ii 709). I have chosen to accept Reed's dating, though the presence of drafts in the same MS dating from Jan. 1806 and after (see Cornell *Benjamin* 5) might suggest an even later date. See also Cornell *Lyrical Ballads* xxiv-v; Reed ii 625-7; Cornell *Home at Grasmere* 139-41.

413. Voltaire, François-Marie Arouet de, *Dictionnaire Philosophique*
Suggested date of reading: by Jan. 1815
References: *Prose Works* iii 68-9, 89
W alludes to Voltaire's phrase, 'le plus méprisable bouffon' in his *Essay, Supplementary to the Preface*, indicating that he had seen this work by Jan. 1815.

414. Waller, Edmund, *Poems, &c., Written upon Several Occasions* (5th edn, 1686)
Suggested date of reading: by Jan. 1815
References: *Prose Works* iii 71, 93
W reveals that this volume was in his possession by 1815 in his *Essay, Supplementary to the Preface*. Later in the *Essay* he quotes from Waller's *Of Love* (*Prose Works* iii 81). Shaver lists the 7th edn of 1705, but not that of 1686 (Shaver 267).

415. Walton, Izaak, and Charles Cotton
(i) *The Complete Angler* ed. John Sidney Hawkins (6th edn, 1797)
Suggested date of reading: the evening of 3 Jan. 1808 onwards
References: *MY* i 186; Shaver 268
On 3 Jan. 1808 DW wrote to Lady Beaumont: 'today arrives your note enclosed in the parcel with Walton's complete Angler'. She added: 'My Brother has seized upon the Book for his own reading this night, as he fancies that the imagery and sentiments accord with his own train of thought at present, in connection with his poem, which he is just upon the point of finishing' (*MY* i 187). The 'poem' was *The White Doe of Rylstone*.[1] This copy of Walton is now in the possession of Christopher Wordsworth. The second front flyleaf contains the following inscription in ink, in the hand of Sir George Beaumont:

> From Sir George Beaumont to
>   Dorothy Wordsworth
>   Grasmere January 10th
>   1808

The volume contains pencilled marginalia on pages 37 and 40. On page 40 either W or DW has marked Walton's comments on Sir Henry Wotton, which DW discusses in her letter to Lady Beaumont (see *MY* i 187). Beaumont's dating of the inscription as 10 January 1808 is somewhat puzzling as he is not known to have been in Grasmere at that time.

There is a hint in Lamb's letter to W of 5 March 1803 that W either had read or at least knew of Walton's *Angler* by that earlier date: 'You know Cotton, who wrote a 2d part to Walton's Angler' (Marrs ii 98). Interestingly, Hazlitt commented in his account of W in *The Spirit of the Age* (1825) that 'He approves of Walton's Angler, Paley, and some other writers of an inoffensive modesty of pretension' (p. 246).

(ii) *The Complete Angler*
Suggested date of reading: c. May 1812
References: *Love Letters* 154
'I wish you could buy the Complete Angler for me', MW wrote to her husband on 13 May 1812, 'I want to make Tom a present of it' (*Love Letters* 154). During his short life Tom

---

[1] Comparetti discusses the relation of Walton to *The White Doe* (Comparetti 117-18).

Wordsworth was a keen fisherman; he was approaching his sixth birthday in May 1812. W was evidently sending books to Mary during her stay at Hindwell, as she wrote on 23 May to thank him for 'the 2^d. Book you have sent enclosed in a blank cover' (*Love Letters* 181). He appears not to have acquired a new copy by 29 May when MW wrote: 'I repeat that I very much wish you could buy for me the Compleat Angler - I want to give it to Tom, whom I think it would please very much' (*Love Letters* 196). W soon put things to rights, for on 3-4 June 1812, he replied: 'I hope that Davy will let me have an Angling Rod, and I will take care to bring Isaac Walton' (*Supp.* 110). He saw Davy on several occasions during his stay in London, including meetings on 8, 22, 30 May (when they probably spoke about angling; see *Supp.* 89-90). At least three copies of *The Complete Angler* were retained at Rydal Mount (Shaver 268).

416. Warner, Richard, *A Tour Through the Northern Counties of England, and the Borders of Scotland* (2 vols., Bath and London, 1802)

Suggested date of reading: c. July 1802
References: Griggs ii 826-7; Bicknell 43
Describing Keswick, Warner takes the opportunity to mention W and C:

> The animated, enthusiastic, and accomplished Coleridge, whose residence at Keswick gives additional charms and interest to its impressive scenery, inspired us with terror, whilst he described the universal uproar that was awakened through the mountains by a sudden burst of involuntary laughter in the heart of their precipices; an incident which a kindred intellect, his friend and neighbour at Grasmere, Wordsworth, (whose 'Lyrical Ballads,' exclusively almost of all modern compositions, breathe the true, nervous, and simple spirit of poetry) has worked up into the following admirable effusion: [Warner then quotes *To Joanna* 38-76.] (*Tour* ii 100-2)

C had seen Warner's volume by 27 July 1802, when he wrote to SH:

> Could you believe now, that the Rogue made up all this out of my telling him, that Wordsworth's Echo, tho' purposely beyond Nature, was yet only an *exaggeration* of what really would happen - for that I myself with John Wordsworth & William had laughed aloud at Stickle Tarn in Langdale, & that the effect was quite enough to justify the Poem from being more extravagant, than it was it's purpose to be. - Whatever I told him, the Fellow has murdered in this way - a book fuller of Lies & Inaccuracies & Blunders was, I believe, on my conscience, never published. From foolish men, that write Books, Lord deliver me! - It has been my Lot to be made a Fool of by Madmen, & represented as a Madman by Fools! (Griggs ii 827)

W and DW were by this date in Hull on their way to London, but they must shortly after have encountered Warner's *Tour*. And they can be expected to have heard of C's disgruntlement at it on meeting him again on 13 Oct., after W's wedding. The Wordsworths were both acquainted with Warner from earlier years (see *WR* 143-4; Reed i 242). There is no evidence that a copy of the *Tour* ever entered W's possession.

417. Warton, Joseph, *An Essay on the Writings and Genius of Pope* **[2 vols., 1756-82]**
Suggested date of reading: by Jan. 1815
References: *Prose Works* iii 73-4, 96
In his *Essay, Supplementary to the Preface*, W observed that the characteristics of Thomson's genius went unrecognized 'till the elder Warton, almost forty years after the publication of the Seasons, pointed them out in a note in his Essay on the Life and Writings of Pope' (*Prose Works* iii 73-4).

418. Warwick, Sir Philip, *Memoires of the reigne of Charles I with a continuation to the happy restauration of King Charles II* **(1701)**
Suggested date of reading: by 26 March 1809
References: *Prose Works* i 336, 405
W's quotations from Warwick in *The Convention of Cintra* were added, apparently, at the same time as those from Vaughan (see note 407). The terminal date for his reading of Vaughan, 26 March 1809, therefore provides a point by which he may be presumed to have read Warwick. It may be presumed also that he had by that time acquired the copy of the *Memoires* later retained at Rydal Mount (Shaver 269).

419. Watson, Thomas, works
Suggested date of reading: by 17 Sept. 1814
References: *MY* ii 153
In his letter to Robert Anderson of 17 Sept. 1814, W suggests that an enlarged edn of Anderson's *British Poets* should include Watson. This indicates that he was aware of his works by 17 Sept. 1814.

420. Weever, John, *Ancient Funerall Monuments with the United Monarchie of Great Britaine, Ireland, and the Ilands adjacent* **(1631)**
Suggested date of reading: Nov.-Dec. 1809; by 22 Feb. 1810
References: *Prose Works* ii 101; CC *Friend* ii 336
Owen and Smyser describe Weever as a 'major source' for W's *Essays Upon Epitaphs*. It is ascertained by Owen, on the evidence of a misprint, that W used the 1631 edn. C may have been referring to the same volume in Nov.-Dec. 1809 (*Notebooks* iii 3647n); W referred Basil Montagu to it in Feb. 1840 (*LY* iv 29).[1]

---

[1] The editor of *LY* iv notes, erroneously, that W's reference to 'Wever's Funeral Monuments' is to Robert Weaver, *Monumenta Antiqua* (1840) (*LY* iv 29n2).

421. West, Thomas
(i) *The Antiquities of Furness* **(1774)**
Suggested date of reading: 1810
References: *Prose Works* ii 194; Bicknell 9.1
W quotes from West's *Antiquities* in his *Select Views*, composed 1810. This is, so far as I can find, his earliest reference to this title. Owen and Smyser note that, although a copy of the 1805 edn was retained at Rydal Mount (Shaver 271), W was using that of 1774 - 'for twice, when the 1805 text is improved, he continues to quote the 1774 text'. They add that 'in 1810 he was oblivious to, if not ignorant of, the 1805 edition' (*Prose Works* ii 402).

All the same, W must soon after have acquired the copy of the 2nd edn of 1805 which is now in the possession of Paul F. Betz (Betz 130). It was given to him by Jane Penny, the celebrated belle of Windermere, who married John Wilson in 1811. She visited W in Aug. 1810, and may have presented it then. Graver suggests that W knew the *Antiquities* as early as his schooldays: 'A young boy who rode on horseback to Furness Abbey, and who had such a lively recollection of several of its artifacts, probably read the standard history of the place' (letter to me).

(ii) *A Guide to the Lakes in Cumberland, Westmorland, and Lancashire*
(9th edn, Kendal, 1807)
Suggested date of reading: 1810
References: *Prose Works* ii 380; Bicknell 13.9; Shaver 271; Gordan 334
West's *Guide* was of major importance during W's work on *Select Views* in 1810. As Owen and Smyser note,

> A copy of the ninth edition (Kendal, 1807) with Wordsworth's name and the date '1814' inscribed on the title-page is in the Berg Collection of the New York Public Library. . . . Since the date on the title-page does not preclude Wordsworth's having used, earlier than 1814, either this copy or another copy of the same edition, and since it was the most recent when he was composing *Select Views*, we shall ordinarily cite the 1807 edition . . . (*Prose Works* ii 380)

W had of course known this work since his schooldays (see *WR* 146 7).

(iii) *A Guide to the Lakes in Cumberland, Westmorland, and Lancashire*
(9th edn, Kendal, 1807)
Suggested date of reading: between Sept. 1811 and Nov. 1812
References: *Prose Works* ii 436
West was an important source for W's *Unpublished Tour*, composed between Sept. 1811 and Nov. 1812. Owen and Smyser note: 'Apparently it was Wordsworth's intention to print in an

appendix an abridgement of West's *Guide*, pp. 25-31, including, no doubt, Cockin's long and interesting footnote on the journey over the Sands [of Morecambe Bay]' (*Prose Works* ii 437).

(iv) *The Antiquities of Furness* (1774)
Suggested date of reading: between Sept. 1811 and Nov. 1812
References: *Prose Works* ii 438, 443
The *Antiquities* provided a source for W's *Unpublished Tour*, composed between Sept. 1811 and Nov. 1812.

422. *Westmorland Advertiser, or Kendal Chronicle*
(i)
Suggested date of reading: by about July 1813 and from then onwards
References: *MY* ii 102
W's letter to George Thompson of about July 1813 suggests that he was by then acquainted with the *Westmorland Advertizer* and its editor, Mr Shaw.

The paper always had radical leanings, and its opposition to the Lowthers in 1818 led W to associate it with 'Jacobinical principles', a point of view echoed by Southey a year later (*MY* ii 407; Curry ii 197).

(ii)
Suggested date of reading: 1, 22 Oct. 1814
References: see note
On 22 Oct. 1814, MW told DW: 'The Kendal paper today has given a judicious transcript from the Poem - the description of the Valley Funeral - they have often given a lump from it' (*MWL* 20). Indeed, on 22 Oct. 1814 the *Westmorland Advertiser* published *Excursion* ii 546-92, and on 1 Oct. they had published *Excursion* vi 1-74. W must have seen these 'lumps'.

(iii) 12, 19 Nov. 1814
Suggested date of reading: 12, 19 Nov. 1814
References: see note
On 12 Nov. 1814 the *Westmorland Advertiser* published an obituary for a local clergyman, the Revd. Matthew Murfitt:

> DIED
>
> At the Vicarage-house early on Monday morning last, after a short but severe indisposition, the Rev. Matthew Murfitt, M.A. Vicar of this parish, formerly fellow of Trinity College, Cambridge. Amiable in his private life, zealous in the discharge of his public duties, peculiarly eloquent and impressive in the pulpit, learned, humane, and pious, he was a splendid example of that truly dignified character, a christian pastor. His numerous hearers, in common with all his friends, will long regret their severe loss, and deeply lament the sudden catastrophe which has deprived society of so bright an ornament, and the church of so staunch a supporter.

W evidently read this, for it inspired him to write a poem, *Written upon a blank leaf in a copy of the Excursion by the author, upon reading an account of a recent death in Kendal*. He composed it on 13 Nov. and sent it to the *Westmorland Advertiser*, which published this early text on 19 Nov.:

> To public notice, with reluctance strong,
> Did I deliver this unfinished song,
> Yet with one happy issue - and I look
> With self-congratulation on the Book
> Which pious, learned Murfitt saw and read; -
> Upon my thoughts his saintly Spirit fed;
> He con'd the new-born Lay, with grateful heart,
> Foreboding not how soon he must depart,
> Unweeting that to him the joy was giv'n
> Which good Men take with them from Earth to Heav'n.
>   Nov. 13th 1814

The poem appeared in the 1815 *Poems*, and was included in subsequent collections. Its first appearance in the *Westmorland Advertiser* has not hitherto been recorded. Little is known of W's acquaintance with Murfitt - though the poem indicates that they did know each other. It is interesting to note that Murfitt was elected a member of the Kendal Coffee Room and Library in Nov. 1806, and that he was present at the committee meeting of 27 Jan. 1807 when it was decided to order a copy of W's *Poems, in Two Volumes* - significantly, it seems to me, some months before publication on 28 April. Had Murfitt been tipped off by the author? Had he, perhaps, seen some of its contents?

From 26 April 1834 this paper published as the *Kendal Mercury and Northern Advertiser*, and remained regular reading for W (see, for instance, *LY* iv 631 and n).

423. Whitaker, Thomas Dunham
(i) ***An History of the Original Parish of Whalley, and Honour of Clitheroe*** **(1801)**
Suggested date of reading: 16 Oct. 1807 onwards
References: *MY* i 167

On 18 Oct. 1807 DW told Jane Marshall: 'I cannot express how much pleasure my Brother has already received from Dr. Whitaker's Books, though they have been only two days in his possession - Almost the whole time he has been greedily devouring the History of Craven, and, (what is of more importance) he has found all the information which he wanted for the prosecution of his plan' (*MY* i 167). The Marshalls, who knew Whitaker, had evidently borrowed from him, on W's behalf, copies of his two *History*s. W's 'plan' was *The White Doe of Rylstone*, and he was frank about its influence on the poem in his notes (see Cornell *White Doe* 150-64). The story of the white doe appears at p. 383. The subscribers to Whitaker's *History of Craven* included Lord Lowther, Sir Gilfrid Lawson, and William

Rawson (DW's distant 'uncle'; see *WR* 118). W seems never to have acquired his own copies of Whitaker's volumes; he had returned those borrowed on his behalf by Dec. 1808 (*MY* i 281). Intriguingly, he felt such a debt to Whitaker that he sent him a MS copy of the *White Doe* in Feb. 1808 (*MY* i 198).

(ii) *The History and Antiquities of the Deanery of Craven* (1805)
Suggested date of reading: 16 Oct. 1807 onwards
References: *MY* i 167
See preceding note, though it is possible that W saw a copy before 16 Oct. Dugas says that 'Wordsworth must have seen a copy of Whitaker's *History of Craven* before he composed this poem [*The Force of Prayer*]' (Cornell *White Doe* 147); according to Reed ii 45, W's *The Force of Prayer* was composed *c*. 18 Sept. 1807. W may have seen Whitaker's book briefly in Sept. 1807, and then attempted to borrow one from the author through the Marshalls (see preceding note).

(iii) *The History and Antiquities of the Deanery of Craven* (1805)
Suggested date of reading: Nov. 1809
References: see note
Nabholtz, 'Wordsworth's *Guide to the Lakes* and the Picturesque Tradition', *MP* 61 (1964) 288-97, argues for Whitaker's influence on W's *Select Views*, composed early Nov. 1809.

424. White, Henry Kirke
(i) *Clifton Grove: A Sketch in Verse, with Other Poems* (1803)
Suggested date of reading: *c*. 21 Feb. 1804
References: see note
In his preface to White's *Remains* (2 vols., 1807), Southey describes the adverse critical reception granted to *Clifton Grove*, before recalling how he showed the volume to two friends: 'The poems which had been thus condemned, appeared to me to discover strong marks of genius. I had shewn them to two of my friends, than whom no persons living better understand what poetry is, nor have given better proofs of it; and their opinion coincided with my own' (i 24-5). W. A. Cox, 'Kirke White', *N&Q* 5 (1906) 427, 496-8, was the first to suggest that these two friends were C and W. Southey moved into Greta Hall in Sept. 1803, and is likely to have shown *Clifton Grove* to W and C shortly after. His earliest known visit to DC dates from 21 Feb. 1804 (Reed ii 253), providing a likely terminal date for W's first encounter with Kirke White's poetry.

A month before, on 23 Jan., Southey had told his brother Herbert:

> A little volume of poems by Henry Kirke White, of Nottingham, has excited some interest in me for the author, who is very young, and has published them in the hope of obtaining help to pursue his studies and graduate for orders. . . . There is a wild little

poem there to a Rosemary bush, which affected me. The poor boy is sickly, and will, I suppose, die of consumption. . . . In the "Annual" I have been his friend.

(Warter i 252)

True to his word, Southey composed a favourable review of *Clifton Grove* in the *Annual Review* 2 (1803) 552-4, describing its contents as 'extraordinary productions of early genius' (p. 552). White's *To the herb Rosemary*, which Southey mentions in his letter, is reprinted entire in his review, with the comment: 'This is a most interesting poem. We know no production of so young a poet that can be compared to it, and when we say this, we remember Cowley and Pope and Chatterton' (p. 554). I can now reveal here for the first time that this poem is that which, hitherto unidentified, appears in the Wordsworth Commonplace Book (DC MS 26, 36v-37r), beginning with the lines, 'Sweet scented flow'r! who'rt wont to bloom / On January's front severe'. The copy is very rough, and pays little heed to indentations, punctuation, or capitals, and it contains at least two variants to be found in neither of the available printed texts. Both of the variants, however, can be accounted for by scribal error. Dating the copy, Reed notes: 'In the absence of more specific evidence, [it] may be regarded as dating between Mar 1804 and 11 Feb 1805' (Reed ii 706). With this new evidence I would argue for a date of c. 21 Feb. 1804.

(ii) *The Remains of Kirke White, of Nottingham*, **ed. Robert Southey (2 vols., 1807)**
Suggested date of reading: probably 1807; certainly by 13 May 1812
References: Morley i 82
Having been shown Kirke White's 1803 volume by Southey, W would have been interested in his editing of the literary remains. In his preface, Southey recalls their arrival at Greta Hall: 'Mr. Coleridge was present when I opened them, and was, as well as myself, equally affected and astonished at the proofs of industry which they displayed. . . . There were papers upon law, upon electricity, upon chemistry, upon the Latin and Greek languages, from their rudiments, to the higher branches of critical study, upon history, chronology, divinity, the fathers, &c. Nothing seemed to have escaped him. His poems were numerous' (*Remains* i 51). Even if W did not see these MSS, he would have heard about them from C. On 13 May 1812 Robinson recorded in his diary that W spoke of White 'as a man of more talents than genius' (Morley i 82). Further clues might one day turn up in W's lost correspondence with Southey, 1807-8.[1] The *Remains* were deservedly popular, and went into their 5th edn by 1811.

425. Wilberforce, William, *A Practical View of the Prevailing Religious System of Professed Christians* **(1797)**
Suggested date of reading: by 19 Jan. 1801
References: Griggs ii 666-7; *EY* 684-5

---

[1] They were in contact in 1808, as a transcript of part of one letter survives (*MY* i 162).

C composed the letter which W copied out to send to Wilberforce with a copy of *Lyrical Ballads* (1800). In it, he mentions 'your religious treatise', describing himself as 'a Fellow-labourer with you in the same Vineyard'. Although C was responsible for this letter, it is possible that W had read Wilberforce's pamphlet. C may have known it as early as 1797 (*Notebooks* i 80n).

The Wordsworths must have read Wilberforce's publications over the years; certainly, DW's remark on 23 July 1806 to Catherine Clarkson indicates some familiarity with his writings: 'I was much interested with your account of the Wilberforces and glad to find your opinion of Mr. W. correspond so exactly with my own' (*MY* i 60). W and Wilberforce met only in 1815 (Reed ii 605).

426. Wilkinson, Thomas, of Yanwath
(i) poems copied by
Suggested date of reading: probably after 19 Jan. 1801
References: Reed ii 704; Moorman *N&Q* 402
Two poems in Wilkinson's hand, *I Love to Be Alone* and *Lines Written on a Paper Wrapt round a Moss-rose Pulled on New-years Day, and sent to M. Wilson*, copied onto a duodecimo double sheet, have been pasted into the Wordsworth Commonplace Book (DC MS 26, 18r-18v). Robert Woof observes that they 'must surely date from a time after Wordsworth's first meeting with Thomas Wilkinson which cannot be before the arrival at Grasmere, 1799' (Woof PhD 233). W's earliest known meeting with Wilkinson occurred on 19 Jan. 1801 (Reed ii 110).

(ii) *A Lamentation on the Untimely Death of Roger, in the Cumberland Dialect*
Suggested date of reading: between 19 Jan. 1801 and 25 March 1804
References: Reed ii 705; Moorman *N&Q* 402-3
This poem, by Wilkinson, in his own hand, was pasted into the Wordsworth Commonplace Book (DC MS 26, 28r-29v) after 19 Jan. 1801, the date of W's first known meeting with Wilkinson.

(iii) *Tours to the British Mountains* **in MS**
Suggested date of reading: by 5 Nov. 1805
References: see note
W noted that *The Solitary Reaper*, composed 5 Nov. 1805, 'was suggested by a beautiful sentence in a MS. Tour in Scotland written by a Friend, the last line being taken from it *verbatim*' (Cornell *Poems 1800-7* 415). In a letter to Lady Beaumont of 7 Nov., DW also notes that it 'was suggested by a very beautiful passage in a Journal of a Tour among the Highlands, by Thomas Wilkinson' (*EY* 639).

W hung onto Wilkinson's MS for quite a while after Nov. 1805. He cannot have finished reading it in July 1806, when Wilkinson called at DC (Reed ii 328), for it was still at Grasmere in Oct. when the Wordsworths left for Coleorton, as W confessed in a letter to

Wilkinson the following month: 'but what shall I say in apology for your Journal, which is now locked up with my manuscripts in Grasmere' (*MY* i 104). The Wordsworths remained at Coleorton until June 1807, so that the MS could not have been returned till then at the earliest.

After his return to DC, and before giving the MS back to Wilkinson, W copied from it the passage which had inspired *The Solitary Reaper*, alongside another related to *The Excursion*, into his Commonplace Book (DC MS 26, 48v):

> Pass'd by a Female who was reaping alone, she sung in Erse as she bended over her sickle, the sweetest human voice I ever heard. Her strains were tenderly melancholy & felt delicious long after they were heard no more -
> But take courage return to thy Fathers rise with the Lark, climb the summits of thy surrounding Hills, roll the stone in thunder from the mountain, and follow with all thy might the Wild Goats of Ben Vorlach, so shalt thou return weary to thy Cottage & thy rest will be as quiet as mine.

The second of these extracts inspired *Excursion* iv 491-504, the earliest known date of composition for which, according to Reed, is between Dec. 1809 and March 1812: the draft in the Commonplace Book almost certainly preceded drafting of the relevant *Excursion* lines. Wilkinson's *Tours* was not published until 1824.

(iv) *To My Thrushes, Blackbirds, etc.*
Suggested date of reading: 13 June 1809
References: *MY* i 362
On 7 July 1809, W told Thomas Wilkinson that 'Mr Coleridge showed me a little poem of yours upon your Birds which gave us all very great pleasure' (*MY* i 362). C arrived at Allan Bank on 13 June having come from Wilkinson (Reed ii 430); the Wordsworths must have seen the poem on or around that date. It is published in Mary Carr, *Thomas Wilkinson* (1905), pp. 75-7.

427. Williams, Helen Maria, *Letters Written in France, in the Summer 1790* (1790)
Suggested date of reading: by late autumn 1804
References: see note
The misfortunes of Monsieur and Madame du Fossé, as reported by Williams, provided an important source for the Vaudracour and Julia story in *Thirteen-Book Prelude*; see F. M. Todd, *Politics and the Poet* (1958), pp. 222-4. See also *WR* 150.

428. Willoughby, Henry, works
Suggested date of reading: by 17 Sept. 1814
References: *MY* ii 153

In his letter to Robert Anderson of 17 Sept. 1814, W suggests that an enlarged edn of Anderson's *British Poets* should include 'Willoby'. This indicates that he was aware of his works, most probably *Willobie's Avisa* [1594], by 17 Sept. 1814.

429. Wilson, Elizabeth, MS album
Suggested date of reading: c. 22 Oct. 1814
References: *MWL* 18-19; *MY* ii 168
W copied his poem to Gillies ('From the dark chambers of dejection freed')[1] into Elizabeth Wilson's MS album between 22 Oct. and 12 Nov. 1814. Ketcham thinks that 'the autumn was well advanced before . . . WW's sonnet . . . was composed and written into the album after it reached Rydal Mount' (Cornell *Poems 1807-20* 528). For the album's other contents, including works by R. P. Gillies and 'a rig-ma-role about some beast' by James Hogg, see *MWL* 18-19.

430. Wilson, John
(i) *The Angler's Tent* in MS
Suggested date of reading: c. 29 June 1809
References: Reed ii 432-3 and n46
After the boating expedition on Windermere, c. 29 June 1809, W helped Wilson with *The Angler's Tent*, later published in *The Isle of Palms* (1812).[2] Reed suggests that this might conceivably have occurred as late as 8-13 Sept. (Reed ii 437), though the June date seems as likely. On 13 May 1812, W told Robinson that he had 'tried to get Wilson to compress' *The Angler's Tent* - presumably recalling this occasion (Morley i 82).

(ii) MS poems including *To a Sleeping Child*
Suggested date of reading: between 1809 and May 1812
References: Morley i 82
On 13 May 1812, Robinson asked W about Wilson's recently-published volume, *The Isle of Palms*: 'He said he had seen only a few'. W added that 'Wilson's poems are an attenuation of mine. Everything he had he owes to me' (Morley i 82). W took the same line in his letter to MW of 23 May, which mentions one of Wilson's poems 'which we had in Mss, to the sleeping Child and which is but an Attenuation of my ode to the Highland Girl' (*Supp.* 91). These remarks indicate that W knew a number of the poems in *The Isle of Palms* from MS - including *To a Sleeping Child* (published *The Isle of Palms*, pp. 280-9). The most likely time for him to have read these MS works would be between 1809 and 1812.

---

[1] See Cornell *Poems 1807-20* 140, 528.
[2] The principal source for this information is Mary Gordon, *Christopher North* (2 vols., 1862), i 129-30, reproduced Cornell *Poems 1807-20* 596-7. See also Reed's observations on her account, Reed ii 433n46.

(iii) *Letter of 'Mathetes', The Friend* **no. 17 (14 Dec. 1809)**
Suggested date of reading: probably early Nov. 1809
References: Reed ii 49; *Prose Works* ii 3ff; CC *Friend* ii 222-32
Reed suggests that W's *Reply to 'Mathetes'* was composed between early Nov. and early Dec. 1809; W must therefore have read Wilson's *Letter* in early Nov.

(iv) *The Isle of Palms, and Other Poems* **(1812)**
Suggested date of reading: probably by 23 May 1812
References: Supp. 91
There was a copy of *The Isle of Palms* at Rydal Mount (Shaver 275), which W probably acquired close to the date of publication. On 23 May 1812 he told MW that 'Mr Wilson is reviewed' (*Supp.* 91), referring to Jeffrey's account in the *Edinburgh Review*. Although his phrasing is not unambiguous, it sounds as if he had acquired a copy of Wilson's volume by that date; even if he hadn't, he probably did so soon after. W's relations with Wilson were still cordial at this period (see Reed ii 510).

431. Winstanley, William, *England's Worthies: Select Lives of the most Eminent Persons from Constantine the Great to the Death of Oliver Cromwell late Protector* **(1684)**
Suggested date of reading: by 22 Feb. 1810
References: *Prose Works* ii 108; Shaver 276
Owen and Smyser note that W's source for the Marquis of Montrose's epitaph on Charles I was Winstanley. W had presumably acquired his copy by 1810; it was later retained at Rydal Mount.

432. Wither, George, works
Suggested date of reading: by 17 Sept. 1814
References: *MY* ii 153
In his letter to Robert Anderson of 17 Sept. 1814, W suggests that an enlarged edn of Anderson's *British Poets* should include Wither, whose works he had known since at least Dec. 1797 (*WR* 150-1). Four extracts from Wither's works appear in the album W compiled for Lady Mary Lowther in 1819 (*Album* 33-41).

433. Withering, William, *An Arrangement of British Plants according to the latest Improvements of the Linnean System and an Introduction to the Study of Botany* **(3rd edn, 4 vols., Birmingham, 1796)**
Suggested date of reading: Aug. 1800 onwards
References: Reed ii 77-8; *EY* 321 and n; Shaver 276
'Oh! that we had a book of botany', DW wrote in her journal on 16 May 1800, 'all flowers now are gay & deliciously sweet' (*Grasmere Journals* 2). The need was shared by W, and on 7 Aug. his account with Longman was charged £2.16.0 for '2 Withering's Botany boards',

and £1.7.0 for '2 Microscope' (see p. 265, below). The books and microscopes can be presumed to have been sent to W later that month, although he did not acknowledge them until 27 March 1801 when he wrote to Longman: 'Mr Coleridge and I conjointly are in your debt for two Copies of Withering's Botany and two botanical microscopes' (*EY* 321).

As Reed ii 174n45 observes, DW's detailed accounts of flora in her journals indicate that she frequently consulted Withering - as do her marginalia in the volumes themselves, now at the Wordsworth Library.[1] The half-title of vol. 1 bears an inscription in ink, 'WW', and the title-page bears the inscription, 'W Wordsworth'. Before 1800 W and C might have known Withering from the copy in the Bristol Library Society in 1797-8 (*BLS* 109). See also D. E. Coombe, 'The Wordsworths and Botany', *N&Q* 197 (1952) 298-9.

434. Wordsworth, Christopher
(i) *Six Letters to Granville Sharp, Esq. Respecting his Remarks on the Uses of the Definitive Article, in the Greek Text of the New Testament* **(1802)**
Suggested date of reading: probably by July 1802
References: see note
On 26 July 1802 C wrote to Estlin about some of the matters raised by CW's *Six Letters* (Griggs ii 820). Chambers suggested that C even reviewed the volume in the *British Critic*, but Griggs points to C's letter to Poole of 28 Jan. 1810: 'On the first appearance of Christopher Wordsworth's Book on the Subject I studied the matter seriously; [and] but for accidents should have published on it' (Griggs iii 282-3). C's copy, which contains a note on the endpaper, is now at Victoria University Library (Dendurent 568).[2] I cannot say for certain whether W had a copy but it would be extraordinary if he did not. In any case, C's copy was later retained at Rydal Mount (Shaver 362).

(ii) *Ecclesiastical Biography, or Lives of Eminent Men connected with the History of Religion in England* **vol. 1 only (1810)**
Suggested date of reading: by 19 Feb. 1810
References: *MY* i 388
'Have you seen my Brother Christopher's publication?' DW asked Jane Marshall on 19 Feb. 1810, 'I am reading it with great inter[est]. The lives of Cardinal Wolsey and Sir Thomas More are delightful' (*MY* i 388). Lady Beaumont was another early admirer of the volume (*MY* i 392). In one of his notes to *The Excursion* (1814), p. 428, W refers his readers to CW's account of Baxter (see also *PW* v 424). W's copy was retained at Rydal Mount (Shaver 278); a copy of vol. 1 is now on display in Rydal Mount in what used to be the poet's study. It contains some pencilled annotations but no ownership inscription, or anything that would

---

[1] There is a note in pencil, in DW's hand, on the front flyleaf, dated 30 May 1802.
[2] For more comments on this book by C, see Griggs ii 820-1, 829, *Notebooks* iii 3275.

confirm it to have been W's. In 1814 CW presented a copy of this work, on W's behalf, to William Johnson (*MY* ii 171 and n2).

(iii) *Reasons for declining to become a subscriber to the British and Foreign Bible Society* **(1810)**
Suggested date of reading: by 27 March 1811
References: *MY* i 472-3
Writing to Wrangham on 27 March 1811, W offers a critique of the work of the British and Foreign Bible Society that is evidently influenced by CW's pamphlet. He adds: 'I think the last 50 or 60 Pages of my Brother's pamphlet merit the serious consideration of all persons of the established Church' (*MY* i 473).

(iv) *Sermons* **(2 vols., 1814)**
Suggested date of reading: by 25 Feb. 1815 onwards
References: *MY* ii 206
On 18 Feb. 1815 DW believed that CW was 'sending us his sermons - but we have not yet received them' (*MY* ii 202). On 27 Feb. she told Priscilla Wordsworth:

> The day before yesterday Miss Alne dined with us, and from her we learned that Chris's sermons were just arrived at Brathay, so William walked to B. with Miss A. and borrowed one volume - It is the second. William and Mary have read several of the sermons and are very much delighted with them . . . (*MY* ii 206)

DW gives special mention to Sermon VI in vol. 2, on 'Paul and Felix' (at pp. 121-45),[1] 'which I heard my Brother preach at Binfield, a pleasure which I shall never forget' (*MY* ii 206). That occasion was almost certainly her visit to the Cooksons at Binfield near Windsor, 13-19 Oct. 1810, where she met CW and his wife. No more is heard of CW's sermons, though it may be presumed that W chased up vol. 1 and read that too, soon after finishing with vol. 2. Or perhaps CW sent W a copy of his own.

435. Wordsworth, Dorothy
(i) *Grasmere journals in MS*
Suggested date of reading: 24 Dec. 1801
References: *Grasmere Journals* 52
'Thoughts of last year - I took out my old journal' (DW's journal, 24 Dec. 1801). It is likely that W might also have renewed his acquaintance with DW's journals for 1800 at this time - or, indeed, at any point during the DC years.

---

[1] The sermon is on Paul and Felix, not Paul and Festus, as DW mistakenly writes (see *MY* ii 206 and n1).

(ii) Recollections of a Tour in Scotland in MS

Suggested date of reading: late Sept. 1803-31 May 1805
References: *EY* 421

DW's *Recollections* were written between late Sept. 1803 and 31 May 1805 (see Reed ii 35). Her brother was almost certainly reading them as they were composed, and they inspired a number of poems based on the 1803 tour; see also *EY* 421, 451, 463, 598. Like much else by DW, the *Recollections* circulated in MS for years after composition (see, for instance, *MY* ii 38). Despite moves to print it in 1822 (see *LY* i 152-3, 180-1), it was not published in full until 1874.

(iii) poetry in MS

Suggested date of reading: c. 1805 onwards
References: see note

DW mentions in her Grasmere journal of 18 March 1802 that she 'tried to write verses but alas!' (*Grasmere Journals* 81). It is not known whether any of her extant poems date from that early moment, but *A Cottage in Grasmere Vale* and *The Cottager to her Infant* date from c. 1805;[1] *Address to a Child, During a Boisterous Winter Evening* dates from 1806, and *The Mother's Return* from 1807.[2] She composed poems intermittently throughout the DC and Allan Bank years, and would have shown these to her brother. *Address to a Child*, *The Mother's Return*, and *The Cottager to her Infant*, were published in W's *Poems* (1815), and reprinted in subsequent edns of his collected works; *Loving and Liking* and *The Floating Island* were added 1836 onwards.

(iv) children's stories and verse

Suggested date of reading: between ?summer/autumn 1803 and spring 1806; by 20 April 1806
References: *MY* i 24

In her letter to Lady Beaumont of 20 April 1806, DW remarked, with characteristic self-deprecation: 'Do not think that I was ever bold enough to hope to compose verses for the pleasure of grown persons. Descriptions, Sentiments, or little stories for children was all I could be ambitious of doing, and I did try one story, but failed so sadly that I was completely discouraged' (*MY* i 24). The handful of poems by DW surviving from this period evidently represent only a part of her writing for children. She had amassed a number of miscellaneous pieces by May 1804 when Lamb wrote to ask her whether she had anything to contribute to a childrens' book being prepared by his friend, Eliza Fenwick. On 2 June he wrote to thank her for helping out: 'We are all sensibly obliged to you for the little scraps (Arthur' o Bower and his brethren) which you sent up; the bookseller has got them, and paid Mrs. Fenwick for them. So while some are authors for fame, some for money, you have commenced author for

---

[1] See *Romanticism: An Anthology*, ed. Duncan Wu (1994), pp. 498-9, and *PW* ii 50.
[2] See *PW* i 229-30, i 230-2. DW recalls the composition of *Address to a Child* and *The Cottager to her Infant* in her letter to Lady Beaumont of 29 April 1806 (*MY* i 24).

charity' (Marrs ii 138). Arthur o' Bower was not by DW, but she is, according to the Opies, the earliest written source for the rhyme.[1] It was among her contributions to Fenwick's volume, some of which may have been original works by DW. The 'bookseller' mentioned by Lamb was perhaps Mrs Godwin who, in 1809, published Charles and Mary Lamb's *Poetry for Children*.

(v) *Narrative Concerning George and Sarah Green* **in MS**
Suggested date of reading: between 22 April and 4 May 1808 or shortly after
References: see note
DW's *Narrative* was composed between 22 April and 4 May 1808, and her brother would have seen it in MS either during, or shortly after, composition. Though formally published only in 1936, it circulated in MS long after it was written (see, for instance, *MY* ii 46, 641).

(vi) passages composed for Joseph Wilkinson's *Select Views in Cumberland, Westmoreland, and Lancashire* **(1810)**
Suggested date of reading: 12 Nov. 1810 and thereafter
References: *MY* i 449
W provided the letterpress for Wilkinson's *Select Views*, which was published in twelve monthly instalments. On 12 Nov. 1810 DW told Catherine Clarkson: 'I wrote so far last night after W. and M. were gone to bed; for in the evening Wm. employed me to compose a description or two for the finishing of his work for Wilkinson' (*MY* i 449). Owen and Smyser find the description of Wastwater to be in DW's hand (see *Prose Works* ii 126, 278-80). Other passages are detectable as hers on stylistic grounds but without textual evidence.

(vii) passages composed for Andrew Bell, *Elements of Tuition, Part II. The English School* **in MS**
Suggested date of reading: Aug. 1812
References: Reed ii 509
Bell's MS was virtually rewritten by DW during Aug. 1812, and was presumably read by W. Few of her alterations were incorporated by Bell. See notes 37(iii) and (iv).

436. Wordsworth, William and Samuel Taylor Coleridge
(i) *The Voice from the Side of Etna; or, The Mad Monk*
Suggested date of reading: c. 13 Oct 1800
References: Reed ii 94
This poem, largely by C, with contributions by W, appeared in the *Morning Post*, 13 Oct. 1800. W certainly read it, as it influenced the *Ode*. Various critics have disputed the poem's

---

[1] See *The Oxford Dictionary of Nursery Rhymes*, ed. Iona and Peter Opie (1951), pp. 57-8. The Wordsworths were probably read 'Arthur o' Bower' as children; W copies it out for Allan Cunningham in his letter of 23 Nov. 1825 (*LY* i 402).

authorship, the truth of which continues to be a matter for conjecture. See the summary of the arguments thus far and the *Morning Post* text in Cornell *Lyrical Ballads* 802-6.

(ii) *Lyrical Ballads* (2 vols., 1800)
Suggested date of reading: 26 March 1801 onwards
References: *EY* 321
W acknowledged receipt of the second edn of *Lyrical Ballads* on 27 March 1801; it had been formally published *c*. 25 Jan.

(iii) *Lyrical Ballads* (2 vols., 1802)
Suggested date of reading: 22 June 1802 onwards
References: *Grasmere Journals* 114
'The LB arrived' (DW's journal, 22 June 1802). This was W's first sighting of the 1802 edition, published *c*. 16 June.

437. Wrangham, Francis
(i) four sonnets and *Song*, *Annual Anthology* (1800)
Suggested date of reading: between 31 July 1800 and late Feb. 1801
References: *EY* 318
Writing to Wrangham in late Feb. 1801, W remarked: 'I read with great pleasure a very elegant and tender poem of yours in the 2nd Vol: of the anthology' (*EY* 318). As Shaver notes, Wrangham contributed four sonnets and a *Song* to the *Annual Anthology* (1800), a copy of which arrived at DC on 31 July 1800 (see note 11, above).

(ii) *Thirteen Practical Sermons; Founded Upon Doddridge's Rise and Progress of Religion in the Soul. To which are annexed Rome is fallen! a sermon preached 1798, with notes and illustrations, &c.* (1800)
Suggested date of reading: shortly after late Feb. 1801
References: *EY* 318
In late Feb. 1801 W sent Wrangham what amounts to a plea for copies of his latest publications. After claiming that 'I have not seen a single book since I came here [i.e. to DC], now 13 months ago', W goes on to add: 'You will not therefore be surprized if your sermons, neither the Rome is fallen, nor the Vol: have found their way to us' (*EY* 318). This refers to Wrangham's recently published *Thirteen Practical Sermons* (1800). C's copy was retained at Rydal Mount and is now at Victoria University Library (Shaver 362; Dendurent 571). It is inconceivable that Wrangham gave one to C and not to W; presumably he sent a copy to W shortly after receiving the letter of late Feb. 1801.

(iii) *The Holy Land* (1800)
Suggested date of reading: after late Feb. 1801
References: *EY* 318

In late Feb. 1801 W wrote to Wrangham to say how few books he read, and that he has not seen 'your poem' - meaning Wrangham's recently published *The Holy Land*. He goes on to suggest: 'When you visit this country mind you bring your poems along with you, also your sermons, if possible' (*EY* 318). With no further evidence one cannot be certain, but it seems probable that W saw *The Holy Land* not long after this letter was written.

(iv) *Poems* (1795)
Suggested date of reading: 1802
References: see note
Despite the date on its title-page, this book took a long time to emerge from the press. Sadleir notes: 'One may assume that the volume was actually issued in 1802. It was certainly "out" by 1803, as it is advertised as available at 4*s*. in boards on A2 verso of *The Disadvantages of Diffused Knowledge*, a sermon published in 1803.'[1] In *WR* 154 I speculated that W and C, both of whom had poems in the volume, saw parts of it prior to its eventual publication; they must both have seen, and, one supposes, been given, copies of the finished work. No copy is listed in Shaver. It was reviewed by Southey, *Annual Review* 1 (1802) 655-7 (Southey *SC* 3050).

(v) *A Sermon on the Translation of the Scriptures into the Oriental Languages* (Cambridge, 1807)
Suggested date of reading: after 12 July 1807
References: *MY* i 155 and n2
Writing to Wrangham on 12 July 1807, W said: 'Pray let a copy of your sermon be sent by Mawman to Longman's, to be forwarded by him in the first parcel of books he sends to Southey' (*MY* i 155). There is no further evidence, but it is likely that Wrangham obliged.

(vi) *Human Laws best supported by the Gospel: An Assize Sermon* (York, 1808)
Suggested date of reading: between 17 April and 5 June 1808
References: *MY* i 246-7
On 5 June 1808, W told Wrangham

> I have read your sermon (which I lately received from Longman) with much pleasure. I only gave it a cursory perusal, for since it arrived our family has been in great confusion, we having removed to another House, in which we are not yet half settled. The Appendix I had received before in a frank, and of that I feel myself more entitled to speak, because I had read it more at leisure. (*MY* i 247)

W had ordered a copy of the sermon by 17 April, but he had not at that date received it (*MY* i 212). Reed dates the Wordsworths' removal to Allan Bank to *c*. 24 May; evidently, the sermon arrived shortly before then. As for the appendix, it appears that W had been sent this

---

[1] *Archdeacon Francis Wrangham 1769-1842* (Oxford, 1937), p. 33.

in a letter some time between 17 April and the time when he received a copy of the sermon itself. W discusses Wrangham's ideas on education at some length; see *MY* i 247-9.

(vii) *The Gospel best Promulgated by National Schools* **(York, 1808)**
Suggested date of reading: 1-3 Dec. 1808
References: *MY* i 277
'Your sermon did not reach me till the night before last', W told Wrangham on 3 Dec. 1808, 'I believe we have all read it, and are much pleased with it' (*MY* i 277).

438. York Herald
Suggested date of reading: probably 1799 onwards; by Oct. 1802
References: Grasmere Journals 126
On their way back to DC from W's wedding, DW recorded that they 'put a Letter into the Post office for the York Herald' (DW's journal, 4 Oct. 1802). Reed ii 196n71 mentions that notices of the wedding appeared in the *York Herald* on 9 Oct. and the *York Courant* on 11 Oct. This intriguing detail suggests that the *York Herald* was the local paper of choice for the Hutchinson family. As such it would probably have been known to W from 1799 onwards.

439. Young, Edward, *Night Thoughts*
Suggested date of reading: 12 March 1805
References: EY 556-7
The thirteen-line quotation from *Night Thoughts* in W's letter to Beaumont of 12 March 1805 (*EY* 556-7) was probably copied from the printed text. The Wordsworths may have been reading the poem as consolation in the wake of JW's untimely death.

Appendix I

Wordsworth's reading 1770-1799

1. Additions

AI1. Barbauld, Anna Laetitia, *A Summer Evening's Meditation*
Suggested date of reading: c. 25 Jan. 1798
References: see note
In his note, 'Wordsworth's "A Night-Piece" and Mrs Barbauld', *N&Q* NS 40 (1993) 40-1, David Chandler argues for the influence of Barbauld's *A Summer Evening's Meditation* on W's *A Night-Piece*, composed shortly after 25 Jan. 1798. Barbauld's poem first appeared in her *Poems* (1773). In his forthcoming note, '"A tongue in every star": Wordsworth and Mrs Barbauld's "A Summer Evening's Meditation"', Damian Walford Davies lends support to Chandler's argument by pointing out a reference to Barbauld's poem in a draft in the Alfoxden notebook of c. March-April 1798. 'Has every star a tongue?' W asks in 'Are there no groans no breeze or wind' (Cornell *Lyrical Ballads* 284) - following Barbauld's question: 'Is there not / A tongue in every star that talks to man . . ?' These notes would suggest that W had access to a copy of Barbauld's *Poems* at Alfoxden. C almost certainly owned one, as he had been a fervent admirer of her work since at least 1796.

AI2. Beattie, James, *Original Poems and Translations* **(1760)**
Suggested date of reading: 1794
References: see note
A reading of this work is recorded in *WR* 11, dated '1779-87; certainly by 1787'. Graver points out that W's translation of Horace's *Ode* III xiii ('o fons Bandusiae'), probably composed 1794 (see Cornell *Evening Walk* 135), echoes Beattie's translation, published in the 1760 volume. Beattie was the only eighteenth-century translator, other than W, to render 'loquaces' as 'loquacious'. Both render 'desiliunt' as 'leap away', and W's poem echoes Beattie's translation in lines 1, 4, 5, and 6 as well. Thus a 1794 reading of *Original Poems and Translations* is possible. I would add only that it is just possible that W's translation of the ode, though its terminal date is 1794, may have been executed in earlier years, perhaps at Cambridge.

AI3. Bentley, Richard, *Dissertation on the Epistles of Phalaris . . .*
and the Fables of Aesop **(1697)**
Suggested date of reading: probably 1787-91
References: *LY* iii 503
On 23 Dec. 1837 W wrote to Dyce to thank him for the gift of *The Works of Richard Bentley* ed. Dyce (3 vols., 1836-8). It evidently contained Bentley's *Dissertation*, which W mentions in his letter:

Appendix I

How much do I regret that I have neither learning nor eyesight thoroughly to enjoy Bentley's masterly *Dissertation on the Epistles of Phalaris*; many years ago I read the work with infinite pleasure. As far as I know, or rather am able to judge, it is without a rival in that department of literature; a work of which the English nation may be proud as long as acute intellect, and vigorous powers, and profound scholarship shall be esteemed in the world. (*LY* iii 503)

W's dating of this reading is vague, but the most likely guess would be that it took place during his Cambridge years, or shortly afterwards.

AI4. Bourne, Vincent, *Miscellaneous Poems: Consisting of Originals, and Translations* (1772)
Suggested date of reading: late 1780s onwards
References: *EY* 657
See note 53, above. Evidently this volume came into W's possession before 1800, probably during his Cambridge years.

AI5. Burns, Robert, *Poems* (Kilmarnock, 1786)
Suggested date of reading: 1786
References: *FN* 170
In *WR* 23 I could not be certain as to whether W had seen the Kilmarnock volume on publication; in fact, a MS note prepared for the 1842 text of *At the Grave of Burns* confirms that he did: 'With the Poems of Burns I became acquainted almost immediately upon their first appearance in the volume printed at Kilmarnock in 1796 [*a mistake for* 1786]' (*FN* 170).

AI6. Chetwynd, John, *Anthologia historica, containing fourteen centuries of memorable passages and remarkable occurrents, collected out of the English, Spanish, Imperial, and Jewish histories, and several other authors and writers* (1674)
Suggested date of reading: c. 1799
References: see note
W's copy is now at Cornell University Library (Shaver 53). Abbie F. Potts, 'Wordsworth and William Fleetwood's *Sermons*', *Studies in Philology* 26 (1929) 444-56, described the volume, which, she noted, contains a note in W's hand which she dated to 'about 1799-1800': 'See Fleetwood of Self-Murder'. This also reveals, of course, that W was acquainted with Fleetwood's *Sermons* by that date.

AI7. Fleetwood, William, *The Relative Duties of Parents and Children, Husbands and Wives, Masters and Servants, Considered in Sixteen Sermons* (1705)
Suggested date of reading: c. 1799
References: see note

See preceding note. Potts traces Fleetwood's influence back to *Salisbury Plain* (1793). There is no mention of this title in Shaver.

AI8. Habington, William, *Description of Castara*
Suggested date of reading: by 28 Dec. 1798
References: Stein 154; Potts 203-17
C. Lawrence Ford, 'Wordsworthiana', *N&Q* 9th Ser. 4 (1899) 321-3, 342-3, was the first to observe that *She dwelt among th' untrodden ways* has a source in Habington's *Castara*:

> Like the violet, which alone
>   Prospers in some happy shade,
> My Castara lives unknown,
>   To no looser eye betrayed.

Potts 203-17 argues vigorously for Habington's influence on W from 1798 onwards.

AI9. Horatius Flaccus, Quintus, *Odes, Epodes, Satires, Epistles, and Ars Poetica*
Suggested date of reading: c. 1787-91
References: see note
Though not listed by Shaver, W's copy is on display at Rydal Mount in what used to be the poet's study. It is a duodecimo volume, without title-page or prelims, containing Horace's complete works: four books of *Odes*, one book of *Epodes*, two books of *Satires*, two books of *Epistles*, and the *Ars Poetica*. Although it contains no title-page, the typeface and paper indicate that it was published in the 1770s or, more likely, 1780s. The inscription 'Wm Wordsworth' appears on page 1, which is the first page in the book, in an early hand, similar to that on other books owned by W at Cambridge. On the inside back board of the volume W has practised writing his name in a neat hand - again indicating that the book was an early acquisition. The text itself is quite well used. In particular, *Ode* I xxxi, *To Apollo*, which W translated at Cambridge, contains a number of inked corrections. *Ode* III xiii, to the Blandusian fountain, follows the spelling 'B*l*andusian', which W duplicated in his rendering (see Cornell *Evening Walk* 135 and n).

AI10. Hutchinson, William, *The History and Antiquities of the County Palatine of Durham* **(Carlisle, 1794)**
Suggested date of reading: between late April and 17 Dec. 1799
References: Reed ii 708-9
At some time between late April and 17 Dec. 1799, DW copied the epitaph of Sir George Vane at the parish church of Long Newton, Durham, as published in Hutchinson, into DC MS 20. This MS transcription was probably W's source for its appearance in the second of the *Essays Upon Epitaphs* (*Prose Works* ii 69, 107-8).

Appendix I

AI11. Lemprière, John, *Bibliotheca classica; or, a classical dictionary*
Suggested date of reading: mid-1790s onwards
References: Shaver 156
W's copy is now at the Wordsworth Library. The front flyleaves and prelims are missing. However, the book contains an early ownership inscription, in ink, 'W Wordsworth'. This appears to me to date from the mid-1790s, like that on W's copy of Walker's *Universal Gazetteer* (*WR* 143). My guess is that this book was in his possession by the time he moved into DC.

AI12. Lucretius Carus, Titus, *His Six Books of Epicurean Philosophy, done into English Verse, with Notes*, **tr. Thomas Creech (1699)**
Suggested date of reading: ?1780s onwards
References: see note
W's copy was auctioned at the Wordsworth Summer Conference, 1994, and is now in the possession of Paul F., Betz. It contains an early set of initials on the title-page, 'W:W.' A note entered in pencil on the flyleaf says: 'This copy formerly belonged to Wordsworth, and was purchased at the sale of his Library. See his initials on the Titlepage.' With only the initials to go on, it is not easy to put a precise date on W's ownership, but the mid to late 1780s onwards is about right. I am puzzled by the pencilled inscription, as this volume is not listed by the Shavers, and does not appear, so far as I can find, in Wordsworth *SC*. However, there can be no doubt as to its authenticity.

AI13. Martin, Martin, *A Voyage to St. Kilda* **(4th edn, 1753)**
Suggested date of reading: late 1780s onwards
References: Shaver 171
W's copy is now at St John's College, Cambridge. It survives in its original vellum binding, and bears the title-page inscription, in ink: 'Wordsworth St Johns'. Immediately beneath this, he has added 'very scarce'. On pages 63-4, W has written, in a very late hand, in pencil:

> This separate pamplet which I
> suppose to be exceedingly scarce
> is furthermore valuable as con-
> taining particulars of S^t. Kilda
> w^h are not found in the account
> of that place given by the same
> author in his Vol. concerning the
> Western Isles - Collins the poet
> had read this pamplet -
> Wm Wordsworth

From W's letters to Dyce of Nov. 1828 onwards it is evident that he mislaid this book for a while, finding it only in mid-June 1830 (see *LY* i 650, ii 236, 291).

AI14. Randolph, Thomas, *Poems, with the Muses looking-glass, and Amyntas,* **ed. Robert Randolph (5th edn, Oxford, 1668)**
Suggested date of reading: mid-1790s onwards
References: Shaver 211
W's copy is now at the Wordsworth Library. It bears an ownership inscription on its title-page, in ink: 'W. Wordsworth'. This is early, and dates, I think, from the mid-1790s.

AI15. Ritson, Joseph, ed., *A Collection of Scotch Songs, with the airs* **(2 vols., 1794)**
Suggested date of reading: by 23 Feb. 1799
References: Moorman i 429; Shaver 216
W's *Ellen Irwin, of the Braes of Kirtle* tells the story given in the Scots ballad *Helen of Kirkconnell*, which Moorman suggests W read in Ritson's *Scotch Songs*. Butler and Green endorse this suggestion, as Ritson's volume also contains a quotation from Pennant's *Tour in Scotland* on which W also appears to have drawn (Cornell *Lyrical Ballads* 382-3). *Ellen Irwin* was probably composed between 6 Oct. 1798 and 23 Feb. 1799, providing a terminal date for W's reading of this volume, a copy of which was retained at Rydal Mount.

AI16. Seneca, Lucius Annaeus, *L. Annei Senecæ Cordubensis. Tragœdiæ X.* **(Basle, 1550)**
Suggested date of reading: c. late 1780s onwards
References: see note
W's copy is now at the Wordsworth Library. It contains an early ownership inscription on the title-page, in ink, by W. There can be no certainty, as it is undated, but I would guess the inscription to date from W's Cambridge years.

AI17. Sotheby, William, *Sonnet VIII. A Fancy Sketch,* **in** *A Tour through parts of Wales, Sonnets, Odes, and other Poems* **[Bath, 1790]**
Suggested date of reading: shortly before 1797
References: *MY* ii 515
On 6 Feb. 1827 W told Sotheby:

> I was gratified the other day by meeting in Mr Alaric Watts' Souvenir with a very old acquaintance, a Sonnet of yours, which I had read with no little pleasure more than 30 years ago. 'I knew a gentle Maid'.

W probably saw Sotheby's sonnet in *Poems* (1790), reprinted 1794; if his dating is correct, he must have read it shortly before 1797.

> I knew a gentle maid: I ne'er shall view
>   Her like again: and yet the vulgar eye
>   Might pass the charms I traced, regardless by;
> For pale her cheek, unmarked with roseate hue;
>   Nor beamed from her mild eye a dazzling glance;
> Nor flashed her nameless graces on the sight;
> Yet beauty never woke such pure delight.
>   Fine was her form, as DIAN's in the dance;
> Her voice was music, in her silence dwelt
>   Expression, every look instinct with thought:
>   Though oft her mind by youth to rapture wrought
> Struck forth wild wit, and fancies ever new,
> The lightest touch of woe her soul would melt:
>   And on her lips, when gleamed a lingering smile,
>   Pity's warm tear gushed down her cheek the while:
> Thy like, thou gentle maid! I ne'er shall view.

C knew some of the contents of the 1790 volume almost by heart, so he claimed in Aug. 1802 (Griggs ii 855); perhaps he discussed, or even introduced W to, Sotheby's poem.

AI18. Tacitus, Caius Cornelius, *C. Cornelii Taciti Opera quae extant omnia, ad editionem optimam Joh. Fre. Gronovii . . . expressa* **(2 vols., Glasgow, 1743)**
Suggested date of reading: 1787 onwards
References: Shaver 251

W's copy is now at St John's College, Cambridge, surviving in its original leather boards. It contains the flyleaf inscription, 'Wordsworth St John's', and, directly underneath, 'C. Wordsworth'. The second flyleaf bears the much later inscription, 'W. Wordsworth', probably entered during the late 1810s or early 1820s, and underneath that of 'C. C. Cookson'. The volume contains numerous marginalia in pencil not in W's hand.

Christopher Crackanthorpe Cookson entered his name in this volume well before W - and I would suggest that he was its first owner. He was born in 1745, and might well have acquired this book while at University himself. At any rate, he seems to have presented it to W when he went up to St John's in 1787. W would have found it useful, as Tacitus' *De Moribus Germanorum* was on the College examination syllabus in June 1788 (see *WR* 167). CW was admitted to Trinity College, Cambridge, in Aug. 1792, when presumably W passed it on to him. It returned to W's possession at some point, as it was retained at Rydal Mount in later years.

AI19. 'Mr Taylor's tour'
Suggested date of reading: by 24 Dec. 1799

References: *EY* 680

Writing to C on 24 Dec. 1799, W describes his recent journey from Sockburn to Grasmere and mentions 'one of the waterfalls of which I read you a short description in Mr Taylor's tour' (*EY* 680). Shaver records that 'This book has not been identified', but I wonder whether it could have been Joseph Taylor's *A Journey from Edenborough in Scotland 1705*, unpublished until 1903 when it was edited by W. Cowan. The description of the waterfall may be that of the 'dropping well' of Knaresborough, pp. 47-8 of the published text.

2. *Points of information*

p. 23, note 42 (ii): Burns' *Epistle to J.L.* is used as the epigraph to *Ruined Cottage* MS B, not MS D.

p. 25, note 46: Graver suggests that W's references to Benjamin Flower in letters of 1809 support the argument that he read the *Cambridge Intelligencer* (see *MY* i 327, 332).

p. 28, note 54: Graver suggests that the copy of Cicero's Orations kept at JW Sr's library at Cockermouth, later retained by Richard Wordsworth of Branthwaite, and sent to W in 1805 (note 54 [i]), was the copy of *De officiis, Cato Major* and *Laelius* now retained at the Wordsworth Library (note 54 [ii]).

p. 44, note 74 (ii): Desmond King-Hele points out that further echoes of Darwin at *Descriptive Sketches* 70-1 may be found at the beginning of *The Loves of the Plants* Canto III, which contains such phrases as 'to the cross', 'with hideous laugh', 'two imps', 'in mock devotion' (lines 36, 29, 15, 35).

p. 50, last line: R. W. Clancey points out that although Dyer 'may have' attended Bennett's lectures, it is not certain. This applies also to the reiteration of this claim on p. 163. Clancey adds that Dyer certainly called Bennett his tutor.

Appendix II

Wordsworth's reading 1800-1815: some queries

AII1. Buchanan, Claudius, *Christian Researches in Asia; with notices of the translation of the Scriptures into the Oriental Languages* **(Cambridge and London, 1811)**
Suggested date of reading: after Nov. 1811
References: see note
In Nov. 1811, Lady Beaumont wrote to W:

> let me know if you have seen Mrs Grant's view of the superstitions of the Highlanders, I am enchanted with the wildness of her simplicity which is quite practical, and unstudied, some of her literal translations from the Galic I am sure would please you, in particular a dialogue between the Hunter & owl. have you seen Buchanan's Christian Researches in India, a most interesting work . . .
>
> (Wordsworth Library WLL/Beaumont, G. H./37)

It is not clear whether W saw either of these volumes, but Lady Beaumont would hardly have brought them to his attention had she not been prepared to either show them to him, perhaps on a visit to London, or to send them to him at Grasmere.

AII2. Dibdin, Charles, the younger, *Edward and Susan, or The Beauty of Buttermere* **(1803)**
Suggested date of reading: between 1803 and 13 June 1804
References: Marrs ii 117
Dibdin's play is mentioned at *Thirteen-Book Prelude* vii 321-7 - lines composed, Reed suggests, between late March and 13 June 1804. Although the *Prelude* lines imply otherwise, W is unlikely to have seen this play, as it opened at Sadler's Wells on Easter Monday, 11 April 1803, and he did not visit London between then and the time at which he composed the *Prelude* lines. W's principal source of information was Mary Lamb, whose letter to DW of 9 July 1803 describes the details mentioned in the *Prelude* (Marrs ii 117). However, it is just possible that W also read the play, which went into print in 1803. He and C had an interest in its subject, and they might have wanted to see what Dibdin had made of it. For further details of the production of 1803 see E. Rimbault Dibdin, 'Sadler's Wells Play Alluded to by Wordsworth', *N&Q* 10th Ser. 1 (1904) 136-7.

AII3. Grant, Anne, *Essays on the Superstitions of the Highlanders of Scotland; to which are added, translations from the Gaelic* **(2 vols., 1811)**
Suggested date of reading: after Nov. 1811
References: see note
In Nov. 1811, Lady Beaumont wrote to W:

let me know if you have seen Mrs Grant's view of the superstitions of the Highlanders, I am enchanted with the wildness of her simplicity which is quite practical, and unstudied, some of her literal translations from the Galic I am sure would please you, in particular a dialogue between the Hunter & owl. have you seen Buchanan's Christian Researches in India, a most interesting work . . .

(Wordsworth Library WLL/Beaumont, G. H./37)

It is not clear whether W saw either of these volumes, but Lady Beaumont would hardly have brought them to his attention had she not been prepared to either show them to him, perhaps on a visit to London, or to send them to him at Grasmere. He might have become further acquainted with Mrs Grant's writing through her sketches of manners and scenery in America, lent to the Wordsworths by Southey in summer 1813 (see note 186).

AII4. Kant, Immanuel, works
Suggested date of reading: see note
References: see note

There is a wealth of excellent critical writing available on the subject of Kant's influence on the Romantics in general, and on W in particular. But, while there may be grounds for thinking that W was aware of some of Kant's ideas, there seems little reason to question his insistence to Robinson in 1840 that he had 'never read a word of German metaphysics, thank Heaven!' (*LY* iv 49). His comment to Henry Reed of 23 Dec. 1839 is typical: 'German transcendentalism . . . would be a woeful visitation for the world were it not sure to be as transitory as it is pernicious' (*LY* iii 752).

'Kant, Schelling, Fichte; Fichte, Schelling, Kant: all this is dreary work and does not denote progress', he commented in 1844 (Peacock 76). I am struck by the fact that C was studying all three of these authors - and especially Kant (see CC *Marginalia* iii 263) - during his intermittent residence at Allan Bank, 1809-10, and it is likely that much of what W knew of them was gleaned from him at this time. None of this, however, constitutes proof of readings by W. It should be borne in mind that many of the writers read by C during 1809-10 were not read by W, nor had they any impact on his thinking. It is doubtful whether his grasp of German ever equalled that of C, whose expertise was well up to the standard required to read Kant and Fichte in the original. At most, W may have seen translations (as, perhaps, he had done in 1798 - see *WR* 80-1), but I suspect that what he knew of the Germans was largely picked up from C. Hazlitt's comments, too, on W's intellectual talents, have a bearing on the likelihood of W's knowledge of Kant: 'Mr. Wordsworth's power is not that of analysis or illustration' (Howe ix 5).

Owen and Smyser cite Kant in notes to W's *Sublime and Beautiful*, composed between Sept. 1811 and Nov. 1812. But Owen warns: '"Cf." doesn't necessarily mean that W read Kant, but that W and Kant had the same idea and/or used similar phrasing' (letter to me). This caution is supported by the occasion when Sir William Hamilton told W how he had been struck by the similarity of certain ideas in *The Excursion* to those of Kant, to which W replied that he had no knowledge of Kant. Useful discussion of Kantianism in W is provided by Stallknecht, *Strange Seas of Thought* (1958), pp. 206-12.

AII5. 'Letters to Don Francisco Rigueline'
Suggested date of reading: 1 April 1809 onwards
References: Jordan 121
According to a letter by De Quincey to DW, 28 March 1809, this was sent to Grasmere by De Quincey in a consignment that arrived 1 April. I have been unable to identify this volume; or perhaps it was part of a newspaper or periodical article, though my searches through the files of the *Courier* of this period have revealed nothing by that name. According to De Quincey Rigueline was 'commander of the 3rd. division of Blake's Army'.

AII6. Oldham, John, *Works*
Suggested date of reading: perhaps 1800s
References: see note
In early 1823 Samuel Rogers wrote to DW:

> I have lately met with a remarkable instance of your Brother's sagacity - He had always maintained that Gray's line 'And leave us leisure to be good' was not his own - It is in Oldham. 'I have not yet the leisure to be good.' He is said to have been scrupulous in quoting, but he never did so, but when he wanted an authority. 'Slow tolls the village-clock the drowsy hour' is in H^y V.th 'The clocks do toll, & the third hour of drowsy morning came.' (WL/A/Rogers/3)

The reference is to Oldham's *The Satyr Against Vertue. Pindarique Ode* 119 and Gray's *Hymn to Adversity* 20 (see *LY* i 189). W referred again to this piece of erudition in a letter to Rogers of *c*. 17 Feb. 1836, when he added: 'You recollect that long ago I said to you I was sure the line would be found somewhere, and if I am not mistaken you told me, some time after, you had met with it in Owen Feltham's prose' (*LY* iii 172). All of which provides little enough evidence to date W's first reading of Oldham; he could have made his learned remark to Rogers at any time from May/June 1801 onwards, when they first met (Reed ii 119). I would guess in any case that W was *au fait* with Oldham's work by the 1800s. Perhaps Wrangham might have referred W to Oldham during composition of their *Imitation of Juvenal*, 1795. Oldham's *Works* (1692) was at Rydal Mount (Shaver 189).

AII7. Sharp, Richard, poem in MS
Suggested date of reading: see note
References: *EY* 469
On 29 April 1804 W wrote to Sharp: 'You did flatter me with a sort of hope that I should receive from you an Ms Poem of your own, which I have expected with no little eagerness;

but as you did not mention it in your Letter I rather conclude that you have not sent it along with the Books, a loss which I shall the less regret' (*EY* 469). Did Sharp ever send W his MS poem? He continued to correspond with W, and visited DC in July or Aug. 1805, when he might well have brought some of his poetry (Reed ii 292). His *Epistles in Verse* (1828) was at Rydal Mount (Shaver 233).

AII8. Ussher, James, Archbishop of Armagh, *Clio*
Suggested date of reading: see note
References: Rogers 207

'There are passages in Wordsworth where I can trace his obligations to Usher's *Clio*', Rogers once remarked (*Rogers* 207). Really? I find no specific mention of Ussher in W's letters or works, but Rogers must have had cause for this observation, and may even have discussed it with W.

AII9. Vaughan, Henry
Suggested date of reading: see note
References: see note

Ever since the anonymous author of 'Tennyson's Maud', *National Review* 1 (Oct. 1855) 377-410, noted the similarity in thought between W's *Ode: Intimations of Immortality* and Vaughan's *The Retreat*, numerous critics have sought similarities between the two poems.[1] The only piece of circumstantial evidence in favour of W's reading of Vaughan was his alleged annotated copy of *Silex Scintillans*, which in fact never existed.[2] Indeed, there is no evidence either that W knew Vaughan's work at the time he composed the *Ode*, or that he read it in succeeding years. I turn to the letter to Anderson, 17 Sept. 1814, as indicating the range of W's poetic knowledge up to that point: Vaughan is conspicuously absent from a list that includes Herbert, Marvell, and Herrick - who, one would have thought, would have reminded W of Vaughan had he known of his work (*MY* ii 151-5). J. Sturrock observes: 'As Wordsworth and Southey include such poets as minor as John Chalkhill and Abraham Fraunce, it is most unlikely that the omission of Vaughan is based on a low opinion of his work. It surely argues for their ignorance of his work at that time.'[3] Furthermore, the Rydal Mount library did contain a copy of Herbert's *Remains* (1652), but no copy of any volume containing Vaughan. There are no references to Vaughan in any of W's writings or spoken

---

[1] See also George Macdonald, *England's Antiphon* iii (Dec. 1868) 255-6, 261-2, 303-7; Richard Chenevix Trench, *A Household Book of English Poetry* (1869); J. C. Shairp, 'Friendship in English Poetry', *North American Review* 138 (Feb. 1884) 120-37; Anon., 'Henry Vaughan', *Spectator* 59 (18 Sept. 1886) 1245-7; John Dennis, 'Children and the Poets', *Leisure Hour* 39 (Jan. 1890) 182-6; John G. Dow, 'Poets and Puritans', *Macmillan's magazine* 61 (April 1890) 457-64; Quiller-Couch, 'A Literary Causerie: Wordsworth's "Ode"', *Speaker* 17 (14 May 1898) 611-13, to name only the nineteenth-century advocates of this argument.

[2] Helen McMaster, 'Vaughan and Wordsworth', *RES* 11 (1935) 313-25.

[3] 'Wordsworth and Vaughan', *N&Q* 222 (1977) 322-3, p. 323.

utterances. For further useful discussion of this matter see John T. Shawcross, 'Kidnapping the Poets: the Romantics and Henry Vaughan', *Milton, the Metaphysicals, and Romanticism*, ed. Lisa Low and Anthony John Harding (Cambridge, 1994), pp. 185-203.

Appendix III

The Longman accounts

Two articles by W. J. B. Owen provide the central sources of information about W's dealings with Longman.[1] However, to the best of my knowledge the Longman account for 1800-12 remains unpublished. As it provides an important source for several of the notes in the main list, above, I thought it worth presenting here. It survives at the Wordsworth Library, where it is catalogued as WLMS Box 6/Bundle 8/1. The account is dated 'London Jany 16 1812', and is prefaced by a letter.

Dear Sir,

We have above stated your account, agreeable to your request, which leaves a balance in our favour of £3.8.5.

We have 261 copies remaining of your Poems: but we have no sets of the Lyrical Ballads.

> We are
> Dear Sir
> Yrs truly
> Longman

1800				
Aug. 7	2 Withering's Botany boards	2.	16.	0
	2 Microscope	1.	7.	0
	wharfage		1.	4
1801				
Jan 23	3 Lyrical Ballads boards M^r RW			
	7 do to Sundries and order			
	1 do Vol 2 Mr Stoddart			
26	6 do 2 Vols Mr Hutchinson			
	1 Davy's Researches, 8° boards		9.	6
29	1 Lyrical Ballads 2 Vols Mr Lambe[2]			
Feb 10	1 do do bds			

---

[1] 'Letters of Longman & Co. to Wordsworth, 1814-36', *The Library* 9 (1954) 25-34; 'Costs, Sales, and Profits of Longman's Editions of Wordsworth', *The Library* 12 (1957) 93-107.

[2] For deductions stemming from the entries for Jan. 1801 see my article, 'Lamb's Reading of *Lyrical Ballads* (1800)', *CLB* 92 (1995) 224-5.

1802
June 16   8 do   do   bds
            4 do   do   M^r RW

1803
July 20   Postage   9

1805
Sept 13   4 Lyrical Ballads 2 Vols bds
            1 do W Scott Esq[1]

1806
Feb 15   1 Massingers Works boards   1.   19.   0

1807[2]
May 2   To paid Coach hire   1.   11.   6
            Crusoes Life - Sheep   1.   3.   0
April 14   1 Decameron 4to used calf   15.   0

1812
Jan 14   2 Goldsmiths England per Mr Jameson   5.   10

---

[1] A copy of *Lyrical Ballads* (1805) was probably promised to Scott during the brief walking-tour of early Aug. (Reed ii 296). Scott had given W a copy of *The Lay of the Last Minstrel* in Jan. (see note 349[iv]).

[2] The entries for 1807 relate to W's stay in London. Though not listed in this statement, W made other calls on his account with Longman at this time; see Reed ii 352 and n11.

Appendix IV

Libraries used by Wordsworth

A number of book clubs and libraries were established in the Lake District during the late eighteenth and early nineteenth centuries:

> Carlisle had a subscription library as early as 1768; the Kendal one was founded in 1794 and by 1829 there were libraries of this kind in Cockermouth, Workington, Penrith (with over 1,000 volumes), Alston, Kirkby Lonsdale and Ulverston. In addition, books clubs, the members of which each expended from 10 shillings to a guinea a year on books, which circulated among the members and were then sold, were founded in Kendal (1761), Appleby (1790), Kirkby Lonsdale (1794) and Orton (1828). Such clubs performed systematically a service that might operate informally among friends in a village.[1]

John Gavin tells me that the Kirkby Lonsdale Book Club had sixty subscribers (paying 14 shillings per annum), and a library of 'upwards of 500 complete works' in 1828. In 1851 it still owned 500 volumes stored at the house of John Forster, Bookseller and Printer.

Grasmere Subscription Library
The Wordsworths were using books belonging to the Library in Jan. 1805; see note 336. This library still exists, now known as the Red Book Club.

Ambleside Book Society
The Ambleside Book Society was established in 1828 to serve the inhabitants of Ambleside, Rydal, Grasmere, and Langdale. Wordsworth was a member from its inception. Subscription costs were one guinea. At an annual sale all books circulated during the year were auctioned. It is interesting to find Dora Wordsworth complaining in 1828 of precisely the same thing that DW mentions in her letter of 1805 about the Grasmere Book Club: the short loan period. On 30 December 1828 Dora told Edward Quillinan:

> My Father is a subscriber to a book club in Ambleside what think you of the march of Intellect in this northern clime - ? exceedingly interested in the book we are now reading - Genl Miller's - the worst is we were only allowed seven days for a vol: which makes it a hurry scurrying business and we can only half enjoy an interesting book when we have it - It does not suit our Poet at all. When he is at work he cannot read. So he has petitioned to be allowed to keep the book beyond the time & pay his fine.
> (Wordsworth Library WLL/Wordsworth, Dora/17)

---

[1] C. M. L. Bouch and G. P. Jones, *A Short Economic and Social History of the Lake Counties 1500-1830* (Manchester, 1961), p. 208.

Appendix IV

John Miller's *Memoirs* (2 vols., 1828) were later retained at Rydal Mount (Shaver 174), having been purchased at the annual auction. Other purchases included Samuel Pepys, *Memoirs*, ed. Richard, Lord Braybrooke (2nd edn, 5 vols., 1828) (Shaver 198); Thomas Colley Grattan, *Traits of Travel* (3 vols., 1829) (Shaver 107);[1] Lady Anne Fanshawe, *Memoirs of Lady Fanshawe* (1829); John Evelyn, *Memoirs of John Evelyn*, rev. William Upcott (5 vols., 1827); Sydney Owenson, Lady Morgan, *The Book of the Boudoir* (2 vols., 1829) and *The O'Briens and the O'Flahertys* (4 vols., 1827). I suspect that the volumes not mentioned by Shaver (i.e. Fanshawe, Evelyn, and the two Owensons) were given to Dora. Records of the Book Club are to be found at the Armitt Library, Ambleside.

Kendal Coffee Room and Library
The Wordsworths were using the Kendal Book Club by July 1809. They were permitted to do so only by the grace of an existing member, as they were never elected to memberships themselves. When Dorothy visited the Coffee Room in July 1809 she consulted its copy of the *Edinburgh Review*. It is likely that she and her brother had been using these facilities for some years. The Coffee Room took a selection of newspapers and periodicals that would have enabled them to stay in touch with current affairs and literary developments; the Library was located in the same building, and retained a comprehensive stock of books. It is most intriguing that the Library ordered a copy of *Poems, in Two Volumes* nearly three months prior to publication; they must have been tipped off either by the poet, or by an admirer (see p. 239, above).

The earliest surviving visitors' book to the Book Club dates from 1826; it is now at Kendal Record Office. Wordsworth signed himself in on 23 January 1827; 27 January 1827; and 13 November 1827. He was accompanied by his son John on these occasions; in addition, John went on his own on 24 November 1827. Each time, the member of the Book Club who admitted them was Thomas Cookson, the Kendal friend of the Wordsworths (see note 103[v]). Cookson sponsored a visit by John Monkhouse, also in 1827. Among other acquaintances of the Wordsworths, Charles Lloyd signed the visitors' book between 3 and 6 October 1824, and John Thelwall on 6 May 1829.[2] For a brief history of the Kendal Coffee Room, News Room, and Book Club, see S. C. Noble, *The Kendal Newsroom* (1909).

---

[1] W's copy is now at the Beineke Library, Yale University.
[2] He did not, apparently, visit Wordsworth on that occasion (see *LY* iii 640).

Appendix V

Fugitive texts read by Wordsworth, 1800-1815

It is no part of my present task to reprint fugitive works known to Wordsworth - a pleasant one no doubt, that could provide material for an entire book in itself. However, there are some which it is necessary to present here as an essential adjunct to the notes that record W's reading of them.

AV1. John Codrington Bampfylde, *On the Evening* **and** *Written at a Farm*
These poems were published in 1778, but not apparently known to W when transcribed for him by Sir George Beaumont in May 1808 (see note 22). The texts are taken from Beaumont's letter to W of 1 May 1808 (Wordsworth Library WLL/Beaumont, G. H./27); they are hitherto unpublished.

Sonnet
Slow sinks the glimmering beam from western sky,
The woods & hills, obscured by Evening gray,
Vanish from mortal sight, and fade away.
Now, with the flocks and yearlings, let me hie
To Farm or Cottage lone; where perch'd hard by,
On mossy pale the Red-breast tunes his lay
Soft twittering, and bids farewell to Day -
Then whilst the watch-dog barks & ploughmen lie
Lull'd by the rocking winds, let me unfold
Whate'er in rhapsody, or strain most holy,
The hoary Minstrel sang in times of old;
For, well I ween, from Them the nine inspire
Wisdom shall flow, and Virtue's sacred fire,
And Peace & Love, and heav'nly Melancholy.

Sonnet
Written at a Farm
Around my porch & lonely casement spread,
The Myrtle never sear, and gadding vine
With fragrant sweet-briar love to intertwine;
And in my garden's box encircled bed
The pansies pied, & muskrose white and red.
The pink and tulip, and honied woodbine,
Fling odours round; the flaunting eglantine
Decks my trim fence, 'neath which, by silence led,
The wren hath wisely placed her mossy cell;

And, far from noise, in courtly land so rife,
Nestles her young to rest, & warbles well.
Here, in this safe retreat, & peaceful glen,
I pass my sober moments, far from men,
Nor wishing Death too soon, nor asking life.

AV2. C., *The Comet, 1811*

This poem, published under the initial 'C' in *The Courier* for 16 Nov. 1811, was thought by W to be by Coleridge (see note 385[xxxviii]). The significance of this is evident when one has read the poem - a task possible only for those with access to a newspaper library. As it is not easy to come by I present it here, in the *Courier* text.

THE COMET, 1811
Mysterious visitant! whose beauteous light
    Among the wondering stars so strangely gleams;
Like a proud banner in the train of Night,
    The unblazoned flag of Deity it streams;
    Infinity is written in thy beams;
And Thought in vain would thro' the pathless sky
    Explore thy secret course; thy circle seems
Too vast for Time to grasp: - O can that eye
Which numbers hosts like thee, this atom earth descry?

O THOU my every hope; my only fear;
    Father of Lights, round whom the systems roll,
With all their Suns and Comets, sphere on sphere,
    Thy all-pervading energy, the soul.
    Thyself the centre of the mighty whole!
When Death shall purge the film of sense away,
    And Truth with irresistible control
Shall seize my ravish'd mind, - that awful day
How shall my soul sustain, - that infinite survey?

Then shall I shudder at the guilty past,
    And feel thy awful presence on my heart:
Was it at thee, O God, my sins I cast?
    Oh! on my trembling soul thy mercy dart
    For now I feel how terrible thou art!
Thou wert All-present, and I saw thee not;
    Thou art my bliss, and yet I said, 'Depart;'

Murmured, tho' boundless mercy fixed my lot: -
And wilt thou own the soul that thee so oft forgot?

O wond'rous thought, the high and holy One,
    Inhabiting Eternity, will make
The humble soul his dwelling place; the sun
    Whose rising beams on orbs innumerous break,
    Doth shine as much for the poor reptile's sake;
To HIM is nothing great - is nothing small;
    He fills a world, - he bids the insect take
His being full of bliss; - he formed them all;
He guides the Comet's course, - He marks the Sparrow's fall.

Man - Man, tho' in the dust his insect birth,
    Beholds his nature unto God allied,
Link'd to the golden throne this creature earth
    By ties that shall eternally abide;
    Let suns, let systems perish - Jesus died;
Nor shall one vital spark be quenched in night,
    Which God has kindled: - Here my soul confide,
Safe in the arms of everlasting Might,
And circled with the beams of uncreated Light.
            C.

AV3. Sir George Beaumont, MS poem on the death of his mother
This poem was transcribed by Beaumont for W in a letter of 20 Nov. 1814. This unpublished work is presented in a text taken from Beaumont's transcription (see note 34[ii]).

The dreaded hour is come - tis come tis past!
That gentle sigh - dear Mother was thy last -
And now diffus'd among the blest above
Glows the pure spirit of maternal love
Ting'd by whose beams, my very failings show
Grac'd in thy eyes with something not their own -
No more affection shall thy Fancy cheat,
Or warp thy judgement, when again we meet.
But every action, in its native hue
Rise undisguis'd & open to thy view -
May every action then, be duely weigh'd
Each Virtue cherish'd, & each duty paid -

Then when my Soul shall wing her trembling flight
Thro Deaths dark valley, to the realms of light -
She may expect, tho no false lights beguile
The approving look, & *that* accustom'd smile
Blest smile! - becoming her sublime abode
And Harbinger of pardon from my God! -

Appendix VI

Tale Imitated from Gower: MS text

Who composed the *Tale Imitated from Gower*? It appears in *Prelude* MS W (DC MS 38, 10r-12r), and comprises a reworking of the tale of the travellers and the angel from Gower's *Confessio Amantis* ii 291-364. The fact that it is in DW's hand might suggest that it is by her - if so, it is an oddity, as it resembles nothing else she ever wrote. Another factor - that it follows immediately after the fair copy of Marvell's *Horatian Ode*, which apparently dates from the Wordsworths' visit to the Lambs in September 1802 (see note 273[ii]) - suggests an alternative possibility. If the copy of the *Tale* dates from the same moment, it could have been the work of Mary Lamb, other poems of whose it seems to resemble in points of content and style.[1] That readers may judge for themselves, I include a transcription of the MS text here.

The *Tale* follows Gower's text quite closely. There are few departures from the original, usually no more than minor amplifications or clarifications. MS punctuation, capitalization, and orthography are preserved in my transcription. Alternative readings are accepted provided they are accompanied by deletion of the original. Ampersands have been preserved.

Tale Imitated from Gower. Friend and Contemporary of Chaucer.

In antient Books I find it written
Of Jupiter, that he was smitten
(Such prayers from day to day he heard,
Such plaints from night to morn preferr'd)
With fatherly desire to know   5
How his[2] poor creatures far'd below,
That outrage might be set aside,
And wrong conditions rectified.
And, for this purpose, downward went
An Angel, on commission sent,   10
To inquire, and use what means he could
Fairly to see how matters stood.
About the world he took his way,
And it befel upon a day
This Angel, who should Jove inform,   15
Was clothed in a human form;
And overtook, I understand,

---

[1] Compare, in particular, Mary Lamb's *The Boy and Snake*, *The Broken Doll*, and *The Reproof*. Like the *Tale*, all of these are written in octosyllabic couplets, and all contain a rather pointed moral.

[2] **his** deleted in MS, but no alternative provided.

Appendix VI

    Two men who journey'd overland
Through whom he thought the truth to espy,
And goes with them in company.   20
With his discourses and words wise
This Angel them in sundry guise
Opposeth; words he had, now soft,
Now loud, and made them wrangle oft;
Each had his reason in his head,   25
And thus with tales, the pair he led;
Till he with good examination
Learn'd their condition & their station,
What kind of men both were & knew
(For he had look'd them through & through) 30
That one was covetous by nature,
And th' other was an envious creature.
When he had learn'd them thus by heart
Anon he feign'd he must depart,
And said that he must forward wend;   35
But hearken what befel in the end.
For then he gave them understanding
He was a Traveller of Jove's sending;
And said that, for their kindness, fain
He'd be to do some grace again;   40
And bade that one of them should say
What thing he'd liefer;[1] & straitway
That he should have it on the spot,
Done perfectly, nor sconc'd a jot;
And further to this tune, no doubt   45
Most sweet, he adds another note,
Saying, that what was wish'd by one
Should twice be for the other done,
The double what his Comrade asketh,
And thus to them his grace he taxeth.   50
The covetous man was wondrous glad;
And he to his Companion said,
'Yours of this kindness the first use is'
And added, he'd have no excuses;

---

[1] **he'd liefer** he would rather [have]. Cf. Coleridge, *Piccolomini* IV v 160: 'Far liever would I face about . . .'

Tale imitated from Gower: MS text

For he supposeth that he would 55
Make his entreaty for world's good,
But then he knew well how it stood,
For he himself by double weight
Shall after take; & thus by sleight
To the intent that he might win, 60
He bade his Comrade first begin.
The envious Man saying, 'God hinder
That courtesy, which moves my wonder,
Should want like courtesy to meet it',
Entreats as he had been entreated. 65
But, at the bottom, big & bigger
His heart grew; wily, and more eager
To have his asking first. He thought
That, if he power or profit sought,
His Comrade would have double dues; 70
That would he in no manner chuse,
But then he sheweth what he was,
His own true heart! for in the case[1]
He to that Angel thus did say,
And for his gift he this did pray, 75
To take from him his one eye's sight,
Be but his Comrade blind outright.
   The word no sooner said, anon
The single eye he had was gone:
Forthwith, his Comrade was also 80
Blind as a stone of both his two.
Then was the Envious glad enough.
The one did weep, the other did laugh;
He set his one eye at no cost,
Whereof the other had two lost. 85

---

[1] **case** an imperfect rhyme, but nonetheless the one used by Gower.

Bibliography

This Bibliography does not duplicate titles included in *Wordsworth's reading 1770-1799*; it lists only items not mentioned there, and used in preparation of the present volume. Works are listed under the following headings:
1. Manuscripts and ephemera
2. Texts by the Wordsworths
3. Works cited, quoted, or referred to
4. Bibliographies, catalogues, etc.

1. Manuscripts and ephemera

Wordsworth Library, Grasmere
Wordsworth Commonplace Book: DC MS 26
Wordsworth manuscripts: DC MSS 20, 24, 28, 31, 38
Sir George Howland Beaumont, Bart., to Wordsworth, WL/Beaumont, G. H.
Benjamin Robert Haydon to Wordsworth, 29 December 1815, WL/MS A/Haydon/3
Samuel Rogers to Dorothy Wordsworth, 1822, WL/A/Rogers/3
Thomas Clarkson to Henry Taylor, 31 May 1808, WL/A/Clarkson, T.
Dora Wordsworth to Edward Quillinan, WL/Wordsworth, Dora/17
Accounts of T. N. Longman with Wordsworth, WL/Box 6/Bundle 8
Dorothy Wordsworth, Recollections of a Tour in Scotland, transcribed by Sara Hutchinson, DC MS 55; one of the earliest extant MSS of the tour, watermarked 1803

Kendal Record Office
Kendal Coffee Room: subscribers and proceedings, 1794 onwards; WD/K/189
Kendal Library: proceedings, 1794 onwards; WD/K/192
Kendal Coffee Room: visitors' book, 1824 onwards; WD/K/303
Files of the *Westmorland Advertiser, or Kendal Chronicle*

Carlisle Record Office
Files of *The Cumberland Pacquet*

2. Texts by the Wordsworths

Wordsworth, Dora. *Dora Wordsworth her book.* Ed. F. V. Morley. London: Selwyn and Blount Ltd., 1924
Wordsworth, Dorothy. *Journals of Dorothy Wordsworth.* Ed. Mary Moorman. 2nd edn. Oxford: Oxford University Press, 1971
Wordsworth, John. *The Letters of John Wordsworth.* Ed. Carl H. Ketcham. Ithaca, NY: Cornell University Press, 1969
Wordsworth, Mary. *The Letters of Mary Wordsworth 1800-1855.* Ed. Mary E. Burton. Clarendon Press: Oxford, 1958

Wordsworth, William. *Lyrical Ballads, and Other Poems, 1797-1800*. Ed. James Butler and Karen Green. Ithaca, NY: Cornell University Press, 1992

The Excursion. London, 1814

The Letters of William and Dorothy Wordsworth VIII: A Supplement of New Letters. Ed. Alan G. Hill. Oxford: Clarendon Press, 1993

The White Doe of Rylstone by William Wordsworth. Ed. Alice Pattee Comparetti. Ithaca, NY: Cornell University Press, 1940

Wordsworth's Preface to Lyrical Ballads. Ed. W. J. B. Owen. Westport, Conn.: Greenwood Press, Inc., 1979

The Fenwick Notes of William Wordsworth. Ed. Jared Curtis. London: Bristol Classical Press, 1993

3. Works cited, quoted, or referred to

Bagchi, P. 'A Note on Wordsworth's Sonnet, "I heard (alas! 'twas only in a dream)"'. *N&Q* 218 (1973) 44

Bampfylde, John Codrington. *The Poems of John Bampfylde*. Ed. Roger Lonsdale. Oxford: The Perpetua Press, 1988

Barton, Anne. 'The Road from Penshurst: Wordsworth, Ben Jonson and Coleridge in 1802'. *Essays in Criticism* 37 (1987) 209-33

Beer, John. *Coleridge's Poetic Intelligence*. Houndmills, Basingstoke: Macmillan, 1977

Betz, Paul F. 'Wordsworth's First Acquaintance with Blake's Poetry'. *Blake Newsletter* 3 (1970) 84-9

Blunden, Edmund. *Leigh Hunt: A Biography*. London: Cobden-Sanderson, 1930

Bonjour, Adrien. *Coleridge's 'Hymn Before Sunrise': A Study of Facts and Problems Connected with the Poem*. Lausanne: Imprimerie La Concorde, 1942

Bouch, C. M. L., and G. P. Jones. *A Short Economic and Social History of the Lake Counties 1500-1830*. Manchester: Manchester University Press, 1961

Burns, Robert. *The Songs of Robert Burns*. Ed. Donald Low. London: Routledge, 1993

The Letters of Robert Burns. Ed. J. DeLancey Ferguson. Rev. G. Ross Roy. 2 vols. Oxford: Clarendon Press, 1985

Byrom, John. *The Poems of John Byrom*. Ed. Adolphus William Ward 3 vols. Manchester: Chetham Society, 1894-1913

Byron, George Gordon, 6th Baron. *The Complete Poetical Works*. Ed. Jerome J. McGann and Barry Weller. 7 vols. Oxford: Clarendon Press, 1980-93

Carr, Mary. *Thomas Wilkinson: A Friend of Wordsworth*. London: Headley Brothers, 1905

Chandler, David. '"Twisted in Persecution's Loving Ways": Peter Bayley Reviewed by Southey, Wordsworth and Coleridge'. *WC* 24 (1993) 256-61

'Wordsworth's "A Night-Piece" and Mrs Barbauld'. *N&Q* NS 40 (1993) 40-1

Clancey, Richard W. 'Wordsworth, Horace, and the Preface to *Lyrical Ballads*'. *CLB* NS 68 (1989) 131-8
   'Wordsworth's *Cintra* Tract: Politics, the Classics, and the Duty of the Poet. *Rhetorical Traditions and British Romantic Literature*. Ed. Don Bialostosky and Lawrence Needham. Bloomington, Indiana: Indiana University Press, 1995, pp. 79-93
Coe, Charles Norton. 'Wordsworth acknowledges his debt to Travel Books'. *N&Q* 194 (1949) 234-5
   'A Note on Wordsworth's "The Solitary Reaper"'. *MLN* 63 (1948) 493
Coleman, Deirdre. *Coleridge and The Friend (1809-10)*. Clarendon Press: Oxford, 1988
Coleridge, Samuel Taylor. *Coleridge's Dejection*. Ed. Stephen Maxfield Parrish. Ithaca, NY: Cornell University Press, 1988
   Seven Lectures on Shakespeare and Milton. Ed. John Payne Collier. London, 1856
Coombe, D. E. 'The Wordsworths and Botany'. *N&Q* 197 (1952) 298-9
Cooper, Lane. 'Wordsworth Sources. Bowles and Keate'. *The Athenaeum* 4043 (22 April 1905) 498-500
   'A Glance at Wordsworth's Reading'. *MLN* 22 (1907) 83-9, 110-17
   'Wordsworth's Knowledge of Plato'. *MLN* 33 (1918) 497-9
Courtney, Winifred F. *Young Charles Lamb 1775-1802*. London and Basingstoke: Macmillan Press, 1982
Cox, W. A. 'Kirke White'. *N&Q* 10th Ser. 6 (1906) 427, 496-8
Crawford, Walter B. 'A Three-Decker Novel in Wordsworth's Library, 1802'. *N&Q* NS 11 (1964) 16-17
Curry, Kenneth. 'The Library of Robert Southey'. *Tennessee Studies in Literature Special Number: Studies in Honor of John C. Hodges and Alwin Thaler*. Knoxville, Tenn.: The University of Tennessee Press, 1961. Pp. 77-86
   'Southey's Contributions to the *Annual Review*'. *Bulletin of Bibliography* 16 (1939) 195-7
   'Southey's Contributions to *The Quarterly Review*'. *WC* 6 (1975) 261-72
   'The Contributors to *The Annual Anthology*'. *Papers of the Bibliographical Society of America* 42 (1948) 50-65
Curtis, Jared R. *Wordsworth's Experiments with Tradition: The Lyric Poems of 1802*. Ithaca, NY: Cornell University Press, 1971
Davies, Damian Walford. '"A tongue in every star": Wordsworth and Mrs Barbauld's "A Summer Evening's Meditation"'. *N&Q* (forthcoming)
De Quincey, Thomas. *Confessions of an English Opium-Eater and Other Writings*. Ed. Grevel Lindop. Oxford: Oxford University Press, 1985
Dibdin, E. Rimbault. 'Sadler's Wells Play Alluded to by Wordsworth'. *N&Q* 10th Ser. 1 (1904) 136-7
Engell, James, ed. *Coleridge: The Early Family Letters*. Oxford, 1994

Bibliography

Farington, Joseph. *The Diary of Joseph Farington*. Ed. Kathryn Cave. Vol. 9. New Haven and London: Yale University Press, 1982
The Diary of Joseph Farington. Ed. Kathryn Cave. Vol. 13. New Haven and London: Yale University Press, 1984
Field, Barron. *Barron Field's Memoirs of Wordsworth*. Ed. Geoffrey Little. Sydney: Sydney University Press, 1975
Ford, C. Lawrence. 'Wordsworthiana'. *N&Q* 9th Ser. 4 (1899) 321-3, 342-3
Gavin, John. 'Westmorland Literary Institutions to 1850'. *Bibliothek* (forthcoming)
Ginsberg, David. 'Wordsworth's *Poems, in Two Volumes* (1807) and the Epideictic Tradition'. *Rhetorical Traditions and British Romantic Literature*. Ed. Don Bialostosky and Lawrence Needham. Bloomington, Indiana: Indiana University Press, 1995, pp. 108-21
Gordon, Mary. *Christopher North: A Memoir of John Wilson*. 2 vols. Edinburgh, 1862
Gower, John. *Confessio Amantis*. Ed. Russell A. Peck. Toronto: University of Toronto Press, 1980
Graver, Bruce E. 'The Oratorical Pedlar'. *Rhetorical Traditions and British Romantic Literature*. Ed. Don Bialostosky and Lawrence Needham. Bloomington, Indiana: Indiana University Press, 1995, pp. 94-107
 'Wordsworth's Georgic Pastoral: *Otium* and *Labor* in "Michael"'. *European Romantic Review* 1 (1991) 119-34
 Review of Duncan Wu, *Wordsworth's Reading 1770-1799*, *CLB* NS 91 (1995) 164-7
Harshberger, Scott. 'The Rhetoric of Improvisation: *Michael* and Quintilian's *Institutio Oratoria*'. *WC* 25 (1994) 37-40
Heath, William. *Wordsworth and Coleridge: A Study of their Literary Relations in 1801-1802*. Oxford: Clarendon Press, 1970
Hodgson, John A. *Wordsworth's Philosophical Poetry, 1797-1814*. Lincoln: University of Nebraska Press, 1980
Hussey, Cyril C. 'Fresh Light on the Poems of Mary Lamb'. *Supplement to Charles Lamb Society Bulletin* 213 (January 1972)
Hutchinson, Sara. *The Letters of Sara Hutchinson*. Ed. Kathleen Coburn. London: Routledge and Kegan Paul, 1954
Jacobus, Mary. *Romanticism, Writing and Sexual Difference: Essays on* The Prelude. Oxford: Clarendon Press, 1989
Jones, Stanley. *Hazlitt: A Life*. Oxford: Clarendon Press, 1989
Jordan, John E. *De Quincey to Wordsworth: A Biography of a Relationship*. Berkeley and Los Angeles: University of California Press, 1962
Kaufman, Paul. 'Wordsworth's "Candid and Enlightened Friend"'. *N&Q* 207 (1962) 403-8

Knight, William, Ed. *Memorials of Coleorton, being letters from Coleridge, Wordsworth and his sister, Southey, and Sir Walter Scott, to Sir George and Lady Beaumont of Coleorton, Leicestershire 1803 to 1834*. 2 vols. Edinburgh: David Douglas, 1887

Lamb, Charles, and Mary Lamb. *The Works of Charles and Mary Lamb*. Ed. E. V. Lucas. 7 vols. London: Methuen, 1903-5

Landon, Carol. 'Wordsworth, Coleridge, and the *Morning Post*: An Early Version of "The Seven Sisters"'. *RES* 11 (1960) 392-402

Langbaum, Robert. 'The Evolution of Soul in Wordsworth's Poetry'. *PMLA* 82 (1967) 265-72

Letters from the Lake Poets to Daniel Stuart. Ed. Mary Stuart. London: West, Newman and Co., 1889

Lindsay, Julian Ira. 'A Note on the Marginalia'. *HLQ* 1 (1937-8) 95-9

Liu, Alan. *Wordsworth: The Sense of History*. Stanford, Calif.: Stanford University Press, 1989

Mabbott, Thomas Ollive. 'Landor on Chatterton and Wordsworth: Marginal Notes'. *N&Q* 156 (1929) 168-9

Mann, Peter. 'Two Unpublished Letters of Robert Southey'. *N&Q* NS 22 (1975) 397-9

Maxwell, J. C. 'Wordsworth and Prospero'. *N&Q* 194 (1949) 477

Montluzin, Emily Lorraine de. *The Anti-Jacobins 1798-1800: The Early Contributors to the 'Anti-Jacobin Review'*. Houndmills: Macmillan Press, 1988

Musgrove, S. *Unpublished Letters of Thomas De Quincey and Elizabeth Barrett Browning*. Auckland University College Bulletin No. 44 English Series No. 7 1954

Nabholtz, John R. 'Wordsworth's Interest in Landscape Design and an Inscription Poem of 1800'. *Papers on Language and Literature* 2 (1966) 265-9

'Wordsworth's *Guide to the Lakes* and the Picturesque Tradition'. *MP* 61 (1964) 288-97

Newlyn, Lucy. 'The Little Actor and his Mock Apparel'. *WC* 14 (1983) 30-9

Nicoll, Allardyce. *A History of English Drama 1660-1900*. 4th edn. Cambridge: Cambridge University Press, 1952-9

Noble, S. C. *The Kendal Newsroom*. Kendal, 1909 (privately printed)

Opie, Iona and Peter Opie, eds. *The Oxford Dictionary of Nursery Rhymes*. Oxford: Clarendon Press, 1951

Owen, W. J. B. 'Wordsworth, the Problem of Communication, and John Dennis'. *Wordsworth's Mind and Art: Essays*. Ed. A. W. Thomson. Edinburgh: Oliver and Boyd, 1969. Pp. 140-56.

'Wordsworth and Jeffrey in Collaboration'. *RES* 15 (1964) 160-7

'Some Wordsworthian Borrowings'. *N&Q* 193 (1948) 429-30

'Understanding *The Prelude*'. *WC* 22 (1991) 100-9

'Manuscript Variants of Wordsworth's Poems'. *N&Q* 203 (1958) 308-10

'Letters of Longman & Co. to Wordsworth, 1814-36'. *The Library* 9 (1954) 25-34

'Costs, Sales, and Profits of Longman's Editions of Wordsworth'. *The Library* 12 (1957) 93-107

Parnell, Thomas. *Collected Poems of Thomas Parnell*. Ed. Claude Rawson and F. P. Lock. London and Toronto: Associated University Presses, 1989

Peacock, Markham L. *The Critical Opinions of William Wordsworth*. New York: Octagon Books, 1969

Potts, Abbie Findlay. 'Wordsworth and William Fleetwood's *Sermons*'. *Studies in Philology* 26 (1929) 444-56

Price, Sir Uvedale, Bart. *Sir Uvedale Price on the Picturesque*. Ed. Sir Thomas Dick Lauder, Bart. Edinburgh and London, 1842

Purton, Valerie. *A Coleridge Chronology*. Houndmills, Basingstoke: Macmillan, 1993

Rawson, C. J. '"Tom Jones" and "Michael": A Parallel'. *N&Q* 212 (1967) 13

Reed, Mark L. 'Blake, Wordsworth, Lamb, etc.: Further Information from Henry Crabb Robinson'. *Blake Newsletter* 3 (1970) 76-84

Rees, Joan. 'Wordsworth and Samuel Daniel'. *N&Q* 204 (1959) 26-7

Richardson, Joanna, ed. *Letters from Lambeth: the correspondence of the Reynolds family with John Freeman Milward Dovaston 1808-1815*. Suffolk: The Royal Society of Literature, 1981

Rogers, Samuel. *Recollections of the Table-Talk of Samuel Rogers*. London: Edward Moxon, 1856

St Clair, William. *The Godwins and the Shelleys: The Biography of a Family*. London: Faber and Faber, 1989

Senex. 'Wordsworth and Greek'. *N&Q* 177 (1939) 366-7

'Wordsworth and Greek'. *N&Q* 178 (1940) 172-3

Shawcross, John T. 'Kidnapping the Poets: the Romantics and Henry Vaughan'. *Milton, the Metaphysicals, and Romanticism*. Ed. Lisa Low and Anthony John Harding. Cambridge: Cambridge University Press, 1994. Pp. 185-203

Shearer, Edna Aston. 'Wordsworth and Coleridge Marginalia in a Copy of Richard Payne Knight's *Analytical Inquiry into the Principles of Taste*. *HLQ* 1 (1937-8) 63-94

Snyder, Alice D. *Coleridge on Logic and Learning*. New Haven: Yale University Press, 1929

Sotheby, William. *Lines suggested by the third meeting of the British Association for the Advancement of Science . . . with a short memoir of his life*. 1834

Southey, Robert. *History of Brazil*. London, 1810

Southey, Robert, and Charles Cuthbert Southey. *The Life of the Revd. Andrew Bell*. 3 vols. London, 1844

Sturrock, J. 'Wordsworth and Vaughan'. *N&Q* 222 (1977) 322-3

Sutton, Denys. 'Unpublished Letters From Sir George and Lady Beaumont to the Wordsworths'. *N&Q* 175 (1938) 146-9

Taylor, Joseph. *A Journey to Edenborough in Scotland 1705*. Ed. W. Cowan. Edinburgh: William Brown, 1903

Turnbull, John M. 'Wordsworth's "Flying Tailor"'. *TLS* (24 Oct. 1929), p. 846

'Wordsworth's Part in the Production of Lamb's "Specimens"'. *N&Q* 154 (1928) 114-15

W., T. 'A Lesson for Laureates'. *N&Q* 2nd Ser. 2 (1856) 487

Wardle, Ralph M. 'Basil and Anna Montagu: Touchstones for the Romantics'. *Keats-Shelley Journal* 34 (1985) 131-71

Wedd, Mary. 'Industrialization and the Moral Law in Books VIII and IX of *The Excursion*'. *CLB* NS 81 (1993) 5-25

Whalley, George. *Coleridge and Sara Hutchinson and the Asra Poems*. London: Routledge and Kegan Paul, 1955

'Samuel Taylor Coleridge: Library Cormorant'. PhD thesis, 2 vols., University of London, 1950

White, Henry Kirke. *The Remains of Henry Kirke White, of Nottingham*. Ed. Robert Southey. London, 1807

Wilson, Edward. 'An Echo of St Paul and Words of Consolation in Wordsworth's "Elegiac Stanzas"'. *RES* 43 (1992) 75-80

Woof, Pamela. 'Dorothy Wordsworth, Writer'. *WC* 17 (1986) 95-110

Woof, R. S. 'A Coleridge-Wordsworth Manuscript and "Sarah Hutchinson's Poets"'. *SIB* 19 (1966) 226-31

Wu, Duncan, ed. *Romanticism: An Anthology*. Oxford: Blackwell, 1994

Wordsworth's Reading 1770-1799. Cambridge: Cambridge University Press, 1993

'Lamb's Reading of *Lyrical Ballads* (1800)'. *CLB* 92 (1995) 224-5

'Wordsworth's Fisher King'. *CLB* (forthcoming)

4. Bibliographies, catalogues, etc.

Barnes, F., and J. L. Hobbs. *Handlist of Newspapers Published in Cumberland, Westmorland, and North Lancashire* (Cumberland and Westmorland Antiquarian and Archaeological Association Society Tract Series XIV). Kendal, 1951

Betz, Paul F. 'Manuscripts, Books, and Related Pictures of the Paul Betz Collection'. *British Romantic Art*. Jonathan Wordsworth, Robert Metzger, and Paul Betz. Lewisburg, Pennsylvania: Bucknell University in association with the Wordsworth Trust, 1990. Pp. 38-47

Britton, Jane. *Catalogue of the Bertram R. Davis Robert Southey Collection*. Waterloo, Ontario: University of Ontario Library, 1990

Coe, Charles Norton. 'Wordsworth and the Literature of Travel: A Bibliography'. *N&Q* 197 (1952) 429-33, 457

Egerer, J. W. *A Bibliography of Robert Burns*. Edinburgh and London: Oliver and Boyd, 1964

Fullmer, June Z. *Sir Humphry Davy's Published Works*. Cambridge, Mass.: Harvard University Press, 1969

Gordan, John D. 'William Wordsworth 1770-1850: An Exhibition'. *BNYPL* 54 (1950) 333-48, 384-96

Hammond, Eleanor Prescott. *Chaucer: A Bibliographical Manual*. New York: Peter Smith, 1933

Hedgecock, Deborah K. *A Handlist to the Charles Lamb Society Collection at Guildhall Library*. Supplement to *CLB* NS 89 (1995)

Jackson, J. R. de J. *Romantic Poetry by Women: A Bibliography 1770-1835*. Oxford: Clarendon Press, 1993

Johnson, C. R. *Provincial Poetry 1789-1839 British Verse Printed in the Provinces: The Romantic Background*. London: Jed Press, 1992

Nineteenth Century Short Title Catalogue 1801-1815. 5 vols. Avero: Newcastle-upon-Tyne, 1984-5

Quaritch, Bernard. *A General Catalogue of Books*. 7 vols. London, 1887-92

Roff, Renée. *A Bibliography of the Writings of Charles and Mary Lamb*. Bronxville, NY: Nicholas T. Smith, 1979

Smith, Simon Nowell. *Wordsworth to Robert Graves and Beyond*. Oxford: Bodleian Library, 1983

Snyder, Alice D. *Coleridge on Logic and Learning*. New Haven: Yale University Press, 1929

Sotheby, S. Leigh. *Bibliotheca Heberiana. Catalogue of the Library of the Late Richard Heber, Esq.* 13 Parts. London: Sotheby, 1834-7

Catalogue of the First and Second Portions of the Extensive and Valuable Library of the Venerable Archdeacon Wrangham. London: Sotheby, 1843

Ward, William S. *Literary Reviews in British Periodicals 1798-1820: A Bibliography*. 2 vols. New York and London: Garland Publishing Inc., 1972

Whalley, George. 'Note 315. Coleridge Marginalia Lost'. *The Book Collector* 18 (1969) 223

Wordsworth, Jonathan, and Stephen Hebron. *Romantic Women Writers*. Grasmere: The Wordsworth Trust, 1994

Zall, P. M., and E. W. Zall. 'Wordsworth in the Huntington Library: A Preliminary Checklist'. *WC* 1 (1970) 141-60

Index

A., *Dr. Adam Smith*, 1
Adam Bell, 1
Adam, Thomas, *Private Thoughts on Religion*, 1
Addison, Joseph, 86; *The Spectator*, 1; *see also* Steele, Sir Richard, and Joseph Addison
Advocates' Library, 192
Aikin, Lucy,
WORKS
poems, 2
periodical poetry (*Monthly Magazine*), 2
Poetry for Children, 2
Alfieri, Vittorio, Count, *The Tragedies of Vittorio Alfieri*, 2
Alfoxden, 85, 104
Allan Bank, 13, 72, 87, 215; young Coleridges stay there, 7; books at, 9, 26, 16, 38, 44, 64, 70, 98, 100, 102, 110, 113, 120, 135, 141, 148, 159, 160, 165, 167, 187, 199, 219, 222, 224; C resident there, 26, 27, 31, 59-60, 67, 75-6, 87, 116, 141, 159, 166, 177, 216, 261; John Wilson visits, 59; De Quincey resident there, 133; Stuart visits, 152
Allen, William, 222
Allestree, Richard, *The Ladies Calling*, 2-3
Alloa, 217
Ambleside, 7, 44-5; Lloyd moves to, 6
Amherst College, 161
Amory, Thomas, *The Life of John Buncle*, 3
An Authentic Narrative of the Loss of the Earl of Abergavenny, East-Indiaman, 3
Anderson, Robert, W's letter to, 28, 45, 46, 50, 54, 62, 80, 81, 88, 89, 95, 99, 100, 103, 108, 110, 112, 132, 136, 143, 144, 149, 153, 159, 161, 173, 174, 191, 193, 200, 207, 208, 228, 232, 232-3, 236, 244, 245; *The Works of the British Poets*, 3-4, 5, 7, 31-2, 33, 45, 46, 47, 49-50, 51, 54, 62, 68, 69, 75, 76, 77, 78, 81, 88, 89, 95, 99, 100, 102, 103, 108, 110, 112, 121, 132, 136, 139, 143, 144, 149, 153, 159, 161, 162, 173, 174, 191, 193, 194, 200, 201, 202, 203, 207, 208, 227, 228, 232, 232-3, 236, 244, 245; JW reads, 135
Anderson, Robert, of Carlisle, *Ballads in the Cumberland Dialect*, 4
Annual Anthology, 4, 179, 250
Annual Register, 4-5, 224
Annual Review, 2, 11, 13, 14, 15, 30, 32, 40, 54, 66, 89, 95, 115, 150, 181, 203, 225, 241, 251
An unfortunate Mother to her infant at her Breast, 6
Appleby, 55
Arbuthnot, John, *Miscellaneous Works*, 6

Ariosto, Ludovico
WORKS
Opere, 6
Orlando Furioso, 6; tr. John Harington, 6-7
Aristotle, 'From Aristotle's Synopsis of the virtues and vices', 7; *Ethics and Politics* tr. John Gillies, 7
Armstrong, John, *The Art of Preserving Health*, 7-8; *Sketches; or, Essays on Various Subjects. By Launcelot Temple, Esq.*, 8
Arnold, Samuel James, *The Devil's Bridge*, 8
Arthuriana, *see Sir Ysumbras, Sir Gowther, Sir Amadas*; Malory, Sir Thomas
Arthur o'Bower, 248-9
Ashburner, Molly, 207
Ashburner, Sarah, 88
Ashby de la Zouch, 75
Ashe, Thomas, *Travels, in America*, 8
Ayscough, Samuel, 188

Babes in the Wood, 124
Bacon, Francis, Lord Verulam, 8-10
WORKS
Advancement of Learning, 9
Advertisement touching the Controversies of the Church of England, 9
Essays, 9
Essays, Moral, Economical, and Political, 10
Meditationes Sacrae, 9
Of Atheism, 9-10
Of Studies, 8-9
On Revenge, 9
Works, 9
Bailey, Nathan, 160
Baillie, Joanna, 11
ballads, 1
Ballantyne, James, gives book to Southey, 96
Bampfylde, John Codrington
WORKS
On the Evening, 10; text given, 269
Sixteen Sonnets, 10
To the River Teign, 10
Written at a Farm, 10; text given, 269-70
Barbauld, Anna Laetitia, 176-7
WORKS
A Summer Evening's Meditation, 253
Eighteen Hundred and Eleven, 11
Hymn to Content, 10-11
review of Lamb's *John Woodvil*, 11, 30
Barker, Mary
WORKS
Lines Addressed to a Noble Lord, 11-12

285

Index

Barnard Castle, 229
Barnard, Thomas, *An account of an English Hermit, by a respectable Clergiman* in MS, 12
Barrington, Daines, *Observations on the More Ancient Statutes*, 12, 102
Barrow, Isaac
  WORKS
  sermon, 12
  Several Sermons Against Evil-Speaking, 12
Barrow, John
  WORKS
  Travels in China, 12-13
  Travels in South Africa, 13-14
Bartolozzi, Francesco, 62
Barton, Anne, 121-2, 191
Bartram, William, *Travels Through North and South Carolina*, 14, 167-8
Bateson, F. W., 24
Bayley, Peter, 197; suspected of having written *English Bards and Scotch Reviewers*, 40
  WORKS
  Poems, 14-15
  The Forest Fay, 15
Beattie, James
  WORKS
  Original Poems and Translations, 253
  The Minstrel, 15, 221
Beaumont, Francis (of Coleorton), 15-16
  WORKS
  To his . . . friend, Mr. Thomas Speght, 16
  Upon the following Poems of my deare Father, 15-16
Beaumont, Francis, and John Fletcher
  WORKS
  Dramatick Works, 16
  Fifty Comedies and Tragedies, 16, 17-18
  Love's Pilgrimage, 16
  Works, 16
Beaumont, Sir George Howland, 7th bart, 1, 12, 30, 44, 61, 63, 94, 114, 120-1, 151, 157, 164, 173, 197, 225, 226, 252; sends W poems, 10, 16, 17; lends books to W, 19-20, 67; W gives book to, 23-4; gives books to W, 61, 115, 175-6; library, 61, 98, 133, 139, 226, 231; gives books to C, 67; read to by W, 147; visits theatre with W, 160; gives book to DW, 234
  WORKS
  poem on his mother's death, 17; text given, 271-2
  review, 17
  review of books on William Betty, 152
Beaumont, Sir John; W to edit his poetry, 19; W reads books belonging to, 24-5, 32
  WORKS
  An Act of Hope, 19
  An Epitaph on my dear brother, 17-18
  Bosworth-field, 16, 18, 19-20
  poems, 18
  The Crown of Thorns, 19
  The Shepherdesse, 18
Beaumont, Margaret (Willes), Lady, DW gives book to, 37; sends book to DW, 124; 2, 5, 7, 13, 14, 18-19, 28, 32, 49, 60, 61, 67, 69, 83, 89, 95, 96, 97, 111, 115, 117, 118n2, 120-1, 123, 124, 147, 150, 151, 152, 161, 164, 171, 176, 180-1, 197, 208, 210, 216, 217, 225, 234, 246, 248, 260
Beaver, Philip, *African Memoranda*, 20
Beckford, William, 145
Beddoes, Thomas, 71
Beer, John, 75
Bell, Andrew, corresponds with C, 21; W encouraged to read by C, 130
  WORKS
  Elements of Tuition, 21-2, 249
  Experiment in Education, 21
  The Madras School, 20-21
Bell, John, *Poets of Great Britain*, 22, 47, 48, 64, 78
Bentley, Richard, *Dissertation on the Epistles of Phalaris*, 253-4
Bessie Bell and Mary Gray, 22
Betty, William, 17, 30, 152
Betz, Paul F., 24, 25n1, 72, 140, 150, 184, 237, 256
Bewick, Thomas, works, 22
  WORKS
  British Birds, 22
  Quadrupeds, 22
  Select Fables, 22
Bible, 22-3; C and W's approval of Old Testament, 120-1
Bibliothèque Portative de Voyageur, 26, 126, 174
Bickerstaff, Isaac, *see* Steele, Sir Richard, and Joseph Addison
Bingley, William, *North Wales*, 23
Birch, Thomas, 174; *Heads and Characters*, 23-4
Blair, Hugh, *Lectures on Rhetoric and Belles Lettres*, 24
Blake, William, 139
  WORKS
  A Dream, 25
  A Little Boy Lost, 25
  America, 25
  Dedication for Blair's *Grave*, 25
  Earth's Answer, 25
  Europe, 25
  Holy Thursday (Innocence), 24

Index

How Sweet I Roamed, 24
I love the jocund dance, 24
Introduction, 25
Jerusalem, 25
Laughing Song, 24
Night, 25
The Chimney Sweeper, 25
The Divine Image, 24
The Garden of Love, 25
The Human Abstract, 25
The Little Black Boy, 25
The Poison Tree, 25
The Sick Rose, 25
The Sunflower, 25
The Tyger, 24
To the Muses, 25
Blakeney, Robert, 161
Bloomfield, Robert, *The Farmer's Boy*, 25
Blunden, Edmund, 114n1
Boccaccio, Giovanni, *Il Decamerone*, 26
Bodleian Library, 75, 131
Boie, Heinrich Christian, 206
Boileau-Despréaux, Nicolas, *Œuvres*, 26
Bonaparte, Lucien, *Charlemagne*, 26
Bonaparte, Napoleon, 146, 154, 158, 213; escape from Elba, 218n1
Bonjour, Adrien, 33
Bonneval, Claude Alexandre de, Count, *Memoirs*, 26
Book of Common Prayer, 27
books, pass from C to W, 1; jointly purchased by C and W, 39; W's treatment of, 56
borderer, John Armstrong as, 8
Borrowdale, 77-8
Boston Athenæum, 207
Boston Public Library, 129
Boswell, James, *Life of Johnson*, 27
Bourne, Vincent
WORKS
Epitaph on a Dog, 28
Miscellaneous Poems, 27-8, 254
Works, 28
Bowles, William Lisle, daughter of, 161; *The Two Sailors*, 28
Bragg, Joshua, 24, 27
Breton, Nicholas, works, 28
Bristol, Southey meets Landor, 131
Bristol Library Society, 52, 123, 164
British Critic, 28-9, 206, 246
British Library, 1, 16, 17-18, 63, 81, 87, 103, 115, 188, 198-9, 208, 220; catalogue, 96; Lamb burrows away in, 127
Brookhouse, Christopher, 192

Brougham, Henry, review of Byron, 29-30; W meets, 114, 115
Brown, John, *Barbarossa*, 30
Brown, Thomas, review of Lamb, *John Woodvil*, 30
Browne, Sir Thomas
WORKS
Enquiries into Vulgar and Common Errors, 31
Pseudodoxia Epidemica, 31, 115
Religio Medici, 30-31
Browne, William, *Britannia's Pastorals*, 31-2
Bruce, James, *Travels to the Nile*, 32
Bruce, Michael, 46, 78
WORKS
Lochleven, 32-3
Elegy, 33
Brun, Frederika
WORKS
Chamouny beym Sonnenaufgange, 33
Die sieben Hügel, 33
Gedichte, 33
Brydges, Sir Samuel Egerton, 70; *The Ruminator*, 33
Buchanan, Claudius, *Christian Researches in Asia*, 260
Buchanan, George, 1
WORKS
Eclog of Crownes, 34
Maiae Calendae, 34
Opera Omnia, 34
poems, 33-4
Buchanan, John Lanne, *Travels in the Western Hebrides*, 34
Bunyan, John
WORKS
Pilgrim's Progress, 34
The Holy War, 34-5
Bürger, Gottfried August
WORKS
Der wilde Jäger, 35
Die Entführung, 35
Burges, James Bland, *Richard Coeur de Lion*, 35
Burgh, James, *Political Disquisitions*, 35
Burn, Richard, *see* Nicolson, Joseph, and Richard Burn
Burne, Nicol, *Leader-Haughs and Yarow*, 35
Burnet, Gilbert, *History of his Own Time*, 36
Burnet, Thomas, *Telluris Theoria Sacra*, 36-7
Burns, Robert, 33-4, 49, 80, 177, 205; letters, 96, 177n1; reviewed by Jeffrey, 117-18
WORKS
Poems, 37, 38, 254
Poetical Works, 38
The Ode to Ruin, 37

Index

The Vision, 38
Works, 37
Burton, Robert, *Anatomy of Melancholy*, 38
Busby, Thomas, 82
Butler, James A., 22, 35, 107, 181, 227-8, 257
Butler, Samuel, *Hudibras*, 38-9
Buxtorfius, Johannes, *Lexicon Hebraicum et Chaldaicum*, 39
Byrom, John, *Epigram on the Feuds Between Handel and Bononcini*, 39-40
Byron, Annabella Milbanke, Lady, W dines alone with, 40
Byron, George Gordon, 6th Baron, 25, 40-1; cordial meetings with W, 40; opinion of Thurlow, 227n1
WORKS
Beppo, 41
Childe Harold's Pilgrimage I, III and IV, 40-1
Don Juan, 41
English Bards and Scotch Reviewers, 40, 141
Hours of Idleness, 29-30
Lara, 41
The Corsair, 41
The Prisoner of Chillon, 41
Works, 41

C., *The Comet, 1811*, 216-17; text given, 270-1
Calais, 26, 126, 174
Calne, 103
Calvert, William, 85
Calvin, Jean, *Institutio Christianae Religionis*, 42
Cambridge, 62, 70, 74, 88, 93, 142, 149, 208, 253, 255, 257; St John's College, 44, 107, 144, 256, 258
Campbell, Thomas
WORKS
Gertrude of Wyoming, 42-3
Hohinlinden, 43
The Exile of Erin, 42, 108, 153
The Pleasures of Hope, 42
Carleton, George, *The Memoirs of Captain George Carleton*, 43, 102
Carlisle Cathedral Library, 74-5, 167
Carter, Elizabeth, 164
Cartwright, John, *People's Barrier*, 76
Carver, Jonathan, *Travels*, 43-4
Cave, William
WORKS
Apostolici, 44
Scriptorum, 44
Centlivre, Susanna, 'the Volume', 44
Cervantes Saavedra, Miguel de, *Don Quixote*, 44-5
Cevallos, Don Pedro, *Exposition of the Arts and Machinations*, 45
Chalkhill, John, 45
Chalmers, Alexander, 38; *Works of the English Poets*, 39-40, 45-6, 120, 191, 193, 228
Chamberlayne, William, 46
Chambers, E. K., 246
Chandler, David, 15, 209, 253
Chapman, George, 46
WORKS
Homer, 46, 111-12
Charles II, moralists of his day, 62
Chatterton, Thomas
WORKS
The Excellent Ballade of Charitie, 46
Works, 46-7
Chaucer, Geoffrey, 47-9, 77, 78; works attributed to, 51
WORKS
General Prologue, 48
The Canterbury Tales, 47
The Knight's Tale, 48, 78
The Manciple's Tale, 47
The Man of Law's Tale, 48
The Miller's Tale, 48
The Prioress' Tale, 47
Troilus and Criseyde, 47
Works, 49
Chetwynd, John, *Anthologia historica*, 254
Chiabrera, Gabriello, *Delle Opere di Gabriello Chiabrera*, 49
children's books, 49
Churchill, Awnsham and John Churchill, *Voyages and Travels*, 61
Churchill, Charles, 49-50
WORKS
Independence, 49-50
Rosciad, 50
Churchyard, Thomas, 50; *The Legend of Shore's Wife*, 50
churns, advertisement for, 13-14; quoted, 215-16
Cibber, Colley, *Apology*, 50; adaptations of Shakespeare, 50
Cicero, Marcus Tullius
WORKS
De Divinatione, 50-1
De Natura Deorum, 51
De Oratore, 51
In Catilinam, 51
Tusculan Disputations, 51
Clancey, Richard W., 112
Clanvowe, John, *Of the Cuckowe and the Nightingale*, 51
Clarendon, Earl of, *see* Hyde, Edward

Index

Clarke, James, *Survey of the Lakes*, 51-2
Clarkson, Catherine, 2, 3, 9, 29, 39, 43, 73, 96, 105, 118, 122, 125, 127, 128, 133, 148, 151, 158, 179, 183, 197, 199, 218, 242; lends books to W, 24, 179, 222
Clarkson, Thomas, 52-4; stays at DC, 53
WORKS
Essay on the Impolicy of the African Slave-Trade, 52
Essay on the Slavery and Commerce of the Human Species, 52
History of the Slave-trade, 53-4
Memoirs of William Penn, 54
Portraiture of Quakerism, 52-3
Claudianus, Claudius, works, 54
Cleveland, John, works, 54
Clifford, D. J. H., 55
Clifford, Lady Anne, Countess of Pembroke, 'Memoirs', possibly in MS, 54-5
Clym of the Clough, 1
Cobbett, William
WORKS
Cobbett's Parliamentary Debates, 56
Weekly Political Register, 55-6
Cobham, 34
Coburn, Kathleen, 21, 32, 59, 69, 74, 98, 116, 167, 172, 175, 188
Cochrane, Thomas, Lord (later 10th Earl of Dundonald), 219
Cockin, William, 237-8
Coe, Charles N., 8, 14, 109
Coffman, Ralph J., 139, 145, 166
Cole, John, 140
Coleorton, 1, 14, 19, 20, 24, 32, 34, 67, 88, 89, 96, 98, 111, 115, 129, 139, 147, 225
Coleridge, Derwent, 7
Coleridge, George, 60, 121
Coleridge, Hartley, 72, 73, 90; infant marginalia, 7; borrows books from Rydal Mount, 169; corresponds with Mrs Skepper, 177
Coleridge, N. F. D., 70
Coleridge, Samuel Taylor, 3, 10, 25, 31, 46, 49, 71, 118, 141, 227, 241; refers W to Adam Smith, 1; influenced by Addison, 2; lends books to W, 3, 9, 171; gives books to W, 4; studies Bacon, 9; notes referred to by W, 9; writes to Beaumont, 12; writes to Andrew Bell, 21; refers to Bonneval, 26; borrows Lamb's books, 38, 98; 'abused' by Byron, 40; lends book to Godwin, 42; reading, 53, 69, 75, 102, 186, 198; reviews Clarkson, 53; attacks Cobbett, 55; makes entry in Wordsworth Commonplace Book, 66, 206-7; acts as Davy's agent, 71; gives book to Thomas Hutchinson, 84; corresponds with John Edwards, 84; falling-out with W, 52, 54, 75, 112, 118n2, 163, 166, 169, 177, 198, 199; inscription by, 26, 31, 50, 53, 90, 144; sent books by Lamb, 103; reading Herbert, 107; borrows W's books, 116, 172; on Jeffrey, 118; reads Johnson, 120; argues with W about Jonson, 122; meets G. F. Leckie, 132; reads Malthus, 141; transcribes Marvell for SH, 142; introduces W to Josiah Wade, 145; acquainted with Pasley, 163; at Christ's Hospital, 167; meets Roscoe, 181; gives book to SH, 188; stays with Hutchinsons at Gallow Hill, 197; gives book to turnpike man, 205; plagiarism, 206; servile adulation of the Wellesleys, 216; attacked by Tytler, 229; visits John Hatfield, 229, described by Warner, 235; reads CW, 246
WORKS
A Letter to Sara Hutchinson, 58
Christabel, 57, 59, 184; W reads, 59
Dejection: An Ode, 58, 155
essays for *Morning Post*, 154, 155
essays for *The Courier*, 210, 216
Hymn Before Sunrise, 33
Inscription for a Fountain on a Heath, 57
Inscription on a jutting Stone, over a Spring, 57
In the Manner of Spenser, 58
Kubla Khan, 173
lectures, 11, 36, 121, 124, 130, 144
Letters on the Spaniards, 60
Logic, MSS on, 60
Logosophia, 60
marginalia, 1, 4, 16, 26, 31, 44, 46, 65, 75-6, 98-9, 103, 115, 129, 132, 139, 141, 144, 177, 178, 183, 187, 188, 191, 195, 199
Notebooks, 1, 6, 38, 39, 40, 55, 56, 56-7, 59, 59-60, 61, 65, 66, 67, 68, 73-4, 74-5, 75n2, 76, 78, 110, 116, 131, 144-5, 150, 152, 166, 167, 175, 177, 193, 227; SH copies into, 142
Ode to the Rain, 57-8
On a Cataract, 206
Organum verè Organum, 60
Poems on Various Subjects, 58
Prospectus of The Friend, 59
Religious Musings, 32
Remorse, 196
Sibylline Leaves, 57
The Ancient Mariner, 107, 173
The Day-Dream, 58
The Death of Wallenstein, 182
The Friend, 2, 31, 42, 54, 56, 59, 76, 84, 87, 102, 121, 133, 163, 165, 169, 177, 208n2, 222
The Language of Birds, 58

Index

The Voice from the Side of Etna, 249-50
This Lime-tree Bower my Prison, 4
To Mr. Justice Fletcher, 60-1, 217
Wallenstein, 151
See also Southey, Robert, and Samuel Taylor Coleridge *and* Wordsworth, William, and Samuel Taylor Coleridge
Coleridge, Sara (wife of C), 20, 60, 87; Thelwall presents book to, 220
Coleridge, Sara (daughter of C), 59
Coleridge, W. H. P., 42
Coleridge, William (brother of C), 75
Coleridge, William Hart (nephew of C), 75n1
Collier, John Payne, 83
Colly, Mr, 24
Colman, George, 16
Columbus, Christopher, 61
Columbus, Ferdinand, *History of Christopher Columbus*, 61
Commentaries on the Scriptures, 61
Comparetti, Alice Pattee, 165, 185, 234n1
Condillac, Etienne Bonnot de, 60
Congreve, William, 61-2
Constable, Henry, works, 62
Convention of Cintra, 198, 210; *see also Copy of the Proceedings upon the Inquiry relative to the Armistice and Convention, &c. made and concluded in Portugal, in August 1808, between the Commanders of the British and French Armies*
Cook, Capt. James, *Voyage*, 62
Cooke, G. F., 137
Cookson, Christopher Crackanthorpe, 258
Cookson, Elizabeth, 53-4
Coomb, D. E., 246
Cooper, Anthony Ashley, 3rd Earl of Shaftesbury, 157
  WORKS
  Characteristicks, 62
  The Moralists, 62
Cooper, Lane, 14n1, 122
Copy of the Proceedings upon the Inquiry relative to the Armistice and Convention, &c. made and concluded in Portugal, in August 1808, between the Commanders of the British and French Armies, 63, 215
Cora Linn, 62
Corbet, Richard, *To Francis Beaumont*, 63
Corn Laws, 158
Cornell Wordsworth Collection, 33, 35, 37, 187, 254
Cottle, Amos, death of, 154
Cottle, Joseph, 71, 154, 196

WORKS
Alfred, 63-4, 139
Works of Chatterton, 46-7
Cotton, Charles
  WORKS
  Cn. Cornelii Galli; vel potius Maximiani Elegia I. Trans., 64
  Odes, 46, 120
  Poems on Several Occasions, 64
  Winter, 64
  See also Walton, Izaac, and Charles Cotton
Courtenay, Rt. Hon. Thomas Peregrine, *Observations on the American Treaty*, 64-5
Courtney, Winifred, 206
Covent Garden Theatre, 190
Cowley, Abraham, 121, 152; *Works*, 65
Cowper, William, translates Bourne, 28
  WORKS
  Homer, 111
  Life and Posthumous Writings, 28, 66, 66-7
  On the Loss of the Royal George, 66
  poems, 65
  To Mary, 66
  Verses by Alexander Selkirk, 65-6
  Yardley Oak, 66, 66-7
Cox, W. A., 240
Crabbe, George, *Poems*, 67
Creech, Thomas, 256
Critical Review, 13, 131
Croker, John Wilson, 11
Cromwell, Oliver, 107 and n1
Crump, J. G., 181, 224
Culpeper, Nicholas, *English Family Physician*, 67-8
Currie, Dr James, 37
Curry, Kenneth, 96
Curtis, Jared, 5, 32, 36, 46, 53, 77, 107, 109, 120, 122-3, 142, 201, 202, 229

Dallaway, James, 149-50
Dalmeida, William, 3
Dalyell, Sir John Graham, 113
Dampier, William, *New Voyage round the World*, 68
Daniel, Samuel
  WORKS
  Epistle to the Countess of Cumberland, 68-9, 187
  History of the Civil Wars, 68
  Hymen's Triumph, 69
  Musophilus, 68, 69
  The Poetical Works, 68, 69
  The Queenes Arcadia, 69
Dante Alighieri, *Divina Commedia*, 69-70
Danvers, Charles, 32, 37

Index

d'Aquino, Carlo, 70
Darwin, Erasmus, *The Botanic Garden* Part II, *The Loves of the Plants*, 70
Davies, Damian Walford, 253
Davies, Sneyd, *Against Indolence. An Epistle.*, 70, 86
Davy, Humphry, 71-2; proofreader for *Lyrical Ballads*, 71; presented book to W, 131; angling with W, 235
WORKS
Researches on Nitrous Oxide, 71
Syllabus of a Course of Lectures, 72
Davy, Lady Jane, 122
Davy, Dr John, 198
Dawes, Revd. John, 7
Day, Thomas, *Sandford and Merton*, 72
Decius, 64-5
Defoe, Daniel, *Robinson Crusoe*, 72
Delille, Jacques, *Discours Preliminaire, Georgiques*, 73
Dennis, John, works, 73
De Quincey, Thomas, 6, 9, 20, 35, 36, 39, 43, 45, 56, 60, 63, 64-5, 72, 76, 84, 91, 108, 118, 123, 133, 141, 152, 153, 160, 163, 182, 186, 216, 232; moves into DC, 60, 101; requested to send books to W, 9, 26, 36, 45, 63, 64, 76, 98, 101, 108, 116, 123, 125, 148, 168, 230, 262; gives book to W, 35; requested to bring C's MSS, 60; borrows book from W, 87; acquainted with Pasley, 163; supervises printing of *Convention of Cintra*, 213, 224; shares newspapers with the Wordsworths, 217; sends newspapers to Wordsworths, 219, 222; *Recollections of the Lakes and the Lake Poets*, 133
Derby, 84
Derham, William, works, 73-4
Descartes, Rene, 74
De Selincourt, Ernest, 36, 37, 50, 51-2, 109, 112, 115, 140-1, 141, 170, 201, 202, 203, 205
De Vega, Lope, 89
Dibdin, Charles, the younger, *Edward and Susan*, 260
Dibdin, E. Rimbault, 260
Dickson, Dorothy, 149
dictionary, 74
Digby, Kenelm, *Two Treatises*, 74-5, 167
Diogenes Laërtius, *Diogenis Laertii de vitis*, 75
D'Israeli, Isaac, *Curiosities of Literature*, 75
Dodsley, Robert, *Select Collection of Old Plays*, 142
Donne, John, *LXXX Sermons*, 75-6
Douglas, Thomas, 5th Earl of Selkirk, *A Letter Addressed to John Cartwright*, 76

Dove Cottage, 85; books at, 14, 22, 27, 31, 52-3, 55, 124, 141, 159, 160, 203, 206, 242-3, 250, 256; Anthony Harrison stays at, 12, 101; Clarksons visit, 52, 53; C at, 55, 59, 69, 74, 75-6, 78, 141, 167, 172, 182; readings at, 57, 78; Richard Sharp visits, 184, 263; Sotheby visits, 195; Southey visits, 197, 240; Stoddart visits, 205-6
Drayton, Michael, 76-8
WORKS
Elegy to Henry Reynolds, 76-7
Moses's Birth and Miracles, 77
Nymphida: The Court of Fairy, 77
Poly-Olbion, 4, 76, 77-8
The Muses Elysium, 77
Drury Lane Theatre, 30, 190, 228
Drury Lane Company, 8
Dryden, John, 6, 78-9, 102, 110
WORKS
Absalom and Achitophel, 78, 157
Alexander's Feast, 78
Essay of Dramatic Poesy, 79
MacFlecknoe, 6, 188
Ode to Mrs Killigrew, 79
Palamon and Arcite, 78
Religio Laici, 79
The Indian Emperor, 79
To my dear Friend Mr. Congreve, 79
translations from Boccaccio, 78
works, 78
Works, 79, 110
Du Bartas, Guillaume de Saluste
WORKS
A Summarie Upon his Famous Poeme, 80
Dubartas his Second Weeke, 79-80
Oeuvres, 80
Works, 80
Dugas, Kristine, 10, 240
Dunbar, William, poems, 80
Duppa, Richard, *Life and Works of Michelangelo*, 80-1
D'Urfey, Thomas, works, 81
Dwight, Timothy, *The Conquest of Canäan*, 81
Dyce, Alexander, 70-1, 180, 193, 253, 256; collection, 80, 96, 180
Dyer, George
WORKS
Gilberto Wakefield, 82
On the Death of Gilbert Wakefield, 82
Poems (1792), 82
Poems (1800), 81
Poems (1801), 81, 82
Poems (1802), 82

Index

Dyer, Gilbert (bookseller), 9
Dyer, John, *The Fleece*, 83

Eachard, Laurence, *The History of England*, 83, 232
Earl of Abergavenny, 3
East India House, 3
Eclectic Review, 150
Edgeworth, Maria, W meets, 84; *Castle Rackrent*, 83-4
Edinburgh, 37, 111, 229
Edinburgh Magazine, 229
Edinburgh Review, 29-30, 30, 43, 53, 84, 116-19, 126
 reviews of Campbell, *Gertrude of Wyoming*, 84; More, *Coelebs in Search of a Wife*, 84, 152-3
Edwards, John, sends Montgomery's review of *The Excursion* to W, 150
 WORKS
 All Saints' Church, 84
 poems in MS, 84-5
Edwards, Richard
 WORKS
 Amantium iræ amoris redintigratia est ('In goyng to my naked bedde'), 85
 The Paradyse of Daynty Devices, 85
Egmont, John James Perceval, 3rd Earl of, 1
Eildon Hills, 36n1
Elleray, 117
Ellwood, James, presents book to W, 226
Ellwood, Jane, 226
Encyclopaedia Britannica, 85
Enfield, William
 WORKS
 Is Verse Essential to Poetry?, 85
 The Speaker, 70-1, 85-6
Epitaphs, 86
Estlin, John Prior, 246
Euripides, *Iphigenia at Aulis*, 86
European Magazine, 1, 193
Eusemere, 53
eutrapelia, 12

Fairfax, Edward, 208
Farington, Joseph, diary, 120-1, 151, 208
Fawcett, Joseph, death of, 137-8; *The Art of War*, 138
Fenwick, Eliza, 248
Fergusson, Robert, *Poetical Works*, 86-7
Ferriar, John, 144
Fichte, Johann Gottlieb, *Das System der Sittenlehre*, 87
Fielding, Henry, 87-8
 WORKS

Amelia, 87
Joseph Andrews, 87-8
Tom Jones, 87
Works, 88
Finch, Anne, Countess of Winchelsea, works, 88
Fitzwilliam Library, Cambridge, 116, 145
Flatman, Thomas, *Poems and Songs*, 88
Fleetwood, William, *Relative Duties*, 154-5
Fletcher, Phineas or Giles Fletcher, works, 88
Flodden Field, in Nine Fits, 88-9
Flower, Benjamin, 138
Folger Shakespeare Library, 3, 76, 100, 190-1
Ford, C. Lawrence, 162, 255
Fox, Rt. Hon. Charles James, 173; *To Mrs. Crewe*, 89, 221
Fox, afterwards Vassall, Henry Richard, 3rd Baron Holland, *Life and Writings of L. F. de Vega Carpio*, 89
Foxe, John, *Acts and Monuments*, 89
Fraunce, Abraham, works, 89
Frend, William
 WORKS
 Evening Amusements, 90
 Patriotism, 90
Fuller, Thomas, *History of the Worthies of England*, 121

Galfridus, Monumetensis, *The British History*, 90
Gallow Hill, 22, 140, 178, 197
Gallus Cornelius, 64
gardening, 1-2
Garve, Christian, 171
Gay, John
 WORKS
 Fables, 90-1
 The Shepherd's Week, 91
Gazette, 91
Gehol, description of, 13
gentleman, the need to write like a, 1
Gentleman's Magazine, 138
George III, 106
German Grammar, 91, 134
Gibbon, Edward, *Decline and Fall of the Roman Empire*, 91-2, 139
Gibraltar, 56
Gifford, William, 119, 128, 143-4
Gilbert, William, *The Hurricane*, 92
Gillies, John, 7
Gillies, Robert Pearce, 2, 15, 26, 115, 186, 244; sends books to W, 33, 111
 WORKS
 Albert, 93
 Childe Alarique, 92-3

292

Index

Egbert, 92
Illustrations of a Poetical Character, 92, 93
Gillman, James, books, 144
Gilpin, William
WORKS
Observations on the Lakes, 93
Observations on the Wye, 93
Ginsberg, David, 109
Goalby, Margaret, 149
Godwin, Mary Jane, 249
Godwin, William, 42, 60, 126, 182, 209; diary, 42; C breakfasts with, 163
WORKS
Essay on Sepulchres, 93-4
Lives of Edward and John Philips, 94
Golding, Arthur, 161
Goldsmith, Oliver, unkindly spoken of by Adam Smith, 1
WORKS
An History of England, 94
Retaliation, 94
The Deserted Village, 221
The Traveller, 221
The Vicar of Wakefield, 94
Googe, Barnaby, works, 95
Gordon, Mary, 244
Göttingen, 166
Gower, John, *Tale Imitated from Gower*, 95; text given, 273-5
Graham, James, 1st Marquis of Montrose, *I'll never love thee more*, 95
Grahame, James, gives book to Southey, 230
WORKS
Birds of Scotland, 96
British Georgics, 96
The Sabbath, 95-6
Grahame, Robert, 59, 96
Grant, Anne
WORKS
Essays on the Superstitions, 260
Memoirs of an American Lady, 96
Grasmere Abbey, 194
Grasmere Book Club, 176
Grasmere School, 156
Graver, Bruce, 44, 47, 51, 76, 77, 78, 112, 174, 231, 237, 253
Graves, John, *The History of Cleveland*, 96-7
Gray, Thomas
WORKS
Elegy, 221
Epitaph on Mrs Clark, 97
Hymn to Adversity, 262
Poems, 97

Works, 97
Green, Karen, 22, 35, 107, 181, 257
Greene, Robert, *Ah, What is Love*, 97-8
Greta Bank, 85
Greta Hall, 3, 14, 27, 31, 38, 55, 74, 91, 99, 154, 167, 181, 220; SH visits, 188; Southey moves into, 240
Greville, Fulke, Baron Brooke
WORKS
Remains, 98-9
The Five Years of King James, 99
The Life of the Renowned Sir Philip Sidney, 98
Grey, Zachary, 38
Grimm, Friedrich Melchior von, Baron, *Correspondance littéraire*, 99
Griggs, Earl Leslie, 112n1
Guide to the City of Perth, 99
Guildhall Library, 157
Gutch, J. M., 103
Guyon, Jeanne Marie Bouvières de la Motte, *The Life of Lady Guion*, 99

Habington, William, *Description of Castara*, 155
Hakewill, George, *Apologie or Declaration*, 99-100
Hakluyt, Richard, *The Principall Navigations*, 100, 228
Hall, Joseph
WORKS
A Recollection, 100
satires, 100
Hamburg, 101
Hamilton, Joshua, 68
Hamilton, Sir William, 261-2
Hamilton, William, *The Braes of Yarrow*, 101
Handel, George Frideric, 39-40
Hardinge, George, *Biographical Memoirs of the Rev. Sneyd Davies, D.D.*, 70n3
Hargrave, Francis, *A Complete Collection of State-Trials*, 101
Harington, John, 6-7
Harrison, Anthony, gives W books, 12; gives C books, 169; *Poetical Recreations*, 101-2
Harshberger, Scott, 173-4
Harte, Walter, 102-3
WORKS
Life of Gustavus Adolphus, 102-3
works, 102
Hartley, David, *Observations on Man*, 103
Hatfield, John, bigamist and forger, 229
Hawes, Stephen, works, 103
Hawkesworth, John, *Voyages*, 62
Hawkins, John Sidney, 234
Hawkshead, 46, 51, 61, 76, 165; Grammar School,

293

101, 112, 125, 168, 191, 207, 221, 232
Haydon, Benjamin Robert, 106, 114, 221
Hayley, William, 66
Hays, Samuel, *Practical Treatise*, 103
Hazlitt, William, 261; liking of Blake's poetry, 25; encounters with W, 69; dispute with C and W, 73-4, 175; and Fawcett's death, 137-8
WORKS
A Reply to 'Z', 104
Essay on the Principles of Human Action, 104
review of *Comus*, 106
review of *The Excursion*, 104-5
The Spirit of the Age, 22, 72, 234
Heath, James, *Flagellum*, 106-7
Heath, William, 32; review of *Lyrical Ballads*, 107
Heber, Richard, handsome library of, 193
Hebron, Stephen, 135
Hedgecock, Deborah K., 157n1
Helen of Kirkconnell, 257
Helm Crag, 38
Helvellyn, 191
Henderson, Alexander, 105
Herbert, Edward, Baron Herbert of Cherbury, 107; *Epitaph for Himself*, 107
Herbert, George, 107-8
WORKS
poems, 107-8
Sunday, 108
The Temple, 107
Vertue, 108
Herbert, I., 178
Herd, David, *Ancient and Modern Scottish Songs*, 108, 218
Herodotus, *History*, 108-9
Heron, Robert, *Observations in Scotland*, 109
Herrick, Robert, works, 109-10
Herriot, Miss, 43
Heyne, C. G., 166
Heywood, Thomas
WORKS
A Woman Kill'd with Kindness, 110
poems, 110
Highgate, 70
Hill, Alan G., 61, 70, 236n1
Hill, Herbert, Revd., 138
Hill, John, *A Review of the Works of the Royal Society*, 110
Hindwell, 3, 234
Hoccleve, Thomas, works, 110
Hodgson, John A., 142
Hogg, James, 15
WORKS
The Queen's Wake, 111

The Hunting of Badlewe, 111
Home, John, *Douglas*, 30
Homer
WORKS
The Iliad, 111-12
Odyssey, 111-12
Iliad, Book 24, 111
Hone, William, *Table Book*, sent to W, 128
Horatius Flaccus, Quintus, 34, 112-13, 253
WORKS
Ars Poetica, 112
Epistles, 113
Works, 255
Housman, John, *Tour*, 113
Houghton Library, 69, 75-6
Howe, P. P., 105
Howley, William, 181
Huber, François, *New Observations on the Natural History of Bees*, 113
Hughes, John, 204
Hull, 235
Humboldt, Friedrich Heinrich Alexander von, Baron, *Researches*, 113-14
Hume, David, 194
Hunmanby, home of Francis Wrangham, 140, 178
Hunt, James Henry Leigh, 106, 114-15
WORKS
Descent of Liberty, 114
The Feast of the Poets, 114-15
see also *The Champion*, *The Examiner*, *The Indicator*, *The Reflector*
Huntington Library, 110, 124
Hurdis, James, *The Favorite Village*, 115
Hutchinson, John, 170
Hutchinson, Lucy, *Memoirs of the Life of Colonel Hutchinson*, 115
Hutchinson, Mary (later Mary Wordsworth), 22, 25, 47, 48, 78, 135, 146, 151, 158, 179, 188, 201, 206; reading, 225
Hutchinson, Sara, 2, 11, 13-14, 21, 23, 42, 54, 58, 67, 72, 102, 105, 125, 137, 142, 150, 152, 166, 170-1, 204, 215, 217, 235; C gives books to, 14, 31, 50, 111-12, 188; Sara Hutchinson's Poets, 57, 58; amanuensis to C, 59; journal of Scottish tour, 99, 137; anthology of poetry, 109
Hutchinson, Thomas, 21, 84
Hutchinson, William, *The History and Antiquities of the County Palatine of Durham*, 255
Hyde, Edward, 1st Earl of Clarendon, *The History of the Rebellion and Civil Wars*, 116

Imago primi saeculi societatis Jesu, 116
Indiana, University of, 65, 166

Index

Ingleby, C. M., 132
Isola, Agostino, *Pieces Selected from the Italian Poets*, 116, 145
Italian, C learns, 26 and n1

Jackson, Heather, 124, 139
Jackson, J. R. de J., 194
Jackson, William, 10; library of, 27, 91, 120
Jacobinical principles, 238
Jacobus, Mary, 159, 162n1
James I, 34
Jameson, Mr, bookseller, 94
Jedburgh, 183
Jeffrey, Francis, Lord, 30, 116-19, 151; attacked by Thelwall, 221
  WORKS
  review of Southey's *Thalaba*, 116-17, 141
  review of *Poems, in Two Volumes*, 117
  review of Burns, *Reliques*, 117-18
  review of Scott, *Lady of the Lake*, 118
  review of Wilson, *Isle of Palms*, 118, 245
  review of *The Excursion*, 118-19, 151, 153
Johnie Armstrang, 119-20
John Rylands Library, University of Manchester, 31
Johnson, Joseph, 71
Johnson, Samuel, W's thoughts on, 205
  WORKS
  Life of Addison, 120
  Life of Pope, 121
  Lives of the Poets, 46, 120-1
  The Ant, 120
  The Rambler, 121
  Works, 120
Johnson, William, 247
Jones, Stanley, 105
Jonson, Ben, 88, 121-2
  WORKS
  Discoveries, 122
  Drink to me only with thine eyes, 122
  Epode, 122
  Ode Pindaric, on Sir Lucius Carey, and Sir H. Morison, 122
  poems and Life, 121-2
  The Forest, 122
  To My First Daughter, 121
  To Penshurst, 121-2
  Underwoods, 122
Jordan, Donaldson, and Edwin Judson Pratt, *The Spoiled Child*, 122
Jordan, Dorothea, 122

Kant, Immanuel, works, 261-2
Kaufman, Paul, 27n1

Keate, George, *An Account of the Pelew Islands*, 122-3
Kendal, 135
Kendal Book Club, 84, 176
Kendal Coffee Room, 239
Kendal Record Office, 55
Kendal wagon, 49, 82, 147
Kennedy, George, 174
Kentucky University, Hugh Peal Collection, 195
Keswick, 235
Ketcham, Carl H., 83, 244
Kinsley, James, 188
Kishel, Joseph F., 44
Klopstock, Friedrich Gottlieb
  WORKS
  Memoirs of Frederick and Margaret Klopstock, 123, 176
  The Messiah, 123
Klopstock, Margaret, letters, 123, 176
Knight, Richard Payne, 123-4; C meets, 124
  WORKS
  An Analytical Enquiry into the Principles of Taste, 124
  The Landscape, 123-4
Knox, Vicesimus, 124-5
  WORKS
  Elegant Epistles, 125
  Elegant Extracts, 97, 101, 124-5, 136, 143, 162, 170

Laborde, Alexander Louis Joseph de, Count, *A View of Spain*, 125
Lafontaine, Jean de
  WORKS
  Fables choisis, mise en vers; avec un nouveau commentaire par M. Coste, 126
  Les amours de Psyché et de Cupidon, avec le Poëme d'Adonis, 125-6
Laing, David, 8, 80
Laing, Malcolm, *The History of Scotland*, 126
Laing, Mary, 80
Lamb, Charles, 3, 11, 17-18, 29-30, 31, 93, 195, 196, 227, 234; commissioned to buy books for W, 16, 49, 62, 103, 122, 141-2, 143-4, 147, 172, 189-90, 203; reads Bourne, 28; writes to DW, 31; gives books to C, 31; shows books to W, 32, 63, 69; books pass into W's possession, 38; edits C's *Poems*, 58; sends copies of various works to W, 64, 66, 81, 82, 93-4; source of drafts in W's MSS, 95, 143; books annotated by C, 98-9, 191; commiserates over Jeffrey's attacks, 118-19; sends books to DC, 127; visits theatre with W, 133; reads Hannah

Index

More, 153; Charles Lamb Society Archive, 157; reviews Stoddart's *Remarks*, 205-6
WORKS
A Farewell to Tobacco, 127
A Tale of Rosamund Gray and old blind Margaret, 128
John Woodvil, 11, 30, 126
Juvenile Poetry, 129
On Mary Druit who died aged 19, 127
On the Genius and Character of Hogarth, 129
On the Melancholy of Tailors, 128
review of *The Excursion*, 128-9
Specimens of English Dramatic Poets, 127-8; supplement sent to W, 128
The King and Queen of Hearts, 127
The Londoner, 126-7
Lamb, Charles, and Mary Anne Lamb
WORKS
Mrs. Leicester's School, 129
Poetry for Children, 130, 249
Tales from Shakespear, 129
The Sea Voyage, 129
Lamb, Mary Anne, 8, 94, 127, 190, 260; buys books for the Wordsworths, 74; authorship attribution, 95; goes to the theatre with W, 228
WORKS
Dialogue between a Mother and Child, 130
On the Same, 130
The Lady Blanch, regardless of her lovers' fears, 130
Virgin and Child, 130
Why is he wandering o'er the sea?, 130
Lancaster Castle, 81
Lancaster, Joseph, *Improvements in Education*, 130
Landon, Carol, 179, 221
Landor, Walter Savage, 70; shifting relations with W, 131; inscription, 131
WORKS
Count Julian, 131, 131-2
Gebir, 131
Idyllia, 131
Simonidea, 131
Langhorne, John, *Owen of Carron*, 221
Langland, John, *Piers Plowman*, 132
Laplanders, 226
Law, William, *A Serious Call to a Devout and Holy Life*, 132
Lawson, Charles, 39
Lawson, Sir Gilfrid, 240
Leckie, Gould Francis, *An Historical Survey*, 132-3
Ledyard, John, *A Journal of Captain Cook's Last Voyage to the Pacific*, 133
Lee, Harriet

WORKS
The Canterbury Tales, 133
The German's Tale, 133
Lee, Sophia, 133
Le Fanu, Alicia, *The Sons of Erin*, 133
Lemprière, John, *Bibliotheca classica; or, a classical dictionary*, 256
Leonidas, 109
Le Sage, Alain Rene, *The Adventures of Gil Blas of Santillane*, 133-4
Lessing, Gotthold Ephraim, 91
WORKS
Die Hunde, 134
Fables, 134
Laokoon, 134
Lewis, M. G.
WORKS
Osric the Lion, 134
Poems, 135
Tales of Terror, 134
Tales of Wonder, 35, 134
The Felon, 134-5
The Stranger, 134
Lewthwaite, Barbara, 156
Lickbarrow, Isabella, *Poetical Effusions*, 135
Lienemann, Kurt, 27, 39, 65, 88
Lindsay, J. I., 124
Literary and Masonic Magazine, 152
Littlebury, Isaac, 108-9
Liu, Alan, 32
Llanthony, 131
Lloyd, Charles, 2, 105, 176; lends books to C, 2; translator, 2, 111; lends books to W, 6, 23, 205; subscribes to *British Critic*, 28; sends books to DC, 28; borrows books from DC, 44-5; subscribes to *Edinburgh Review*, 117; *Iliad, Book 24*, 111
Lloyd, David, *State Worthies*, 135
Lloyd, Priscilla (later Wordsworth), 119n1, 128, 150, 247; presents book to W, 111
Lloyd, Robert, 126n1
Lochleven, 32
Lockhart, John Gibson, 36n1
Lodge, Thomas, 80
Logan, John
WORKS
life and poems, 135-6
Ode, 135-6
Ode to the Cuckoo, 135-6
London, W visits, 6, 11, 21, 26, 29, 30, 40, 52, 53, 72, 80, 90, 95, 115, 124, 129, 137, 144, 152, 160, 169, 190, 193, 235; JW in, 14; W sends books to, 24, 44, 70; W sent books from, 26,

Index

27, 36, 45; C returns from, 60; bookstalls in, 65; C goes to, 87, 154; C's books sent to, 112; SH visits, 137
London Review, 179
Longman, Thomas Norton, 4n1, 14, 25, 89, 107, 132, 179, 182, 183, 191, 197, 251; accounts, 26, 71, 72, 94, 144, 245-6, 265-6
Lonsdale, Lord, 217, 219
Lonsdale, Roger, 10n2
Losh, James, 3; diary, 27, 197; sends books to W, 85
Lovelace, Richard, works, 136
Lovell, Robert, 199
Lowes, John Livingston, 145
Lowther family, 55, 238
Lowther Hall, 13n1
Lowther, Lady Mary, 8, 20, 69, 88, 128, 245
Lowther, Lord, 240
Lucanus, Marcus Annaeus, *Pharsalia*, 136
Lucas, E. V., 129
Lucretius Carus, Titus, *His Six Books of Epicurean Philosophy*, 256
Lyceum Theatre, Strand, 8, 228
Lyon, Judson S., 8, 139, 173
Lyttelton, George, Baron Lyttelton
WORKS
Epitaph to the Memory of Lucy Lyttelton, 136
To the Memory of a Lady Lately Deceased, 136-7

Macartney, Lord, 13
Macklin, Charles, *The True-Born Scotsman*, 137
Macpherson, James, 126
WORKS
Fingal, 137
Temora, 137
magazines, 137-8
Maid of Buttermere, 229, 260
Malcolm, Sir John
WORKS
Observations on the Disturbances in the Madras Army, 138
Persia, 138
Sketch of India, 138
Malcolm, Gilbert, 138
Malkin, Benjamin Heath, 133; *Father's Memoirs*, 24, 139
Mallet, David, 9
WORKS
Edwin and Emma, 221
The Excursion, 139
William and Margaret, 221
Mallet, Paul-Henri, *Northern Antiquities*, 139-40
Malone, Edmond, 175

Malory, Sir Thomas, *Morte D'Arthur*, 140
Malta, 73, 165, 166, 220n1, 228
Malthus, Thomas Robert, *An Essay on the Principle of Population*, 140-1
Manchester Grammar School, 39
Manning, Thomas, 127
Mant, Revd. Richard
WORKS
Church Architecture, 141
The Simpliciad; a satirico-didactic poem, 141
Marlowe, Christopher, 'plays & poems', 141-2
Marrs, Edwin W., 127
Marshall, Jane, 3, 179, 239, 246
Marshall, John, gives book to W, 178
Martin, Martin
WORKS
A Description of the Western Islands of Scotland, 142
A Voyage to St Kilda, 142, 256-7
Marvell, Andrew, 34
WORKS
An Horatian Ode, 142-3
On a Drop of Dew, 142
Upon Appleton House, 143
Mason, William, 97, 143
WORKS
Epitaph on Mrs Mason, 143
Epitaph on Miss Drummond, 143
The English Garden, 143
Massinger, Philip
WORKS
The Bashful Lover, 144
Works, 143-4
May, John, 60, 115
May, Thomas, 136; works, 144
Mayne, John, *By Logan's Streams That Run Sae Deep*, 144
Mays, J. C. C., 34n1
McMillan, Dorothy A. Porter, 96
Mela, Pomponius, *De Situ Orbis Libri Tres*, 144-5
Melmoth, William, *The Great Importance of a Religious Life Consider'd*, 145
Mercantile Gazette, 145, 209
Metastasio, Pietro Antonio, sonnets, 145
Michelangelo, sonnets, 145
Miller, John, 225
Milliken, J., 221
Milton, John, 106, 146-9
WORKS
Dedication to *The Doctrine and Discipline of Divorce*, 147
Digression to *The History of Britain*, 147-8
Giovane piano e simpliceto amante, 146-7

Index

History of Britain, 148
Il Penseroso, 146, 147
L'Allegro, 147
Methought I saw my late espoused saint, 146
On Shakespear, 148
Paradise Lost, 149; W gives readings from, 147, 148; Book V, al fresco reading of by W, 148; Book XI, 146
Poems on Several Occasions, 149
Prose Works, 207
Reason of Church Government, 148
sonnets, 146, 147
Works, 147
Minot, Laurence, works, 149
Mirehouse, 55, 56
miscellany, 149
Misopappas, Philanax, see N., S.
Mithridates, 63, 91, 139
Monkhouse, John, 72, 152; gives book to MH, 188
Monkhouse, Mary, 13, 23, 127, 215-16, 217
Monkhouse, Thomas, 102
Monmouth, Geoffrey of, see Galfridus Monumetensis
Montagu, Algernon, 45
Montagu, Basil, 9, 45, 52-3, 177, 185, 236
Montagu, Lady Mary Wortley, Works, 149-50
Montgomery, James, 66
   WORKS
   A Field Flower, 150
   review of The Excursion, 150-1
   The Wanderer of Switzerland, 150
   The World Before the Flood, 151
Monthly Magazine, 2, 85, 209
Monthly Review, 123, 151-2, 229-30
Montluzin, Emily Lorraine de, 107
Moore, Edward, The Gamester, 152
Moore, Sir John, letters, 152, 224
Moorman, Mary, 13, 24, 61, 257
More, Hannah, Coelebs in Search of a Wife, 152-3
More, Henry, works, 153
Morning Chronicle, 8, 42, 153, 156, 195, see also newspapers
Morning Post, 33, 57, 58, 126-7, 145, 146, 154-5, 157, 179, 183, 249-50 see also newspapers
Motte, Thomas, 'Travels to the Diamond Mines of Jumbulpoor in Orissa', 155-6
Murdoch, Patrick, 226
Murfitt, Revd. Matthew, 238-9
Murphy, Arthur, The Grecian Daughter, 156
Murray, John, 11, 41
Murray, Lindley, Introduction to the English Reader, 156
Musgrove, S., 163

N., S., Rawleigh Redivivus, 156-7
Nabholtz, John R., 124, 171, 240
Napoleon see Bonaparte, Napoleon
Nether Stowey, 4
New Annual Register, 157
Newlyn, Lucy, 142
newspapers, 157-8
Newton, Sir Isaac, 28
Newton, John, An Authentic Narrative, 158-9
Newton, Thomas, 149
New York Public Library, 31, 107, 185, 237
Nicolson, Joseph, and Richard Burn, The History and Antiquities of the Counties of Westmorland and Cumberland, 159
nitrous oxide, 71
Norris, John, works, 159
North, Thomas, 168-9
Nowell Smith, Simon, 83-4, 132

Ober, Warren U., 71, 153
Odin, 139
Ogilby, John, 83; translations from Virgil, 83, 231-2
Old Brathay (Low Brathay), 2, 28, 117, 205
Oldham, John, Works, 262
O'Neill, Eliza, 196
Opie, Amelia, Adeline Mowbray, 159-60
Ossian, see Macpherson, James
Otway, Thomas, Venice Preserved, 160; W sees, with Beaumont, 160
Ovidius Naso, Publius
   WORKS
   Electa ex Ovidio, et Tibullo, 161
   Metamorphoses, 160-1
Owen, W. J. B., 24, 25, 27, 43, 44, 49n1, 51, 56, 59-60, 63, 64, 70, 73, 77, 77-8, 79, 81, 85, 91, 97, 103, 109, 112, 118, 120, 125, 135, 149, 156, 159, 174, 175, 186, 194, 204, 230, 236, 237, 245, 261, 265
Oxford, Christ Church, 75; Wadham, 75

Paley, William, 73-4, 234
Palmer, Mrs, 'O hours of peace and comfort, whither fled?', 161
Park, Mungo, Travels in the Interior Districts of Africa, 162
Parnell, Thomas, The Hermit, 162
Parrish, Stephen Maxfield, 58, 134
Parry, Henry, 110
Pasley, Sir Charles William, 138; Essay on the Military Policy and Institutions, 162-3
Patton, Cornelius Howard, 161
Pennant, Thomas, A Tour in Scotland, 1769, 163-4
Pennington, Montagu, Memoirs of the Life of Mrs

Index

Elizabeth Carter, 164
Penny, Jane, belle of Windermere, 237
Penrith, 23, 38, 101, 111-12, 117, 163, 167, 195, 226
Percy, Thomas
WORKS
Reliques, 1, 50, 101, 164-5
The Hermit of Warkworth, 165
Perth, 38, 41; *Guide*, 99
Peterborough, 25
Petrarca, Francesco
WORKS
De Vita Solitaria, 165-6
Dichiarationi, 166
poems, 165
Phaer, Thomas, 232
Philips, Ambrose, *A Collection of Old Ballads*, 166
Pindar, *Carmina*, 166
Piranesi, Giambattista, 111, 166-7
Pitt, William, death of, 158
Pittman, Charles, L., 74, 167-8, 175
Placidi, G. B., 69
Plato, *The Cratylus, Phædo, Parmenides and Timæus of Plato*, 167-8; Platonic ideas in W's poetry, 168 and n2; Platonism in Stolberg, 206
Pliny, *Natural History*, 168
Plutarch, *The Lives of the Noble Grecians and Romans*, 168-9
Poetae Latini minores, 169
Poole, Thomas, 1, 72, 85, 115, 141n1, 148, 154, 155, 193
Pope, Alexander, 112, 120, 150
WORKS
Epitaph. On Mrs. Corbet, 170
Epitaph. On the Honble. Simon Harcourt, 170
Essay on Criticism, 229
Imitation of the 1st Epistle of the 1st Book of Horace, 170
Messiah, 170
Moral Essays, 170
Works of Shakespeare, 189-90
Porter, Anna Maria, *The Recluse of Norway*, 170-1
Potts, Abbie, 254, 255
Pratt, Edwin Judson, *see* Jordan, Donaldson
Price, Sir Uvedale, 1st bart., early reader of *Lyrical Ballads*, 171
WORKS
Essay on Decorations near the House, 171
Essay on the Picturesque, 171
Prior, Matthew, *Charity*, 172
Purchas, Samuel, *Purchas His Pilgrimage*, 172
Pye, Henry James, *Some Observations on Gardening*, 173

Pyrard, François, *Voyage to the East Indies*, 20

Quaritch, Bernard, 208
Quarles, Francis
WORKS
Emblems, 173
works, 173
Quarterly Review, 2, 11, 119, 128-9, 150, 151, 163n2
Quillinan, Dora, 22
Quintilianus, Marcus Fabius, *Institutio Oratoria*, 173-4

Racine, Jean, *Oeuvres*, 174
Raleigh, Sir Walter, *A Vision upon the Fairy Queen*, 174
Ramsay, Allan, 1
Randolph, Thomas, 228; works, 174; *Poems*, 257
Rasbotham, Dorning, 39
Rawson, C. J., 87n1
Rawson, William, 179-80, 240
Ray, John, *Observations*, 175
Reed, Henry, 261
Reed, Mark L., 6, 9, 13, 14, 23, 24, 36, 37, 38, 42, 51, 57, 58, 63, 66, 72, 75, 77, 80, 85, 86, 98, 99, 108, 109, 127, 137, 139-40, 142, 143, 144, 145, 155-6, 162, 164, 169, 178, 182, 201, 202, 206, 213, 229, 233, 240, 241, 244, 245, 246, 251; dating followed, 164, 233
Rees, Joan, 68
Reynolds, John Hamilton, 228n1
Reynolds, Sir Joshua, *Works*, 175-6
Richardson, Samuel, 123; *Correspondence*, 176-7
Rigueline, Don Francisco, letters to, 262
Ritson, Joseph
WORKS
Ancient Songs, 178
Ancient English Metrical Romances, 192n1
A Select Collection of English Songs, 177
Poems by Laurence Minot, 149
Scotish Song, 36, 164, 257
Robert le Diable, *Roberte the Deuyll*, 178
Robertson, Joseph, *A Traveller's Guide through Scotland and its Islands*, 178-9
Robinson, G. and J., 126
Robinson, Henry Crabb, 4, 11, 12, 24, 25, 29-30, 40-1, 53, 64, 67, 91-2, 105, 106, 116, 121, 131, 139, 158, 182, 190, 208, 241, 244, 261; review of *Convention of Cintra*, 179
Robinson, Mary
WORKS
Lyrical Tales, 179
The Haunted Beach, 33, 179

Index

Rogers, Samuel, 28, 42, 65, 67, 70, 183-4, 210, 262, 263; accompanies W to the theatre, 156; W meets, 179-80
WORKS
An Epistle to a Friend, with other poems, 180
Jacqueline, 41, 180
Poems, 180
The Pleasures of Memory, 41, 179-80
The Voyage of Columbus, 180
Rooke, Barbara, 59
Roscoe, William, *The Life and Pontificate of Leo the Tenth*, 180-1
Rosenbach Foundation, 3n1
Rousseau, Jean Jacques, *Discourse on Inequality*, 181
Royal George, 66
Royal Institution, 72
Rubens, Pieter Paul, 93
Rubruquis, William de, *Itinerarium*, 100
Russell, Thomas, *Sonnets and Miscellaneous Poems*, 181
Rydal Mount, 11, 29, 48, 80, 255; books at, 2, 6, 6-7, 8, 10, 16, 22, 26, 31, 32, 34, 36, 37, 38, 39, 41, 42, 43, 44, 45, 50, 52, 54, 59, 61, 62, 65, 67, 72, 74, 81, 87, 89, 90, 92, 93, 97, 100, 101, 105, 108, 110, 111, 112, 113, 114, 115, 120, 124, 125, 126, 128, 130, 131, 132, 135, 141, 143, 147, 153, 157, 158, 162, 163, 165, 166, 167, 173, 175, 176, 180, 183, 185, 187, 188, 195, 195-6, 196, 198, 199, 205, 208, 220, 221, 226, 230, 231, 235, 236, 237, 245, 246, 257, 262, 263; books not at, 8, 23, 109, 159-60, 181, 190, 207, 225, 237; C's books enter, 31, 100, 103, 104, 165, 188, 208, 246, 250; auction of 1859, 87, 101, 166, 167, 181-2; catalogues, 129, 130, 169, 180, 207; Southey stays at, 200

Sackville-West, Vita, 55
Sadler, ---------, of Chippenham, *Wanly Penson*, 181-2
Sadler's Wells, 260
Saragossa, Siege of, 222; boy of, 215; decree of, 219
Sayers, Frank, *Nugae Poeticae*, 209
Scambler, Dr Richard, 67
Schiller, Johann Christoph Friedrich von
WORKS
The Death of Wallenstein, 151, 182
The Piccolomini, or the first part of Wallenstein, 182
Schuyler, Catalina, 96
Scots Magazine, 229
Scott, John

WORKS
A Visit to Paris, 183
review of *The White Doe*, 183
Scott, Walter, 6, 14-15, 25, 35, 36n1, 50, 78, 79, 83, 88-9, 102, 110, 115, 117, 119, 157, 160, 192, 203, 229, 231, 231-2; appointed Clerk of Session, 158
WORKS
Annus Mirabilis, 231
Ballads and Lyrical Pieces, 185
Guy Mannering, 186
Marmion, 185-6
Minstrelsy of the Scottish Border, 119-20, 184
review of *The Works of Edmund Spenser*, 185
Song, 185
The Chase, 35
The Lady of the Lake, 186
The Lay of the Last Minstrel, 183-4, 184-5
The Lord of the Isles, 186
Waverley, 186
Works of Dryden, 6, 50, 79, 157, 188, 231
Selden, John, 4, 76
Seneca, Lucius Annaeus
WORKS
L. Annei Senecæ Cordubensis. Tragœdiæ X., 257
L. Annæi Senecæ Philosophi, et M. Annæi Senecæ Rhetoris quæ extant opera, 187
works, 187
Senex, 86
Sennertus, Daniel, *Opera*, 187
Seward, Anna, 65
WORKS
Original Sonnets, 188
poems, 187
Shadwell, Thomas, *The Virtuoso*, 188
Shaftesbury, 3rd Earl of, *see* Cooper, Anthony Ashley
Shakespeare, William, 11, 50, 86; W comments on, 10
WORKS
A Lover's Complaint, 188-9
As You Like It, 189
A Winter's Tale, 189
Dramatic Works, 188
Hamlet, 30, 189
Henry V, 189
Julius Caesar, 190
Othello, 190
Plays, 190
Richard II, 190
sonnets, 146
Works, 189-90
Sharp, Richard ('Conversation'), 135; MS poem,

Index

172, 262-3; gives book to W, 184
Shaver, Chester L., 7, 16, 149, 176, 203, 259
Shaver, Chester L., and Alice C. Shaver, *Wordsworth's Library*, 38, 64, 68, 71, 90, 100, 116, 148, 149, 153, 166, 167, 174, 188, 191, 199, 208, 209; does not list title, 3, 8, 14, 31, 46-7, 94, 95, 98, 100, 109, 116, 150, 159, 162, 180, 188, 207, 208, 220, 256
Shearer, E. A., 124
Shelton, Thomas, 45
Shelvocke, George, *Voyage*, 173
Shenstone, William, 160
Sidney, Sir Philip, 51, 135
  WORKS
  Arcadia, 51, 191
  Astrophil and Stella, 191
  Defence of Poetry, 190-1
  Works, 191
Simon Fraser University, 162, 229
Simonides, 51, 230
Sinclair, Sir John, *A Statistical Account of Scotland*, 191-2
Sir Ysumbras, Sir Gowther, Sir Amadas, 192
Skelton, John, Southey's interest in, 193n2
  WORKS
  'pieces which have lately come to light', 193
  The Bowge of Court, 192-3
Skepper, Anna Dorothea Benson, 177, 178
Smith, Adam, critical opinions of, 1
  WORKS
  Theory of Moral Sentiments, 193-4
  The Wealth of Nations, 1, 193
Smith, Charlotte
  WORKS
  Elegiac Sonnets, 194
  Ethelinde, 194
Smith, Elizabeth, as translator, 123, 176; *Fragments*, 123, 194
Smollett, Tobias
  WORKS
  life of, 194
  Ode to Leven-water, 194
  Ferdinand Count Fathom, 194-5
Smyser, Jane Worthington, 25, 44, 51, 56, 59-60, 63, 77-8, 79, 81, 97, 109, 112, 125, 135, 149, 156, 159, 187, 194, 204, 230, 236, 237, 245, 261
Sockburn, 154
Somers, Lord, 204
Somerset, W resident in, 4; goods sent from, 123
Sotheby, William, lends books to C and W, 165
  WORKS
  A Fancy Sketch, text given, 257-8

Georgics, 195
Netley Abbey, 195
Oberon, 195
Orestes, 195
Poems, 195, 257
Poetical Epistle to George Beaumont, 195
Saul, 195
tragedies, 196
Soulby, Anthony, 47
Southerne, Thomas, *Isabella; or, the Fatal Marriage*, 196
Southey,˙Edith, 7
Southey, Herbert, 72, 181, 240-1
Southey, Robert, 20, 22, 32, 40, 53, 65, 71, 73, 81, 91, 102, 119n4, 126n1, 128, 132, 163, 173, 191, 192, 206, 238; critical opinions of, 2, 66; reviews, 2, 13, 14, 14-15, 32, 46, 54, 66, 89, 95, 96, 115, 131, 141, 150, 151, 163n2, 164, 225, 251; gives or lends books to W, 4, 8, 11, 20, 23, 32, 46, 67, 113-14, 136, 150, 163, 181, 185, 197, 198, 199, 200, 203, 204, 205, 209, 224; admirer of Bampfylde, 10; W visits, 14; researching Sir John Beaumont, 19; consults Lloyd's copy of *British Critic*, 28; sees William Betty in performance, 30; attacked by Byron, 40; library of, 45, 46, 67, 68, 80, 81, 90, 99, 100, 110, 114, 125, 136, 138, 144, 153, 161, 173, 176, 186, 204-5, 230; reading, 54n2, 80, 182, 204, 205, 222; reactions to Jeffrey, 117; tells W about Landor, 131; shown books by W, 138; books, 140; gives books to C, 198, 198-9; friendship with William Taylor, 209; attacked by Tytler, 229; moves into Greta Hall, 240
  WORKS
  Carmen Triumphale, 199
  Chronicle of the Cid, 198
  Essays Moral and Political, 163n2
  History of Brazil, 198-9
  Joan of Arc, 197-8, 229
  Letters from Spain and Portugal, 196
  Life of Nelson, 199
  Madoc, 197
  Morte D'Arthur, 140
  Ode to His Royal Highness the Prince Regent, 200
  Poems, 199
  Remains of Henry Kirke White, 240, 241
  review of Peter Bayley, 197
  Roderick, 200
  Select Works of the British Poets, 103
  Specimens of the later English Poets, 10
  Thalaba, 197, 198

The Curse of Kehama, 199
The Retrospect, 199
Works of Chatterton, 46-7
Southey, Robert, and Samuel Taylor Coleridge, *Omniana*, 200
Southwell, Robert, poems, 200
Sparrman, Anders, *Voyage to the Cape of Good Hope*, 201
Spedding, John, 55-6
Spenser, Edmund, 100, 201-4
WORKS
Colin Clout's Come Home Again, 202
Faerie Queene, 202, 204, 217
Muiopotmos, 201, 204
Prosopopoia, 202
Prothalamion, 202
The Shepherd's Calendar, 203
View of the Present State of Ireland, 202-3
Virgil's Gnat, 203
works, 201
Works, 203, 204
Staël-Holstein, Anne Louise Germaine de, Baroness
WORKS
A Treatise on Ancient and Modern Literature, 204
Corinne, 204
De l'Allemagne, 204
Stallknecht, Newton P., 62, 262
Stanhope, Philip Dormer, 4th Earl of Chesterfield, *Advice to a Lady in Autumn*, 204-5
Stanyhurst, Richard, 232-3
Staple Inn, 24
Steele, Sir Richard, and Joseph Addison, *The Tatler. By Isaac Bickerstaff*, 205
Stein, Edwin, 32, 142, 209
Stephen, James, *The Crisis of the Sugar Colonies*, 205
Sterne, Laurence, 86; *Tristram Shandy*, 205
Stirling, 37, 38
St Basil, 44
St Clair, William, 93n1
Steevens, George, 190
St Gregory, 44
Stickle Tarn, 235
Stockdale, J. J., 45
Stockdale, Percival, 188
Stoddart, John, 48
WORKS
Remarks on Scotland, 205-6
review of *Lyrical Ballads*, 206
Stoicism, 51
Stolberg, Friedrich Leopold, Graf zu, *On a Cataract*, 206
Stothard, Thomas, 72n1

St Paul, 23
Street, T. G., 103
Stuart, Daniel, 9, 60, 63, 64, 98, 102-3, 138, 154, 183, 217; W requests books from, 98, 132-3; C given books by, 141; visits Allan Bank, 152; sends newspapers to W, 210-11; joins in the 'clamour' against W, 217
Sutton, Denys, 10n1
Swarthmore College, 12
Sydrophel, 38
Sylvester, Joshua, 79-80, 206-7
WORKS
O Holy Peace, 206-7
works, 207
Symmons, Dr Charles, *Life of Milton*, 207
Sympson, Joseph, *Science Revived*, 207

Tacitus, Caius Cornelius, *C. Cornelii Taciti Opera*, 258
Tasso, Torquato, *Godfrey of Bulloigne; or, the recoverie of Jerusalem*, 208
Taylor, Henry, 54
Taylor, Jeremy, 121, 208
WORKS
A Dissuasive from Popery, 208
Holy Dying, 208-9
Holy Living, 208-9
works, 208
Taylor, Joseph, *Tour*, 259
Taylor, Thomas, 167
Taylor, William, 76, 173, 209
WORKS
Bluebeard, 209
Cinderella, 209
English Synonyms Discriminated, 209
The Iris, 209
Temple, Laura Sophia, *Poems*, 209
The Albion, 206
The Anti-Jacobin Review, 107
The Assemble of Ladies, 5
Theatre Royal, Haymarket, 122
The Cabinet, 28, 210
The Champion, 128, 183
The Courier, 23, 60, 60-1, 63, 109, 152, 158, 198, 210-18, 262 *see also* newspapers
The Cumberland Pacquet, 218-19
The Evening Mail, 219
The Examiner, 104-5, 106, 114, 219; W contributes to, 115
The Floure and the Leafe, 5
The Globe, 219-20
The Indicator, 28
Thelwall, John, 30, 116, 155, 220; inscription, 220

302

WORKS
Letter to Francis Jeffray, 221
Lines written at Bridgwater, 220
Paternal Tears, 221
Poems Chiefly Written in Retirement, 220-1
The Peripatetic, 221
The Muse's Pocket Companion, 165, 221
The Philanthropist, 222
The Reflector, 114, 128
The Statesman, 222
The Times, 223-4
The Vision of the Brothers, 224-5
Thiébault, Dieudonné, *Original Anecdotes of Frederick II*, 225
Thomas, W. K., 71, 153
Thompson, Aaron, 90
Thompson, Capt. Edward, 143
Thompson, George, 238
Thomson, James, 33, 80, 225-6
WORKS
Hymn on Solitude, 225-6
The Castle of Indolence, 225, 226
The Seasons, 226, 236
Winter, 226
Works, 226
Thrale, Miss Queeney, 27
Thurlow, Edward Hovell, 2nd Baron, 'a volume of Poems', 227
Tickell, Thomas
WORKS
Kensington-garden, 227
Lucy and Colin, 221
To a Lady before Marriage, 227
Tierra del Fuego, 62
Tobin, James Webbe, 14, 25, 159, 227-8
Tobin, John, 71; *The Honey Moon*, 227-8
Todd, Henry John, 185, 203
Townley, James, *High Life Below Stairs*, 8, 228
Trott, Nicola Zoe, 93, 113
Tuffin, J. F., 190
Turberville, George
WORKS
works, including poems on Russia, 228
works included in Chalmers, 228
Turnbull, John M., 127-8
Turner, William, *A Compleat History of the most Remarkable Providences*, 229
Tyrwhitt, Thomas, 47
Tytler, Henry William
WORKS
Extract of a Letter, 229
The Voyage Home, 230

Ullswater, 62, 71, 85, 149
Underhill, Timothy, 39
Urry, John, 47
Ussher, James, Archbishop of Armagh, *Clio*, 263

Valerius Maximus, Caius, *Facta et Dicta Memorabilia*, 51, 230
Vaughan, Sir Charles Richard, *Narrative of the Siege of Zaragoza*, 230, 236
Vaughan, Henry, 263-4
Victoria and Albert Museum, 80, 96, 139, 180
Victoria University Library, 37, 111, 246, 250
Vieyra Transtagano, Anthony, *A New Portuguese Grammar in Four Parts*, 230
Vincent, Augustine, *A discoverie of errours*, 230-1
V.[incent], T.[homas], *God's Terrible Voice in the City*, 231
Virgilius Maro, Publius, 231-3
WORKS
Aeneid, 232, 232-3
Georgics, 231, 232
Works, 231-2
Volney, Constantin François de Chasseboeuf, comte de, *Travels through Syria and Egypt*, 233
Voltaire, François-Marie Arouet de, *Dictionnaire Philosophique*, 233

Wade, Josiah, 145, 209
Wakefield, Battle of, 55
Walker, Robert, 5
Wallace, William, 206
Waller, Edmund, *Poems, &c., Written upon Several Occasions*, 234
Walsingham, Sir Francis, 191
Walton, Izaac, and Charles Cotton
WORKS
Life of Herbert, 107
The Complete Angler, 45, 64, 234-5
Warner, Richard, *A Tour Through the Northern Counties of England*, 235
Warton, Joseph, *An Essay on the Writings and Genius of Pope*, 236
Warton, Thomas, 149, 191
Warwick, Sir Philip, *Memoires of the reigne of Charles I*, 236
Washington University, 112
Watson, James, *Comic and Serious Scots Poems*, 95
Watson, Thomas, works, 236
Watts, Alaric, 195, 257
Weaver, Robert, *Monumenta Antiqua*, 236n1
Wedd, Mary, 193n3
Wedgwood, Josiah, 75, 115, 141n1, 182
Wedgwood, Thomas, 100, 141n1

Index

Weever, John, *Ancient Funerall Monuments*, 236
Wellesley, Sir Arthur (later Duke of Wellington), 212, 214; C's servile adulation of, 216
West, Thomas
   WORKS
   A Guide to the Lakes, 237-8
   The Antiquities of Furness, 237, 238
   Westmorland Advertiser, 41, 135, 199, 238-9
Whalley, George, 9, 13, 26n1, 31, 42, 44, 49, 57, 58, 70, 73, 98, 103, 111-12, 113, 124, 139, 144-5, 167, 175
Whitaker, Thomas Dunham
   WORKS
   History and Antiquities of Craven, 55, 240
   An History of the Original Parish of Whalley, and Honour of Clitheroe, 239-40
   Piers Plowman (as editor), 132
White, Henry Kirke
   WORKS
   Clifton Grove: A Sketch in Verse, with Other Poems, 240-1
   Remains, 240, 241
   To the herb rosemary, 241
Whitehaven, 161
White Moss, 126
Wickham, D. E., 143
Wieland, Christoph Martin, 195
Wilberforce, William, 158; *A Practical View*, 241-2
Wilkinson, Thomas, 24, 83, 194
   WORKS
   A Lamentation on the Untimely Death of Roger, 242
   poems, 242
   To my Thrushes, 243
   Tours to the British Mountains, 242-3
William of Cloudeslie, 1
Williams, Helen Maria, 113-14; *Letters written in France*, 243
Willoughby, Henry, works, 243-4
Wilson, Edward, 23
Wilson, Elizabeth, MS album, 244
Wilson, John, 193, 237; letter to, 1; tells story about W, 104-5; DW visits, 117
   WORKS
   Letter to 'Mathetes', 245
   poems, 244
   The Angler's Tent, 244
   The Isle of Palms, 244, 245
Windermere, boating expedition, 244
Winstanley, William, *England's Worthies*, 79, 245
Wisbech Museum, 166
Wither, George, works, 245
Withering, William, *An Arrangement of British Plants*, 245-6
Woof, Pamela, 32, 58, 78, 85, 86, 100, 121, 122, 127, 146, 151-2, 154, 155, 179-80, 202
Woof, Robert, 24, 35, 37n1, 42, 57, 58, 67, 68, 154, 164n1, 165, 166, 242
Wordsworth, Catherine, 217
Wordsworth, Charles, 40, 181
Wordsworth, Christopher (brother of W), 2, 27, 111, 138, 258
   WORKS
   Ecclesiastical Biography, 246-7
   Reasons for declining to become a subscriber, 247
   Sermons, 247
   Six Letters to Granville Sharp, 246
Wordsworth, Christopher (nephew of W), 40
Wordsworth, Christopher (of Warminster), 10, 142, 234
Wordsworth, Dora, 22, 49; catalogue of Rydal Mount library, 53, 91, 180; marginalia, 232
Wordsworth, Dorothy, 2, 3, 4, 18, 20, 24, 32, 37, 39, 41, 43, 45, 46, 52-3, 54, 56, 60, 65, 67, 74, 80, 83, 84, 86, 89, 95, 96, 97, 101, 105, 108, 111, 115, 116, 123, 124, 125, 128, 130, 133, 135, 147, 148, 150, 164, 167, 171, 176, 179, 183, 197, 199, 200, 204, 216, 218, 219, 221, 222, 238, 239, 242, 246, 255; makes entry in Commonplace Book, 7, 12, 57-8, 99, 155-6, 166; refers to Brown's *Barbarossa*, 30; meets William Enfield, 86; flyleaf inscriptions, 10, 22, 37, 129; studies German, 91, 195n1; reads Jeffrey, 117; reads to W, 121, 146; translates Lessing, 134; reading, 139, 144, 159-60, 169, 170-1, 186, 198, 199, 200, 201; marginalia, 234, 246n1
   WORKS
   children's stories and verse, 248-9
   Grasmere journals, 2, 4, 27, 32, 33, 34, 44-5, 47, 48, 50, 57, 58, 62, 68, 71, 78, 85, 87, 88, 100, 101, 121, 122, 123-4, 126, 127, 135-6, 137, 146, 147, 151, 154, 155, 157, 181-2, 189, 194, 196, 201, 202, 207, 245-6, 247, 250, 252
   Narrative Concerning George and Sarah Green in MS, 249
   passages composed for Joseph Wilkinson's *Select Views*, 249
   passages composed for Andrew Bell, *Elements of Tuition, Part II. The English School* in MS, 21-1, 249
   poetry in MS, 248
   Recollections of the Scottish tour, 1803, 31, 34-5, 49, 62, 183-4, 194, 195, 205, 206, 248
Wordsworth, Gordon Graham, 232

Index

Wordsworth, John (brother of W), 3, 74, 134, 135, 151, 152, 219, 235; lends books to W, 3-4; visits DC, 3; books lent to, 14; reads Bloomfield, 25; makes entry in Wordsworth Commonplace Book, 98; critical opinions, 135; reads Mary Robinson, 179; death of, 181, 184, 252; advised on purchase of books, 203; sees Stoddart's review of *Lyrical Ballads*, 206

Wordsworth, John (son of W), 49, 72, 86, 94, 127

Wordsworth, John (father of W), library of, 44, 61, 87, 88, 94

Wordsworth, Jonathan, *Romantic Women Writers*, 135; dating followed, 13n2, 100n1, 162n1, 201; donates book to Wordsworth Library, 103

Wordsworth Library, Grasmere, 3, 6, 12, 14, 23, 26, 28, 38, 50, 52, 58, 82, 84, 90, 103, 126, 142, 159, 160, 167, 174, 177, 178, 178-9, 182, 197, 198, 199, 200, 230, 232, 246, 256, 257

Wordsworth, Mary, 3, 7, 8, 9, 10, 21, 22, 24, 28, 31, 36, 37, 40, 41, 48, 53, 60, 67, 69, 76, 78, 102, 105, 118, 122, 129, 137, 144, 158, 161, 196, 200, 205, 217, 227, 228, 234, 238; sees William Betty in performance, 30; reading, 68, 169, 170-1; inscription by, 22, 31; W gives book to, 89, 221; visits theatre with SH, 137; copies into Wordsworth Commonplace Book, 139, 144

Wordsworth, Richard (brother of W), 27, 219; conduit for books, 24, 153

Wordsworth, Richard, 149

Wordsworth, Richard, of Branthwaite (W's uncle), 61

Wordsworth Summer Conference, 256

Wordsworth, Thomas, 94, 234

Wordsworth, William, referred to Adam Smith by C, 1; inscriptions in books, 6, 7, 12, 26, 33, 38, 52, 75, 90, 90-1, 100, 103, 129, 132, 144, 150, 157, 160, 161, 166, 167, 168, 177, 180, 185, 187, 190-1, 198, 208, 229, 230, 237, 246, 256, 257, 258; Commonplace Book (DC MS 26), 7, 13, 24, 34, 37, 42, 57-8, 66, 67, 85, 99, 108, 109, 139, 140, 144, 153, 155-6, 164, 166, 178, 201, 206-7, 241, 242; contributes to Mary Barker's *Lines Addressed to a Noble Lord*, 11; teaches at Grasmere School, 21; uses C's books, 69, 81, 102-3; falling-out with C, 52, 54, 75, 112, 163, 166, 169, 177, 198, 199; translates German, 91, 134; argues with C about Jonson, 122; involvement with Lamb's *Specimens*, 127; visits theatre with SH, 137; wedding, 155, 252; meets Amelia Opie, 160; a natural soldier, 163; purchases book, 205; defence of C's plagiarism, 206; considers journalism, 211; interest in current affairs, 218; sends books to C, 220; Alfoxden notebook, 253; attitude to German metaphysicians, 261

WORKS

1810, 222

Address to my Infant Daughter, 79

A few bold Patriots, Reliques of the Fight, 200

Album for Lady Mary Lowther, 8, 20, 69, 88, 128, 142, 245

Alice Fell, 96, 117

Andrew Jones, 117

Appendix on Poetic Diction, 66, 77, 120, 170, 172, 181

Artegal and Elidure, 90, 148

At the Grave of Burns, 253

Beggars, 201

Benjamin the Waggoner, 38-9, 205, 233

By their floating mill, 77

Character of the Happy Warrior, 5

Dissolution of the Monasteries, 156

Ecclesiastical Sonnets, 156

Effusion, in the Pleasure-Ground, 109

Ejaculation at the Grave of Burns, 37

Elegiac Stanzas, Suggested by a Picture of Peele Castle, 23

Ellen Irwin, 164n1, 257

Essay, Supplementary to the Preface, 10, 26, 27, 33-4, 35, 47, 62, 65, 73, 75, 79, 80, 88, 91, 99, 100, 121, 126, 149, 159, 165, 188, 190, 193-4, 204, 226, 233, 234, 236

Essays Upon Epitaphs, 49, 51, 79, 84, 93, 97, 121, 125, 128, 135, 136, 137, 143, 148, 159, 170, 191-2, 230, 236, 255

Fenwick Notes, 138, 146, 156

From the dark chambers of dejection freed, 244

Guide to the Lakes, 33, 43

Hail Zaragoza! If with unwet eye, 222

Hart-Leap Well, 35, 101-2

Home at Grasmere, 58, 121-2, 148, 201, 231, 233

I find it written of Simonides, 95

I griev'd for Buonaparte, 146

I heard (alas, 'twas only in a dream), 168

Imitation of Juvenal, 34

Immortality Ode, *see* Ode

Indignation of a High-Minded Spaniard 1810, 223

Inscription for the House, 124

It is not to be thought of that the flood, 68

Kendal and Windermere Railway, 175

Laodamìa, 86, 161, 168, 233

Letter to a Friend of Robert Burns, 37

Index

Lyrical Ballads, 4, 11, 14, 16, 35, 57, 135, 156, 171, 173, 231, 235, 242, 250; epigraph, 76; reviewed, 152, 218
marginalia, 4, 76, 94, 107, 124, 234, 246, 254
Methought I saw the footsteps of a throne, 146, 174
Michael, 58, 181, 231, 233; ballad version, 134
November 1806, 98
November 1, 1815, 183
Now that all hearts are glad, all faces bright, 106
October 1803, 184
Ode, 58, 68, 122, 202, 249-50
Ode to Duty, 120, 147
On a Celebrated Event in Ancient History, 169
Pelion and Ossa flourish side by side, 203
Poems (1815), 85, 106, 114, 141, 142, 200, 204-5, 209
Poems, in Two Volumes, 28-9, 239; reviewed by Jeffrey, 117; reviewed in *The Cabinet*, 210
Poems on the Naming of Places, 56
Point Rash-Judgement, 56
Power of Music, 27
Preface to *Lyrical Ballads*, 24, 54, 57, 66, 70, 73, 103, 109, 112, 120, 124, 134, 152, 174, 175, 191
Preface to *Poems* (1815), 64, 73, 83, 113, 129, 143, 209
Prospectus to *The Recluse*, 77
Reply to 'Mathetes', 8, 168, 245
Resolution and Independence, 46, 58
Salisbury Plain, 254-5
Select Views, 43, 59-60, 93, 97, 159, 171, 226, 237, 240
She dwelt among th' untrodden ways, 255
Song, at the Feast of Brougham Castle, 19, 38, 54-5, 159, 230-1
Sonnet on Milton, 207
Sonnet to Thomas Clarkson, 53
sonnets in *Morning Post*, 155
Stanzas Written in My Pocket-Copy of Thomson's 'Castle of Indolence', 225
Strange fits of Passion I have known, 32
The Affliction of Margaret, 122-3
The Blind Highland Boy, 68
The Brothers, 92
The Convention of Cintra, 9, 23, 43, 56, 69, 98, 109, 113, 148, 165, 169, 190, 191, 211, 212, 213, 214, 215, 223, 224, 230, 232, 236; reviewed by Robinson, 179
The Dog: An Idyllium, 137
The Excursion, 4, 8, 21, 26, 29, 37, 41, 43, 51, 57, 61, 62, 69, 82, 92, 102, 104-5, 107, 109, 112, 115, 118n2, 131, 137-8, 141, 162, 169, 173, 174, 187, 193, 199, 208-9, 217, 221, 222, 231, 238, 242-3, 246, 261-2; Preface to, 148; reviewed by Jeffrey, 118-19; reviewed by Lamb, 128-9; reviewed by Montgomery, 150-1; reprinted and reviewed by *Courier*, 217, 218
The Female Vagrant, 106
The Five-Book Prelude, 61, 68, 100, 162, 170
The Force of Prayer, 240
The Forsaken, 122-3
The Green Linnet, 77
The Idiot Boy, 107
The Kitten and the Falling Leaves, 59
The Oak of Guernica, 125
The Pedlar, 118n2
The Pet-lamb, 156
The Recluse, 231
The Redbreast and the Butterfly, 65, 146
There was a boy, 32
The River Duddon, 5, 108, 113-14, 207
The Ruined Cottage, 73, 118n2, 175
The Sailor's Mother, 122
The Seven Sisters, 33, 164n1, 179
The Solitary Reaper, 109, 242
The Sparrow's Nest, 49-50
The Sublime and Beautiful, 25, 176
The Thirteen-Book Prelude, 9, 13, 14, 27, 32, 36, 45, 51, 58, 63, 68, 72, 74, 91, 93, 95, 100, 112, 113, 139-40, 143, 158-9, 169, 170, 172, 191, 193, 201, 203, 225, 231, 243, 260, see also *The Five-Book Prelude*
The Thorn, 108
The Tuft of Primroses, 44
The Two Thieves, 22
The White Doe of Rylstone, 10, 69, 165, 185, 203, 204, 234, 239-40; W reads, 59; read by Mrs Skepper in MS, 177; reviewed by John Scott, 183
The world is too much with us, 202
Tintern Abbey, 41
To H.C., Six Years Old, 43, 142
To Joanna, 14, 76, 235
To R. B. Haydon, 183
To the Daisy, 77, 150
To the Poet, Dyer, 83
Translation from the Italian of Michael Angelo, 80, 145
Translated from the Italian of Milton, 147
translation from Horace, 253
translations from Ariosto, 6
translations from Chaucer, 4, 47, 77, 78
translations from Chiabrera, 49
translations from Metastasio, 116, 145
Unpublished Tour, 5, 15, 52, 69, 77-8, 81, 123,

Index

156, 194, 204, 226, 227, 237-8, 238
Upon the Same Event, 169
View from the Top of Black Comb, 186
With ships the sea was sprinkled, 192-3
Written on a Blank Leaf of The Excursion, text given, 239
Yarrow Unvisited, 35-6, 101
Yew-trees, 66-7
Wordsworth, William, and Samuel Taylor Coleridge
WORKS
Lyrical Ballads, 250
The Voice from the Side of Etna, 249-50
Wordsworth, William, Jr, 26, 38, 50, 67, 198
Worthington, Jane, *see* Smyser, Jane Worthington
Wotton, Sir Henry, 234
Wrangham, Francis, 21, 27, 61, 72, 97, 107, 112, 207, 247, 262; introduces W to the work of Buchanan, 34; library, 115, 139, 140; Cole's catalogue of, 140; Sotheby's sale catalogue, 178

WORKS
A Sermon on the Translation of the Scriptures, 251
four sonnets and *Song*, 250
Human Laws, 251-2
Poems, 251
The Gospel Promulgated, 252
The Holy Land, 250-1
Thirteen Practical Sermons, 250
Wu, Duncan, 57, 93, 113; corrects himself, 52, 173n2
Wynn, C. W. Williams, 90, 140, 150, 176, 192, 203

Yale University, Beineke Library, 168, 200
York Herald, 252
Young, Edward, *Night Thoughts*, 252

Zall, Paul M., 124
Zeno, 60